STANDARD CATA

JAGUAR

Jaguar Heritage — North America

Jaguar founder Sir William Lyons with an XKE coupe.

JOHN GUNNELL

©2007 Krause Publications
Published by

krause publications
An Imprint of F+W Publications

700 East State Street • Iola, WI 54990-0001
715-445-2214 • 888-457-2873
www.krausebooks.com

Our toll-free number to place an order or obtain
a free catalog is (800) 258-0929.

Library of Congress Catalog Number: 2007922989

ISBN 13: 978-0-89689-595-9

Designed by Emily Adler
Edited by Tom Collins

Printed in China

Back cover: 1965 E-type (XK-E) roadster (Andrew Morland);
1954 XK 120 (Dan Lyons); 2001 X-type sedan (Andrew Morland)

Acknowledgments

The heritage of the Standard Catalog (r) series of books continues with a new generation product, *Standard Catalog of® Jaguar.*

The original concept has been carried in a new format that assists the hobbyist, historian, collector and professional dealer in finding helpful information.

Chester L. Krause, founder of the former Krause Publications, created the concept of the Standard Catalog (r) series and David V. Brownell did preliminary work on the project while serving as editor of *Old Cars Weekly* during the 1970s. John A. Gunnell assumed the project in 1978.

This new book concept is a new direction. And it adds to the 2004 work, the *Standard Guide of British Sports Cars.* Jaguar is one of a few British auto manufacturers that still are with us in the 21st century, along with Aston-Martin, Morgan and others. In addition to beautiful images, this book offers a physical description, highlights of equipment, options and original specifications, technical data, historical facts and information about current values.

Standard Catalog of® Jaguar was made possible thanks to the experienced editorial team at Krause Publications, part of the F+W Publications family of companies. The many contributors have included recognized experts, restorers and owners of these cars.

Of particular note in this book are the images of photographers Tom Glatch, Bob Harrington, David Lyon, Dan Lyons, Andrew Morland and John Wheater. Their work complements the design template developed at Krause Publications by the team of Jamie Griffin and Brian Brogaard in 2005.

Owners of special note are Carl and Carrol Jensen and other members of the Wisconsin Jaguar Owners Club Ltd. for their special efforts, especially pulling precious Jaguars from the warmth of storage on cold winter days. The Jaguar Club of North America also shared their wonderful Heritage collection of Jaguar images.

The meticulous Richard Dance Collection of original literature and magazine articles plus literature from the Phil Hall Collection went a long way in completing this book. Also, the staff of the Bergstrom Fox Valley Jaguar of Appleton, WI, particularly Carl F. Davies, offered assistance.

This new book also builds on the work done previously by James M. Flammang and Mike Covello in their respective editions of the *Standard Catalog of® Imported Cars* as well as the 2004 work, the *Standard Catalog of® British Sports Cars.*

Special thanks go to the folks at XKs Unlimited, a Jaguar parts supplier in San Luis Obispo, California. Their catalog entries were a great help in sorting various generations of Jaguar models.

Standard Catalog of® Jaguar is intended to help readers appreciate these rare cars that combine success through innovative racing competition as well as refinement and tasteful distinction. You can hear the growl that is and always has been the Jaguar "Art of Performance."

JAGUAR
Table of Contents

Customs and Classics, Kelly Purdum

Dan Lyons

Tom Glatch

1970s

Andrew Morland

1980s

1990s

2000s

1920s Austin-Swallow 7 tourer *Andrew Morland*

Introduction

JAGUAR

The origin of the world-renowned Jaguar nameplate began in England with William Lyons and the SS company. The Swallow Coachbuilding Company was formed in 1927, five years after Sir William Lyons and William Walmsley joined forces to build motorcycle sidecars.

During the 1920s, the company produced bodies for such cars as the Austin Seven, Morris Cowley, Standard Nine, Swift Ten and Fiat Tipo. One Swallow version had its wings clipped when the MG superseded the rare Morris Swallow.

In 1931, the firm changed its name to SS Cars Ltd. Soon they turned from building special bodies to making complete automobiles. Lyons designed a rakish body for a new Standard chassis that became known as the SS1. It was offered in saloon (sedan), coupe and drophead (convertible) form. With a long hood and styling reminiscent of the huge SSK Mercedes, the SS1 captured attention at the 1931 British Motor Show. The two-seater SS90, produced in 1935, was followed by the even more notable SS100.

That SS100 first came with a 2663-cc overhead-valve six (a Standard engine conversion). Later, a 3485-cc 125-hp engine was used, mainly in the SS. The SS100 was fast and became known for its good road holding, although some observers of that time thought the body work was flamboyant. The gracefully curved front fenders blended beautifully into the running boards and rounded rear fenders. It attracted considerable attention on both sides of the Atlantic. Priced reasonably at 445 Pounds Sterling in Britain, the 3.5-litre SS100 could run from 0 to 60 mph in about 10.5 seconds, and hit a top speed of about 100 mph. Before and after World War II, SS100s raced at Brooklands, rallies and British hill climbs. Some 265 examples of the SS100 roadster were built before the end of WWII.

In the fall of 1935, the Jaguar name was used for the first time, initially on saloons.

Michael Frostick, author of *The Jaguar Tradition* says Standard Swallow executives wanted to change their name before the end of World War II, due in part to the unfortunate association of "SS" with the dreaded Nazi regiments. The model name "Jaguar" was targeted as the official company name. Arrangements had to be made with Armstrong Siddley, a company that had used the Jaguar name for an airplane engine. As post-war auto production resumed, Jaguar would be an active player.

The SS100 made no further appearance, but production of prewar saloons was resumed and these gained surprising popularity in America. Dubbed the Mark IV series, they were powered by 2.5- or 3.5-litre engines. The popular Jaguars spurred the new Mark V saloon in 1949. At home, Jaguar offered a smaller 1.5-litre model, descended in part from the pre-war SSII car series, with a Standard four-cylinder engine. Few of these crossed the Atlantic. When Standard stopped producing the four-cylinder engine, Jaguar elected to drop the small sedans completely.

At the Earl's Court Motor Show in fall 1948, the new Jaguar, the XK-120 roadster created a sensation. Work on it had begun in 1938 with the prototype SS100 coupe. Its name suggested a 120-mph top speed, and the XK soon became the fastest production car in the world. It was powered by a new 3.4-litre six-cylinder engine that delivered 160 hp, enough to send an XK-120 to 60 mph in as little as 10 seconds.

The XK-120 was intended to be a limited-production model used solely to demonstrate the new dual-overhead-camshaft six-cylinder engine, which was slated to be used in future saloons. The sports car's immediate success called for complete body tooling to be created in a hurry. The new roadster was reasonably priced, docile, rode nicely and held the road securely. And it was a classic beauty.

Not everyone believed early claims of the XK-120 Jaguar's virtues, so the company held a high-speed demonstration run on Belgium's Jabbeke highway. An unmodified XK-120 hit 126 mph, then the windshield was then removed and the car did 132 mph.

Pre-war racing competition had made SS cars famous as driven by the likes of Tommy Wisdom. In 1949, three Jaguars entered the British Racing Driver's Club meet at Silverstone. This was a one-hour race for production models. The Jaguars took first and second places. Other victories followed. Stirling Moss won the 1950 Tourist Trophy and the Jaguar tagged NUB 120, driven by Ian Appleyard, often accompanied by his wife, Pat, daughter of Sir William Lyons, won Alpine rallies in 1950, 1951 and 1952.

Three Jaguar XK-120s entered the 1950 Le Mans 24-Hour race with no intention of winning and two of them finished far back in the pack. This attempt revealed that a special design would be needed for victory, which led to the XK-120C or C-Type. This car had a special multi-tube frame. A Jaguar C-Type won the 1951 Le Mans event driven by the team of

1922 Swallow Sidecar

JAGUAR DAIMLER HERITAGE TRUST

Jaguar Heritage—North America

The graceful Standard-Swallow logo

Whitehead and Walker and won it again in 1953 with a 220-hp engine, Dunlop disc brakes and the driver team of Rolt and Hamilton.

Joining the roadster at the 1951 Geneva (Switzerland) Motor Show was a new fixed-head coupe, with a profile similar to the one-of-a-kind 1938 SS100 coupe. More civilized than the roadster, the new coupe was a better choice for long-distance touring. The coupe's more pleasing interior detailing included a veneer-trimmed dashboard and wind-up windows. A Special Equipment model, called XK-120M in the U.S. market, had a 180-hp engine in place of the usual 160-hp six.

In 1953, an XK-120 drophead-coupe with a fully-trimmed convertible top was introduced. In 1954, the D-Type racer was designed to win the Le Mans Grand Prix. It became one of the famous racing sports cars of the 1950s. The wind-tunnel-tested D-Type used a central monocoque chassis designed around aircraft principles. A modified cylinder head with three Weber carburetors produced 250 hp. The rigid rear axle was connected by trailing arms and transverse torsion bars. Dunlop disc brakes were used on all four wheels. The D-Type's first outing at Le Mans produced a second-place finish despite fuel problems. D-Types then took both first and second spots in the Rheims 12-Hour race in France.

The XK-140 debuted in October 1954. Moving its engine forward in the chassis allowed a larger cockpit. The engine also got a boost to 190 hp and rack-and-pinion steering was added.

Jerry and Kathy Nell

1938 SS 100 3.5 litre Graber body coupe

The graceful 1935 SS Airline Sedan

Drophead and fixed-head coupes offered 2+2 seating, although the back seats were best suited for kids.

A factory D-Type had improved aerodynamics with a longer nose and smooth tail. It put out at least 250 hp and won at Le Mans, setting a 122.39-mph lap record. The factory D-Types had trouble at the next year's Le Mans race, but a privately-owned Jaguar racing team won the event. In 1957, the factory dropped out of participation and the same private team, the famous Ecurie Ecosse, won again. A limited-production short nose D-Type became available by 1956. In 1957, a few of them were marketed with minimal road gear and named the XK-SS.

Dunlop 4-wheel disc brakes were the major features of the XK-150 series introduced in 1957. Styling changes included a wider hood, a larger cockpit and a straight feature line back from the fenders. The original swoopy Jaguar profile was gone but engine access was much better. A one-piece windshield replaced the former vee-type. Almost all XK-150s had a 210-hp "special equipment" with 20 hp more than the standard version. Only drophead and fixed-head coupes were sold in 1957, but the roadster became available again in 1958. An "S" engine option with triple S.U. carburetors produced 250 hp. In 1959, displacement of the now 220-hp engine grew to 3781 cc. The "S" version produced 265 hp.

Jaguar's racing D-Type evolved into an E prototype, then into the production E-Type and became known as the XK-E in the U.S. It was introduced in 1961 and proved very popular. The XK-E's pressed-steel monocoque frame had a bolt-on tubular front sub-frame to hold the engine and front suspension. At the rear, another cage-type sub-frame held the final drive member and a new coil-spring independent rear suspension. Under the hood was the "S" variant of the 3.8-litre XK engine. The XK-E's top speed was 150 mph and it could run from 0-60 mph in 6.9 seconds. An open two-seater and a fastback style fixed-head hatchback coupe were offered.

An E-Type Jag driven by Graham Hill won its first race, but sports cars were changing and Jaguar couldn't field cars that rivaled Ferrari and others. Its racing involvement declined, yet a dozen "lightweight" E-Types were built for racing. Some featured an aluminum monocoque chassis. With fuel injection they delivered up to 320 hp. Even top drivers like Jackie Stewart and Graham Hill could only push the lightweight E-Types to modest and brief success.

Saloon editions of the Jaguar continued to have racing success and Jaguar again tooled with the E-Type. A 4235-cc version of the old XK engine went into the E-Type in 1964. This did not boost horsepower, but did produce more torque. The gearbox was now fully synchronized. In 1966, a fixed-head coupe with

1935 SS 100

Jaguar Heritage—North America

a nine-inch longer wheelbase and four-passenger seating was offered. This 2+2 had a more vertical windshield.

By the late 1960s, the name E-Type was used on both sides of the Atlantic, surpassing the XK-E reference. The Series II E-Type, introduced during 1968, dropped the first-generation model's headlight covers and added bigger taillights. The Series II bumpers were also mounted higher, partly as a result of U.S. safety requirements. In 1971, a Series III E-Type with a 5343-cc V-12 engine joined the six-cylinder Series II. It offered up to 314 gross horsepower with a longer wheelbase. A two-seat convertible and 2+2 fixed-head coupe were offered in Series III format. The final E-Types were built in the winter of 1974-1975.

In mid-1975 the Jaguar XJ-S coupe emerged. It also used the V-12 and had full monocoque construction. Its underpan evolved from the XJ12 saloon. The XJ was more of a "boulevard" sportster. Before long, all XJ12s had automatic transmission. An "H.E." version of the engine debuted by 1982. It was more efficient and more economical. In autumn 1983, a XJ-S cabriolet joined the 2+2 coupe in England. It used a fixed roll bar above the seats. A cabriolet took several years to arrive in the U.S. market.

In addition to V-12 power, the 1988 XJ sedans had a new

3.6-litre 225-hp twin-cam six hooked to a five-speed Getrag manual gearbox. Jaguar continued to do well in production touring car races during the 1980s and gave official factory sanction to racing in 1983 and 1984.

It was easy to separate the 1990 Jaguar models. The XJ6 designation was used on six-cylinder-powered four-door sedans. The XJ-S name was used on V-12-motivated two-door models, including a convertible. Those seeking extra luxury could get an XJ-S Collection Rouge Coupe or Sovereign, Vanden Plas and Majestic versions. By this time the priciest Jaguars were in the $60,000 range.

In 1997, things changed. The XJ sedans went to inline six engines, while the sporty new XK8 coupe and convertible (both with a "throw back" XK-E look) had a V-8. Also new was an XJR sedan with a supercharged six. Things changed again in 1998-1999, when only V-8s were used. The sedans became XJ8s (or XJR with a supercharger) and the sports models remained XK8s. For the New Millennium, Jaguar introduced the S-Type sedan and it resembled Jaguar saloons of the 1950s and early 1960s in the 2.4, 3.4 and 3.8 series.

The exciting new XKR version of the XK8 came with a 4.0-litre supercharged V-8. In 2001, an ultra-fast Silverstone edition of the XK8 was offered. Jaguar's new-for-2002 X-Type was a mid-size four-door sedan and the company's first-ever all-wheel-drive car. Jaguar cars produced 126,121 vehicles in England in calendar-year 2003. This total included 26,949 XJS models, 5,656 XK models, 61,609 X-Type models and 31,907 S-Type models. The U.S. car buyer shifted to upscale SUVs and the strength of the British Pound hurt Jaguar business here. Jaguar did launch a new long-wheelbase XJ sedan and the Estate Wagon—called the Sportwagon for the North American market.

And Jaguar continues to design for the future with cars like the Advanced Lightweight Coupe.

Jaguar Heritage—North America

1931 SS1 coupe

Jaguar Heritage—North America

1938 SS 100 Jaguar coupe prototype

By 1946, the SS name was dropped. This is the nose of the Jaguar 1.5-litre saloon.
Andrew Morland

1946

1½ LITRE — FOUR — The styling of the first Jaguars to appear after World War II changed little from those offered during the late 1930s. Both the saloon (sedan) and drophead coupe (convertible) displayed a traditional look that had been used on the SSI, SSII and SS Jaguar cars. They had huge, round, separately-mounted Lucas bulb-type headlights sitting on either side of a bright vertical-bars grille. Tiny round parking lights were mounted on each fender. The bodies had running boards and front-opening "suicide" doors. Solid axles with leaf springs were used at front and rear. The brakes, though new, were still mechanically actuated. Under the bonnet (hood) was an overhead-valve six engine with twin S.U. carburetors and two electric fuel pumps hooked to a four-speed manual transmission. Jaguars had Connolly leather upholstery with plenty of polished walnut wood, but the folding tables offered in prewar models were not installed. Standard equipment included a tachometer, twin electric windshield wipers, "trafficator" (semaphore-style) turn signals, wire wheels, a telescopic steering wheel, twin fog lamps, a heater and defroster, a cigarette lighter and a built-in tool kit. The drophead model's top could be fully raised, fully lowered or raised halfway for a "Coupe' de Ville" look. The left-hand-drive (steering wheel on left side) Jaguars destined for America had overriders (bumper guards). Wire wheels were used and had "JAGUAR" lettering on the knock-off hubs. The 1½-Litre Jaguar was built for "home market" buyers in England, using a smaller, less powerful four-cylinder engine.

2½ LITRE — SIX — The 2½-Litre Jaguar looked similar to the smaller model, but on top of the grille was a "2½ Litre" badge.

3½ LITRE — SIX — The 3½-Litre Jaguar looked similar to both other models. It was the same size as the 2½-Litre model. A "3½ Litre" badge was seen on the grille. A different rear axle ratio was used with the more powerful motor.

I.D. DATA: Chassis serial number is stamped on the front of the frame, and on a plate at side of firewall. Engine numbers are stamped on a boss on the rear of the cylinder block, and on the firewall plate. Starting serial number: (3½ Litre RHD saloon) 610001; (3½ Litre LHD saloon) 630001; (3½ Litre RHD coupe) 617001; (3½ Litre LHD coupe) 637001; (2½ Litre RHD saloon) 510001; (2½ Litre LHD saloon) 530001; (2½ Litre RHD coupe) 517001; (2½ Litre LHD coupe) 537001; (1½ Litre RHD) 410001; (1½ Litre LHD) 430001. Starting engine number: (3/½ Litre) S26; (2½ Litre) P18; (1½ Litre) KB1001.

ENGINES

BASE FOUR 1½ LITRE: Inline, overhead-valve four-cylinder. Cast-iron block and head. Displacement: 108.3 cid (1775 cc). Bore & Stroke: 2.87 x 4.17 in. (73 x 106 mm). Compression

Model	Body Type	Engine/ CID	POE Price	Weight (Lbs.)	Production Total
1½-Litre	4d Saloon-4/5P	I4/108	N/A	2,800	**Note 1**
2½-Litre	4d Saloon-5P	I6/162	N/A	3,528	**Note 1**
3½-Litre	4d Saloon-5P	I6/213	N/A	3,528	**Note 1**

Note 1: A total of 11,952 Jaguars were produced from 1946 to 1949; of that total, 4,166 were intended for export (including 376 of the 3½ Litre models and 31 of the 2½ Litre).

The Mark IV Jaguar saloon was produced from 1946 through 1948. *John Gunnell*

Ratio: 7.50:1. Brake Horsepower: 65 at 4600 rpm. Three main bearings. Solid valve lifters. One S.U. carburetor.

BASE SIX 2½ LITRE: Inline, overhead-valve six-cylinder. Cast-iron block and head. Displacement: 162.4 cid (2664 cc). Bore & Stroke: 2.87 x 4.17 in. (73 x 106 mm). Compression Ratio: 7.60:1. Brake Horsepower: 102 at 4600 rpm. Seven main bearings. Solid valve lifters. Two S.U. sidedraft carburetors. 12-volt electrical system.

BASE SIX 3½ LITRE: Inline, overhead-valve six-cylinder. Cast-iron block and head. Displacement: 212.6 cid (3485 cc). Bore & Stroke: 3.23 x 4.33 in. (82 x 110 mm). Compression Ratio: 7.20:1. Brake Horsepower: 125 at 4250 rpm (or 120 at 4500 rpm). Torque: 184 lbs.-ft. at 2000 rpm. Seven main bearings. Solid valve lifters. Two S.U. sidedraft carburetors. 12-volt electrical system.

CHASSIS

1½ LITRE: Wheelbase: 112.5 in. Overall Length: 173 in. Front Tread: 52 in. Rear Tread: 55 in. Wheel Type: Dunlop center-lock wire; wheel discs (covers) available. Standard Tires: 5.65 x 18.

2½ LITRE: Wheelbase: 120 in. Overall Length: 186 in. Width: 66 in. Front Tread: 54 in. Rear Tread: 56 in. Wheel Type: Dunlop center-lock wire; wheel discs (covers) available. Standard Tires: 5.85 x 18.

3½ LITRE: Wheelbase: 120 in. Overall Length: 186 in. Height: 61 in. Width: 66 in. Front Tread: 54 in. Rear Tread: 56 in. Wheel Type: Dunlop center-lock wire; wheel discs (covers) available. Standard Tires: 5.85 x 18.

TECHNICAL

1½ LITRE: Layout: front-engine, rear-drive. Transmission: Moss four-speed manual, floor lever (synchromesh 2nd/3rd/4th). Standard Final Drive Ratio: 4.87:1. Steering: Burman-Douglas worm and nut. Suspension (front): rigid axle with semi-elliptic leaf springs. Suspension (rear): rigid axle with semi-elliptic leaf springs. Brakes: Girling mechanical, front/rear drum. Body Construction: steel body on box-section steel frame.

2½ LITRE: Layout: front-engine, rear-drive. Transmission: Moss four-speed manual, floor lever (synchromesh 2nd/3rd/4th). Standard Final Drive Ratio: 4.55:1. Steering: Burman-

Douglas worm and nut. Suspension (front): rigid axle with semi-elliptic leaf springs. Suspension (rear): rigid axle with semi-elliptic leaf springs. Brakes: Girling mechanical, front/rear drum. Body Construction: steel body on box-section steel frame.

3½ LITRE: Layout: front-engine, rear-drive. Transmission: Moss four-speed manual, floor lever (synchromesh 2nd/3rd/4th). Standard Final Drive Ratio: 4.27:1. Steering: Burman-Douglas worm and nut. Suspension (front): rigid axle with semi-elliptic leaf springs. Suspension (rear): rigid axle with semi-elliptic leaf springs. Brakes: Girling mechanical, front/rear drum. Body Construction: steel body on box-section steel frame. Fuel Tank: 16.8 gallon.

OPTIONS: (All) Radiator ornament. Ace wheel covers. Optional compression ratios.

PERFORMANCE

1½ LITRE: Top Speed: 71 mph.

2½ LITRE: Top Speed: 87 mph. Acceleration (0-50 mph): 10.6 seconds. Acceleration (quarter-mile): 20.6 seconds.

3½ LITRE: Top Speed: 90+ mph (up to 100 mph claimed).

Acceleration (quarter-mile): 21 seconds. Fuel Mileage (3½ Litre): 18-20 mpg claimed.

CALENDAR YEAR SALES (U.S.): N/A

MANUFACTURER: Jaguar Cars Ltd., Coventry, England.

DISTRIBUTOR: Fergus Motors and The Hoffman Motor Car Co., New York City.

HISTORY: All three models were introduced just after World War II, in September 1945. Only six-cylinder models were officially imported, and those were mainly 3½ Litre Jaguars. The 1946 models were later referred to as Mark IVs. However, their only official name was the "3½ Litre" designation. Export auto sales were very important in England at this time, as the money generated by such business, primarily in North America, was needed to rebuild a British economy that had been devastated during World War II. All of the top-selling imports in the U.S. at this time were British cars – particularly Austin, Hillman and MG – and Jaguar was always high on the charts. In the later 1950s, cars like the Volkswagen Beetle and Renault Dauphine would "come out of nowhere" and knock the British cars down or off the charts. It's a shame, really, that the British makers didn't have a better long-range view because they had such a strong foothold on the early imported car marketplace.

The impressive nose of a 3.0-litre Mk IV Jaguar.

John Wheater

Mural Adams

1947

1½ LITRE — FOUR — The styling of the early postwar Jaguars did not change from that of the 1946 models. During 1947, Jaguar adopted automatic ignition advance. After that the spark advance mechanism was no longer controlled by a lever on the steering wheel.

2½ LITRE — SIX — The 2½-Litre Jaguar looked similar to the smaller model, but on top of the grille was a "2½ Litre" badge.

3½ LITRE — SIX — The 3½-Litre Jaguar looked similar to both other models. It was the same size as the 2½-Litre model. A "3½ Litre" badge was seen on the grille. A different rear axle ratio was used with the more powerful motor.

I.D. DATA: Chassis serial number is stamped on the front of the frame, and on a plate at side of firewall. Engine numbers are stamped on a boss on the rear of the cylinder block, and on the firewall plate. Starting serial number: (3½ Litre RHD saloon) 610001; (3½ Litre LHD saloon) 630001; (3½ Litre RHD coupe) 617001; (3½ Litre LHD coupe) 637001; (2½ Litre RHD saloon) 510001; (2½ Litre LHD saloon) 530001; (2½ Litre RHD coupe) 517001; (2½ Litre LHD coupe) 537001; (1½ Litre RHD) 410001; (1½ Litre LHD) 430001. Starting engine number: (3½ Litre) S26; (2½ Litre) P18; (1½ Litre) KB1001.

ENGINES

BASE FOUR 1½ LITRE: Inline, overhead-valve four-cylinder. Cast-iron block and head. Displacement: 108.3 cid (1775 cc). Bore & Stroke: 2.87 x 4.17 in. (73 x 106 mm). Compression Ratio: 7.50:1. Brake Horsepower: 65 at 4600 rpm. Three main bearings. Solid valve lifters. One S.U. carburetor.

BASE SIX 2½ LITRE: Inline, overhead-valve six-cylinder. Cast-iron block and head. Displacement: 162.4 cid (2664 cc). Bore & Stroke: 2.87 x 4.17 in. (73 x 106 mm). Compression Ratio: 7.60:1. Brake Horsepower: 102 at 4600 rpm. Seven main bearings. Solid valve lifters. Two S.U. sidedraft carburetors. 12-volt electrical system.

BASE SIX 3½ LITRE: Inline, overhead-valve six-cylinder. Cast-iron block and head. Displacement: 212.6 cid (3485 cc). Bore & Stroke: 3.23 x 4.33 in. (82 x 110 mm). Compression Ratio: 7.20:1. Brake Horsepower: 125 at 4250 rpm (or 120 at 4500 rpm). Torque: 184 lbs.-ft. at 2000 rpm. Seven main bearings. Solid valve lifters. Two S.U. sidedraft carburetors. 12-volt electrical system.

CHASSIS

1½ LITRE: Wheelbase: 112.5 in. Overall Length: 173 in. Front Tread: 52 in. Rear Tread: 55 in. Wheel Type: Dunlop center-lock wire; wheel discs (covers) available. Standard Tires: 5.65 x 18.

2½ LITRE: Wheelbase: 120 in. Overall Length: 186 in. Width: 66 in. Front Tread: 54 in. Rear Tread: 56 in. Wheel Type: Dunlop center-lock wire; wheel discs (covers) available. Standard Tires: 5.85 x 18.

3½ LITRE: Wheelbase: 120 in. Overall Length: 186 in. Height: 61 in. Width: 66 in. Front Tread: 54 in. Rear Tread: 56 in. Wheel Type: Dunlop center-lock wire; wheel discs (covers) available. Standard Tires: 5.85 x 18.

TECHNICAL

1½ LITRE: Layout: front-engine, rear-drive. Transmission: Moss four-speed manual, floor lever (synchromesh 2nd/3rd/4th). Standard Final Drive Ratio: 4.87:1. Steering: Burman-Douglas worm and nut. Suspension (front): rigid axle with semi-elliptic leaf springs. Suspension (rear): rigid axle with semi-elliptic leaf springs. Brakes: Girling mechanical, front/rear drum. Body Construction: steel body on box-section steel frame.

2½ LITRE: Layout: front-engine, rear-drive. Transmission: Moss four-speed manual, floor lever (synchromesh 2nd/3rd/4th). Standard Final Drive Ratio: 4.55:1. Steering: Burman-Douglas worm and nut. Suspension (front): rigid axle with semi-elliptic leaf springs. Suspension (rear): rigid axle with semi-elliptic leaf springs. Brakes: Girling mechanical, front/rear drum. Body Construction: steel body on box-section steel frame.

3½ LITRE: Layout: front-engine, rear-drive. Transmission: Moss four-speed manual, floor lever (synchromesh 2nd/3rd/4th). Standard Final Drive Ratio: 4.27:1. Steering: Burman-Douglas worm and nut. Suspension (front): rigid axle with semi-elliptic leaf springs. Suspension (rear): rigid axle with semi-elliptic leaf springs. Brakes: Girling mechanical, front/rear drum. Body Construction: steel body on box-section steel frame. Fuel Tank: 16.8 gallons.

OPTIONS: Radiator ornament. Ace wheel covers. Optional compression ratios.

PERFORMANCE

1½ LITRE: Top Speed: 71 mph.

2½ LITRE: Top Speed: 87 mph. Acceleration (0-50 mph): 10.6 seconds. Acceleration (quarter-mile): 20.6 seconds.

3½ LITRE: Top Speed: 90+ mph (up to 100 mph claimed). Acceleration (quarter-mile): 21 seconds. Fuel Mileage: (3½ Litre) 18-20 mpg claimed.

CALENDAR YEAR SALES (U.S.): N/A

MANUFACTURER: Jaguar Cars Ltd., Coventry, England.

DISTRIBUTOR: Fergus Motors and The Hoffman Motor Car Co., New York City, were the first dealers.

HISTORY: The first Jaguar saloons arrived in the U.S. in January 1947. The first drophead coupes arrived at the end of that year, when they gained considerable popularity. Only six-cylinder models were officially imported and those were mainly 3½ Litre Jaguars. These 1946 to 1948 models were later referred to as "Mark IVs."

1947 Jaguar Mark IV drophead

1948 Jaguar Mk IV saloon *Carl and Carrol Jensen*

1948

1½ LITRE — FOUR — The 1½ Litre Jaguar continued to be produced for English buyers in 1948.

2½ LITRE — SIX — The 2½ Litre Jaguar continued to be produced for English buyers in 1948. There were no significant product changes from 1948.

3½ LITRE — SIX — The 3½ Litre Jaguar continued to be produced for English buyers in 1948. There were no significant product changes from 1948.

I.D. DATA: Chassis serial number is stamped on the front of the frame, and on a plate at side of firewall. Engine numbers are stamped on a boss on the rear of the cylinder block, and on the firewall plate. Starting serial number: (3½ Litre RHD saloon) 610001; (3½ Litre LHD saloon) 630001; (3½ Litre RHD coupe) 617001; (3½ Litre LHD coupe) 637001; (2½ Litre RHD saloon) 510001; (2½ Litre LHD saloon) 530001; (2½ Litre RHD coupe) 517001; (2½ Litre LHD coupe) 537001; (1½ Litre RHD) 410001; (1½ Litre LHD) 430001. Starting engine number: (3½ Litre) S26; (2½ Litre) P18; (1½ Litre) KB1001.

ENGINES

BASE FOUR 1½ LITRE: Inline, overhead-valve four-cylinder. Cast-iron block and head. Displacement: 108.3 cid (1775 cc). Bore & Stroke: 2.87 x 4.17 in. (73 x 106 mm). Compression Ratio: 7.20:1. Brake Horsepower: 65 at 4600 rpm. Three main bearings. Solid valve lifters. One S.U. sidedraft (horizontal) carburetor.

BASE SIX 2½ LITRE: Inline, overhead-valve six-cylinder. Cast-iron block and head. Displacement: 162.4 cid (2664 cc). Bore & Stroke: 2.87 x 4.17 in. (73 x 106 mm). Compression Ratio: 7.30:1. Brake Horsepower: 102 at 4600 rpm. Seven main bearings. Solid valve lifters. Two S.U. sidedraft (horizontal) carburetors. 12-volt electrical system.

BASE SIX 3½ LITRE: Inline, overhead-valve six-cylinder. Cast-iron block and head. Displacement: 212.6 cid (3485 cc). Bore & Stroke: 3.23 x 4.33 in. (82 x 110 mm). Compression Ratio: 7.75:1. Brake Horsepower: 125 at 4250 rpm. Torque: 184 lbs.-ft. at 2000 rpm. Seven main bearings. Solid valve lifters. Two S.U. sidedraft (horizontal) carburetors. 12-volt electrical system.

CHASSIS

1½ LITRE: Wheelbase: 112.5 in. Overall Length: 173 in. Front Tread: 52 in. Rear Tread: 55 in. Wheel Type: Dunlop center-lock wire; wheel discs (covers) available. Standard Tires: 5.65 x 18.

2½ LITRE: Wheelbase: 120 in. Overall Length: 186 in. Width: 66 in. Front Tread: 54 in. Rear Tread: 56 in. Wheel Type: Dunlop center-lock wire; wheel discs (covers) available. Standard Tires: 5.85 x 18.

3½ LITRE: Wheelbase: 120 in. Overall Length: 186 in. Height: 61 in. Width: 66 in. Front Tread: 54 in. Rear Tread: 56 in. Wheel Type: Dunlop center-lock wire; wheel discs (covers) available. Standard Tires: 5.85 x 18.

TECHNICAL

1½ LITRE: Layout: front-engine, rear-drive. Transmission: Moss four-speed manual, floor lever (synchromesh 2nd/3rd/4th). Standard Final Drive Ratio: 4.87:1. Steering: Burman-Douglas worm and nut. Suspension (front): rigid axle with semi-elliptic leaf springs. Suspension (rear): rigid axle with semi-elliptic leaf springs. Brakes: Girling mechanical, front/rear drum. Body Construction: steel body on box-section steel frame.

2½ LITRE: Layout: front-engine, rear-drive. Transmission: Moss four-speed manual, floor lever (synchromesh 2nd/3rd/4th). Standard Final Drive Ratio: 4.55:1. Steering: Burman-Douglas worm and nut. Suspension (front): rigid axle with semi-elliptic leaf springs. Suspension (rear): rigid axle with semi-elliptic leaf springs. Brakes: Girling mechanical, front/rear drum. Body Construction: steel body on box-section steel frame.

3½ LITRE: Layout: front-engine, rear-drive. Transmission: Moss four-speed manual, floor lever (synchromesh 2nd/3rd/4th). Standard Final Drive Ratio: 4.27:1. Steering: Burman-Douglas worm and nut. Suspension (front): rigid axle with semi-elliptic leaf springs. Suspension (rear): rigid axle with semi-elliptic leaf springs. Brakes: Girling mechanical, front/rear drum. Body Construction: steel body on box-section steel frame. Fuel Tank: 16.8 gallons.

OPTIONS: Radiator ornament. Ace wheel covers. Optional compression ratios.

PERFORMANCE

1½ LITRE: Top Speed: 71 mph.

2½ LITRE: Top Speed: 87 mph. Acceleration (0-50 mph): 10.6 seconds. Acceleration: (quarter-mile): 20.6 seconds.

3½ LITRE: Top Speed: 90+ mph (up to 100 mph claimed). Acceleration: (quarter-mile): 21 seconds. Fuel Mileage: (3½ Litre) 18-20 mpg claimed.

CALENDAR YEAR SALES (U.S.): N/A

MANUFACTURER: Jaguar Cars Ltd., Coventry, England.

DISTRIBUTOR: Fergus Motors and The Hoffman Motor Car Co., New York City, were the first dealers.

HISTORY: After the Mark V Jaguar debuted late in 1948, people sometimes referred to the 1946 through 1948 models as Mark IVs. However, their only official name was their litre designation. Production of the 1½-, 2½- and 3½-litre models ceased in March 1949, after the Mark V had already emerged. Jaguar wanted to use pressed steel bodies for its early postwar sedans instead of the prewar-style steel-over-ash body, but pressed steel was scarce in these years. So they soon mixed a new chassis with the old (3.5-litre) engine and mounted a traditional-style "interim" body to create the Mark V saloon. This model lasted until the arrival of the all-new Mark VII. Early Hoffman ads in the U.S. promoted the 1948 Jaguar 3½ Litre convertible (drophead coupe) as "The World's Finest Car in its Class," and "the first British-made luxury car to offer conventional American left-hand drive." Customers were further advised that the car's "fleet, low, European lines…attract admiring glances everywhere." The Jaguar XK-120 Super Sport model was unveiled at the Automobile Show at Earls Court, London, England, late in 1948 (as a 1949 model).

1948 Jaguar Mk IV 2.5-litre saloon

Dan Lyons

Model	Body Type & Seating	Engine Type/CID	P.O.E. Price	Weight (Lbs.)	Production Total
1½-Litre	4d Saloon-4/5P	I4/108	N/A	2,800	Note 1
1½-Litre	2d Drophead Coupe-4/5P	I4/108	N/A	2,800	Note 1
2½-Litre	4d Saloon-5P	I6/162	N/A	3,528	Note 1
2½-Litre	2d Drophead Coupe-5P	I6/162	N/A	3,528	Note 1
3½-Litre	4d Saloon-5P	I6/213	$4,633	3,528	Note 1
3½-Litre	2d Drophead Coupe-5P	I6/213	$4,745	3,528	Note 1

Note 1: A total of 11,952 Jaguars were produced from 1946 to 1949; of that total, 4,166 were intended for export (including 376 of the 3½ Litre models and 31 of the 2½ Litre).

Jerry and Kathy Nell

1948 Jaguar Mk IV drophead

Carl and Carrol Jensen

1948 Jaguar Mk IV saloon

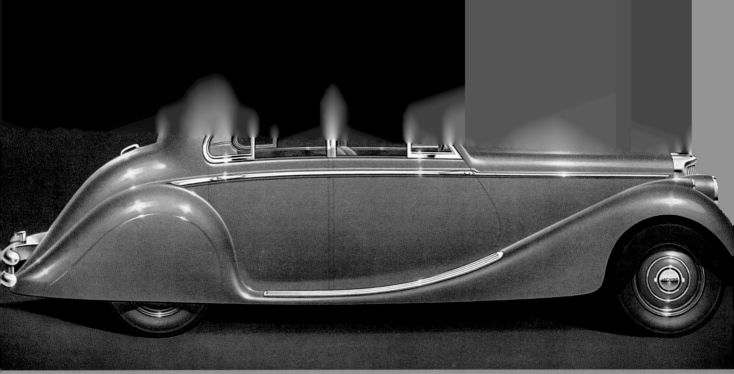

1949

XK-120 — SIX — Jaguar's new XK-120 two-seat roadster quickly became a favorite with American sports car fans. Its name suggested the likely top speed (120 mph). Faired-in sealed-beam headlights sat alongside the narrow oval grille with 13 vertical bars. The grille was flanked by two slim bumpers without overriders. The grille rose as a unit when the narrow, tapered hood was opened. The parking-light nacelles were chrome-plated at first, but were changed to body-color finish about one-third of the way through the production run. After the first 1,772 cars were built, air vents were added to the front fenders. The vents were positioned low on the cowl. At the rear, small taillights stood alongside the long deck lid. Some rear protection was provided by two vertical overriders. More than 200 early models had aluminum bodies on a wooden framework. All Jaguars produced after April 1950 had steel bodies. Leather upholstery was standard and leather was used on the instrument panel and garnish rails. Standard equipment included a twin-blade wiper, twin blended-note horns, two batteries, a 140-mph speedometer, a tachometer and an electric clock. The mohair folding top was concealed behind the seats when lowered. Detachable side screens went into a tray in the top compartment. The new double-overhead-camshaft six-cylinder engine produced 160 hp (150 hp with the lower compression head). It had seven main bearings, hemispherical combustion chambers and a cylinder head made of high-strength aluminum alloy. The two camshafts were driven by a two-stage chain. The engine had inclined overhead valves. Jaguars could be ordered with an optional performance package that included high-lift camshafts, a higher compression ratio, a racing clutch, a dual exhaust system and wire wheels. A mono-screen windshield was available for racing. Fender skirts became a popular option for models with steel disc wheels.

MARK V — SIX — Jaguar's saloon (sedan) changed dramatically with the arrival of the four-door Mark V. The 120-inch-wheelbase chassis featured independent front suspension and hydraulic brakes. The front suspension system relied on upper and lower wishbones with ball joints and longitudinal torsion bars. The rear end retained a rigid axle and semi-elliptic leaf springs. Sealed-beam headlights were semi-faired into the front fenders which also held wing lamps. The front doors featured a particularly elegant curve in their forward edges to complement the angled-back trailing edge of the bonnet (hood). The twin bumpers had overriders. The Mark V wore rakish rear fender skirts. The Mark V's overall appearance was similar to that of the all-new-in-1946 Bentley Mark VI. The Jaguar Mark V also used a Burman steering gear, longer rear leaf springs and a new gearbox. Standard Mark V equipment included two fog lamps, two-blade windshield wipers, self-canceling trafficators and built-in "air conditioning" with a defroster and demister. Sixteen-inch bolt-on pressed-steel disc wheels carried Dunlop 6.70 x 16 tires. The big tires gave the car a low appearance. On the dashboard were two 5-inch gauges, a 0-120 mph speedometer and a tachometer. The new dashboard design made it easier to produce both left-hand-drive and right-hand-drive versions. The Jaguar sedan's windshield no longer opened for ventilation. The car had non-pleated Vaumol leather and Dunlopillo upholstery. The garnish rails, window frames and instrument panel were crafted of polished walnut. A tool kit was stored in a soundproof container stored in the deck lid. A Mark V drophead coupe with large landau bars joined the four-door saloon in September 1949.

I.D. DATA: Chassis serial number for XK-120 is stamped atop the chassis side member, opposite the flywheel housing, and on the front cross member, under the radiator. Chassis number for the Mark V saloon is stamped on front of frame. Starting chassis serial number: (XK-120) 660001 with RHD, 670001 with LHD; (MK V 2.5-Litre RHD saloon) 520001; (MK V 2.5-Litre RHD coupe) 540001; (MK V 2.5-Litre LHD

Model	Body Type & Seating	Engine Type/CID	P.O.E. Price	Weight (lbs.)	Prod. Total
XK-120					
XK-120	2d Roadster-2P	I6/210	$4,745	2,408	**Note 1**
Mark V					
2.5-Litre	4d Saloon-5P	I6/162	N/A	N/A	**Note 2**
2.5-Litre	2d Drophead Coupe-5P	I6/162	N/A	N/A	**Note 2**
3.5-Litre	4d Saloon-5P	I6/213	$4,600	3,500	**Note 2**
3.5-Litre	2d Drophead Coupe-5P	I6/213	$4,950	3,650	**Note 2**

Note 1: Total XK-120 production (1949-1954) came to 12,078 units (7,631 roadsters, 2,678 fixed-head coupes, and 1,769 drophead coupes). Approximately 10,392 were left-hand-drive.

Note 2: Total Mark V production (1949-1951) came to 7,814 3.5-Litre saloons (4,690 for export); 1,647 2.5-Litre saloons (533 for export); 977 3.5-Litre drophead coupes (840 for export); and 28 2.5-Litre drophead coupes (all but one for export).

David Lyon

1949 Jaguar XK120 roadster, top up

saloon) 527001; (MK V 2.5-Litre RHD coupe) 547001; (MK V 3.5-Litre RHD saloon) 620001; (MK V 3.5-Litre RHD coupe) 640001; (MK V 3.5-Litre LHD saloon) 627001; (MK V 2.5-Litre RHD coupe) 647001; Engine number for XK-120 is stamped on oil-filter boss on right side of block, and (on later engines) on rear face of camshaft drive housing on the cylinder head; suffix /7 or /8 denotes compression ratio. Engine number for Mark V is stamped on a boss at the rear of the block. Starting engine number: (XK-120) W1001; (MK V 2.5-Litre) H2001; (MK V 3.5-Litre) T5001. Engine and chassis numbers for both models also appear on a large firewall plate, which also contains body and gearbox numbers.

ENGINES

BASE SIX XK-120: Inline, 70-degree dual-overhead-cam six-cylinder. Cast-iron block and aluminum-alloy head. Displacement: 210 cid (3442 cc). Bore & Stroke: 3.27 x 4.17 in. (83 x 106 mm). Compression Ratio: 7.00:1. Brake Horsepower: 160 at 5000 rpm. Torque: 195 lbs.-ft. at 2500 rpm. Seven main bearings. Solid valve lifters. Two S.U. H6 sidedraft carburetors. Lucas ignition.

BASE SIX MARK V 2.5-LITRE: Inline, overhead-valve six-cylinder. Cast-iron block and head. Displacement: 162.4 cid (2664 cc). Bore & Stroke: 2.48 x 4.17 in. (73 x 106 mm). Compression Ratio: 7.30:1. Brake Horsepower: 102 at 4600 rpm. Seven main bearings. Solid valve lifters. Two S.U. sidedraft (horizontal) carburetors. 12-volt electrical system.

BASE SIX MARK V 3.5-LITRE: Inline, overhead-valve six-cylinder. Cast-iron block and head. Displacement: 212.6 cid (3485 cc). Bore & Stroke: 3.27 x 4.17 in. (82 x 110 mm). Compression Ratio: 6.75:1. Brake Horsepower: 125 at 4250 rpm. Seven main bearings. Solid valve lifters. Two S.U. sidedraft carburetors. 12-volt electrical system. Dual exhaust system.

CHASSIS

XK-120: Wheelbase: 102 in. Overall Length: 168 in. Height: 52.5 in. Width: 61.5 in. Front Tread: 51 in. Rear Tread: 50 in. Wheel Type: pressed steel bolt-on disc. Standard Tires: Dunlop 6.00 x 16.

MARK V 2.5-LITRE: Wheelbase: 120 in. Overall Length: 187 in. Height: 62.5 in. Width: 68.5 in. Front Tread: 56 in. Rear Tread: 57.5 in. Wheel Type: pressed steel bolt-on disc. Standard Tires: Dunlop 6.70 x 16.

MARK V 3.5-LITRE: Wheelbase: 120 in. Overall Length: 187 in. Height: 62.5 in. Width: 68.5 in. Front Tread: 56 in. Rear Tread: 57.5 in. Wheel Type: pressed steel bolt-on disc. Standard Tires: Dunlop 6.70 x 16.

TECHNICAL

XK-120: Layout: front-engine, rear-drive. Transmission: four-speed manual. Overall gear ratios: (1st) 12.29:1; (2nd) 7.22:1; (3rd) 4.98:1; (4th) 3.64:1. Standard Final Drive Ratio: 3.64:1.

Steering: Burman re-circulating ball. Suspension (front): independent; transverse wishbones, long torsion bars and anti-roll bar. Suspension: rigid axle with semi-elliptic leaf springs. Brakes: hydraulic, front/rear drum. Body Construction: steel body on box-section steel frame. Fuel Tank: 18 gallons (U.S.).

MARK V 2.5-LITRE: Layout: front-engine, rear-drive. Transmission: four-speed manual. Overall gear ratios: (1st) 15.35:1; (2nd) 9.01:1; (3rd) 6.21:1; (4th) 4.55:1. Standard Final Drive Ratio: 4.55:1. Steering: Burman re-circulating ball. Suspension (front): independent; transverse wishbones and long torsion bars. Suspension (rear): rigid axle with semi-elliptic leaf springs. Brakes: hydraulic, front/rear drum. Body Construction: steel body on box-section steel frame.

MARK V 3.5-LITRE: Layout: front-engine, rear-drive. Transmission: four-speed manual. Overall gear ratios: (1st) 14.5:1; (2nd) 8.52:1; (3rd) 5.87:1; (4th) 4.3:1. Standard Final Drive Ratio: 4.30:1. Steering: Burman re-circulating ball. Suspension (front): independent; transverse wishbones and long torsion bars. Suspension (rear): rigid axle with semi-elliptic leaf springs. Brakes: hydraulic, front/rear drum. Body Construction: steel body on box-section steel frame.

OPTIONS

XK-120: High-capacity 24-gallon fuel tank. Two spare wheels. Wire wheels. 3.27:1 ratio rear axle. 4.0:1 ratio rear axle. 4.3:1 ratio rear axle. High-compression cylinder head.

PERFORMANCE

XK-120: Top Speed: 122-125 mph. Acceleration (0-60 mph): 10.0 to 11.7 seconds. Acceleration (quarter-mile): 17 to 18.3 seconds at about 74 mph. Fuel Mileage: about 18 to 20 mpg.

In 1949, Jaguar advertised the new Mk V saloon and XK 120 roadster in the U.S.

MARK V 3.5-LITRE: Top Speed: 91 mph. Acceleration (0-50 mph): 9.9 seconds. Acceleration (quarter-mile): 20.2 seconds.

CALENDAR YEAR SALES (U.S.): Approximately 158 Jaguars were registered in the U.S. during 1949.

MANUFACTURER: Jaguar Cars Ltd., Coventry, England.

DISTRIBUTOR: The Hoffman Motor Car Co., New York City; and Charles H. Hornburg Jr., International Motors, Los Angeles, California.

HISTORY: Production of the XK-120 began in July 1949 and continued until September 1954. Initial deliveries on the East Coast began in August 1949, when Hoffman Motors received an example with serial number 670005. West Coast shipments began to arrive in September 1949, going to Charles Hornburg. On May 30, 1949, a standard aluminum-bodied Jaguar XK-120 with 3.5-litre engine, running on ordinary pump fuel, attained a speed of 132.6 mph over a flying mile on the Jabbeke-Aeltre road in Belgium. Officially timed by the Royal Automobile Club of Belgium, it was the fastest run time ever recorded by a standard production car without a supercharger. Jaguars finished first and second in the production-car one-hour race at Silverstone, touted in American ads that advised orders for the car were being filled "in strict rotation." "It is typically British that Jaguars never claimed more than 120 mph for this car," said *California Autonews*. The *British Daily Herald* explained that the XK-120 was "the fastest ever tourer, yet as docile in heavy traffic as the most expensive and biggest saloon." *Country Life* noted that the car "reaches a standard of functional beauty never before achieved by a British manufacturer." At the time, the XK's engine was the most powerful production unit available in Europe.

The XK-120 evolved from a "100" experimental coupe done in 1938, which featured a long hood, sloped tail, and rounded cockpit. The XK-120 copied that profile, but added a narrower oval vertical-bar grille and faired-in headlights. The XK-120 was featured in the September 1949 issue of *Motor Trend* as the "XK 120 Super Sports Model of 3½ litre capacity." A full-page advertisement for the XK-120 on the back cover mentioned the record setting car produced four new speed records on 74 octane fuel. Its price was $4,745. International Motors, Inc., 8536 Sunset Boulevard (On the Strip), said the company's showroom and service department was open evenings and Sundays. The XK-120 design arrived almost by accident, when the company needed a sports roadster body to fit a cut down Mark V chassis for display at the fall 1948 Motor Show. The first aluminum-bodied example was produced in just six weeks. There was a huge demand with most cars produced ultimately heading to the U.S. market. A four-cylinder roadster called the XK-100 was also announced. The Mark V saloon was introduced in September 1948, an interim model available in March 1949 after delivery of new bodies in 1947-1948 had been delayed. The drophead coupe was added in September 1949. A preliminary announcement called the Mark V a "worthy successor to a car which has fully earned the description of being the finest car of its class in the world." A photo and detailed press release about the Jaguar Saloon appeared in the October 1949 issue of *Motor Trend* and according to an International Motors ad in that issue, the price of the XK-120 was lowered to $3,945, while the Saloon was $3,750.

1950

XK-120 — SIX — Appearance and mechanical details of the roadster were the same as 1949. All bodies were now made of steel, and all later models had air vents on trailing ends of the front fenders.

MARK V — SIX — Appearance and mechanical details of the Jaguar saloons were the same as 1949.

I.D. DATA: Chassis serial number for XK-120 is stamped atop the chassis side member, opposite the flywheel housing; and on the front cross member, under the radiator. Chassis number for the Mark V saloon is stamped on front of frame. Starting serial number: (XK-120) 670001; (Mark V) 627251. Starting engine number: (XK-120) W1016; (Mark V) T5626.

ENGINES

BASE SIX XK-120: Inline, 70-degree dual-overhead-cam six-cylinder. Cast-iron block and aluminum-alloy head. Displacement: 210 cid (3442 cc). Bore & Stroke: 3.27 x 4.17 in. (83 x 106 mm). Compression Ratio: 7.00:1. Brake Horsepower: 160 at 5000 rpm. Torque: 195 lbs.-ft. at 2500 rpm. Seven main bearings. Solid valve lifters. Two S.U. H6 sidedraft carburetors. Lucas ignition.

BASE SIX MARK V 2.5-LITRE: Inline, overhead-valve six-cylinder. Cast-iron block and head. Displacement: 162.5 cid (2664 cc). Bore & Stroke: 2.48 x 4.17 in. (73 x 106 mm). Compression Ratio: 7.30:1. Brake Horsepower: 102 at 4600 rpm. Seven main bearings. Solid valve lifters. Two S.U. sidedraft (horizontal) carburetors. 12-volt electrical system.

BASE SIX MARK V 3.5-LITRE: Inline, overhead-valve six-cylinder. Cast-iron block and head. Displacement: 212.6 cid (3485 cc). Bore & Stroke: 3.27 x 4.17 in. (82 x 110 mm). Compression Ratio: 6.75:1. Brake Horsepower: 125 at 4250 rpm. Seven main bearings. Solid valve lifters. Two S.U. sidedraft carburetors. 12-volt electrical system. Dual exhaust system.

CHASSIS

XK-120: Wheelbase: 102 in. Overall Length: 168 in. Height: 52.5 in. Width: 61.5 in. Front Tread: 51 in. Rear Tread: 50 in. Wheel Type: pressed steel bolt-on disc. Standard Tires: Dunlop 6.00 x 16.

MARK V 2.5-LITRE: Wheelbase: 120 in. Overall Length: 187 in. Height: 62.5 in. Width: 68.5 in. Front Tread: 56 in. Rear Tread: 57.5 in. Wheel Type: pressed steel bolt-on disc. Standard Tires: Dunlop 6.70 x 16.

MARK V 3.5-LITRE: Wheelbase: 120 in. Overall Length:

187 in. Height: 62.5 in. Width: 68.5 in. Front Tread: 56 in. Rear Tread: 57.5 in. Wheel Type: pressed steel bolt-on disc. Standard Tires: Dunlop 6.70 x 16.

TECHNICAL

XK-120: Layout: front-engine, rear-drive. Transmission: four-speed manual. Overall gear ratios: (1st) 12.29:1; (2nd) 7.22:1; (3rd) 4.98:1; (4th) 3.64:1. Standard Final Drive Ratio: 3.64:1. Steering: Burman re-circulating ball. Suspension (front): independent; transverse wishbones, long torsion bars and anti-roll bar. Suspension: rigid axle with semi-elliptic leaf springs. Brakes: hydraulic, front/rear drum. Body Construction: steel body on box-section steel frame. Fuel Tank: 18 gallon (U.S.).

MARK V 2.5-LITRE: Layout: front-engine, rear-drive. Transmission: four-speed manual. Overall gear ratios: (1st) 15.35:1; (2nd) 9.01:1; (3rd) 6.21:1; (4th) 4.55:1. Standard Final Drive Ratio: 4.55:1. Steering: Burman re-circulating ball. Suspension (front): independent; transverse wishbones and long torsion bars. Suspension (rear): rigid axle with semi-elliptic leaf springs. Brakes: hydraulic, front/rear drum. Body Construction: steel body on box-section steel frame.

MARK V 3.5-LITRE: Layout: front-engine, rear-drive. Transmission: four-speed manual. Overall gear ratios: (1st) 14.5:1; (2nd) 8.52:1; (3rd) 5.87:1; (4th) 4.3:1. Standard Final Drive Ratio: 4.30:1. Steering: Burman re-circulating ball.

Suspension (front): independent; transverse wishbones and long torsion bars. Suspension (rear): rigid axle with semi-elliptic leaf springs. Brakes: hydraulic, front/rear drum. Body Construction: steel body on box-section steel frame.

OPTIONS

XK-120: High-capacity 24-gallon fuel tank (XK-120). Two spare wheels (XK-120). Wire wheels (XK-120). 3.27:1 ratio rear axle. 4.0:1 ratio rear axle. 4.3:1 ratio rear axle. High-compression cylinder head.

PERFORMANCE

XK-120: Top Speed: 122-125 mph. Acceleration (0-60 mph): 10.0-11.7 seconds. Acceleration (quarter-mile): 17-18.3 seconds at about 74 mph. Fuel Mileage: about 18-20 mpg.

MARK V 3.5-LITRE: Top Speed: 91 mph. Acceleration (0-50 mph): 9.9 seconds. Acceleration (quarter-mile): 20.2 seconds.

CALENDAR YEAR REGISTRATIONS (U.S.): A total of 912 Jaguars were registered in the U.S. during 1950.

HISTORY: A new Mark VII saloon (sedan) replaced the Mark V in October 1950. Several privately owned XK-120s entered the Le Mans race in 1950. In terms of new car registrations in the U.S. market, Jaguar was the sixth best-

Jaguar enjoyed proclaiming its successful racing heritage.

Richard Dance Collection

Model	Body Type & Seating	Engine Type/CID	P.O.E. Price	Weight (lbs.)	Production Total
XK-120					
XK-120	2d Roadster-2P	I6/210	$3,945	2,750	**Note 1**
Mark V					
2.5-Litre	4d Saloon-5P	I6/162	N/A	3,540	**Note 2**
2.5-Litre	2d Drophead Coupe-5P	I6/162	N/A	3,650	**Note 2**
3.5-Litre	4d Saloon-5P	I6/213	$3,750	3,500	**Note 2**
3.5-Litre	2d Drophead Coupe-5P	I6/213	$3,850	3,690	**Note 2**

Note 1: Total XK-120 production (1949 through 1954) came to 12,078 units (7,631 roadsters, 2,678 fixed-head coupes, and 1,769 drophead coupes).

Note 2: Total Mark V production (1949 through 1951) came to 7,814 3.5-Litre saloons (4,690 for export); 1,647 2.5-Litre saloons (533 for export); 977 3.5-Litre drophead coupes (840 for export); and 28 2.5-Litre drophead coupes (all but one for export).

selling imported car in the U.S. in 1950. Austin (5,452) was first, Hillman (3,279) was second, British Ford (1,869) was third, MG Midget (1,576) was fourth, Renault (1,551) was fifth and Jaguar (912) was sixth. By 1951, the popularity of the XK-120 would move Jaguar into the number 5 slot. The April 1950 issue of *Motor Trend* showed a white Jaguar XK-120 roadster on its cover with Audrey Carrigan and a Douglas DC-6A airplane. A three-page article about the Jaguar XK-120 appeared inside the magazine. The car was described as "the outstanding achievement of a distinguished marque." Jaguar was one of over 100 British automobiles featured at the British Automobile and Motorcycle Show held at New York City's Grand Central Palace April 15-23, 1950. This event was organized by Sir William Welsh, a representative for the British Motorcar Industry. In the Jaguar booth at the show, the emphasis was on performance. In September 1950, two Jaguar XK-120s driven by Phil Hill and Jack McAfee placed second and third in a sports car race at Santa Ana, California behind an Allard K-2. "The two Jaguar XK-120s, driven by Hill and McAfee, were very consistent in the hands of these experienced drivers," *Motor Trend* reported in September. "An interesting feature of Phil Hill's campaign was his use of 'asphalt slicks' on the Jaguar. These smooth tread, track-type tires proved very effective and mark a significant innovation in western sports car racing." Soon after the race, two West Coast Allard dealers ran a full page ad showing a photo of an Allard beating an XK-120 to the checkered flag. One of those dealers was Moss Motors, a company now familiar to collectors of Jaguars and other British cars as a leading restoration parts supplier. Elsewhere, the Carson Top Shop, of Los Angeles, California, developed a custom top for the XK-120 that was an improvement on the looks of the factory-style top.

1950 Jaguar Mk V drophead

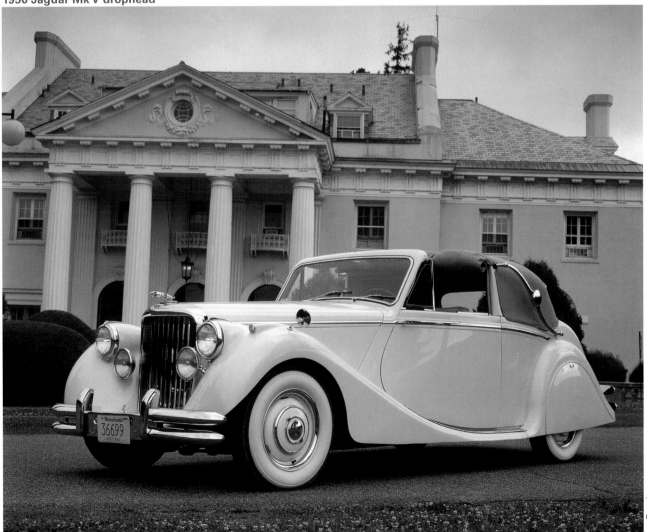

Dan Lyons

Dan Lyons

1950 Jaguar Mk V saloon

Customs and Classics, Kelly Purdum

1950 Jaguar Mk V drophead

1951

XK-120 — SIX — A fixed-head coupe with "hardtop" styling joined the original two-seat roadster in August 1951. The coupe had walnut-veneer dashboard trim, versus leather on the roadster. With its sharply-sloped fender line, the coupe looked particularly streamlined and handsome when wearing the available rounded rear fender skirts. Footwell vents were added this year and a heater became standard on the sports roadster by September 1951. Both steel disc and wire wheels were available. You could not use fender skirts with the wire wheels.

XK-120C (C-TYPE) — SIX — Also added to the sports-car lineup in 1951 was a high-performance, competition-oriented "C-Type" version of the Jaguar sports car. It had a special engine that produced 200 hp. The cylinder head had larger valves and ports than the regular twin-cam six. It also had high-lift camshafts and racing pistons. Unlike the XK-120, the aluminum-bodied C-Type roadster rode a frame made up of welded steel tubes. The rear suspension contained a transverse torsion bar and underslung trailing links. Rack-and-pinion steering was installed and the entire front end was hinged so that it could be tilted forward. The C-Type roadster body had only one door. Initial examples had large side louvers at the cowl, but the production version switched to a set of narrow side louvers. The wheelbase of the C-Type was 96 inches (six inches shorter than the wheelbase of the XK-120).

MARK VII — SIX — The traditionally-styled Mark V saloon was replaced by a completely different Mark VII, which would evolve over the next decade into Mark VIII and Mark IX versions. Up top, some similarity was evident

in roof profile between the Mark V and Mark VII; but below the beltline virtually no resemblance could be noted as the gracefully-sweeping separate fenders and running boards faded into history. Not only the body, but also the power plant was completely different. Identical to the engine installed in the XK-120 roadster and coupe, the motor produced 160 hp. That was enough to give the four-door sedan a top speed above 100 mph. The all-steel body had modern styling and now featured faired-in fenders and front-hinged front doors. A small grille contained thin vertical bars and a two-piece windshield was used. Dual saddle-style gas tanks were installed, as were rear fender skirts. The frame and suspension were identical to those used in the Mark V, but the new XK engine sat five inches farther forward than its predecessor. The brakes had a vacuum booster. Mark VII sedans came with a sunshine roof. The Deluxe model included a radio and heater. The Mark V remained available into 1951, when the Mark VII superceded it.

I.D. DATA: Chassis serial number for XK-120 is located on front left chassis member; for Mark VII, on left side of chassis member, above rear engine mounting bracket. Engine number is stamped on right of engine block above oil filter (XK-120); and on front end of cylinder head (Mark VII). Starting chassis serial number: (XK-120 coupe) 669001 with RHD, 679001 with LHD; (XK-120C C-Type) XKC001; (Mark VII) 730001. Starting engine number: (Mark VII) A-1001.

ENGINES

BASE SIX XK-120: Inline, dual-overhead-cam six-cylinder. Cast-iron block and aluminum-alloy head. Displacement: 210

Model	Body Type & Seating	Engine Type/CID	P.O.E. Price	Weight (Lbs.)	Production Total
XK-120					
XK-120	2d Roadster-2P	I6/210	$4,039	2,750	Note 1
XK-120	2d Coupe-2P	I6/210	$4,065	2,800	Note 1
C-Type					
XK-120C	2d Roadster-2P	I6/210	N/A	2,128	Note 2
Mark VII					
Standard	4d Sedan-5/6P	I6/210	$4,170	3,700	Note 3
Deluxe	4d Sedan-5/6P	I6/210	$4,290	3,775	Note 3

Note 1: Total XK-120 production (1949-1954) came to 12,078 units (7,631 roadsters, 2,678 fixed-head coupes, and 1,769 drophead coupes).

Note 2: A total of 53 C-Types were produced from 1951-1953 (both racing and "production" versions).

Note 3: A total of 20,908 Mark VII sedans were produced from 1951-1955 (12,978 for export).

Dan Lyons

A 1951 Jaguar XK 120 that is ready for racing.

cid (3442 cc). Bore & Stroke: 3.27 x 4.17 in. (83 x 106 mm). Compression Ratio: 8.0:1. Brake Horsepower: 160 at 5000 rpm. Torque: 195 lbs.-ft. at 2500 rpm. Seven main bearings. Solid valve lifters. Two S.U. sidedraft carburetors. Lucas ignition.

BASE SIX C-TYPE: Inline, dual-overhead-cam six-cylinder. Cast-iron block and aluminum-alloy head. Displacement: 210 cid (3442 cc). Bore & Stroke: 3.27 x 4.17 in. (83 x 106 mm). Compression Ratio: 8.0:1. Brake Horsepower: 200 at 5800 rpm. Seven main bearings. Solid valve lifters. Two S.U. sidedraft carburetors. Lucas ignition.

BASE SIX MARK VII: Inline, dual-overhead-cam six-cylinder. Cast-iron block and aluminum-alloy head. Displacement: 210 cid (3442 cc). Bore & Stroke: 3.27 x 4.17 in. (83 x 106 mm). Compression Ratio: 7.0:1. Brake Horsepower: 160 at 5000 rpm. Seven main bearings. Solid valve lifters. Two S.U. sidedraft carburetors. Lucas ignition.

CHASSIS

XK-120: Wheelbase: 102 in. Overall Length: 173.5 in. Height: 52.5 in. Width: 62.0 in. Front Tread: 51 in. Rear Tread: 50 in.

Wheel Type: steel disc. Standard Tires: 6.70 x 16.

XK-120C: Wheelbase: 96 in. Overall Length: 157 in. Width: 64.5 in. Front Tread: 51 in. Rear Tread: 50 in.

MARK VII: Wheelbase: 120 in. Overall Length: 196.5 in. Height: 63.0 in. Width: 73.0 in. Front Tread: 56 in. Rear Tread: 57.5 in. Wheel Type: steel disc. Standard Tires: 7.00 x 16.

TECHNICAL

XK-120: Layout: front-engine, rear-drive. Transmission: four-speed manual. Standard Final Drive Ratio: 3.64:1. Steering: Burman re-circulating ball. Suspension (front): independent; transverse wishbones, long torsion bars and anti-roll bar. Suspension (rear): rigid axle with semi-elliptic leaf springs. Brakes: hydraulic, front/rear drum. Body Construction: steel body on box-section steel frame. Fuel Tank: 18 gallon (U.S.).

XK-120C: Layout: front-engine, rear-drive. Transmission: four-speed manual. Steering: rack-and-pinion. Suspension (front): independent; transverse wishbones, long torsion bars and anti-roll bar. Suspension (rear): Transverse torsion bar

1951 Jaguar Mk VII saloon

with underslung trailing links and angled upper link. Brakes: hydraulic, front/rear drum. Body Construction: Aluminum body on tubular steel frame.

MARK VII: Layout: front-engine, rear-drive. Transmission: four-speed manual. Standard Final Drive Ratio: 4.27:1. Steering: Burman re-circulating ball. Suspension (front): independent; transverse wishbones and long torsion bars. Suspension (rear): rigid axle with semi-elliptic leaf springs. Brakes: hydraulic, front/rear drum. Body Construction: steel body on box-section steel frame.

OPTIONS

XK-120: High-capacity 24-gallon fuel tank (XK-120). Two spare wheels (XK-120). Wire wheels (XK-120). 3.27:1 ratio rear axle. 4.0:1 ratio rear axle. 4.3:1 ratio rear axle. High-compression cylinder head.

PERFORMANCE

XK-120 COUPE: Top Speed: 120 mph. Acceleration (0-60 mph): 9.9 seconds.

C-TYPE: Top Speed: 143 mph. Acceleration (0-60 mph): 6.1

seconds. Acceleration (quarter-mile): 16.2 seconds; (MK VII) 19.3 seconds.

MARK VII: Top Speed: 101 mph. Acceleration (0-60 mph): 13.4 seconds. Acceleration (quarter-mile): 19.3 seconds.

CALENDAR YEAR REGISTRATIONS (U.S.): 1,702 Jaguars were registered in the U.S. during 1951.

MANUFACTURER: Jaguar Cars Ltd., Coventry, England.

DISTRIBUTOR: The Hoffman Motor Car Co., New York City; and Charles H. Hornburg Jr., Los Angeles.

HISTORY: The Mark VII sedan debuted at the 35th International Motor Exhibition at Earls Court in London, in fall 1950. The XK-120 fixed-head coupe debuted at the 1951 Geneva show. One of the new limited-production, high-performance XK-120C roadsters won the Le Mans race this year. In terms of new car registrations in the U.S. market, Jaguar became the fifth best-selling imported car in the U.S. in 1951. Austin (3,800) was first, MG Midget (3,790) was second, Hillman (3,787) was third, British Ford (3,508) was fourth and Jaguar (1,702) was fifth.

1952 Jaguar C-type (also called XK-C) *Jerry and Kathy Nell*

1952

XK-120 — SIX — During 1952, faired-in lights replaced the former chromed sidelight housings on top of the Jaguar XK-120's front fenders. New this year were XK-120M ("M" stood for "modified") versions of the sports car with knock-off wire wheels, no fender skirts, a 180-hp version of the twin-cam engine and dual exhausts. The modified engine had high-lift camshafts from the C-Type racer, stiffer valve springs and a special crankshaft damper. The "M" package also included stiffer front torsion bars and rear springs. It added $395 to the car's price. Meanwhile, the basic engine adopted a thicker head gasket in 1952.

MARK VII — SIX — Production of the four-door sedan continued with little change. Standard MK VII equipment included a 120-mph speedometer, a sliding sunroof, a polished walnut instrument panel, polished walnut interior garnish moldings, twin locking glove boxes, five ashtrays, padded armrests and deep-pile carpeting. The seats were upholstered in Vaumol leather over foam rubber. Either five-passenger or six-passenger seating was available.

I.D. DATA: Chassis serial number for XK-120 is located on front left chassis member; for Mark VII, on left side of chassis member, above rear engine mounting bracket. Engine number is stamped on right of engine block above oil filter (XK-120); and on front end of cylinder head (Mark VII). Starting serial number: (XK C-Type) XKC004; (other models) continued in sequence from prior listings. "Special Equipment" models have a "S" prefix for the chassis number, and "S" suffix added to the engine number.

ENGINES

BASE SIX XK-120: Inline, dual-overhead-cam six-cylinder. Cast-iron block and aluminum-alloy head. Displacement: 210 cid (3442 cc). Bore & Stroke: 3.27 x 4.17 in. (83 x 106 mm). Compression Ratio: 8.0:1. Brake Horsepower: 160 at 5200 rpm. Torque: 195 lbs.-ft. at 2500 rpm. Seven main bearings. Solid valve lifters. Two S.U. sidedraft carburetors. Lucas ignition.

BASE SIX XK-120M: Inline, dual-overhead-cam six-cylinder. Cast-iron block and aluminum-alloy head. Displacement: 210 cid (3442 cc). Bore & Stroke: 3.27 x 4.17 in. (83 x 106 mm). Compression Ratio: 9.0:1. Brake Horsepower: 180 at 5300 rpm. Seven main bearings. Solid valve lifters. Two S.U. sidedraft carburetors. Lucas ignition.

BASE SIX C-TYPE: Inline, dual-overhead-cam six-cylinder. Cast-iron block and aluminum-alloy head. Displacement: 210 cid (3442 cc). Bore & Stroke: 3.27 x 4.17 in. (83 x 106 mm). Compression Ratio: 8.0:1. Brake Horsepower: 200 at 5800 rpm. Seven main bearings. Solid valve lifters. Two S.U. sidedraft carburetors. Lucas ignition.

BASE SIX MARK VII: Inline, dual-overhead-cam six-cylinder. Cast-iron block and aluminum-alloy head. Displacement: 210 cid (3442 cc). Bore & Stroke: 3.27 x 4.17 in. (83 x 106 mm). Compression Ratio: 8.0:1. Brake Horsepower: 160 at 5200 rpm. Seven main bearings. Solid valve lifters. Two S.U. sidedraft carburetors. Lucas ignition.

CHASSIS

XK-120: Wheelbase: 102 in. Overall Length: 173.5 in. Height: 52.5 in. Width: 62.0 in. Front Tread: 51 in. Rear Tread: 50 in. Wheel Type: steel disc. Standard Tires: 6.00 x 16.

XK-120C: Wheelbase: 96 in. Overall Length: 157 in. Width: 64.5 in. Front Tread: 51 in. Rear Tread: 50 in.

MARK VII: Wheelbase: 120 in. Overall Length: 196.5 in. Height: 63.0 in. Width: 73.0 in. Front Tread: 56 in. Rear Tread: 57.5 in. Wheel Type: steel disc. Standard Tires: 6.70 x 16.

TECHNICAL

XK-120: Layout: front-engine, rear-drive. Transmission: four-speed manual. Standard Final Drive Ratio: 3.64:1. Steering: Burman re-circulating ball. Suspension (front): independent; transverse wishbones, long torsion bars and anti-roll bar. Suspension (rear): rigid axle with semi-elliptic leaf springs. Brakes: hydraulic, front/rear drum. Body Construction: steel body on box-section steel frame. Fuel Tank: 18 gallon (U.S.).

XK-120C: Layout: front-engine, rear-drive. Transmission: four-speed manual. Steering: rack-and-pinion. Suspension (front): independent; transverse wishbones, long torsion bars and anti-roll bar. Suspension (rear): Transverse torsion bar with underslung trailing links and angled upper link. Brakes: hydraulic, front/rear drum. Body Construction: Aluminum body on tubular steel frame.

MARK VII: Layout: front-engine, rear-drive. Transmission: four-speed manual. Overall gear ratios: (1st) 14.4:1; (2nd) 8.56:1; (3rd) 5.84:1; (4th) 4.27:1. Standard Final Drive Ratio: 4.27:1. Steering: Burman re-circulating ball. Suspension (front): independent; transverse wishbones and long torsion bars. Suspension (rear): rigid axle with semi-elliptic leaf springs. Brakes: hydraulic, front/rear drum. Body Construction: steel body on box-section steel frame.

OPTIONS

XK-120: High-capacity 24-gallon fuel tank (XK-120). Two spare wheels (XK-120). Wire wheels (XK-120). 3.27:1 ratio rear axle. 4.0:1 ratio rear axle. 4.3:1 ratio rear axle. High-compression cylinder head.

PERFORMANCE

XK-120: Top Speed: 122 mph. Acceleration (0-60 mph): 10.5 seconds. Acceleration (quarter mile): 18.5 seconds.

XK-120M: Top Speed: 124 mph. Acceleration (0-60 mph): 9.0 seconds. Acceleration (quarter mile): 17.0 seconds at 83 mph.

C-TYPE: Top Speed: 145 mph. Acceleration (0-60 mph): 6.5-8.0 seconds. Acceleration (quarter-mile): 15.2-16.2 seconds.

MARK VII: Top Speed: 102 mph. Acceleration (0-60 mph): 13.5 seconds. Acceleration (quarter-mile): 19.3 seconds at 72 mph.

CALENDAR YEAR REGISTRATIONS (U.S.): 3,349 Jaguars were registered in the U.S. during 1952.

MANUFACTURER: Jaguar Cars Ltd., Coventry, England.

DISTRIBUTOR: The Hoffman Motor Car Co., New York City; Charles H. Hornburg Jr., Los Angeles; and Peter Satori, California.

1952 Jaguar XK 120 fixed head coupe *Bob Harrington*

Model	Body Type & Seating	Engine Type/CID	P.O.E. Price	Weight (lbs.)	Production Total
XK-120					
XK-120	2d Roadster-2P	I6/210	$4,039	2,750	**Note 1**
XK-120	2d Coupe-2P	I6/210	$4,065	2,800	**Note 1**
XK-120M (modified)					
XK-120M	2d Roadster-2P	I6/210	$4,434	N/A	**Note 1**
XK-120M	2d Coupe-2P	I6/210	$4,460	N/A	**Note 1**
C-Type					
XK-120C	2d Roadster-2P	I6/210	N/A	2,128	**Note 2**
Mark VII					
Standard	4d Sedan-5/6P	I6/210	$4,170	3,700	**Note 3**
Deluxe	4d Sedan-5/6P	I6/210	$4,290	3,775	**Note 3**

Note 1: Total XK-120 production (1949-1954) came to 12,078 units (7,631 roadsters, 2,678 fixed-head coupes, and 1,769 drophead coupes).

Note 2: A total of 53 C-Types were produced from 1951-1953 (both racing and "production" versions).

Note 3: A total of 20,908 Mark VII sedans were produced from 1951-1955 (12,978 for export).

Equipment Note: Mark VII sedans came with a sunshine roof; Deluxe model included radio and heater.

Greg Hertel

A view of the classic Jaguar XK 120 roadster.

HISTORY: By 1951-1952, factory information sheets describing performance boosts were available to owners who wished to modify their own cars. Jaguar also offered alternative equipment for sporting events, including a 24-gallon fuel tank and dual spare wheels. Brochures issued at the 1952 Paris Salon called the Mark VII "an entirely new car of unparalleled beauty . . . powered by the world famous record-breaking XK120 engine." Some U.S. ads omitted the "120" designation of the sports roadster, promoting it as the "XK Super Sports." In terms of new car registrations in the U.S. market, Jaguar remained the fifth best-selling imported car in the U.S. in 1952. MG (7,449) was first, Austin (4,804) was second, Hillman (4,782) was third, British Ford (3,854) was fourth and Jaguar (3,349) was a close fifth. Volkswagen was way down the list with 601 cars imported, which was up from last year's 390. Unfortunately, the British makers weren't keeping an eye on the German upstart.

A classic Jaguar XK 120 in racing action.

Phil Hall Collection

1953

XK-120 — SIX — A full-fledged drophead coupe joined the roadster and fixed-head coupe for 1953. A 180-hp "Special Equipment" engine was available under the hood of the XK-120M models. Jaguar also offered a selection of other performance options. Throughout the early 1950s, many XK-120s had the optional center-lock wire wheels instead of the standard steel discs. Some of these cars had sleek-looking rear fender skirts.

MARK VII — SIX — An automatic transmission became available for the four-door sedan early in 1953. Then, later in the year, a Laycock de Normanville overdrive was made available. Initially, the Borg-Warner automatic transmission was available only on export models. When overdrive was ordered, a 4.55:1 rear axle was installed. Otherwise, production continued with little change.

I.D. DATA: Serial number is located on front left chassis member (XK-120); on left side of chassis member, above rear engine mounting bracket (Mark VII). Engine number is on right of engine block above oil filter, or on front end of cylinder head. Starting serial number: (XK-120 convertible) 667001 with RHD. "Special Equipment" models have a "S" prefix for the chassis number, and a suffix added to the engine number.

ENGINES

BASE SIX XK-120: Inline, dual-overhead-cam six-cylinder. Cast-iron block and aluminum-alloy head. Displacement: 210 cid (3442 cc). Bore & Stroke: 3.27 x 4.17 in. (83 x 106 mm). Compression Ratio: 8.0:1. Brake Horsepower: 160 at 5200 rpm. Torque: 195 lbs.-ft. at 2500 rpm. Seven main bearings. Solid valve lifters. Two S.U. sidedraft carburetors. Lucas ignition.

BASE SIX XK-120M: Inline, dual-overhead-cam six-cylinder. Cast-iron block and aluminum-alloy head. Displacement: 210 cid (3442 cc). Bore & Stroke: 3.27 x 4.17 in. (83 x 106 mm). Compression Ratio: 9.0:1. Brake Horsepower: 180 at 5300 rpm. Torque: 203 lbs.-ft. at 4000 rpm. Seven main bearings. Solid valve lifters. Two S.U. sidedraft carburetors. Lucas ignition.

BASE SIX C-TYPE: Inline, dual-overhead-cam six-cylinder. Cast-iron block and aluminum-alloy head. Displacement: 210 cid (3442 cc). Bore & Stroke: 3.27 x 4.17 in. (83 x 106 mm). Compression Ratio: 8.0:1. Brake Horsepower: 200 at 5800 rpm. Seven main bearings. Solid valve lifters. Two S.U. sidedraft carburetors. Lucas ignition.

BASE SIX MARK VII: Inline, dual-overhead-cam six-cylinder. Cast-iron block and aluminum-alloy head.

Model	Body Type & Seating	Engine Type/CID	P.O.E. Price	Weight (lbs.)	Production Total
XK-120					
XK-120	2d Roadster-2P	I6/210	$4,039	2,920	**Note 1**
XK-120	2d Coupe-2P	I6/210	$4,065	3,050	**Note 1**
XK-120	2d Convertible-2P	I6/210	$4,250	3,060	**Note 1**
XK-120M (modified)					
XK-120M	2d Roadster-2P	I6/210	$4,434	N/A	**Note 1**
XK-120M	2d Coupe-2P	I6/210	$4,460	3,022	**Note 1**
XK-120M	2d Convertible-2P	I6/210	$4,645	N/A	**Note 1**
C-Type					
XK-120C	2d Roadster-2P	I6/210	$5,860	2,128	**Note 2**
Mark VII					
Standard	4d Sedan-5/6P	I6/210	$4,170	3,700	**Note 3**

Note 1: Total XK-120 production (1949-1954) came to 12,078 units (7,631 roadsters, 2,678 fixed-head coupes, and 1,769 drophead coupes).

Note 2: A total of 53 C-Types were produced from 1951-1953 including both racing and "production" versions.

Note 3: A total of 20,908 Mark VII sedans were produced from 1951-1955 of which 12,978 were export editions. Those were followed by 10,061 MK VIIM sedans of which 3,818 were for export.

John Wheater

1953 Jaguar XK 120 fixed head coupe

Displacement: 210 cid (3442 cc). Bore & Stroke: 3.27 x 4.17 in. (83 x 106 mm). Compression Ratio: 8.0:1. Brake Horsepower: 160 at 5200 rpm. Seven main bearings. Solid valve lifters. Two S.U. sidedraft carburetors. Lucas ignition.

CHASSIS

XK-120: Wheelbase: 102 in. Overall Length: 173.5 in. Height: 52.5 in. Width: 62.0 in. Front Tread: 51 in. Rear Tread: 50.0 in. Wheel Type: steel disc. Standard Tires: 6.00 x 16.

XK-120C: Wheelbase: 96 in. Overall Length: 157 in. Width: 64.5 in. Front Tread: 51 in. Rear Tread: 50 in.

MARK VII: Wheelbase: 120 in. Overall Length: 196.5 in. Height: 63.0 in. Width: 73.0 in. Front Tread: 56 in. Rear Tread: 57.5 in. Wheel Type: steel disc. Standard Tires: 6.70 x 16.

TECHNICAL

XK-120: Layout: front-engine, rear-drive. Transmission: four-speed manual. Standard Final Drive Ratio: 3.64:1. Steering: Burman re-circulating ball. Suspension (front): independent; transverse wishbones, long torsion bars and anti-roll bar. Suspension (rear): rigid axle with semi-elliptic leaf springs. Brakes: hydraulic, front/rear drum. Body Construction: steel body on box-section steel frame. Fuel Tank: 18 gallons (U.S.).

XK-120C: Layout: front-engine, rear-drive. Transmission: four-speed manual. Steering: rack-and-pinion. Suspension (front): independent; transverse wishbones, long torsion bars and anti-roll bar. Suspension (rear): Transverse torsion bar with underslung trailing links and angled upper link. Brakes: hydraulic, front/rear drum. Body Construction: Aluminum body on tubular steel frame.

MARK VII: Layout: front-engine, rear-drive. Transmission: four-speed manual. Overall gear ratios: (1st) 14.4:1; (2nd) 8.56:1; (3rd) 5.84:1; (4th) 4.27:1. Standard Final Drive Ratio: 4.27:1. Steering: Burman re-circulating ball. Suspension (front): independent; transverse wishbones and long torsion bars. Suspension (rear): rigid axle with semi-elliptic leaf springs. Brakes: hydraulic, front/rear drum. Body Construction: steel body on box-section steel frame.

OPTIONS

XK-120: High-capacity 24-gallon fuel tank (XK-120). Two spare wheels (XK-120). Wire wheels (XK-120). 3.27:1 ratio rear axle. 4.0:1 ratio rear axle. 4.3:1 ratio rear axle. High-compression cylinder head.

MARK VII: Automatic transmission: ($280). Overdrive and 4.55:1 ratio rear axle.

PERFORMANCE

XK-120: Top Speed: 122 mph. Acceleration (0-60 mph): 8.5-10.5 seconds. Acceleration (quarter mile): 18.5 seconds.

XK-120M: Top Speed: 124 mph. Acceleration (0-60 mph): 9.0-10.4 seconds. Acceleration (quarter mile): 17.0-17.5 seconds at 83 mph.

C-TYPE: Top Speed: 139-145 mph. Acceleration (0-60 mph): 6.5-8.0 seconds. Acceleration (quarter-mile): 15.2-16.2 seconds.

MARK VII: Top Speed: 102 mph. Acceleration (0-60 mph): 13.5 seconds. Acceleration (quarter-mile): 19.3 seconds at 72 mph.

CALENDAR YEAR REGISTRATIONS (U.S.): 3,914 Jaguars were registered in the U.S. during 1953.

MANUFACTURER: Jaguar Cars Ltd., Coventry, England.

DISTRIBUTOR: The Hoffman Motor Car Co., New York City; and Charles H. Hornburg Jr., Los Angeles.

HISTORY: A special bubble-topped XK-120 roadster hit 172.412 mph in October 1953. Norman Dewis drove this car for the Belgian Royal Automobile Club. Because the engine was essentially stock, the car's performance made Jaguar the world's fastest production car. The Jaguar XK-120 drophead coupe (convertible) debuted for the U.S. market at the New York Automobile Show in spring 1953. *Auto Sportsman* magazine reported that the XK-120C was "sold only to drivers or owners who are consistent competitors." In the U.S. market, Jaguar was the third most imported car in 1953.

A 1953 Hansgen-Jaguar is captured in racing action. *Bob Harrington*

A 1954 Jaguar XK 140 modified for racing. *Bob Harrington*

1954

XK-120 — SIX — Production of the three basic sports-car models continued with little change in what would be their final year, before replacement by the XK-140.

D-TYPE — SIX — Another sports-racing evolution of the XK-120 went into (limited) production in 1954. The D-Type was powered by a hopped-up 250-hp version of the twin-cam six with a new head, a three-plate clutch and a fully-synchronized four-speed gearbox. Only 87 D-Types were produced from 1954-1956. The wheelbase was 90 inches (six inches shorter than the C-Type) and torsion-bar suspensions were used front and rear. The rear suspension was similar to that used on the C-Type, but with upper and lower trailing links at each side. This was the first monocoque (unibodied) Jaguar with steel tube sub frames bolted to an aluminum/magnesium center section, though early models had bodies riveted to a square magnesium tubular frame. Knock-off Dunlop magnesium alloy wheels were standard equipment. Styling features included a short oval nose, a small windshield and a large fin behind the headrest. D-Types were offered only to qualified race drivers.

MARK VII — SIX — Production of Jaguar's full-size sedan continued with little change.

I.D. DATA: Serial number is located on front left chassis member (XK-120); or on left side of chassis member, above rear engine mounting bracket (Mark VII). Engine number is on right of engine block above oil filter, or at front end of cylinder head. Serial number range: (D-Type) XKD401-406. "Special Equipment" models have a "S" prefix for the chassis number, and a suffix added to the engine number.

ENGINES

BASE SIX XK-120: Inline, dual-overhead-cam six-cylinder. Cast-iron block and aluminum-alloy head. Displacement: 210 cid (3442 cc). Bore & Stroke: 3.27 x 4.17 in. (83 x 106 mm). Compression Ratio: 8.0:1. Brake Horsepower: 160 at 5200 rpm. Torque: 195 lbs.-ft. at 2500 rpm. Seven main bearings. Solid valve lifters. Two S.U. sidedraft carburetors. Lucas ignition.

BASE SIX XK-120M: Inline, dual-overhead-cam six-cylinder. Cast-iron block and aluminum-alloy head. Displacement: 210 cid (3442 cc). Bore & Stroke: 3.27 x 4.17 in. (83 x 106 mm). Compression Ratio: 9.0:1. Brake Horsepower: 180 at 5300 rpm. Torque: 203 lbs.-ft. at 4000 rpm. Seven main bearings. Solid valve lifters. Two S.U. sidedraft carburetors. Lucas ignition.

BASE SIX D-TYPE: Inline, dual-overhead-cam six-cylinder. Cast-iron block and aluminum-alloy head. Displacement: 210 cid (3442 cc). Bore & Stroke: 3.27 x 4.17 in. (83 x 106 mm). Compression Ratio: 9.0:1. Brake Horsepower: 250 at 6000 rpm. Seven main bearings. Solid valve lifters. Three Weber sidedraft carburetors. Lucas ignition.

BASE SIX MARK VII: Inline, dual-overhead-cam six-cylinder. Cast-iron block and aluminum-alloy head. Displacement: 210 cid (3442 cc). Bore & Stroke: 3.27 x 4.17 in. (83 x 106 mm). Compression Ratio: 8.0:1. Brake Horsepower: 160 at 5200 rpm. Seven main bearings. Solid valve lifters. Two S.U. sidedraft carburetors. Lucas ignition.

CHASSIS

XK-120: Wheelbase: 102 in. Overall Length: 173.5 in. Height: 52.5 in. Width: 62.0 in. Front Tread: 51 in. Rear Tread: 50.0 in. Wheel Type: steel disc. Standard Tires: 6.00 x 16.

D-TYPE: Wheelbase: 90 in. Overall Length: 154 in. Height: 38 in. Width: 65.8 in. Front Tread: 50 in. Rear Tread: 48 in. Tires: 6.50 x 16.

MARK VII: Wheelbase: 120 in. Overall Length: 196.5 in. Height: 63.0 in. Width: 73.0 in. Front Tread: 56 in. Rear Tread: 57.5 in. Wheel Type: steel disc. Standard Tires: 6.70 x 16.

TECHNICAL

XK-120: Layout: front-engine, rear-drive. Transmission: four-speed manual. Standard Final Drive Ratio: 3.64:1. Steering: Burman re-circulating ball. Suspension (front): independent; transverse wishbones, long torsion bars and anti-roll bar. Suspension (rear): rigid axle with semi-elliptic leaf springs. Brakes: hydraulic, front/rear drum. Body Construction: steel body on box-section steel frame. Fuel Tank: 18 gallons (U.S.).

D-TYPE: Layout: front-engine, rear-drive. Transmission: four-speed manual. Steering: rack-and-pinion. Suspension (front): independent; transverse wishbones, long torsion bars and anti-roll bar. Suspension (rear): Transverse torsion bar with upper and lower trailing links. Brakes: hydraulic, front/rear drum. Body Construction: Body riveted to magnesium-tube chassis or, later, aluminum/magnesium monocoque with steel-tube sub frames.

MARK VII: Layout: front-engine, rear-drive. Transmission: four-speed manual. Overall gear ratios: (1st) 14.4:1; (2nd) 8.56:1; (3rd) 5.84:1; (4th) 4.27:1. Standard Final Drive Ratio: 4.27:1. Steering: Burman re-circulating ball. Suspension (front): independent; transverse wishbones and long torsion bars. Suspension (rear): rigid axle with semi-elliptic leaf springs. Brakes: hydraulic, front/rear drum. Body Construction: steel body on box-section steel frame.

OPTIONS

XK-120: High-capacity 24-gallon fuel tank. Two spare wheels (XK-120). Wire wheels. 3.27:1 ratio rear axle. 4.0:1 ratio rear axle. 4.3:1 ratio rear axle. High-compression cylinder head.

MARK VII: Automatic transmission: ($195). Overdrive and 4.55:1 ratio rear axle.

PERFORMANCE

XK-120: Top Speed: 122 mph. Acceleration (0-60 mph): 8.5-10.5 seconds. Acceleration (quarter mile): 18.5 seconds.

XK-120M: Top Speed: 124 mph. Acceleration (0-60 mph): 9.0-10.4 seconds. Acceleration (quarter mile): 17.0-17.5 seconds at 83 mph.

In 1954, the D-type Jaguar was new and featured a 250-hp engine. *Jaguar Heritage—North America*

Model	Body Type & Seating	Engine Type/CID	P.O.E. Price	Weight (lbs.)	Production Total
XK-120					
XK-120	2d Roadster-2P	I6/210	$3,345	2,690	**Note 1**
XK-120	2d Coupe-2P	I6/210	$3,875	2,744	**Note 1**
XK-120	2d Convertible-2P	I6/210	$3,975	2,800	**Note 1**
XK-120M (Modified)					
XK-120M	2d Roadster-2P	I6/210	$3,545	N/A	**Note 1**
XK-120M	2d Coupe-2P	I6/210	$4,075	3,022	**Note 1**
XK-120M	2d Convertible-2P	I6/210	$4,175	N/A	**Note 1**
D-Type					
D-Type	2d Roadster-2P	I6/210	$10,000	1,904	**Note 2**
Mark VII					
MK VII	4d Sedan-6P	I6/210	$4,255	3,700	**Note 3**

Note 1: Total XK-120 production (1949-1954) came to 12,078 units (7,631 roadsters, 2,678 fixed-head coupes and 1,769 drophead coupes).

Note 2: A total of 87 D-Types were produced from 1954-1956 (including 16 that were converted for road operation, starting in 1957).

Note 3: A total of 20,908 Mark VII sedans were produced from 1951-1955 (12,978 for export). Those were followed by 10,061 MK VIIM sedans (3,818 for export).

Dan Lyons

1954 Jaguar XK 120

D-TYPE: Top Speed: 160 mph. Acceleration (0-60 mph): 4.7 seconds. Acceleration (quarter-mile): 13.7 seconds at 107 mph.

MARK VII: Top Speed: 102 mph. Acceleration (0-60 mph): 13.5 seconds. Acceleration (quarter-mile): 19.3 seconds at 72 mph.

CALENDAR YEAR REGISTRATIONS (U.S.): 3,365 Jaguars were registered in the U.S. during 1954.

MANUFACTURER: Jaguar Cars Ltd., Coventry, England.

DISTRIBUTOR: Hoffman Motor Car Co., New York City; and Charles H. Hornburg Jr., Los Angeles.

HISTORY: Jaguar's replacement for the XK-120, the restyled XK-140, debuted at the British International Motor Show which opened in London, England on October 20, 1954. Sports Cars Unlimited, an exhibition of over 50 automobiles, including Jaguars, opened at the Henry Ford Museum, in Dearborn, Michigan, on January 8, 1954. On February 3, 1954, Jaguar Cars Limited, of Canada, formed a wholly-owned subsidiary called Jaguar Cars North America. In the U.S.A. marketplace, Jaguar was again the third most popular import, but the really interesting change was that the number 1 rank no longer belonged to a British car. Instead, Volkswagen was in first place with 6,344 cars. The MG Midget was in second place with 3,454 cars imported. Jaguar's total was 3,365 registrations.

1955

XK-140 — SIX — Although the basic profile of the XK-140 was similar to that of the XK-120, the new model displayed a number of significant changes. Advertisements pointed out the XK-140's redesigned chassis, larger-diameter torsion bars, new rack-and-pinion steering (replacing the re-circulating ball type), new high-lift camshafts, new oil ignition coil and larger cockpit with increased legroom. The bumpers were bigger and the cast metal grille was made up of fewer (seven), heavier vertical bars. A chrome strip extended the full length of the hood. Tiny wing lights remained atop the front fenders. Additional round lights, mounted in a low position, were positioned just above the bumper. The coupe had a larger backlight, rear quarter windows and taillights. The roadster, fixed-head coupe and drophead coupe were again offered. The roadster kept its side curtains, while the other models carried roll-up windows. The dual-cam 3.4-litre engine was also carried over from the XK-120, but the XK-140 version produced more horsepower than its predecessor. The base engine now was comparable to the "Special Equipment" version offered on later XK-120s. The XK-140 was about 200 pounds heavier but it offered easier handling and a roomier interior. A Laycock de Normanville overdrive and a rarely ordered Borg-Warner automatic transmission were optional. The top speed of an XK-140 with overdrive was close to 130 mph. The optional XK-140 "M" appearance package included a crankshaft damper, wire wheels (either body-colored or chrome), dual exhausts, and twin fog lamps. An "MC" package for $295 above base price included those extras, but also added a "C" type cylinder head that boosted output to 210 hp.

D-TYPE — SIX — Small quantities of the competition Jaguar introduced in 1954 continued to leave the factory in 1955. The D-Type was basically a competition version of the XK sports cars. A hopped-up version of the twin-cam six with a new head, a three-plate clutch and a fully-synchronized four-speed gearbox was used. D-Types had a shortened wheelbase and front and rear torsion-bar suspensions. The D-Type had steel tube sub frames bolted to an aluminum/magnesium center section. Dunlop magnesium alloy knock-off wheels were standard. Styling features included a short oval nose, a small windshield and a large fin behind the headrest. D-Types were offered only to qualified race drivers.

MARK VIIM — SIX — The basic shape of the Jaguar sedan was unchanged, but the MK VIIM had various modifications, starting with a more potent version of the dual-overhead-cam six-cylinder engine, the same used in the new XK-140 sports cars. Appearance modifications included the addition of wraparound bumpers, separately mounted fog lamps above the bumper and new headlights. The round holes below the headlights, now contained horn grilles. The additional horsepower combined with close-ratio gearing made the MK VIIM a quicker car than the MK VII.

I.D. DATA: Chassis serial numbers are stamped on the left frame member, above the rear engine mounting bracket, and contained on a brass identification plate at the firewall. Engine number is on right of engine block, above the oil filter; or on front end of cylinder head. Starting chassis serial number: (XK-140 roadster) 810001; (XK-140 coupe) 814001; (XK-140 convertible) 817001; (D-Type) XKD501; (MK VIIM) 738184. Starting engine number: (XK-140) G1001; (MK VIIM)

Model	Body Type & Seating	Engine Type/ CID	P.O.E. Price	Weight (Lbs.)	Production Total
XK-140					
XK-140	2d Roadster-2P	I6/210	$3,450	2,750	**Note 1**
XK-140	2d Coupe-2+2P	I6/210	$3,795	2,860	**Note 1**
XK-140	2d Convertible-2+2P	I6/210	$3,795	2,970	**Note 1**
XK-140M					
XK-140M	2d Roadster-2P	I6/210	$3,595	2,750	**Note 1**
XK-140M	2d Coupe-2+2P	I6/210	$3,940	2,860	**Note 1**
XK-140M	2d Convertible-2+2P	I6/210	$3,940	2,970	**Note 1**
XK-140MC					
XK-140MC	2d Roadster-2P	I6/210	$3,745	2,750	**Note 1**
XK-140MC	2d Coupe-2+2P	I6/210	$4,090	2,860	**Note 1**
XK-140MC	2d Convertible-2+2P	I6/210	$4,090	2,970	**Note 1**
D-Type					
D-Type	2d Roadster-2P	I6/210	$10,000	1,904	**Note 2**
Mark VIIM					
Mark VIIM	4d Sedan-6P	I6/210	$4,255	3,800	**Note 3**

Note 1: Total XK-140 production (1954-1957) came to 8,884 units (3,347 roadsters, 2,797 fixed-head coupes, and 2,740 drophead coupes). Only 385 of the drophead coupes (convertibles) and 396 of the fixed-head coupes had automatic transmissions.
Note 2: A total of 87 D-Types were produced from 1954-1956 (including 16 that were converted for road operation, starting in 1957).
Note 3: A total of 10,061 Mark VIIM sedans were produced through the full model run (including 3,818 for export).

Richard Dance Collection

1955 Jaguar XK 140 fixed head coupe

D4958. The XK-140M had an "A" prefix in its serial number. The XK-140MC could be identified by a red plaque on each camshaft cover, and had an "S" prefix in its serial number when exported to the U.S. Engines with the "C" head also had that letter cast into the head top.

ENGINES

BASE SIX XK-140, MARK VIIM: Inline, dual overhead-cam six-cylinder. Cast-iron block and aluminum-alloy head. Displacement: 210 cid (3442 cc). Bore & Stroke: 3.27 x 4.17 in. (83 x 106 mm). Compression Ratio: 8.0:1. Brake Horsepower: 190 at 5500 rpm. Torque: 210 lbs.-ft. at 2500 rpm (213 lbs.-ft. at 4000 rpm with "C" head). Seven main bearings. Solid valve lifters. Two S.U. sidedraft carburetors. Lucas ignition.

BASE SIX XK-140M, XK-140C (C-Type Head): Inline, dual overhead-cam six-cylinder. Cast-iron block and aluminum-alloy head. Displacement: 210 cid (3442 cc). Bore & Stroke: 3.27 x 4.17 in. (83 x 106 mm). Compression Ratio: 8.0:1. Brake Horsepower: 210 at 5750 rpm. Torque: 213 lbs.-ft. at 4000 rpm. Seven main bearings. Solid valve lifters. Two S.U. sidedraft carburetors. Lucas ignition.

BASE SIX D-TYPE: Inline, dual-overhead-cam six-cylinder.

Cast-iron block and aluminum-alloy head. Displacement: 210 cid (3442 cc). Bore & Stroke: 3.27 x 4.17 in. (83 x 106 mm). Compression Ratio: 9.0:1. Brake Horsepower: 250 at 6000 rpm. Seven main bearings. Solid valve lifters. Three Weber sidedraft carburetors. Lucas ignition.

CHASSIS

XK-140: Wheelbase: 102 in. Overall Length: 176.0 in. Height: 55.0 in. Width: 64.5 in. Front Tread: 51.5 in. Rear Tread: 50.5 in. Wheel Type: steel disc. Standard Tires: 6.00 x 16.

D-TYPE: Wheelbase: 90 in. Overall Length: 154 in. Height: 38 in. Width: 65.8 in. Front Tread: 50 in. Rear Tread: 48 in. Tires: 6.50 x 16.

MARK VII: Wheelbase: 120 in. Overall Length: 196.5 in. Height: 63.0 in. Width: 73.0 in. Front Tread: 56 in. Rear Tread: 57.5 in. Wheel Type: steel disc. Standard Tires: 6.70 x 16.

TECHNICAL

XK-140: Layout: front-engine, rear-drive. Transmission: four-speed manual. Standard Final Drive Ratio: 3.54:1. Steering: Rack-and-pinion. Suspension (front): independent; transverse wishbones, long torsion bars and anti-roll bar. Suspension (rear): rigid axle with semi-elliptic leaf springs. Brakes: hydraulic, front/rear drum. Body Construction: steel body on box-section steel frame. Fuel Tank: 18 gallon (U.S.).

D-TYPE: Layout: front-engine, rear-drive. Transmission: four-speed manual. Steering: rack-and-pinion. Suspension (front): independent; transverse wishbones, long torsion bars and anti-roll bar. Suspension (rear): Transverse torsion bar with upper and lower trailing links. Brakes: hydraulic, front/rear drum. Body Construction: Aluminum/magnesium monocoque with steel-tube sub frames.

MARK VII: Layout: front-engine, rear-drive. Transmission: four-speed manual. Overall gear ratios: (1st) 14.4:1; (2nd) 8.56:1; (3rd) 5.84:1; (4th) 4.27:1. Standard Final Drive Ratio: 4.27:1. Steering: Re-circulating ball. Suspension (front): independent; transverse wishbones and long torsion bars. Suspension (rear): rigid axle with semi-elliptic leaf springs. Brakes: hydraulic, front/rear drum. Body Construction: steel body on box-section steel frame.

OPTIONS

XK-140: Automatic transmission: ($240). Overdrive: ($160).

MARK VIIM: Automatic transmission: ($195). Overdrive: ($160).

PERFORMANCE

XK-140: Top Speed: 120+ mph (near 130 mph with overdrive). Acceleration (quarter-mile): 17.4 seconds

XK-140M: Acceleration (0-60 mph): under 8.5 seconds.

D-TYPE: Top Speed: 160 mph. Acceleration (0-60 mph): 4.7 seconds. Acceleration (quarter-mile): 13.7 seconds at 107 mph.

CALENDAR YEAR REGISTRATIONS (U.S.): 3,573 Jaguars were registered in the U.S. during 1955. This represented 6.1 percent of all imported car registrations. Jaguar was second in exports to the United States, behind Volkswagen's 28,907 cars. MG Midget was third with 3,001 cars exported.

MANUFACTURER: Jaguar Cars Ltd., Coventry, England.

DISTRIBUTOR: Hoffman Motor Car Co., New York City; and Charles H. Hornburg Jr., Los Angeles.

HISTORY: The Mark VIIM debuted in September 1954. On December 2, 1954, the 1955 Jaguars were introduced in New York City. They were promoted as being priced $80 to $160 below 1954 models. Jaguars were featured in the third annual "Sports Cars International" show that opened at the Henry Ford Museum, in Dearborn, Michigan, on January 14, 1955.

1955 Jaguar Mk VII saloon *John Wheater*

1956

XK-140 — SIX — Production of the three body styles continued with little change. As before, both an "M" appearance package and an "MC" performance package were available.

D-TYPE — SIX — Small numbers of the competition Jaguar continued to be built.

2.4 — SIX — In 1956, a smaller four-door Jaguar joined the full-sized sedan. It was powered by a 2483-cc short-stroke version of the twin-cam six-cylinder engine and had a 107.4-inch wheelbase. The engine produced 112 hp, giving the 2.4-litre sedan a top speed beyond 100 mph. Its 0-60 mph acceleration time was in the neighborhood of 14.5 seconds. Styling features of the unibody sedan included inboard headlights, wing lights with parking lamp and blinker functions and a narrow vertical-bars grille. The car's overall profile differed considerably from that of the Mark VIIM. It had with a straight-through fender line, thick roof pillars and thick window frames. The 2.4's unibody construction was a "first" for Jaguar and its suspension also was new. It featured coil springs up front and a rigid axle with cantilever springs at the rear.

MARK VIIM — SIX — Production of the full-size four-door sedan continued with little change.

I.D. DATA: Chassis numbers of the XK-140 and Mark VIIM are located on front left chassis member, above rear engine mounting bracket. Chassis number for the 2.4 sedan is on body channel under the hood on the right side, ahead of the radiator header tank. Engine number is on right of engine block above the oil filter, or at front end of cylinder head. Serial numbers are also found on a brass plate on the firewall. Starting serial number: (XK-140 and MK VIIM) continued from prior year; (D-Type) XKD601 to XKD606, plus leftovers in the XKD500 series; (2.4-Litre) 940001. Starting engine number: (2.4) BB-1001.

ENGINES

BASE SIX 2.4: Inline, dual overhead-cam six-cylinder. Cast-iron block and aluminum-alloy head. Displacement: 151.5 cid (2483 cc). Bore & Stroke: 3.27 x 3.01 in. (83 x 76.5 mm). Compression Ratio: 8.0:1. Brake Horsepower: 112 at 5750 rpm. Torque: 140 lbs.-ft. at 2000 rpm. Seven main bearings. Solid valve lifters. Two Solex downdraft carburetors.

BASE SIX XK-140, MARK VIIM: Inline, dual overhead-cam six-cylinder. Cast-iron block and aluminum-alloy head. Displacement: 210 cid (3442 cc). Bore & Stroke: 3.27 x 4.17 in. (83 x 106 mm). Compression Ratio: 8.0:1. Brake Horsepower: 190 at 5500 rpm (210 at 5750 rpm with "C" type head). Torque: 210 lbs.-ft. at 2500 rpm (213 lbs.-ft. at 4000 rpm with "C" head). Seven main bearings. Solid valve lifters. Two S.U. sidedraft carburetors.

BASE SIX XK-140M, XK-140C (C-Type Head): Inline, dual overhead-cam six-cylinder. Cast-iron block and aluminum-alloy head. Displacement: 210 cid (3442 cc). Bore

Model	Body Type & Seating	Engine Type/CID	P.O.E. Price	Weight (Lbs.)	Production Total
XK-140					
XK-140	2d Roadster-2P	I6/210	$3,595	2,750	**Note 1**
XK-140	2d Coupe-2+2P	I6/210	$3,995	2,860	**Note 1**
XK-140	2d Convertible-2+2P	I6/210	$3,995	2,970	**Note 1**
XK-140M					
XK-140M	2d Roadster-2P	I6/210	$3,755	2,750	**Note 1**
XK-140M	2d Coupe-2+2P	I6/210	$4,160	2,860	**Note 1**
XK-140M	2d Convertible-2+2P	I6/210	$4,160	2,970	**Note 1**
XK-140MC					
XK-140MC	2d Roadster-2P	I6/210	$3,910	2,750	**Note 1**
XK-140MC	2d Coupe-2+2P	I6/210	$4,315	2,860	**Note 1**
XK-140MC	2d Convertible-2+2P	I6/210	$4,315	2,970	**Note 1**
D-Type					
D-Type	2d Roadster-2P	I6/210	$10,000	1,904	**Note 2**
2.4 Litre					
2.4 Litre	4d Sedan-5/6P	I6/151	$3,795	2,800	**Note 3**
Mark VIIM					
MK VIIM	4d Sedan-6P	I6/210	$4,440	3,800	**Note 4**

Note 1: Total XK-140 production for 1954-1957 came to 8,884 units (3,347 roadsters, 2,797 fixed-head coupes, and 2,740 drophead coupes). Only 385 of the drophead coupes (convertibles) and 396 of the fixed-head coupes had automatic transmissions.
Note 2: A total of 87 D-Types were produced from 1954-1956 (including 16 that were converted for road operation, starting in 1957).
Note 3: Approximately 19,400 2.4-litre sedans were produced from 1956-1959.
Note 4: A total of 10,061 Mark VIIM sedans were produced through the full model run, including 3,818 for export.

& Stroke: 3.27 x 4.17 in. (83 x 106 mm). Compression Ratio: 8.0:1. Brake Horsepower: 210 at 5750 rpm. Torque: 213 lbs.-ft. at 4000 rpm. Seven main bearings. Solid valve lifters. Two S.U. sidedraft carburetors. Lucas ignition.

BASE SIX D-TYPE: Inline, dual-overhead-cam six-cylinder. Cast-iron block and aluminum-alloy head. Displacement: 210 cid (3442 cc). Bore & Stroke: 3.27 x 4.17 in. (83 x 106 mm). Compression Ratio: 9.0:1. Brake Horsepower: 250 at 6000 rpm. Seven main bearings. Solid valve lifters. Three Weber sidedraft carburetors. Lucas ignition.

CHASSIS

XK-140: Wheelbase: 102 in. Overall Length: 176.0 in. Height: 55.0 in. Width: 64.5 in. Front Tread: 51.5 in. Rear Tread: 50.5 in. Wheel Type: steel disc. Standard Tires: 6.00 x 16.

D-TYPE: Wheelbase: 90 in. Overall Length: 154 in. Height: 38 in. Width: 65.8 in. Front Tread: 50 in. Rear Tread: 48 in. Tires: 6.50 x 16.

2.4: Wheelbase: 107.4 in. Overall Length: 180.75 in. Height: 57.5 in. Width: 66.75 in. Front Tread: 54.6 in. Rear Tread: 50.1 in. Wheel Type: steel disc. Standard Tires: 6.40 x 15.

MARK VII: Wheelbase: 120 in. Overall Length: 196.5 in. Height: 63.0 in. Width: 73.0 in. Front Tread: 56 in. Rear Tread: 57.5 in. Wheel Type: steel disc. Standard Tires: 6.70 x 16.

TECHNICAL

XK-140: Layout: front-engine, rear-drive. Transmission: four-speed manual. Standard Final Drive Ratio: 3.54:1. Steering: Rack-and-pinion. Suspension (front): independent; transverse wishbones, long torsion bars and anti-roll bar. Suspension (rear): rigid axle with semi-elliptic leaf springs. Brakes: hydraulic, front/rear drum. Body Construction: steel body on box-section steel frame. Fuel Tank: 18 gallons (U.S.).

D-TYPE: Layout: front-engine, rear-drive. Transmission: four-speed manual. Steering: rack-and-pinion. Suspension (front): independent; transverse wishbones, long torsion bars and anti-roll bar. Suspension (rear): Transverse torsion bar with upper

1956 XK 140SE roadster *Dan Lyons*

and lower trailing links. Brakes: hydraulic, front/rear drum. Body Construction: Aluminum/magnesium monocoque with steel-tube sub frames.

2.4: Layout: front-engine, rear-drive. Transmission: four-speed manual. Standard Final Drive Ratio: 4.55:1. Steering: Re-circulating ball. Suspension (front): independent; wishbones with coil springs. Suspension (rear): rigid axle with cantilever springs. Brakes: hydraulic, front/rear drum. Body Construction: steel unibody.

MARK VII: Layout: front-engine, rear-drive. Transmission: four-speed manual. Overall gear ratios: (1st) 14.4:1; (2nd) 8.56:1; (3rd) 5.84:1; (4th) 4.27:1. Standard Final Drive Ratio: 4.27:1. Steering: Re-circulating ball. Suspension (front): independent; transverse wishbones and long torsion bars. Suspension (rear): rigid axle with semi-elliptic leaf springs. Brakes: hydraulic, front/rear drum. Body Construction: steel body on box-section steel frame.

OPTIONS

XK-140: Automatic transmission: ($260). Overdrive: ($175).

MARK VIIM: Automatic transmission: ($200). Overdrive: ($160).

PERFORMANCE

XK-140: Top Speed: 120+ mph (near 130 mph with overdrive). Acceleration (quarter-mile): 17.4 seconds

XK-140M: Acceleration (0-60 mph): under 8.5 seconds.

D-TYPE: Top Speed: 160 mph. Acceleration (0-60 mph): 4.7 seconds. Acceleration (quarter-mile): 13.7 seconds at 107 mph.

2.4: Top Speed: 100+ mph. Acceleration (0-60 mph): 13.4-14.5 seconds. Acceleration (quarter-mile): 19.2 seconds at 71 mph.

CALENDAR YEAR REGISTRATIONS (U.S.): 3,685 Jaguars were registered in the U.S. during 1956. This was 3.7 percent of total U.S. imports. Jaguar was the number 4 import behind Volkswagen, Metropolitan and MG in order.

MANUFACTURER: Jaguar Cars Ltd., Coventry, England.

DISTRIBUTOR: Jaguar Cars North American Corp., New York City.

HISTORY: Jaguar's 1956 models were introduced to the U.S. market on September 1, 1955. A central parts depot opened in the U.S. in January 1956. Other British automakers were not enjoying the same success as Jaguar in the U.S. market. On January 9, 1956, Austin, Standard and Rootes' Humber Hawk curtailed production due to reduced demand for British cars.

The 1956 Jaguar lineup (top to bottom): Mark VII saloon, 2.4 saloon, plus XK 140s in drophead, fixed head coupe and roadster versions.

Jaguar Heritage—North America

1957 Jaguar XK 150 fixed head coupe *Dan Lyons*

1957

XK-140 — SIX — Production of Jaguar's sports car continued with little change. As before, three body styles were offered, with "M" and "MC" packages available.

XK-SS — SIX — The XK-SS was created as the road version of the D-Type competition roadster that won the French Grand Prix at Le Mans in 1955, 1956 and 1957. Each of the 16 XK-SS models built before the tooling was destroyed had right-hand-drive and were made from leftover D-Type components. The XK-SS was the fastest street Jag ever. With three Weber carburetors, the 3442-cc six produced some 260 hp. Styling included a curved windshield and a rear-deck luggage rack. The seats were upholstered in leather. To make the XK-SS road legal, turn signals and mufflers were provided. A disastrous fire at the Browns Lane factory ended production prematurely. Owners of Jaguar XK-SS roadsters included actors Hugh O'Brien (star of "Wyatt Earp") and Steve McQueen (star of "Wanted: Dead or Alive"). McQueen bought back his car for many times what he paid for it. He planned to restore it before he died. In 2003, the XK-SS was offered for $1 million at the Barrett-Jackson Auction.

2.4 — SIX — Jaguar continued to produce its small sedan without changing anything major.

3.4 — SIX — The body of the Jaguar 3.4 Saloon was essentially the same as that used on the 2.4 model, but this new model carried a bigger engine. Round parking lights were mounted on the outboard side of the headlights. Wire wheels were optional. The top speed of this car approached 120 mph with the 210-hp twin-cam engine. The 3.4 sedan could accelerate to 60 mph in close to 9 seconds. It was produced in response to American demand for more power in the smaller sedan.

MARK VIIM — SIX — Production of the Mark VIIM sedan continued into 1957. Then, the Jaguar Mark VIII sedan replaced it.

MARK VIII — SIX — Evolution into Mark VIII form brought only a handful of significant changes including a one-piece windshield and modest revisions to the cylinder head which was now in "B" (green) tune. A new grille had a thicker chrome surround molding and flatter appearance. It was decorated with a "leaping Jaguar" grille mascot. A Dual-Range Borg-Warner automatic transmission was optional.

I.D. DATA: Chassis serial number for XK-140 and Mark VIIM are located on front left chassis, above the rear engine-mounting bracket; for 2.4/3.4 sedans, on body channel under

Model	Body Type & Seating	Engine Type/CID	P.O.E. Price	Weight (lbs.)	Production Total
XK-140					
XK-140	2d Roadster-2P	I6/210	$3,645	2,750	**Note 1**
XK-140	2d Coupe-2+2P	I6/210	$4,045	2,860	**Note 1**
XK-140	2d Convertible-2+2P	I6/210	$4,045	2,970	**Note 1**
XK-140M					
XK-140M	2d Roadster-2P	I6/210	$3,755	2,750	**Note 1**
XK-140M	2d Coupe-2+2P	I6/210	$4,160	2,860	**Note 1**
XK-140M	2d Convertible-2+2P	I6/210	$4,160	2,970	**Note 1**
XK-140MC					
XK-140MC	2d Roadster-2P	I6/210	$3,960	2,750	**Note 1**
XK-140MC	2d Coupe-2+2P	I6/210	$4,365	2,860	**Note 1**
XK-140MC	2d Convertible-2+2P	I6/210	$4,365	2,970	**Note 1**
XK-SS					
XK-SS	2d Roadster-2P	I6/210	$6,900	1,960	16
2.4 Litre					
2.4 Litre	4d Sedan-5/6P	I6/151	$3,845	2,800	**Note 2**
3.4 Litre					
3.4 Litre	4d Sedan-5/6P	I6/210	$4,530	3,164	**Note 3**
Mark VIIM					
MK VIIM	4d Sedan-6P	I6/210	$4,465	3,800	**Note 4**
Mark VIII					
Luxury	4d Sedan-6P	I6/210	$5,770	3,752	**Note 5**

Note 1: Total XK-140 production (1954-1957) came to 8,884 units (3,347 roadsters, 2,797 fixed-head coupes, and 2,740 drophead coupes). Only 385 of the drophead coupes (convertibles) and 396 of the fixed-head coupes had automatic transmissions.

Note 2: Approximately 19,400 2.4-litre sedans were produced from 1956 through 1959.

Note 3: Approximately 17,340 3.4-litre sedans were produced from 1957 through 1959.

Note 4: A total of 10,061 Mark VIIM sedans were produced through the full model run including 3,818 for export.

Note 5: A total of 6,212 Mark VIII sedans were produced from 1957 through 1959 including 2,448 for export.

Jerry and Kathy Nell

1957 Jaguar XK-SS

the hood on the right side, ahead of the radiator header tank. Engine number is on right of engine block above oil filter or front end of cylinder head. Serial numbers are also found on a brass plate on the firewall. Starting serial number: (XK-140, 2.4, Mark VIIM) continued from prior listings; (XK-SS) XKSS701; (3.4) 985001; (Mark VIII with LHD) 780001. Starting engine number: (3.4) KE1001. Irrespective of motor or serial numbers, the model year of Jaguars was determined by the year appearing on the first registration made for each car.

ENGINES

BASE SIX 2.4: Inline, dual overhead-cam six-cylinder. Cast-iron block and aluminum-alloy head. Displacement: 151.5 cid (2483 cc). Bore & Stroke: 3.27 x 3.01 in. (83 x 76.5 mm). Compression Ratio: 8.0:1. Brake Horsepower: 112 at 5750 rpm. Torque: 140 lbs.-ft. at 2000 rpm. Seven main bearings. Solid valve lifters. Two Solex downdraft carburetors.

BASE SIX XK-140, MARK VIIM SEDAN: Inline, dual overhead-cam six-cylinder. Cast-iron block and aluminum-alloy head. Displacement: 210 cid (3442 cc). Bore & Stroke: 3.27 x 4.17 in. (83 x 106 mm). Compression Ratio: 8.0:1. Brake Horsepower: 190 at 5500 rpm. Torque: 210 lbs.-ft. at 2500 rpm. Seven main bearings. Solid valve lifters. Two S.U. sidedraft carburetors.

BASE SIX XK-140MC: Inline, dual overhead-cam six-cylinder. Cast-iron block and aluminum-alloy head. Displacement: 210 cid (3442 cc). Bore & Stroke: 3.27 x 4.17 in. (83 x 106 mm). Compression Ratio: 8.0:1. Brake Horsepower: 210 at 5750 rpm. Torque: 213 lbs.-ft. at 4000 rpm. Seven main bearings. Solid valve lifters. Two S.U. sidedraft carburetors.

BASE SIX XK-SS: Inline, dual overhead-cam six-cylinder. Cast-iron block and aluminum-alloy head. Displacement: 210 cid (3442 cc). Bore & Stroke: 3.27 x 4.17 in. (83 x 106 mm). Compression Ratio: 9.0:1. Brake Horsepower: 260 at 6000 rpm. Seven main bearings. Solid valve lifters. Three 45 mm diameter Weber DCO3 double choke carburetors. Lucas ignition.

BASE SIX 3.4 SEDAN, MARK VIII SEDAN: Inline, dual overhead-cam six-cylinder. Cast-iron block and aluminum-alloy head. Displacement: 210 cid (3442 cc). Bore & Stroke: 3.27 x 4.17 in. (83 x 106 mm). Compression Ratio: 8.0:1. Brake Horsepower: 210 at 5500 rpm. Torque: 215 lbs.-ft. at 3000 rpm. Seven main bearings. Solid valve lifters. Two S.U. sidedraft carburetors.

CHASSIS

XK-140: Wheelbase: 102 in. Overall Length: 176.0 in. Height: 55.0 in. Width: 64.5 in. Front Tread: 51.5 in. Rear Tread: 50.5 in. Wheel Type: steel disc. Standard Tires: 6.00 x 16.

XK-SS: Wheelbase: 90.63 in. Overall Length: 168.0 in. Height: 31.5 in. to base of windscreen. Width: 65.63 in. Front Tread: 50.0 in. Rear Tread: 50.0 in. Wheel Type: Dunlop light alloy, center lock disc wheels. Standard Tires: 6.50 x 16.

2.4: Wheelbase: 107.4 in. Overall Length: 180.75 in. Height: 57.5 in. Width: 66.75 in. Front Tread: 54.6 in. Rear Tread: 50.1 in. Wheel Type: steel disc. Standard Tires: 6.40 x 15.

3.4: Wheelbase: 107.4 in. Overall Length: 180.75 in. Height: 57.5 in. Width: 66.75 in. Front Tread: 54.6 in. Rear Tread: 50.1 in. Wheel Type: steel disc. Standard Tires: 6.40 x 15.

MARK VIIM: Wheelbase: 120 in. Overall Length: 196.5 in.

Height: 63.0 in. Width: 73.0 in. Front Tread: 56 in. Rear Tread: 57.5 in. Wheel Type: steel disc. Standard Tires: 6.70 x 16.

MARK VIII: Wheelbase: 120 in. Overall Length: 196.5 in. Height: 63.0 in. Width: 73.0 in. Front Tread: 56 in. Rear Tread: 57.5 in. Wheel Type: steel disc. Standard Tires: 6.70 x 16.

TECHNICAL

XK-140: Layout: front-engine, rear-drive. Transmission: four-speed manual. Standard Final Drive Ratio: 3.54:1. Steering: Rack-and-pinion. Suspension (front): independent; transverse wishbones, long torsion bars and anti-roll bar. Suspension (rear): rigid axle with semi-elliptic leaf springs. Brakes: hydraulic, front/rear drum. Body Construction: steel body on box-section steel frame. Fuel Tank: 18 gallons (U.S.).

XK-SS: Layout: front-engine, rear-drive. Transmission: four-speed manual gearbox, synchromesh on upper three (overall ratios 3.54, 4.52, 5.82 and 7.61 to 1). Alternative ratios available, Central control. Clutch: Borg and Beck 7.5-inch diameter dry, triple-plate clutch. Standard Final Drive Ratio: 3.54:1 (hypoid bevel gear; alternative ratios available). Steering: rack-and-pinion. Suspension (front): Independent wishbone and torsion bar. Suspension (rear): Trailing links and torsion bar with live axle. Brakes: Dunlop hydraulic 12.75-inch disc brakes, three-pad front discs, two-pad rear discs. Body Construction: Steel body on box-section steel frame. Fuel tank: 37 gallons in two flexible tanks.

2.4: Layout: front-engine, rear-drive. Transmission: four-speed manual. Standard Final Drive Ratio: 4.55:1. Steering: Re-circulating ball. Suspension (front): independent; wishbones with coil springs. Suspension (rear): rigid axle with cantilever springs. Brakes: hydraulic, front/rear drum. Body Construction: steel unibody.

1957 Jaguar XK 150 drophead

Jaguar Heritage – North America

1957 Jaguar D-type racer *Bob Harrington*

3.4: Layout: front-engine, rear-drive. Transmission: four-speed manual. Standard Final Drive Ratio: 3.77:1. Steering: Re-circulating ball. Suspension (front): independent; wishbones with coil springs. Suspension (rear): rigid axle with cantilever springs. Brakes: hydraulic, front/rear drum. Body Construction: steel unibody.

MARK VIIM: Layout: front-engine, rear-drive. Transmission: four-speed manual. Overall gear ratios: (1st) 14.4:1; (2nd) 8.56:1; (3rd) 5.84:1; (4th) 4.27:1. Standard Final Drive Ratio: 4.27:1. Steering: Re-circulating ball. Suspension (front): independent; transverse wishbones and long torsion bars. Suspension (rear): rigid axle with semi-elliptic leaf springs. Brakes: hydraulic, front/rear drum. Body Construction: steel body on box-section steel frame.

MARK VIII: Layout: front-engine, rear-drive. Transmission: four-speed manual. Standard Final Drive Ratio: 4.27:1. Steering: Re-circulating ball. Suspension (front): independent; transverse wishbones and long torsion bars. Suspension (rear): rigid axle with semi-elliptic leaf springs. Brakes: hydraulic, front/rear drum. Body Construction: steel body on box-section steel frame.

PERFORMANCE

XK-140: Top Speed: 121 mph. Acceleration (0-60 mph): 12.6 seconds for coupe. Acceleration (quarter-mile): 17.4 seconds for roadster; 18.7 seconds for coupe.

XK-140MC: Acceleration (0-60 mph): under 9.1 seconds.

XK-SS: Top speed: 170 mph. Acceleration (0-60 mph): 5.2 seconds. Acceleration (0-100 mph): 13.6 seconds. Acceleration (quarter-mile): 14.1 seconds.

2.4: Top Speed: 100 mph. Acceleration (quarter-mile): 19.2 seconds at 71 mph.

3.4: Top Speed: 120 mph. Acceleration (0-60 mph): 9.0-10.7 seconds. Acceleration (quarter-mile): 17.7 seconds.

MARK VIII: Top Speed: 106 mph. Acceleration (quarter-mile): 18.4 seconds

CALENDAR YEAR REGISTRATIONS (U.S.): 3,800 Jaguars were registered in the U.S. during 1957.

MANUFACTURER: Jaguar Cars Ltd., Coventry, England.

DISTRIBUTOR: Jaguar Cars North American Corp., New York City.

HISTORY: Jaguar's 1957 models were introduced to the U.S. market on September 1, 1956. The XK-150 debuted in mid-1957, replacing the XK-140. The first XK-SS left England in January 1957 and was sent to New York City. The XK-SS was not for sale, but a $6,900 price was publicized. In 1957, import car sales in the United States topped the American independent automakers for the first time in history.

1957 LISTER-JAGUAR

LISTER-JAGUAR – SIX – Sports racing car builder Brian Lister produced the 1957 Lister-Jaguar. It was based on the chassis of the Lister-Bristol that Archie Scott-Brown raced in 1954 and 1955. Lister installed a D-Type Jaguar engine, tuned by a specialist Don Moore. (Michael Head's Cooper-Jaguar was another special car.) The first Lister Jaguar, with its rounded rear end and streamlined fairing, had a touch of the Maserati. The twin tube chassis was constructed so that all body panels could be removed in three minutes. The race car was painted dark green with a yellow stripe.

I.D. DATA: Unknown.

ENGINES

BASE SIX LISTER-JAGUAR: Inline, dual-overhead-cam six-cylinder. Cast-iron block and aluminum-alloy head. Displacement: 210 cid (3442 cc). Bore & Stroke: 3.27 x 4.17 in. (83 x 106 mm). Compression Ratio: 9.0:1. Brake Horsepower: 250 at 6000 rpm in standard form. Seven main bearings. Solid valve lifters. Three Weber sidedraft carburetors. Lucas ignition.

OPTIONAL SIX LISTER-JAGUAR: Inline, dual-overhead-cam six-cylinder. Cast-iron block and aluminum-alloy head. Displacement: 210 cid (3442 cc). Bore & Stroke: 3.27 x 4.17 in. (83 x 106 mm). Compression Ratio: 10.0:1. Brake Horsepower: 300 hp. Seven main bearings. Solid valve lifters. Three twin-choke Weber sidedraft carburetors. Lucas ignition. Dry sump lubrication.

CHASSIS

LISTER-JAGUAR: Wheelbase: 89.0 in. Overall Length: 156.0 in. Height at scuttle: 29.0 in. Width: 59.0 in. Front Tread: 50.0 in. Rear Tread: 50.0 in. Wheel Type: Dunlop bolt-on light alloy, perforated disc. Early Tires: Dunlop racing 5.50 x 16 front, 6.50 x 16 rear. Later Tires: 6.00 x16 front, 7.00 x 16 rear.

TECHNICAL

LISTER-JAGUAR: Layout: front-engine, rear-drive. Transmission: Standard Jaguar D-Type four-speed manual. (Three-plate racing clutch in car with Don Moore tuning). Standard Final Drive: Salisbury unit incorporating a ZF differential. Ratios available: 2.93, 3.31, 3.54, 3.77, 4.09 and 4.27 to 1. Steering: Rack-and-pinion. Suspension (front): Coil springs enclosing telescopic dampers and equal length wishbones. Suspension (rear): Coil springs enclosing telescopic dampers and de Dion axle. Brakes: Girling single-pad 10-in. diameter discs. Body Construction: Twin-tube type chassis with removable bodies and fuel tanks. Fuel Tank: 18 gallons (U.S.).

PERFORMANCE

LISTER-JAGUAR: Top Speed: 145 mph. Acceleration: (0-60 mph): 4.6 seconds. Acceleration: (quarter-mile) 13.2 seconds.

CALENDAR YEAR REGISTRATIONS (U.S.): Probably one car raced by Archie Scott-Brown in 1957.

MANUFACTURER: Brian Lister (Light Engineering, Ltd.), Abbey Road, Cambridge, England.

HISTORY: The Lister-Jaguar had a power-to-weight ratio of over 350 hp per ton. Archie Scott-Brown set the fastest lap at Snetterton in his car (despite a faulty hydraulic clutch cylinder). Scott-Brown's car also set records or established marks at Gulton Park, Silverstone, Aintree and Goodwood. During the 1957 season the car was entered in 14 races and won 11 of them. The car appeared in the English magazine *Motor* on May 22, 1957 and was road tested in *Autosport's* October 18, 1957 issue.

A Lister-Jaguar "Knobbly" Racer in the pits.

Andrew Morland

Model	Body Type & Seating	Engine Type/ CID	P.O.E. Price	Weight (lbs.)	Prod. Total
Lister-Jaguar					
Lister	2d Roadster-2P	I6/210	N/A	1,904	N/A

1958 XK 150 drophead coupe *Dan Lyons*

1958

XK-150 — SIX — A new XK sports car arrived in 1958 wearing new sheet metal and displaying a revised (higher) belt line. The front fenders were taller at the cowl and a curved one-piece windshield and the roof styling were also new. The coupe had a slightly curved, wraparound back window. Up front was a grille wider than the one used on the XK-140. The front bumper dipped downward at the center, ahead of the grille. A wide hood with a raised center section sloped toward the front of the car. The license-plate housing was on the deck lid, allowing the bumper to stretch between vertical guards and wrap around the rear fenders. A fire in the factory delayed roadster production. It debuted nine months later, but was more convertible with wind-up windows and non-cutaway doors. It was more refined and roomier inside, but the XK-150 also gained weight. Inside, the coupe and convertible adopted the leather long used in the roadster. Optional Dunlop four-wheel disc brakes with servo-assist were installed on virtually all cars. Under the hood was the same 190-hp engine but the 210-hp "Special Equipment" option became more popular. The new B-type (Blue Top) cylinder head on the Special Equipment engine was painted blue. In the spring of 1958, a more potent "S" engine became available with its straight-port head, three

big two-inch-diameter S.U. carburetors, a higher compression ratio, more radical cam timing and a 250-hp rating. All XK-150S models had the manual gearbox with overdrive. The "S" engine had a gold-colored cylinder head. A small "S" went on the upper front corner of each door. Standard equipment included a manual ratchet jack and tool kit, fog lamps, and a rev counter (tach) with inset clock. A car radio was optional.

3.4 — SIX — Production of the 3.4 sedan continued with little change, except that disc brakes became optional equipment.

MARK VIII — SIX — Production of the full-size sedan continued with little change, except that disc brakes and wire wheels became optional equipment.

I.D. DATA: Chassis serial number of XK-150 is stamped on the frame, adjacent to the rear engine mounting; for 3.4 sedan, on body channel under the hood on the right side, ahead of radiator header tank; for Mark VIII, stamped atop frame member above the rear engine mounting bracket. Engine number is on right of engine block, above the oil filter. Starting chassis serial number: (XK-150 coupe) 834001; (XK-

150 convertible) 83700; (3.4) 985001; (Mark VIII) 780001. Starting engine number: (XK-150) V-1001-8; (3.4) KE-1001-8; (Mark VIII) N-6001-8. Starting engine number: (XK-150) VE1001; (XK-150S) VS1001. Engine and chassis number also appear on a brass plate on the firewall.

ENGINES

STANDARD SIX XK-150: Inline, dual overhead-cam six-cylinder. Cast-iron block and aluminum-alloy head. Displacement: 210 cid (3442 cc). Bore & Stroke: 3.27 x 4.17 in. (83 x 106 mm). Compression Ratio: 8.0:1. Brake Horsepower: 190 at 3500 rpm. Seven main bearings. Solid valve lifters. Two S.U. sidedraft carburetors.

SPECIAL EQUIPMENT "SE" SIX XK-150, 3.4 SEDAN, MARK VIII SEDAN: Inline, dual overhead-cam six-cylinder. Cast-iron block and aluminum-alloy head. Displacement: 210 cid (3442 cc). Bore & Stroke: 3.27 x 4.17 in. (83 x 106 mm). Compression Ratio: 8.0:1. Brake Horsepower: 210 at 5500 rpm. Torque: 216 lbs.-ft. at 3000 rpm. Seven main bearings. Solid valve lifters. Two S.U. HD6 sidedraft carburetors.

BASE SIX XK-150S: Inline, dual overhead-cam six-cylinder. Cast-iron block and aluminum-alloy head. Displacement: 210 cid (3442 cc). Bore & Stroke: 3.27 x 4.17 in. (83 x 106 mm). Compression Ratio: 9.0:1. Brake Horsepower: 252 at 5500 rpm. Torque: 240 lbs.-ft. at 4500 rpm. Seven main bearings. Solid valve lifters. Two S.U. HD8 sidedraft carburetors.

CHASSIS

XK-150: Wheelbase: 102 in. Overall Length: 177.0 in. Height: 55.0 in. (roadster 52.5 in.) Width: 64.5 in. Front Tread: 51.6 in. Rear Tread: 51.6 in. Wheel Type: steel disc. Standard Tires: 6.00 x 16.

3.4: Wheelbase: 107.4 in. Overall Length: 180.75 in. Height: 57.5 in. Width: 66.75 in. Front Tread: 54.6 in. Rear Tread: 50.1 in. Wheel Type: steel disc. Standard Tires: 6.40 x 15.

MARK VIII: Wheelbase: 120 in. Overall Length: 196.5 in. Height: 63.0 in. Width: 73.0 in. Front Tread: 56 in. Rear Tread: 57.5 in. Wheel Type: steel disc. Standard Tires: 6.70 x 16.

TECHNICAL

XK-150: Layout: front-engine, rear-drive. Transmission: four-speed manual. Standard Final Drive Ratio: 3.54:1. Steering: Rack-and-pinion. Suspension (front): wishbones and torsion bars with anti-roll bar. Suspension (rear): rigid axle with semi-elliptic leaf springs. Brakes: hydraulic, front/rear discs. Body Construction: steel body on box-section steel frame. Fuel tank: 17 gallons (U.S.).

XK-150S: Layout: front-engine, rear-drive. Transmission: four-speed manual with overdrive. Standard Final Drive Ratio: 4.09:1. Steering: Rack-and-pinion. Suspension (front): wishbones and torsion bars with anti-roll bar. Suspension (rear): rigid axle with semi-elliptic leaf springs. Brakes: hydraulic, front/rear discs. Body Construction: steel body on box-section steel frame. Fuel Tank: 17 gallons (U.S.)

3.4: Layout: front-engine, rear-drive. Transmission: four-speed manual with overdrive. Standard Final Drive Ratio: 3.54:1. Steering: Re-circulating ball. Suspension (front): independent; wishbones with coil springs. Suspension (rear): rigid axle with cantilever springs. Brakes: hydraulic, front/rear drum. Body Construction: steel unibody.

MARK VIII: Layout: front-engine, rear-drive. Transmission: four-speed manual. Standard Final Drive Ratio: 4.27:1. Steering: Re-circulating ball. Suspension (front): independent; transverse wishbones and long torsion bars. Suspension (rear): rigid axle with semi-elliptic leaf springs. Brakes: hydraulic, front/rear drum. Body Construction: steel body on box-section steel frame.

OPTIONS

XK-150: Automatic transmission: ($260). Overdrive: ($175). 3.54:1 axle ratio. SE package with Blue Top head.

3.4 SEDAN: Automatic transmission: ($250).

MARK VIII SEDAN: Automatic transmission ($250). Overdrive: ($165).

Jaguar proclaimed its racing victories in this XK 150 badge. *Andrew Morland*

Model	Body Type & Seating	Engine Type/CID	P.O.E. Price	Weight (Lbs.)	Production Total
XK-150					
XK-150	2d Roadster-2P	I6/210	$4,520	3,066	**Note 1**
XK-150	2d Coupe-2+2P	I6/210	$4,475	3,000	**Note 1**
XK-150	2d Convertible-2+2P	I6/210	$4,595	2,900	**Note 1**
XK-150S					
XK-150S	2d Roadster-2P	I6/210	$5,120	3,190	**Note 2**
3.4 Litre (Overdrive)					
3.4 Litre	4d Sedan-5P	I6/210	$4,460	3,200	**Note 3**
Mk VIII					
Mk VIII	4d Sedan-6P	I6/210	$5,445	3,808	**Note 4**

Note 1: Total XK-150 production (1957-1960) came to 7,929 units. Of these, 1,339 were roadsters (42 with 3.8-litre engine), 4,101 were fixed-head coupes (656 with 3.8-litre engine), and 2,489 were drophead coupes (586 with 3.8-litre engine).

Note 2: Total XK-150S production (1958-1961) came to 1,466 units. Of these, 924 were roadsters (36 with 3.8-litre engine), 349 were fixed-head coupes (150 with 3.8-litre engine), and 193 were drophead coupes (89 with 3.8-litre engine).

Note 3: Approximately 17,340 3.4-litre sedans were produced from 1957-1959.

Note 4: A total of 6,212 Mark VIII sedans were produced from 1957-1959 (including 2,448 for export).

Andrew Morland

A 1958 Jaguar Mk VIII saloon goes racing.

PERFORMANCE

XK-150: Top Speed: 120+ mph. Acceleration (0-60 mph): 8.5 seconds. Acceleration (quarter-mile): 16.9 seconds at 82 mph Fuel Mileage: (manual) 18 to 20 mpg, (overdrive) 22 mpg.

XK-150S: Top Speed: 132.3 mph. Acceleration (0-60 mph): 7.4 seconds. Acceleration (quarter-mile): 16.2 seconds. Fuel Mileage: 17 to 18 mpg.

3.4 SEDAN: Top Speed: 120 mph. Acceleration (0-60 mph): 10.4 seconds; (MK VIII) 11.6 seconds.

MARK VIII: Top Speed: 106 mph. Acceleration (0-60 mph): 11.6 seconds.

CALENDAR YEAR REGISTRATIONS (U.S.): A total of 4,607 Jaguars were registered in the U.S. during the year ending July 1958.

MANUFACTURER: Jaguar Cars Ltd., Coventry, England.

HISTORY: Jaguar's 1958 models were introduced to the U.S. market on September 1, 1957. Production of the XK-150 began in May 1957 and continued until October 1960. Production of the 2.4-litre sedan (with 2483-cc engine) continued into 1959, when it was replaced by a MK II version. In 1958, Jaguar had a total of 393 U.S. retail sales outlets. The importers had carved out a 3.5 percent share of the market in 1957. In 1958, import sales wound up at 378,517 cars, or 8.13 percent of the total U.S. market.

1958 LISTER-JAGUAR

LISTER-JAGUAR – SIX – The Lister-Jaguar was changed in 1958 to better comply with Appendix C of the International Sporting Code which stated "coachwork must be completely finished and offer no makeshift element – floor boards, tubes and castings must be properly jointed together and firmly fixed." The head fairing was removed, a full-width windscreen was fitted, headlights were faired in and the hood was lowered. A 300-hp Jaguar 3.8-liter "works" engine was neatly installed.

I.D. DATA: Unknown.

ENGINES

BASE SIX LISTER-JAGUAR: Inline, dual-overhead-cam six-cylinder. Cast-iron block and aluminum-alloy head. Displacement: 210 cid (3442 cc). Bore & Stroke: 3.27 x 4.17 in. (83 x 106 mm). Compression Ratio: 10.0:1. Brake Horsepower: 300 hp at 5600 rpm. Seven main bearings. Solid valve lifters. Three twin-choke Weber sidedraft carburetors. Lucas ignition. Dry sump lubrication.

CHASSIS

LISTER-JAGUAR: Wheelbase: 89.0 in. Overall Length: 156.0 in. Height at scuttle: 29.0 in. Width: 61.0 in. Front Tread: 50.5 in. Rear Tread: 52.0 in. Wheel Type: Dunlop bolt-on light alloy, perforated disc. Early Tires: Dunlop racing 6.00 x 16 front, 6.50 x 16 rear.

TECHNICAL

LISTER-JAGUAR: Layout: front-engine, rear-drive. Transmission: Standard Jaguar D Type four-speed manual. Dry three-plate Borg & Beck clutch. Standard Final Drive: Salisbury unit incorporating a ZF differential. Final drive ratio: 3.73 to 1. Steering: Rack-and-pinion. Suspension (front): Coil springs enclosing telescopic dampers and equal length wishbones. Suspension (rear): Coil springs enclosing telescopic dampers and de Dion axle. Brakes: Girling single-pad 11-in. (front) 10-in. (rear) diameter discs. Body Construction: Twin-tube type chassis with removable bodies and fuel tanks. Fuel **Tank:** 18 gallons (U.S.).

PERFORMANCE

LISTER-JAGUAR: Top Speed: 135 mph. Acceleration (0-100 mph): 10.0 seconds. Acceleration (quarter-mile): 13.0 seconds at 100 mph.

PRODUCTION/SALES: Prototype for production model.

MANUFACTURER: Brian Lister (Light Engineering, Ltd.), Abbey Road, Cambridge, England.

HISTORY: A lengthy article titled "Let Loose with the Lister" appeared in *The Autocar* (November 1, 1957). An artist's rendering showed "next year's 'production' cars" and noted that the production model would be "well trimmed and fitted inside."

A Lister-Jaguar prepares for racing action.

Andrew Morland

Model	Body Type & Seating	Engine Type/CID	P.O.E. Price	Weight (Lbs.)	Production Total
Lister- Jaguar					
Lister	2d Roadster-2P	I6/210	N/A	1,904	**N/A Note 1**

Note 1: An article in *Autocar* (November 1957) quoted Brian Lister as saying the price of a production car without engine would be £2,750.

A 1959 Jaguar 3.4 saloon shows its racing form. *Bob Harrington*

1959

XK-150 — SIX — Production of the XK-150 sports car continued with little change. As before, a more potent "S" version was available. Standard equipment included two six-volt batteries (one in each wing), a manual jack, a very complete kit of tools, fog lamps, directional indicators, Lucas two-speed self-canceling windshield wipers, Trico vacuum-operated windshield washers, headlight and low-fuel indicator lights, an overdrive switch (on cars with overdrive), a petrol filler lock, glove lockers, door map pockets, a parcel shelf, interior lights, leather upholstery, and a heater and demister. A radio was optional.

3.4 — SIX — Production of the smaller 3.4-litre sedan on 107.4-inch wheelbase continued with little change. A manual transmission with overdrive was standard.

MARK IX — SIX — A larger 3.8-litre in-line six powered the new full-size Jaguar Saloon. U.S. market cars came standard with automatic transmission and power steering, as well as four-wheel disc brakes. The 3781-cc 220-hp six delivered a top speed of nearly 115 mph. A "MK IX" emblem decorated the trunk lid, but the new model's appearance was similar to the Mark VIII. The Saloon again had burl-walnut interior trim and picnic tables.

I.D. DATA: The chassis serial number of the XK-150 is stamped on the frame, adjacent to the rear engine mounting. For the 3.4 sedan, it is on the body channel under the hood on the right side, ahead of radiator header tank. For the Mark IX, it is stamped atop the frame member above the rear engine mounting bracket. The engine number is on right of engine block. Starting chassis serial numbers: (XK-150, 3.4) continued from prior listings; (Mark IX with LHD) 790001. Engine and chassis numbers also appear on a brass firewall plate.

ENGINES

STANDARD SIX XK-150, 3.4 SEDAN: Inline, dual overhead-cam six-cylinder. Cast-iron block and aluminum-alloy head. Displacement: 210 cid (3442 cc). Bore & Stroke: 3.27 x 4.17 in. (83 x 106 mm). Compression Ratio: 8.0:1. Brake Horsepower: 210 at 5500 rpm. Torque: 216 lbs.-ft. at 3000 rpm. Seven main bearings. Solid valve lifters. Two S.U. HD6 sidedraft carburetors.

BASE SIX XK-150S: Inline, dual overhead-cam six-cylinder. Cast-iron block and aluminum-alloy head. Displacement: 210 cid (3442 cc). Bore & Stroke: 3.27 x 4.17 in. (83 x 106 mm). Compression Ratio: 9.0:1. Brake Horsepower: 250 at 5500

Model	Body Type & Seating	Engine Type/CID	P.O.E. Price	Weight (lbs.)	Production Total
XK-150					
XK-150	2d Roadster-2P	I6/210	$4,520	3,066	**Note 1**
XK-150	2d Coupe-2+2P	I6/210	$4,500	3,108	**Note 1**
XK-150	2d Convertible-2+2P	I6/210	$4,620	3,108	**Note 1**
XK-150S					
XK-150S	2d Roadster-2P	I6/210	$5,120	3,164	**Note 2**
3.4 Litre (Overdrive)					
3.4 Litre	4d Sedan-5P	I6/210	$4,567	3,136	**Note 3**
Mark IX					
MK IX	4d Sedan-5/6P	I6/231	$6,020	3,976	**Note 4**

Note 1: Total XK-150 production (1957-1960) came to 7,929 units. Of these, 1,339 were roadsters (42 with 3.8-litre engine), 4,101 were fixed-head coupes (656 with 3.8-litre engine), and 2,489 were drophead coupes (586 with 3.8-litre engine).

Note 2: Total XK-150S production (1958-1961) came to 1,466 units. Of these, 924 were roadsters (36 with 3.8-litre engine), 349 were fixed-head coupes (150 with 3.8-litre engine), and 193 were drophead coupes (89 with 3.8-litre engine).

Note 3: Approximately 17,340 3.4-litre sedans were produced from 1957 through 1959.

Note 4: A total of 10,009 Mark IX sedans were produced from 1959 through 1961 (including 4,647 for export).

The interior of a 1959 Jaguar Mk I saloon.

Bob and Linda Budlow

rpm. Torque: 240 lbs.-ft. at 4500 rpm. Seven main bearings. Solid valve lifters. Two S.U. HD8 sidedraft carburetors.

BASE SIX MARK IX: Inline, dual overhead-cam six-cylinder. Cast-iron block and aluminum-alloy head. Displacement: 230.6 cid (3781 cc). Bore & Stroke: 3.425 x 4.17 in. (87 x 106 mm). Compression Ratio: 8.0:1. Brake Horsepower: 220 at 5000 rpm. Torque: 240 lbs.-ft. at 4000 rpm. Seven main bearings. Solid valve lifters. Two S.U. sidedraft carburetors.

CHASSIS

XK-150: Wheelbase: 102 in. Overall Length: 177.0 in. Height: 55.0 in. (roadster 52.5 in.) Width: 64.5 in. Front Tread: 51.6 in. Rear Tread: 51.6 in. Wheel Type: steel disc. Standard Tires: 6.00 x 16.

3.4: Wheelbase: 107.4 in. Overall Length: 180.75 in. Height: 57.5 in. Width: 66.75 in. Front Tread: 54.6 in. Rear Tread: 50.1 in. Wheel Type: steel disc. Standard Tires: 6.40 x 15.

MARK IX: Wheelbase: 120 in. Overall Length: 196.5 in.

Height: 63.0 in. Width: 73.0 in. Front Tread: 56.5 in. Rear Tread: 58.0 in. Wheel Type: steel disc. Standard Tires: 6.70 x 16.

TECHNICAL

XK-150: Layout: front-engine, rear-drive. Transmission: four-speed manual. Standard Final Drive Ratio: 3.54:1. Steering: Rack-and-pinion. Suspension (front): wishbones and torsion bars with anti-roll bar. Suspension (rear): rigid axle with semi-elliptic leaf springs. Brakes: hydraulic, front/rear discs. Body Construction: steel body on box-section steel frame. Fuel tank: 17 gallons (U.S.).

XK-150S: Layout: front-engine, rear-drive. Transmission: four-speed manual with overdrive. Standard Final Drive Ratio: 4.09:1. Steering: Rack-and-pinion. Suspension (front): wishbones and torsion bars with anti-roll bar. Suspension (rear): rigid axle with semi-elliptic leaf springs. Brakes: hydraulic, front/rear discs. Body Construction: steel body on box-section steel frame. Fuel Tank: 17 gallons (U.S.)

1959 Jaguar saloon *Bob and Linda Budlow*

3.4: Layout: front-engine, rear-drive. Transmission: four-speed manual with overdrive. Standard Final Drive Ratio: 3.77:1. Steering: Re-circulating ball. Suspension (front): independent; wishbones with coil springs. Suspension (rear): rigid axle with cantilever springs. Brakes: hydraulic, front/rear drum. Body Construction: steel unibody.

MARK IX: Layout: front-engine, rear-drive. Transmission: Automatic. Standard Final Drive Ratio: 4.27:1. Steering: Re-circulating ball. Suspension (front): independent; wishbones and torsion bars. Suspension (rear): rigid axle with semi-elliptic leaf springs. Brakes: hydraulic, front/rear discs. Body Construction: steel body on box-section steel frame.

PERFORMANCE

XK-150: Top Speed: 126 mph. Acceleration (0-60 mph): 8.5 seconds. Acceleration (quarter-mile): 16.9 seconds at 82 mph. Fuel Mileage: (manual) 18-20 mpg, (overdrive) 22 mpg.

XK-150S: Top Speed: 132.3 mph. Acceleration (0-60 mph): 7.4 seconds. Acceleration (quarter-mile): 16.2 seconds. Fuel Mileage: 17-18 mpg.

3.4 SEDAN: Top Speed: 120 mph. Acceleration (0-60 mph): 10.4 seconds.

MARK IX: Top Speed: 115 mph. Acceleration (0-60 mph): 11.2 seconds. Acceleration (quarter-mile): 18.1 seconds at 79 mph)

CALENDAR YEAR REGISTRATIONS (U.S.): A total of 5,596 Jaguars were exported to the U.S. during the year ending July 1959. Approximately 5,839 Jaguars were registered in the U.S. during 1959.

ADDITIONAL MODELS: Production of the 2.4-litre sedan (with 2483-cc engine) continued into 1959, when it was replaced by a MK II version. Only the larger-engined version was commonly exported to the U.S.

MANUFACTURER: Jaguar Cars Ltd., Coventry, England.

DISTRIBUTOR: Jaguar Cars Inc., New York City. Johannes Eerdmans was president of Jaguar Cars, Inc., headquartered at 32 East 57th St., New York City. Jaguar Cars, Inc. was a national subsidiary of Jaguar Cars Limited of Coventry, England.

HISTORY: Jaguar's 1959 models were introduced to the U.S. market on September 1, 1958. The Mark IX debuted at the London show in fall 1958. By the fall of 1959, the larger (3.8-litre) engine used in a new Jaguar Mark IX Saloon also became available for the XK-150 sports car. It produced 220 hp in standard (Special Equipment) form and 265 hp in the "S" version. Cars with this engine were considered 1960 models, although some may have been registered as 1959 models. Jaguar had 409 retail outlets in the U.S. in 1959.

1959 LISTER-JAGUAR

LISTER-JAGUAR – SIX – The 1959 Lister-Jaguar featured an aerodynamic new body designed by Frank Costin of Maserati and Lotus fame, the chief body designer for the Brian Lister engineering company. The wheels were enclosed to nearly hub level. The car featured a unique "bag" tonneau that enclosed the passenger side of the cockpit and was inflated by air trapped by a high-pressure area of the body. The hood was low, with blisters allowing clearance for the cam covers. Air ducts routed air for brake and engine oil cooling. The low-slung car had a ladder-type tube frame, a wishbone front suspension and a de Dion rear. New Dunlop disc brakes were the major chassis change.

ENGINES

BASE SIX LISTER-JAGUAR: Inline, dual-overhead-cam six-cylinder. Cast-iron block and aluminum-alloy head. Displacement: 210 cid (3442 cc). Bore & Stroke: 3.27 x 4.17 in. (83 x 106 mm). Compression Ratio: 9.0:1. Brake Horsepower: 250 hp at 6000 rpm. Seven main bearings. Solid valve lifters. Three twin-choke Weber sidedraft carburetors. Lucas ignition. Dry sump lubrication.

OPTIONAL SIX LISTER-JAGUAR: Inline, dual overhead-cam six-cylinder. Cast-iron block and aluminum-alloy head. Displacement: 230.6 cid (3781 cc). Bore & Stroke: 3.425 x 4.17 in. (87 x 106 mm). Compression Ratio: 10.0:1. Brake Horsepower: 300 at 5600 rpm. Seven main bearings. Solid valve lifters. Three twin-choke Weber sidedraft carburetors. Lucas ignition. Dry sump lubrication.

CHASSIS

LISTER-JAGUAR: Wheelbase: 90.75 in. Overall Length: 172.75 in. Height at scuttle: 31.0 in. Width: 67.0 in. Front Tread: 52.0 in. Rear Tread: 53.25 in. Wheel Type: Dunlop bolt-on light alloy, perforated disc. Early Tires: Dunlop racing 6.00 x 16 front, 6.50 x 16 rear.

TECHNICAL

LISTER-JAGUAR: Layout: front-engine, rear-drive. Transmission: Standard Jaguar D-Type four-speed manual. Dry three-plate Borg & Beck clutch. Standard Final Drive: Salisbury unit incorporating a ZF differential. Final drive ratio: 3.73 to 1. Steering: Rack-and-pinion. Suspension (front): Coil springs enclosing telescopic dampers and equal length wishbones. Suspension (rear): Coil springs enclosing telescopic dampers and de Dion axle. Brakes: Dunlop single-pad 12-in. (front) 12-in. (rear) diameter discs. Body Construction: Twin-tube type chassis with removable bodies and fuel tanks. Fuel Tank: 38 gallon (Imperial).

OPTIONS

LISTER-JAGUAR: 3.4-liter engine. 3.8-liter engine.

PERFORMANCE

LISTER-JAGUAR 3.4: Top Speed: 135 mph. Acceleration (0-100 mph): 10.0 seconds. Acceleration (quarter-mile): 13.0 seconds at 100 mph.

CALENDAR YEAR REGISTRATIONS (U.S.): N/A

MANUFACTURER: Brian Lister (Light Engineering, Ltd.), Abbey Road, Cambridge, England.

HISTORY: An article about the 1959 Lister-Jaguar appeared in *Autosport* (January 9, 1959). A second article about the 1959 Lister-Jaguar appeared in *Motor Racing* (February, 1959). The 1959 Lister-Jaguar was also featured in the January 9, 1959 issue of *The Autocar*.

Model	Body Type & Seating	Engine Type/ CID	P.O.E. Price	Weight (lbs.)	Production Total
Lister-Jaguar					
Lister	2d Roadster-2P	I6/210	NA	1,904	**NA Note 1**

Note 1: An article in *Autocar* (November 1957) quoted Brian Lister as saying the price of a production car without engine would be £2,750.

The dramatic lines of a 1959 Costin Lister-Jaguar at racing speed. *Bob Harrington*

1960

XK-150 — SIX — For the 1960 model year, the 3.8-litre engine was made available in the XK-150 and XK-150S. The "S" version engine differed from the normal 3.8 engine in having the special "straight-port" cylinder head that was used with a three-piece intake manifold carrying triple Model HD8 S.U. carbs with trumpet inlets and low-restriction air cleaners. The XK-150S came standard with a manual gearbox and overdrive. This year the "S" engine was available in all body styles and the XK-150S coupe was described as "...easily the fastest closed car ever subjected to a full-range road test by *The Motor* in 1959." The 3.4-litre engine remained an available option through the end of XK-150 production.

3.4 — MK II — SIX — Disc brakes were standard on the revised Mark II version of the 3.4-litre sedan, which had a larger rear window, bright trim on the window frames and thinner windshield pillars. A manual gearbox with overdrive was standard. An automatic transmission was optional.

3.8 — MK II — SIX — A bigger-engined Mark II version of Jaguar's smaller sedan debuted for 1960 with an overdrive as standard equipment and an optional automatic transmission. Windshield pillars were thinner than prior models. With the 220-hp engine, a 3.8 could accelerate to 60 mph in as little as 8.5 seconds and hit 125 mph or more.

MARK IX — SIX — Production of the full-size sedan continued with little change. For the U.S. market, an automatic transmission and power steering were standard equipment.

I.D. DATA: The chassis serial number of XK-150 is stamped on the frame, adjacent to the rear engine mounting. For the 3.4 sedan, it's on the body channel under the hood on the right side, ahead of radiator header tank. For the Mark IX, it's stamped atop the frame member above the rear engine mounting bracket. The engine number is on the right of engine block, above the oil filter.

ENGINES

BASE SIX XK-150 3.4, BASE SIX 3.4 MK II SEDAN: Inline, dual overhead-cam six-cylinder. Cast-iron block and aluminum-alloy head. Displacement: 210 cid (3442 cc). Bore & Stroke: 3.27 x 4.17 in. (83 x 106 mm). Compression Ratio: 8.0:1. Brake Horsepower: 210 at 5500 rpm. Torque: 216 lbs.-ft. at 3000 rpm. Seven main bearings. Solid valve lifters. Two S.U. sidedraft carburetors.

BASE SIX XK-150S 3.4: Inline, dual overhead-cam six-cylinder. Cast-iron block and aluminum-alloy head. Displacement: 210 cid (3442 cc). Bore & Stroke: 3.27 x 4.17 in. (83 x 106 mm). Compression Ratio: 9.0:1. Brake Horsepower: 250 at 5500 rpm. Torque: 240 at 4000 rpm. Seven main bearings. Solid valve lifters. Three S.U. carburetors.

Model	Body Type & Seating	Engine Type/CID	P.O.E. Price	Weight (lbs.)	Production Total
XK-150					
XK-150SE	2d Roadster-2P	I6/210	$4,520	3,020	**Note 1**
XK-150SE	2d Coupe-2+2P	I6/210	$4,643	2,912	**Note 1**
XK-150SE	2d Convertible-2+2P	I6/210	$4,763	3,020	**Note 1**
XK-150S	2d Roadster-2P	I6/210	$5,120	3,035	**Note 2**
XK-150S	2d Coupe-2+2P	I6/210	$5,075	3,248	**Note 2**
XK-150S	2d Convertible-2+2P	I6/210	$5,195	N/A	**Note 2**
3.4 Mk II (Overdrive)					
3.4	4d Sedan-5P	I6/210	$4,568	3,136	**Note 3**
3.8 Mk II					
3.8	4d Sedan-5P	I6/231	$4,765	3,136	**Note 4**
Mk IX					
Mk IX	4d Sedan-5/6P	I6/231	$6,020	3,976	**Note 5**

Note 1: Total XK-150 production (1957 through 1960) came to 7,929 units. Of these, 1,339 were roadsters (42 with 3.8-litre engine), 4,101 were fixed-head coupes (656 with 3.8-litre engine), and 2,489 were drophead coupes (586 with 3.8-litre engine).
Note 2: Total XK-150S production (1958 through 1961) came to 1,466 units. Of these, 924 were roadsters (36 with 3.8-litre engine), 349 were fixed-head coupes (150 with 3.8-litre engine), and 193 were drophead coupes (89 with 3.8-litre engine).
Note 3: Approximately 28,660 3.4-litre (MK II) sedans were produced from 1960 through 1967.
Note 4: A total of 30,070 3.8-litre (MK II) sedans were produced from 1960 through 1967.
Note 5: A total of 10,009 Mark IX sedans were produced from 1959 through 1961 (including 4,647 for export).

The nose of the classic 3.8-litre Jaguar. *Jaguar Fox Valley*

1960 Jaguar Mk 2 3.8-litre saloon *Jaguar Heritage—North America*

BASE SIX MARK IX SEDAN 3.8, BASE SIX 3.8 MK II SEDAN, BASE SIX XK-150 3.8: Inline, dual overhead-cam six-cylinder. Cast-iron block and aluminum head. Displacement: 230.6 cid (3781 cc). Bore & Stroke: 3.425 x 4.17 in. (87 x 106 mm). Compression Ratio: 8.0:1. Brake Horsepower: 220 at 5500 rpm. Torque: 240 lbs.-ft. at 4000 rpm. Seven main bearings. Solid valve lifters. Two S.U. sidedraft carburetors.

BASE SIX XK-150S 3.8: Inline, dual overhead-cam six-cylinder. Cast-iron block and aluminum head. Displacement: 230.6 cid (3781 cc). Bore & Stroke: 3.425 x 4.17 in. (87 x 106 mm). Compression Ratio: 9.0:1. Brake Horsepower: 265 at 5500 rpm. Torque: 260 at 4500 rpm. Seven main bearings. Solid valve lifters. Three S.U. carburetors.

CHASSIS

XK-150: Wheelbase: 102 in. Overall Length: 177.0 in. Height: 55.0 in. (roadster 52.5 in.) Width: 64.5 in. Front Tread: 51.6 in. Rear Tread: 51.6 in. Wheel Type: steel disc. Standard Tires: 6.00 x 16.

3.4 MK II, 3.8 MK II: Wheelbase: 107.4 in. Overall Length: 180.75 in. Height: 57.5 in. Width: 66.75 in. Front Tread: 55.7 in. Rear Tread: 54.1 in. Wheel Type: steel disc. Standard Tires: 6.40 x 15.

MARK IX: Wheelbase: 120 in. Overall Length: 196.5 in. Height: 63.0 in. Width: 73.0 in. Front Tread: 56.5 in. Rear Tread: 58.0 in. Wheel Type: steel disc. Standard Tires: 6.70 x 16.

TECHNICAL

XK-150: Layout: front-engine, rear-drive. Transmission: four-speed manual. Standard Final Drive Ratio: 3.54:1. Steering: Rack-and-pinion. Suspension (front): wishbones and torsion bars with anti-roll bar. Suspension (rear): rigid axle with semi-elliptic leaf springs. Brakes: hydraulic, front/rear discs. Body Construction: steel body on box-section steel frame. Fuel tank: 17 gallons (U.S.).

XK-150S: Layout: front-engine, rear-drive. Transmission: four-speed manual with overdrive. Standard Final Drive Ratio: 4.09:1. Steering: Rack-and-pinion. Suspension (front): wishbones and torsion bars with anti-roll bar. Suspension (rear): rigid axle with semi-elliptic leaf springs. Brakes: hydraulic, front/rear discs. Body Construction: steel body on box-section steel frame. Fuel tank: 17 gallons (U.S.).

3.4 MK II, 3.8 MK II: Layout: front-engine, rear-drive. Transmission: four-speed manual with overdrive. Standard Final Drive Ratio: 3.54:1. Steering: Re-circulating ball. Suspension (front): independent; wishbones with coil springs.

Suspension (rear): rigid axle with cantilever springs. Brakes: hydraulic, front/rear discs. Body Construction: steel unibody.

MARK IX: Layout: front-engine, rear-drive. Transmission: Automatic. Standard Final Drive Ratio: 4.27:1. Steering: Re-circulating ball. Suspension (front): independent; wishbones and torsion bars. Suspension (rear): rigid axle with semi-elliptic leaf springs. Brakes: hydraulic, front/rear discs. Body Construction: steel body on box-section steel frame.

OPTIONS

XK-150: Automatic transmission: ($250). Overdrive: ($165).

3.4 MK II, 3.8 MK II SEDAN: Automatic transmission: ($150).

PERFORMANCE

XK-150 3.4: Top Speed: 126 mph. Acceleration (0-60 mph): 8.5 seconds. Acceleration (quarter-mile): 16.9 seconds at 82 mph. Fuel Mileage: (manual) 18 to 20 mpg, (overdrive) 22 mpg.

XK-150 3.8: Top Speed: N/A. Acceleration (0-60 mph): 8.3 seconds. Acceleration (quarter-mile): 16.7 seconds at 82 mph. Fuel Mileage: (manual) 18 to 20 mpg, (overdrive) 22 mpg.

XK-150S 3.4: Top Speed: 132.3 mph. Acceleration (0-60 mph): 8.6 seconds. Acceleration (quarter-mile): 16.2 seconds. Fuel Mileage: 17 mpg.

XK-150S 3.8: Top Speed: 135 mph. Acceleration (0-60 mph): 7.0 seconds. Acceleration (quarter-mile): 15.3 seconds at 87 mph.

3.4 MK II SEDAN: Top Speed: 120 mph. Acceleration (0-60 mph): 10.4 seconds.

3.8 MK II SEDAN: Top Speed: 125 mph. Acceleration (0-60 mph): 8.5 to 9.2 seconds.

MARK IX: Top Speed: 115 mph. Acceleration (0-60 mph): 11.2 seconds. Acceleration (quarter-mile): 18.1 seconds at 79 mph.

PRODUCTION/SALES: Approximately 23,000 Jaguars were produced in England during 1960. A total of 4,934 Jaguars were exported to the U.S. during the company's financial year, which ended in July 1960. A total of 5,369 new-car registrations in the U.S. were recorded for Jaguar.

ADDITIONAL MODELS: A Mark II version of the 2.4-litre sedan with 120-hp engine also became available, but was not ordinarily exported to the U.S. A total of 25,070 were produced from 1960-1967.

MANUFACTURER: Jaguar Cars Ltd., Coventry, England.

DISTRIBUTOR: Jaguar Cars, Inc., New York City. Johannes Eerdmans was president of Jaguar Cars, Inc., headquartered at 32 East 57th St., New York City. Jaguar Cars, Inc. was a national subsidiary of Jaguar Cars Limited of Coventry, England. Regional distributors were located throughout the U.S.

HISTORY: Jaguar's 1960 models were introduced on September 1, 1959. Jaguar acquired Daimler in 1960. Jaguar used the 2.5 liter Daimler V-8 in a Jaguar shell and sold such cars as the Daimler SP250 and the Daimler Majestic. Jaguar entered the bus market with the purchase of Daimler and produced the popular Fleetline double-decker buses in England. Imported car sales in the U.S. hit a record 498,785 units this year and represented 7.51 percent of the total market.

1960 Jaguar E prototype *Jaguar Heritage—North America*

1961 Jaguar XK-E roadster *Greg Hertel*

1961

XK-150 — SIX — This would be the final season for the XK-150 sports car.

XK-E (E-TYPE) — SIX — The new projectile-shaped XK-E roadster and hatchback coupe were completely different in appearance than previous XK models and were 400 pounds lighter than the XK-150. The XK-E debuted in March 1961 at the Geneva Motor Show in Switzerland. Its styling was reminiscent of the 1950s D-Type racing car. The most potent XK-150 engine became standard in the XK-E and produced top speeds near 150 mph. The E-Type used a monocoque unibody bolted to a multi-tube front structure. The front end tilted forward like that of the D-Type racer. The XK-E was styled by Malcolm Sayer, an aerodynamicist and was the first Jaguar not designed by Sir William Lyons, who still provided "much input" the company said. The headlights were recessed into nacelles. A slim wraparound rear bumper, narrow taillights and center-exit dual exhausts were in back. The XK-E had new independent rear suspension and four-wheel disc brakes. Painted wire wheels were standard and chrome wire wheels were optional. Early XK-Es had unpainted center dashboard sections. The car was referred to as the "XK-E" in the U.S. and the "E-Type" in Europe. Standard equipment included a battery under the bonnet on the right side, a manual 3-stage screw jack, a complete tool kit (including an adjustable spanner, a plug spanner, three box spanners, four o.e. [original

equipment] spanners, a grease gun, a hub mallet, a tire gauge, a distributor screw driver, a feeler gauge and a valve extractor), and a tachometer with clock.

3.8 MK II — SIX — "The 3.8 is strictly fabulous," raved the British magazine *Cars Illustrated* in its December 1960 issue, in which the 1961 Jaguar 3.8 sedan was put to the test. Writer Douglas Armstrong determined the car combined the performance of a racing machine, the looks and finish of a luxury-quality car and the manners of a product worth twice its price. Standard equipment included leather upholstery, full instrumentation, a two-spoke steering wheel, Dunlop 4-wheel disc brakes, polished wood tables in the seat backs, twin fog lights and a dipping mirror.

MARK IX — SIX — In its final year before replacement by the Mark X, the full-size sedan continued with little change. U.S. versions came with standard automatic transmission and Burman power steering. Also included were twin petrol tanks in the rear, mudguards (fenders), a walnut veneer instrument panel, a lockable document container, two clocks, spot and fog lights and an optional radio with wind-up aerial.

I.D. DATA: The chassis serial number of the XK-150 is stamped on the frame, adjacent to the rear engine mounting. It is on right frame cross member of the XK-E, above the shock absorber mounting. For the 3.8 sedan, it is on the body channel under the hood on the right side, ahead of radiator header tank. For the Mark IX, it is stamped atop the frame member above the rear engine mounting bracket. The engine number is right of the engine block. Engine and chassis numbers also appear on a firewall plate.

ENGINES

BASE SIX XK-150 3.4, BASE SIX 3.4 MK II SEDAN: Inline, dual overhead-cam six-cylinder. Cast-iron block and aluminum-alloy head. Displacement: 210 cid (3442 cc). Bore & Stroke: 3.27 x 4.17 in. (83 x 106 mm). Compression Ratio: 8.0:1. Brake Horsepower: 210 at 5500 rpm. Torque: 216 lbs.-ft. at 3000 rpm. Seven main bearings. Solid valve lifters. Two S.U. sidedraft carburetors.

BASE SIX XK-150S 3.4: Inline, dual overhead-cam six-cylinder. Cast-iron block and aluminum-alloy head. Displacement: 210 cid (3442 cc). Bore & Stroke: 3.27 x 4.17 in. (83 x 106 mm). Compression Ratio: 9.0:1. Brake Horsepower: 250 at 5500 rpm. Torque: 240 at 4000 rpm. Seven main bearings. Solid valve lifters. Three S.U. carburetors.

BASE SIX MARK IX SEDAN 3.8, BASE SIX 3.8 MK II SEDAN, BASE SIX XK-150 3.8: Inline, dual overhead-cam six-cylinder. Cast-iron block and aluminum head. Displacement: 230.6 cid (3781 cc). Bore & Stroke: 3.425 x 4.17 in. (87 x 106 mm). Compression Ratio: 8.0:1. Brake Horsepower: 220 at 5500 rpm. Torque: 240 lbs.-ft. at 4000 rpm. Seven main bearings. Solid valve lifters. Two S.U. sidedraft carburetors.

BASE SIX XK-150S 3.8; BASE SIX XK-E: Inline, dual overhead-cam six-cylinder. Cast-iron block and aluminum head. Displacement: 230.6 cid (3781 cc). Bore & Stroke: 3.425 x 4.17 in. (87 x 106 mm). Compression Ratio: 9.0:1. Brake Horsepower: 265 at 5500 rpm. Torque: 260 at 4500 rpm. Seven main bearings. Solid valve lifters. Three S.U. carburetors.

CHASSIS

XK-150: Wheelbase: 102 in. Overall Length: 177.0 in. Height: 55.0 in. (roadster 52.5 in.) Width: 64.5 in. Front Tread: 51.6 in. Rear Tread: 51.6 in. Wheel Type: steel disc. Standard Tires: 6.00 x 16.

XK-E: Wheelbase: 96 in. Overall Length: 175.3 in. Height: 48.0 in. (roadster 52.5 in.) Width: 65.25 in. Front Tread: 50.0 in. Rear Tread: 50.0 in. Wheel Type: steel disc. Standard Tires: 6.40 x 15.

3.4 MK II, 3.8 MK II: Wheelbase: 107.4 in. Overall Length: 180.75 in. Height: 57.5 in. Width: 66.75 in. Front Tread: 55.0 in. Rear Tread: 53.4 in. Wheel Type: steel disc. Standard Tires: 6.40 x 15.

MARK IX: Wheelbase: 120 in. Overall Length: 196.5 in. Height: 63.0 in. Width: 73.0 in. Front Tread: 56.5 in. Rear Tread: 58.0 in. Wheel Type: steel disc. Standard Tires: 6.70 x 16.

TECHNICAL

XK-150: Layout: front-engine, rear-drive. Transmission: four-speed manual. Standard Final Drive Ratio: 3.54:1. Steering: Rack-and-pinion. Suspension (front): wishbones and torsion bars with anti-roll bar. Suspension (rear): rigid axle with semi-

1961 Jaguar Mk IX saloon *Karmela Moneta*

Model	Body Type & Seating	Engine Type/CID	P.O.E. Price	Weight (Lbs.)	Production Total
XK-150					
XK-150	2d Roadster-2P	I6/210	$4,520	3,020	Note 2
XK-150	2d Coupe-2+2P	I6/210	$4,643	2,912	Note 1
XK-150	2d Convertible-2+2P	I6/210	$4,763	3,020	Note 1
XK-150S	2d Roadster-2P	I6/210	$5,120	3,035	Note 2
XK-150S	2d Coupe-2+2P	I6/210	$5,142	3,248	Note 2
XK-150S	2d Convertible-2+2P	I6/210	$5,162	3,035	Note 2
XK-E (E-Type)					
XK-E	2d Roadster-2P	I6/231	$5,595	2,464	Note 3
XK-E	2d Coupe-2P	I6/231	$5,895	2,520	Note 3
3.8 Mk II (Overdrive)					
3.8	4d Sedan-5P	I6/231	$4,915	3,136	Note 4
Mark IX					
MK IX	4d Sedan-5/6P	I6/231	$6,070	3,976	Note 5

Note 1: Total XK-150 production (1957 through 1960) came to 7,929 units. Of these, 1,339 were roadsters (42 with 3.8-litre engine), 4,101 were fixed-head coupes (656 with 3.8-litre engine), and 2,489 were drophead coupes (586 with 3.8-litre engine).

Note 2: Total XK-150S production (1958 through 1961) came to 1,466 units. Of these, 924 were roadsters (36 with 3.8-litre engine), 349 were fixed-head coupes (150 with 3.8-litre engine), and 193 were drophead coupes (89 with 3.8-litre engine).

Note 3: Total XK-E (E-Type) production from 1961 through 1964 (First Series) amounted to about 7,820 roadsters and 7,670 fixed-head coupes.

Note 4: A total of 30,070 3.8-litre (MK II) sedans were produced from 1960 through 1967.

Note 5: A total of 10,009 Mark IX sedans were produced from 1959 through 1961 (including 4,647 for export).

Andrew Morland

1961 Jaguar E-type (XK-E) roadster

elliptic leaf springs. Brakes: hydraulic, front/rear discs. Body Construction: steel body on box-section steel frame. Fuel tank: 17 gallons (U.S.).

XK-150S: Layout: front-engine, rear-drive. Transmission: four-speed manual with overdrive. Standard Final Drive Ratio: 4.09:1. Steering: Rack-and-pinion. Suspension (front): wishbones and torsion bars with anti-roll bar. Suspension (rear): rigid axle with semi-elliptic leaf springs. Brakes: hydraulic, front/rear discs. Body Construction: steel body on box-section steel frame. Fuel tank: 17 gallons (U.S.)

XK-E: Layout: front-engine, rear-drive. Transmission: four-speed manual with overdrive. Standard Final Drive Ratio: 3.31:1. Steering: Rack-and-pinion. Suspension (front): wishbones and torsion bars with anti-roll bar. Suspension (rear): independent with lower wishbones, coil springs and anti-roll bar. Brakes: hydraulic, front/rear discs. Body Construction: steel unibody. Fuel tank: 17 gallons (U.S.)

3.4 MARK II, 3.8 MARK II: Layout: front-engine, rear-drive. Transmission: four-speed manual with overdrive.

Standard Final Drive Ratio: 3.54:1. Steering: Re-circulating ball. Suspension (front): independent; wishbones with coil springs. Suspension (rear): rigid axle with cantilever springs. Brakes: hydraulic, front/rear discs. Body Construction: steel unibody.

MARK IX: Layout: front-engine, rear-drive. Transmission: Automatic. Standard Final Drive Ratio: 4.27:1. Steering: Re-circulating ball. Suspension (front): independent; wishbones and torsion bars. Suspension (rear): rigid axle with semi-elliptic leaf springs. Brakes: hydraulic, front/rear discs. Body Construction: steel body on box-section steel frame.

OPTIONS

XK-E: HMV Radiomobile radio. R5 racing tires. A detachable hardtop for the roadster.

XK-150: Automatic transmission: ($250). Overdrive: ($165).

3.4 MARK II, 3.8 MARK II: Automatic transmission: ($150). Power steering ($130).

PERFORMANCE

XK-E: Top Speed: 150 mph. Acceleration (0-60 mph): 6.9 seconds. Acceleration (quarter-mile): 15.3 seconds at 93 mph. Fuel Mileage: 19.1 to 21.3 mpg.

XK-150 3.4: Top Speed: 126 mph. Acceleration (0-60 mph): 8.5 seconds. Acceleration (quarter-mile): 16.9 seconds at 82 mph. Fuel Mileage: (manual) 18 to 20 mpg, (overdrive) 22 mpg.

XK-150 3.8: Top Speed: 126. Acceleration (0-60 mph): 8.3 seconds. Acceleration (quarter-mile): 16.7 seconds at 82 mph. Fuel Mileage: (manual) 18 to 20 mpg, (overdrive) 22 mpg.

XK-150S 3.4: Top Speed: 132.3 mph. Acceleration (0-60 mph): 8.6 seconds. Acceleration (quarter-mile): 16.2 seconds. Fuel Mileage: 17 mpg.

XK-150S 3.8: Top Speed: 135 mph. Acceleration (0-60 mph): 7.0 seconds. Acceleration (quarter-mile): 15.3 seconds at 87 mph.

3.4 MK II SEDAN: Top Speed: 120 mph. Acceleration (0-60 mph): 10.4 seconds.

3.8 MK II SEDAN: Top Speed: 125 mph. Acceleration (0-60 mph): 8.5 to 9.2 seconds. Acceleration (quarter-mile): 17.6 seconds. Fuel Mileage: 15 to 19 mpg.

MARK IX: Top Speed: 115 mph. Acceleration (0-60 mph): 11.2 seconds. Acceleration (quarter-mile): 18.1 seconds at 79 mph.

PRODUCTION/SALES: Approximately 25,000 Jaguars were produced during 1961. A total of 3,422 Jaguars were exported to the U.S. during the company's financial year starting in July 1960 and ending July 1961. Close to 44,000 XK-E (E-Type) Jaguars would be sold in the U.S. from 1961 through 1975, out of a total of 72,520 produced.

ADDITIONAL MODELS: The 3.4-litre sedan was dropped this year from the U.S. market, but remained available in Britain.

MANUFACTURER: Jaguar Cars Ltd., Coventry, England.

DISTRIBUTOR: Jaguar Cars Inc., New York City. Johannes Eerdmans was president of Jaguar Cars, Inc., headquartered at 32 East 57th St., New York City. Jaguar Cars, Inc. was a national subsidiary of Jaguar Cars Limited of Coventry, England. Jaguar had 323 retail outlets in the United States in 1961.

HISTORY: Jaguar's 1961 models were introduced to the U.S. market on September 1, 1960. The XK-E appeared at the New York International Auto Show in April 1961, shortly after its debut at the Geneva (Switzerland) show in March. Autocar called the E-Type a "breakthrough in design of high-performance vehicles." In 1961, Jaguar bought venerable Guy Motors of Wolverhampton, England. Founded by Sidney Guy in 1913, the company was famous for its Arab buses, plus the Guy Warrior and Invincible heavy duty trucks. In 1964, the Guy-built Big J series trucks debuted. Original Big Js were powered by a new Cummins V-6 diesel engine but problems with it meant a return to other diesel choices and modification of the Big J cab-over-engine design. Guy Trucks were part of Jaguar's merger with British Motor Corporation in 1966. Big Js were built through 1971, then rebadged as Leylands. Their durable chassis was used on the 1970s BMC Mastiff truck series. Guy also produced Scammell tractors until production was terminated in 1978. A Guy-built Big J truck is in the collection of the National Transport Museum of Ireland in Dublin.

1961 Jaguar XK 150S roadster

Tom Glatch

1962

XK-E (E-TYPE) — SIX — Production of the sleek roadster and hatchback coupe, introduced in 1961, continued with little change. Power again came from a 3.8-litre twin-cam six with three carburetors. Standard equipment included a battery under the bonnet on the right side, a manual 3-stage screw jack, a complete kit of tools, directional indicators with amber flashers, three-blade two-speed self-parking windshield wipers, a speedometer with trip and distance recorders, a tachometer with clock, a fuel contents gauge, a coolant thermometer, an oil pressure gauge, an ammeter, headlight and low-fuel indicator lights, an ignition lock, key-type door locks, a glove locker on passenger side of fascia, a parcel shelf, Vaumol leather upholstery, and a fresh air heater and demister with two-speed fan.

3.8 MK II — SIX — Jaguar's sportier sedan was back again. Standard equipment included an adjustable steering column, individual front seats, a rear bench seat with a folding armrest, leather upholstery, thick-pile carpeting, door armrests and storage pockets, full instrumentation, an automatic choke, complete interior lighting and controls, a console, a heater and demister, a two-spoke steering wheel, self-canceling two-speed windshield wipers, an overdrive switch and light (on cars with overdrive), Dunlop 4-wheel disc brakes, a remote gear lever, folding tables with polished wood surfaces in the seat backs, electric screen washers, a map light, twin fog lights and a dipping mirror.

MARK X — SIX — The Mark IX sedan faded away as the 1962 model year began, leaving only the XK-E coupe and roadster and 3.8 (Mark II) sedan in Jaguar's lineup. At midyear, a new full-size Mark X sedan arrived. It rode the same 120-inch wheelbase as its predecessor, but it featured unibody construction. On U.S. models buyers had a choice of a manual gearbox with overdrive or an automatic transmission. The styling of the new sedan differed considerably from that of the Mark IX. Gone was the distinctive Jaguar fender line that extended through the front and rear doors to meet a bulging rear fender. Instead, the Mark X had a straight-through look. Under the hood was the more powerful version of the 3.8-litre engine also used in the XK-E. A new coil spring suspension was used up front. Also new was an independent rear suspension with a transverse leaf spring. Standard equipment included 12-volt lighting and starting, a speedometer and electric rpm counter, an ammeter, a water temperature gauge, an oil pressure gauge, a fuel gauge, a high-temperature heating system, a demister and defroster with booster fans, a cold air system, twin wind horns, folding tables built into seat backs and leather upholstery.

I.D. DATA: The serial number for the XK-E is stamped on the right frame cross member, above the front shock absorber mounting. For the 3.8 sedan, the serial number is stamped at the side of the engine compartment, just ahead of the radiator header tank. The serial number of the Mark X sedan is stamped atop the right front wheel's inner panel. The engine number for the XK-E is stamped in two places: on the right side of the block above the oil filter, and at the front end of the cylinder head. A suffix (slash plus digit) in the engine number indicates the engine's compression ratio ("/8"= 8.0:1; "/9"= 9.0:1). Engine and chassis numbers also appear on a firewall plate.

ENGINE

BASE SIX XK-E: Inline, dual overhead-cam six-cylinder. Cast-iron block and aluminum-alloy head. Displacement: 230.6 cid (3781 cc). Bore & Stroke: 3.425 x 4.17 in. (87 x 106 mm). Compression Ratio: 9.0:1. Brake Horsepower: 265 at 5500 rpm. Torque: 260 lbs.-ft. at 4000 rpm. Seven main bearings. Solid valve lifters. Three HD8 S.U. sidedraft carburetors.

BASE SIX 3.8 MK II: Inline, dual overhead-cam six-cylinder. Cast-iron block and aluminum head. Displacement: 230.6 cid (3781 cc). Bore & Stroke: 3.425 x 4.17 in. (87 x 106 mm). Compression Ratio: 8.0:1. Brake Horsepower: 220 at 5500 rpm. Torque: 240 lbs.-ft. at 4000 rpm. Seven main bearings. Solid valve lifters. Two S.U. sidedraft carburetors.

BASE SIX MK X: Inline, dual overhead-cam six-cylinder. Cast-iron block and aluminum-alloy head. Displacement: 230.6 cid (3781 cc). Bore & Stroke: 3.425 x 4.17 in. (87 x 106 mm). Compression Ratio: 9.0:1. Brake Horsepower: 265 at 5500 rpm. Torque: 260 lbs.-ft. at 4000 rpm. Seven main bearings. Solid valve lifters. Three HD8 S.U. sidedraft carburetors.

CHASSIS

XK-E: Wheelbase: 96 in. Overall Length: 175.3 in. Height: 48.0 in. (roadster 52.5 in.) Width: 65.25 in. Front Tread: 50.0 in. Rear Tread: 50.0 in. Wheel Type: steel disc. Standard Tires: 6.40 x 15.

3.8 MK II: Wheelbase: 107.4 in. Overall Length: 180.75 in.

Height: 57.5 in. Width: 66.75 in. Front Tread: 55.0 in. Rear Tread: 53.4 in. Wheel Type: steel disc. Standard Tires: 6.40 x 15.

MARK X: Wheelbase: 120 in. Overall Length: 202.0 in. Height: 54.5 in. Width: 76.0 in. Front Tread: 58.0 in. Rear Tread: 58.0 in. Wheel Type: steel disc. Standard Tires: 7.50 x 14.

TECHNICAL

XK-E: Layout: front-engine, rear-drive. Transmission: four-speed manual with overdrive. Standard Final Drive Ratio: 3.31:1. Steering: Rack-and-pinion. Suspension (front): wishbones and torsion bars with anti-roll bar. Suspension (rear): independent with lower wishbones, coil springs and anti-roll bar. Brakes: hydraulic, front/rear discs. Body Construction: steel unibody. Fuel tank: 17 gallons (U.S.).

3.8 MK II: Layout: front-engine, rear-drive. Transmission: four-speed manual with overdrive. Standard Final Drive Ratio: 3.54:1. Steering: Re-circulating ball. Suspension (front): independent; wishbones with coil springs. Suspension (rear): rigid axle with cantilever springs. Brakes: hydraulic, front/rear discs. Body Construction: steel unibody.

MARK X: Layout: front-engine, rear-drive. Transmission: four-speed manual with overdrive. Standard Final Drive Ratio: 3.77:1. Steering: Re-circulating ball. Suspension (front): independent; wishbones with coil springs. Suspension (rear):) independent, with transverse leaf spring. Brakes: hydraulic, front/rear discs. Body Construction: steel unibody.

OPTIONS

XK-E: HMV Radiomobile radio. R5 racing tires. A detachable hardtop for the roadster ($252).

1962 Jaguar XK-E (E-type) roadster *John Wheater*

MODEL	BODY TYPE & SEATING	ENGINE TYPE/CID	P.O.E. PRICE	WEIGHT (LBS.)	PRODUCTION TOTAL
XK-E					
XK-E	2d Roadster-2P	I6/231	$5,595	2,460	**Note 1**
XK-E	2d Coupe-2P	I6/231	$5,895	2,520	**Note 1**
3.8 Mk II (Overdrive)					
3.8	4d Sedan-5P	I6/231	$5,045	3,276	**Note 2**
Mk X					
Mk X	4d Sedan-5P	I6/231	$7,384	3,926	**Note 3**

Note 1: Total XK-E (E-Type) production from 1961 through 1964 (First Series) amounted to about 7,820 roadsters and 7,670 fixed-head coupes.

Note 2: A total of 30,070 3.8-litre (MK II) sedans were produced from 1960 through 1967.

Note 3: A total of 13,382 Mark X sedans with 3.8-litre engine were produced from 1962 through 1964 (including 5,775 for export).

Racing and Jaguars have always gone together, like this 1962 Mk 2 saloon. *Bob Harrington*

3.8 MK II SEDAN: Automatic transmission and power steering: ($150). Power steering ($130).

PERFORMANCE

XK-E: Top Speed: 150 mph. Acceleration (0-60 mph): 6.9 seconds. Acceleration (quarter-mile): 15.3 seconds at 93 mph. Fuel Mileage: 19.1 to 21.3 mpg.

3.8 MK II SEDAN: Top Speed: 125 mph. Acceleration (0-60 mph): 8.5 to 9.2 seconds. Acceleration (quarter-mile): 17.6 seconds. Fuel Mileage: 15 to 19 mpg.

MARK X: Top Speed: 120 mph. Acceleration (0-60 mph): 10.6 seconds. Acceleration (quarter-mile): 19.9-18.3 seconds. Fuel Mileage: 14 to 17 mpg.

PRODUCTION/SALES: Approximately 28,000 Jaguars were produced during 1962. A total of 6,716 Jaguars were exported to the U.S. during the year ending July 1962. In calendar-year 1962, Jaguar sales to U.S. buyers, including tourist deliveries, totaled 4,680 cars. A total of 4,442 new Jaguars were registered in the U.S. during 1962.

MANUFACTURER: Jaguar Cars Ltd., Coventry, England.

DISTRIBUTOR: Jaguar Cars Inc., New York City. Johannes Eerdmans was president of Jaguar Cars, Inc., headquartered at 32 East 57th St., New York City. Jaguar Cars, Inc. was a national subsidiary of Jaguar Cars Limited of Coventry, England. Regional distributors were located throughout the U.S.

HISTORY: Jaguar's 1962 XKE and MK II 3.8 models were introduced to the U.S. market on September 1, 1961. The Jaguar Mark X debuted on February 15, 1962. The popular new XK-E and Mk IX models put Jaguar back in the list of Top 10 imported cars. Jaguar had a 1.3 percent share of the imported car market and was 10th behind Volkswagen, Renault, Standard Triumph, Mercedes-Benz, Austin-Healey, Fiat, MG and Peugeot in order. It was the first time since 1958 that Jaguar appeared on the charts.

1963

XK-E (E-TYPE) — SIX — The 1963 XK-E had a number of improvements. One was a higher (numerically lower) rear axle ratio which added about five miles per hour to top speed. Additional insulation made the '63 model quieter and cooler. A thermostat-driven electric fan replaced the engine-driven type. The brakes were revised to give increased servo assistance. The brake system had a revised pedal linkage and disc pads made of a different material designed to bring the car to a halt with less pedal pressure. The coupe's seats were revised so they slid further back and provided additional leg room. A back-up light became standard equipment. Details of the heating and fresh air system were revised. Standard equipment included a battery, a jack, a complete tool kit, a number plate lamp, triple-blade two-speed self-parking windshield wipers, Lucas windshield washers, a tachometer with clock, Vaumol leather upholstery, imitation leather trim, an improved fresh air heater and demister with two-speed fan.

3.8 MK II — SIX — The smaller sedan now had sealed headlights. It was again powered by a 220-hp version of the twin-cam six-cylinder engine. An overdrive was standard equipment. An automatic transmission was optional. Standard equipment included an adjustable steering column, individual front seats, a rear bench seat with a folding armrest, leather upholstery, thick-pile carpeting, door armrests and storage pockets, full instrumentation, an automatic choke, a heater and demister, a two-spoke steering wheel, self-canceling two-speed windshield wipers, Dunlop 4-wheel disc brakes, a remote gear lever, folding tables in the seat backs, twin fog lights and a dipping mirror.

MARK X — SIX — Production of the large four-door saloon continued with little change. Standard equipment included 12-volt lighting and starting, a high-temperature heating system, a demister and defroster with booster fans, a cold air system, a cigar light, a map light, a panel light, an interior light, twin wind horns, folding tables built into seat backs and leather upholstery.

I.D. DATA: The serial number for the XK-E is stamped on the right frame cross member, above the front shock absorber mounting. The 3.8 sedan serial number is stamped at the side of the engine compartment, just ahead of the radiator header tank. The Mark X sedan number is stamped atop the right front wheel's inner panel. The engine number for the XK-E is stamped on the right side of the block above the oil filter, and at the front end of the cylinder head. A suffix (slash plus digit) in the engine number indicates the engine's compression ratio ("/8" = 8.0:1; "/9" = 9.0:1). Engine and chassis numbers also appear on a firewall plate.

ENGINE

BASE SIX XK-E: Inline, dual overhead-cam six-cylinder. Cast-iron block and aluminum-alloy head. Displacement: 230.6 cid (3781 cc). Bore & Stroke: 3.425 x 4.17 in. (87 x 106 mm). Compression Ratio: 9.0:1. Brake Horsepower: 265 at 5500 rpm. Torque: 260 lbs.-ft. at 4000 rpm. Seven main bearings. Solid valve lifters. Three HD8 S.U. sidedraft carburetors.

BASE SIX 3.8 MK II: Inline, dual overhead-cam six-cylinder.

Cast-iron block and aluminum head. Displacement: 230.6 cid (3781 cc). Bore & Stroke: 3.425 x 4.17 in. (87 x 106 mm). Compression Ratio: 8.0:1. Brake Horsepower: 220 at 5500 rpm. Torque: 240 lbs.-ft. at 4000 rpm. Seven main bearings. Solid valve lifters. Two HD 6 S.U. sidedraft carburetors.

BASE SIX MK X: Inline, dual overhead-cam six-cylinder. Cast-iron block and aluminum-alloy head. Displacement: 230.6 cid (3781 cc). Bore & Stroke: 3.425 x 4.17 in. (87 x 106 mm). Compression Ratio: 9.0:1. Brake Horsepower: 265 at 5500 rpm. Torque: 260 lbs.-ft. at 4000 rpm. Seven main bearings. Solid valve lifters. Three HD8 S.U. sidedraft carburetors.

CHASSIS

XK-E: Wheelbase: 96 in. Overall Length: 175.3 in. Height: 48.0 in. (roadster 52.5 in.) Width: 65.25 in. Front Tread: 50.0 in. Rear Tread: 50.0 in. Wheel Type: steel disc. Standard Tires: 6.40 x 15.

3.8 MK II: Wheelbase: 107.4 in. Overall Length: 180.75 in. Height: 57.5 in. Width: 66.75 in. Front Tread: 55.0 in. Rear Tread: 53.4 in. Wheel Type: steel disc. Standard Tires: 6.40 x 15.

MARK X: Wheelbase: 120 in. Overall Length: 202.0 in. Height: 54.5 in. Width: 76.0 in. Front Tread: 58.0 in. Rear Tread: 58.0 in. Wheel Type: steel disc. Standard Tires: 7.50 x 14.

TECHNICAL

XK-E: Layout: front-engine, rear-drive. Transmission: four-speed manual with overdrive. Standard Final Drive Ratio: 3.07:1. Steering: Rack-and-pinion. Suspension (front): wishbones and torsion bars with anti-roll bar. Suspension (rear): independent with lower wishbones, coil springs and anti-roll bar. Brakes: hydraulic, front/rear discs. Body Construction: steel unibody. Fuel tank: 17 gallons (U.S.)

3.8 MK II: Layout: front-engine, rear-drive. Transmission: four-speed manual with overdrive. Standard Final Drive Ratio: 3.54:1. Steering: Re-circulating ball. Suspension (front): independent; wishbones with coil springs. Suspension (rear): rigid axle with cantilever springs. Brakes: hydraulic, front/rear discs. Body Construction: steel unibody.

MARK X: Layout: front-engine, rear-drive. Transmission: four-speed manual with overdrive. Standard Final Drive Ratio: 3.77:1. Steering: Re-circulating ball. Suspension (front): independent; wishbones with coil springs. Suspension (rear): independent, with transverse leaf spring. Brakes: hydraulic, front/rear discs. Body Construction: steel unibody.

OPTIONS

XK-E: HMV Radiomobile radio. R5 racing tires. A detachable hardtop for the roadster ($252).

3.8 MK II SEDAN: Automatic transmission and power steering: ($150). Power steering ($120).

PERFORMANCE

XK-E: Top Speed: 150 mph. Acceleration (0-60 mph): 6.5 to 7.0 seconds. Acceleration (quarter-mile): 14.8 to 15.3 seconds at 93 to 97 mph. Fuel Mileage: 19.1 to 21.3 mpg.

3.8 MKII SEDAN: Top Speed: 115 to 118 mph. Acceleration (0-60 mph): 8.5 to 9.2 seconds. Acceleration (quarter-mile): 17.6 seconds. Fuel Mileage: 15 to 19 mpg.

MARK X: Top Speed: 120 mph. Acceleration (0-60 mph): 10.6 seconds. Acceleration (quarter-mile): 17.2 seconds at 80 mph. Fuel Mileage: 14 to 17 mpg.

PRODUCTION/SALES: Approximately 22,500 Jaguars were produced during 1963. In calendar-year 1963, Jaguar sales to U.S. buyers, totaled 4,582 cars with 4,421 retailed by U.S.

A 1963 Jaguar XK-E factory lightweight coupe goes racing. *Bob Harrington*

Model	Body Type & Seating	Engine Type/CID	P.O.E. Price	Weight (lbs.)	Production Total
XK-E					
XK-E	2d Roadster-2P	I6/231	$5,595	2,464	Note 1
XK-E	2d Coupe-2P	I6/231	$5,895	2,520	Note 1
3.8 Mk II					
3.8	4d Sedan-5P	I6/231	$4,890	3,136	Note 2
Mark X					
Mk X	4d Sedan-5P	I6/231	$6,990	3,920	Note 3

Note 1: Total XK-E (E-Type) production from 1961 through 1964 (First Series) amounted to about 7,820 roadsters and 7,670 fixed-head coupes.

Note 2: A total of 30,070 3.8-litre (Mk II) sedans were produced from 1960 through 1967.

Note 3: A total of 13,382 Mark X sedans with 3.8-litre engine were produced from 1962 through 1964 (including 5,775 for export).

A 1963 Jaguar MK IX basks in the California sun.

dealers. A total of 4,113 Jaguars were registered in the U.S. during the year ending July 1963.

MANUFACTURER: Jaguar Cars Ltd., Coventry, England.

DISTRIBUTOR: Jaguar Cars Inc., New York City. Johannes Eerdmans was president of Jaguar Cars, Inc., headquartered at 32 East 57th St., New York City. Jaguar Cars, Inc. was a national subsidiary of Jaguar Cars Limited of Coventry, England. Regional distributors included Auto Distributors of New York, Briggs S. Cunningham president; Royston Distributors, Inc. of Philadelphia, Pennsylvania; Roosevelt Automobile Company, Inc., of Washington, D.C.; Overseas Motors Corporation of Ft. Worth, Texas; Charles H. Hornburg, Jr., Inc., of Los Angeles, California; British Motor Car Distributors, Ltd., of San Francisco, California; Mid-States Jaguar, Inc., Chicago, Illinois; Falvey Motor Sales Company of Detroit, Michigan; and Automotive Imports Corp., of Cleveland Heights, Ohio.

HISTORY: Jaguar's 1963 models were introduced on September 1, 1962. In 1963, Jaguar acquired Coventry-Climax, an engine-builder in Great Britain since 1903. Lord Shackleton used Coventry-Simplex engines in his 1914 Antarctic Expedition. The company built engines for Swift, Standard, and Morgan cars. In the Great Depression, the renamed Coventry-Climax company produced its famous Godiva fire pump engine line. After World War II, Coventry-Climax engines were used in racing and the company also produced engines for the All-British Fork Lift Truck. Their overhead-cam engines gained fame on and off European race tracks in Lotus, Kieft and TVR cars. Coventry-Climax was advertised as "The fire pump that wins races." The firm also made marine and military engines. Former Jaguar employee Walter Hassan returned to Jaguar and became the Group Chief Engineer (Power Units). His expertise was helpful with OHC engine technology. Before going to Coventry-Climax in 1950, Hassan influenced the use of Lockheed brakes in the Jaguar XK-120 series.

1964 Jaguar E-type (XK-E) 4.2-litre coupe *Andrew Morland*

1964

XK-E (E-TYPE) — SIX — In May 1964, *Car and Driver* magazine selected the Jaguar XK-E as "Best GT/Sports Car $3,000-$6,000" and "Best All-Round Car." The magazine stated, "The simplest thing that can be said about the Jaguar XK-E is that it is like a Ferrari, a Maserati or an Aston Martin – but costs half as much." Objections the magazine had to the XK-E were a cramped cockpit, a lack of creature comforts, heavy controls (except steering) and a non-synchro first gear in the manual transmission. Little was new with the XK-E roadster or coupe. A 4.2-litre engine would arrive late in the calendar year for 1965 models. Some 4.2s may have been registered in 1964 and titled as 1964 cars. Standard equipment included a battery, a jack, a tool kit, a tachometer with clock, key-type door locks, a glove locker, a parcel shelf, an ashtray, leather seats, and imitation leather trim.

3.8 MK II — SIX — The smaller Jaguar sedan again came with either a manual gearbox with overdrive or an automatic transmission. Standard equipment included power steering, an adjustable steering column, individual front seats, a rear bench seat with a folding armrest, leather upholstery, thick-pile carpeting, door armrests and storage pockets, full instrumentation, an automatic choke, complete interior lighting and controls, a two-spoke steering wheel, self-cancelling two-speed windshield wipers, an overdrive switch and light (on cars with overdrive), Dunlop 4-wheel disc brakes, a remote gear lever, folding tables with polished wood surfaces in the seat backs, a map light, twin fog lights and a dipping mirror.

3.8 TYPE S — SIX — A longer "S-Type" version of the 3.8 MKII sedan became available this year. It was a car that bridged the market gap between the small sedan and the full-size MK X. The Type S had independent rear coil springs replacing the former cantilevered units. The S-Type also had a different rear-end look with flattened (lower) wheel openings, slimmer bumpers, shrouded headlights, teardrop-shaped turn signals indicators outside the parking lights and a straight deck lid. Inside, the S-Type dashboard had walnut in its center. In the engine compartment the S-Type had a transverse air cleaner.

MARK X — SIX — Jaguar's full-size sedan continued with minimal change. Standard equipment included automatic transmission, power steering, 12-volt lighting and starting, a speedometer and electric rpm counter, a high-temperature heating system, a demister and defroster with booster fans, a cold air system, twin wind horns, folding tables built into seat backs and leather upholstery. A 4.2-litre engine arrived late in the calendar year for 1965 models. Some 4.2s may have been registered in 1964 and titled as 1964 cars.

I.D. DATA: The serial numbers are in the same locations as 1962 and 1963.

ENGINE

BASE SIX XKE: Inline, dual overhead-cam six-cylinder. Cast-iron block and aluminum-alloy head. Displacement: 230.6

cid (3781 cc). Bore & Stroke: 3.425 x 4.17 in. (87 x 106 mm). Compression Ratio: 9.0:1. Brake Horsepower: 265 at 5500 rpm. Torque: 260 lbs.-ft. at 4000 rpm. Seven main bearings. Solid valve lifters. Three HD8 S.U. sidedraft carburetors.

BASE SIX 3.8 MKII: Inline, dual overhead-cam six-cylinder. Cast-iron block and aluminum head. Displacement: 230.6 cid (3781 cc). Bore & Stroke: 3.425 x 4.17 in. (87 x 106 mm). Compression Ratio: 8.0:1. Brake Horsepower: 220 at 5500 rpm. Torque: 240 lbs.-ft. at 4000 rpm. Seven main bearings. Solid valve lifters. Two HD 6 S.U. sidedraft carburetors.

BASE SIX MK X: Inline, dual overhead-cam six-cylinder. Cast-iron block and aluminum-alloy head. Displacement: 230.6 cid (3781 cc). Bore & Stroke: 3.425 x 4.17 in. (87 x 106 mm). Compression Ratio: 9.0:1. Brake Horsepower: 265 at 5500 rpm. Torque: 260 lbs.-ft. at 4000 rpm. Seven main bearings. Solid valve lifters. Three HD8 S.U. sidedraft carburetors.

CHASSIS

XK-E: Wheelbase: 96 in. Overall Length: 175.3 in. Height: 48.0 in. (roadster 52.5 in.) Width: 65.25 in. Front Tread: 50.0 in. Rear Tread: 50.0 in. Wheel Type: steel disc. Standard Tires: 6.40 x 15.

3.8 MK II: Wheelbase: 107.4 in. Overall Length: 180.75 in. Height: 57.5 in. Width: 66.75 in. Front Tread: 55.0 in. Rear Tread: 53.4 in. Wheel Type: steel disc. Standard Tires: 6.40 x 15.

3.8 S-Type: Wheelbase: 107.4 in. Overall Length: 187.75 in. Height: 57.5 in. Width: 66.75 in. Front Tread: 55.25 in. Rear Tread: 54.25 in. Wheel Type: steel disc. Standard Tires: 6.40 x 15.

MARK X: Wheelbase: 120 in. Overall Length: 202.0 in. Height: 54.5 in. Width: 76.0 in. Front Tread: 58.0 in. Rear Tread: 58.0 in. Wheel Type: steel disc. Standard Tires: 7.50 x 14.

TECHNICAL

XK-E: Layout: front-engine, rear-drive. Transmission: four-speed manual with overdrive. Standard Final Drive Ratio: 3.07:1. Steering: Rack-and-pinion. Suspension (front): wishbones and torsion bars with anti-roll bar. Suspension (rear): independent with lower wishbones, coil springs and anti-roll bar. Brakes: hydraulic, front/rear discs. Body Construction: steel unibody. Fuel tank: 17 gallons (U.S.)

3.8 MK II: Layout: front-engine, rear-drive. Transmission: four-speed manual with overdrive. Standard Final Drive Ratio: 3.54:1. Steering: Re-circulating ball. Suspension (front): independent; rigid axle with cantilever leaf springs. Suspension (rear): independent with coil springs. Brakes: hydraulic, front/rear discs. Body Construction: steel unibody.

3.8 MK S-TYPE: Layout: front-engine, rear-drive. Transmission: four-speed manual with overdrive. Standard Final Drive Ratio: 3.77:1. Steering: Re-circulating ball. Suspension (front): independent; wishbones with coil springs. Suspension (rear): independent with coil springs. Brakes: hydraulic, front/rear discs. Body Construction: steel unibody.

MARK X: Layout: front-engine, rear-drive. Transmission: automatic. Standard Final Drive Ratio: 3.54:1. Steering: Re-circulating ball with standard power assist. Suspension (front): independent; wishbones with coil springs. Suspension (rear): independent, with transverse leaf spring. Brakes: hydraulic, front/rear discs. Body Construction: steel unibody.

OPTIONS

XK-E: HMV Radiomobile radio. R5 racing tires. A detachable hardtop for the roadster ($252).

3.8 MK II: Automatic transmission and power steering: ($150). Power steering ($120).

PERFORMANCE

XK-E: Top Speed: 150 mph. Acceleration (0-60 mph): 6.5 to

Various Jaguar Mk 2 saloons are on display together. *Greg Hertel*

Model	Body Type & Seating	Engine Type/CID	P.O.E. Price	Weight (lbs.)	Production Total
XK-E					
XK-E	2d Roadster-2P	I6/231	$5,325	2,464	**Note 1**
XK-E	2d Coupe-2P	I6/231	$5,525	2,520	**Note 1**
3.8 Mk II					
3.8	4d Sedan-5P	I6/231	$5,220	3,248	**Note 2**
3.8 S-Type					
S-Type	4d Sedan-5P	I6/231	$5,850	3,440	**Note 3**
Mark X					
MK X	4d Sedan-5P	I6/231	$6,990	3,976	**Note 4**

Note 1: Total XK-E (E-Type) production from 1961 through 1964 (First Series) amounted to about 7,820 roadsters and 7,670 fixed-head coupes.
Note 2: A total of 30,070 3.8-litre (Mk II) sedans were produced from 1960 through 1967.
Note 3: A total of 15,070 3.8 S-Type sedans were produced from 1964 through 1968.
Note 4: A total of 13,382 Mark X sedans with 3.8-litre engine were produced from 1962 through 1964 (including 5,775 for export).

A 1964 Jaguar Mk 2 3.8-litre saloon from the front.

7.0 seconds. Acceleration (quarter-mile): 14.8 to 15.3 seconds at 93 to 97 mph. Fuel Mileage: 19.1 to 21.3 mpg.

3.8 MK II: Top Speed: 115 to 118 mph. Acceleration (0-60 mph): 8.5 to 9.2 seconds with manual transmission. Acceleration (0-60 mph): 10.8 seconds with automatic transmission. Acceleration (quarter-mile): 17.6 seconds with manual transmission. Acceleration (quarter-mile): 17.2 seconds with automatic transmission. Fuel Mileage: (manual transmission) 15 to 19 mpg. Fuel Mileage: (automatic transmission) 14 to 17 mpg.

MARK X: Top Speed: 120 mph. Acceleration (0-60 mph): 10.6 seconds. Acceleration (quarter-mile): 17.2 seconds at 80 mph. Fuel Mileage: 14 to 17 mpg.

PRODUCTION/SALES: Approximately 20,000 Jaguars were produced during 1964. A total of 4,037 Jaguars were exported to the U.S. during the year ending July 1964. In calendar-year 1964, Jaguar sales to U.S. buyers, including tourist deliveries, totaled 4,018 cars.

MANUFACTURER: Jaguar Cars Ltd., Coventry, England.

DISTRIBUTOR: Jaguar Cars Inc., New York City. Johannes Eerdmans was president of Jaguar Cars, Inc., headquartered at 32 East 57th St., New York City. Jaguar Cars, Inc. was a national subsidiary of Jaguar Cars Limited of Coventry, England. Regional distributors were located across the United States.

HISTORY: Jaguar's 1964 models were introduced to the U.S. market on September 1, 1963. At the end of 1964, there were 282 retail Jaguar outlets in the United States. Jaguar sales were no longer among the top 10 imports. In 1964, the company acquired the Henry Meadows Company of Wolverhampton, England. Meadows began in 1920, producing quality three-speed transmissions, and soon began producing engines for cars like Lagonda, Invicta, Lea-Francis and Frazer-Nash. Later, the company made diesel locomotive engines. In 1957, Meadows introduced the short-lived Frisky Sport three-cylinder mini car. Meadows also made water craft gearboxes. Jaguar XK engines were used in boat racing.

1965 Jaguar E-type (XK-E) roadster *Andrew Morland*

1965

E-TYPE — SIX — A 4.2-litre six-cylinder engine become available this year. This engine had a new intake manifold. A new heavy-duty copper crossflow radiator with a thermostatically-controlled electric fan was used. Perhaps the year's biggest improvement was the new, all-synchromesh, four-speed gearbox. A new Laycock 10-in. diaphragm clutch was fitted. Jaguar reverted to a 3.07:1 rear axle. New sealed beam headlights had improved high and low beam intensity. Entirely new bucket seats featured curved seat backs, increased seat-adjuster movement, soft, deep cushions and better rake position adjustment. Combined with deeper footwells, the seats greatly increased driver comfort. A new Lucas alternator was used. The exhaust system was improved to decrease noise level. The brake system was improved with a bigger servo unit. Lettering on the trunk lid spelled out "E TYPE JAGUAR 4.2." Standard equipment included a hand choke, a battery, a jack, a tool kit, two headlights, two side lights and flashers, two taillights and stop lights, a number plate lamp, a backing lamp, electrical fuses, directional indicators with amber flashers, triple-blade two-speed self-parking windshield wipers, Lucas windshield washers, a speedometer with odometer and trip odometer, a tachometer with clock, a fuel gauge, a temperature gauge, an oil pressure gauge, an ammeter, headlight and low-fuel indicator lights, directional signals, an ignition lock, key-type door locks, a glove locker, a parcel shelf, an ashtray, a cigar lighter, interior lights, leather seats, imitation leather trim, carpets and a fresh air heater and demister with two-speed fan.

3.8 MK II — SIX — Change was minimal on the smaller sedan, which continued with the 3781-cc twin-cam engine. Power steering was standard. Wire wheels and air conditioning were optional. Standard equipment included power steering, an adjustable steering column, individual front seats, a rear bench seat with a folding armrest, leather upholstery, thick-pile carpeting, door armrests and storage pockets, full instrumentation, an automatic choke, complete interior lighting and controls, a console, a heater and demister, a two-spoke steering wheel, self-cancelling two-speed windshield wipers, an overdrive switch and light, Dunlop 4-wheel disc brakes, a remote gear lever, folding tables with polished wood surfaces in the seat backs, electric screen washers, a cigar lighter, a map light, twin fog lights and a dipping mirror.

3.8 TYPE S — SIX — The 3.8 Type S sedan was 7 inches longer than the 3.8 Mk II and had a different rear-end appearance, with flattened rear wheel openings and straight deck lid (similar to the larger Mark X sedan).

MARK X — 4.2 — SIX — The 4.2-litre engine went into Jaguar's full-size sedan even before it appeared under E-Type (E-Type) hoods. Some sources called the revised model, simply, "4.2," although "Mark X" remained part of its name. Standard equipment included variable-ratio power steering, Borg-Warner dual-range automatic transmission, a limited-slip differential, and built-in walnut tables. The "Mark X" portion of its designation was not always used in these final years. Standard equipment included a 12-volt battery (negative ground), four Lucas sealed beam headlights, two automatic reversing lamps, eight electric fuses, dual two-speed self-parking windshield wipers, Lucas windshield washers, a fresh air heater with two-speed fan and rear compartment air corridor, safety belt anchorages, leather interior trim, a cloth headliner, pile carpeting, a screw-pillar jack and twin 20-gallon fuel tanks.

I.D. DATA: The chassis serial number for the E-Type is stamped on the right frame cross member, above the shock absorber mounting. The Mark II (3.8) serial number is stamped in the hood latch channel, ahead of the radiator. The Mark X serial number is stamped atop the right front wheel's inner panel. The engine number is stamped on the right side of the block, above the oil filter; and at the front of the cylinder head. Suffix '8' or '9' indicates the engine's compression ratio. The starting serial numbers: (E-Type 4.2 roadster) 1E.10001 or 1R.7001; (E-Type 4.2 coupe) 1E.300001 or 1R.25001; (Mark X 4.2) 1D.75001.

ENGINES

BASE SIX 3.8 MK II, BASE SIX 3.8 S-TYPE: Inline, dual overhead-cam six-cylinder. Cast-iron block and aluminum-alloy head. Displacement: 230.6 cid (3781 cc). Bore & Stroke: 3.425 x 4.17 in. (87 x 106 mm). Compression Ratio: 8.0:1. Brake Horsepower: 220 at 5500 rpm. Torque: 240/245 lbs.-ft. at 3000 rpm. Seven main bearings. Solid valve lifters. Two S.U. sidedraft carburetors.

BASE SIX E-TYPE, BASE SIX MARK X: Inline, dual overhead-cam six-cylinder. Cast-iron block and aluminum-alloy head. Displacement: 258.4 cid (4235 cc). Bore & Stroke: 3.625 x 4.17 in. (92.1 x 106 mm). Compression Ratio: 9.0:1. Brake Horsepower: 265 at 5400 rpm. Torque: 283 lbs.-ft. at 4000 rpm. Seven main bearings. Solid valve lifters. Three S.U. sidedraft carburetors.

CHASSIS

E-TYPE: Wheelbase: 96 in. Overall Length: 175.3 in. Height: 48.0 in. (roadster 52.5 in.) Width: 65.25 in. Front Tread: 50.0 in. Rear Tread: 50.0 in. Wheel Type: steel disc. Standard Tires: 6.40 x 15.

3.8 MK II: Wheelbase: 107.4 in. Overall Length: 180.75 in. Height: 57.5 in. Width: 66.75 in. Front Tread: 55.0 in. Rear Tread: 53.4 in. Wheel Type: steel disc. Standard Tires: 6.40 x 15.

3.8 S-Type: Wheelbase: 107.4 in. Overall Length: 187.75 in. Height: 57.5 in. Width: 66.75 in. Front Tread: 55.25 in. Rear Tread: 54.25 in. Wheel Type: steel disc. Standard Tires: 6.40 x 15.

MARK X: Wheelbase: 120 in. Overall Length: 202.0 in. Height: 54.5 in. Width: 76.0 in. Front Tread: 58.0 in. Rear Tread: 58.0 in. Wheel Type: steel disc. Standard Tires: 205R x 14.

TECHNICAL

E-TYPE: Layout: front-engine, rear-drive. Transmission: four-speed manual with overdrive. Standard Final Drive Ratio: 3.07:1. Steering: Rack-and-pinion. Suspension (front): wishbones and torsion bars with anti-roll bar. Suspension (rear): independent with lower wishbones, coil springs and anti-roll bar. Brakes: hydraulic, front/rear discs. Body Construction: steel unibody. Fuel tank: 17 gallons (U.S.)

3.8 MK II: Layout: front-engine, rear-drive. Transmission: four-speed manual with overdrive. Standard Final Drive Ratio: 3.54:1. Steering: Re-circulating ball. Suspension (front): independent; rigid axle with cantilever leaf springs. Suspension (rear): independent with coil springs. Brakes: hydraulic, front/rear discs. Body Construction: steel unibody.

3.8 MK S-TYPE: Layout: front-engine, rear-drive. Transmission: four-speed manual with overdrive. Standard Final Drive Ratio: 3.77:1. Steering: Re-circulating ball. Suspension (front): independent; wishbones with coil springs. Suspension (rear): independent with coil springs. Brakes: hydraulic, front/rear discs. Body Construction: steel unibody.

1965 Jaguar XJ-13 V-12 prototype

Model	Body Type & Seating	Engine Type/CID	P.O.E. Price	Weight (lbs.)	Production Total
E-Type					
E-Type	2d Roadster-2P	I6/258	$5,384	2,464	Note 1
E-Type	2d Coupe-2P	I6/258	$5,580	2,520	Note 1
3.8 Mk II					
3.8	4d Sedan-5P	I6/231	$5,419	3,136	Note 2
3.8 S-TYPE					
3.8S	4d Sedan-5P	I6/231	$5,933	3,438	Note 3
Mark X					
4.2	4d Sedan-6P	I6/258	$6,990	3,920	Note 4

Note 1: Total E-Type (E-Type) production from 1965 through 1968 amounted to about 9,550 roadsters and 7,770 fixed-head coupes (plus 5,600 2+2 coupes).

Note 2: A total of 30,070 3.8-litre (Mk II) sedans were produced from 1960 through 1967.

Note 3: A total of 15,070 3.8S sedans were produced from 1964 through 1968.

Note 4: A total of 5,119 Mark X sedans with 4.2-litre engine were produced in 1965 through 1966 (including 2,291 for export), plus 18 limousines.

1965 Jaguar Mark X saloon

Richard Dance Collection

MARK X: Layout: front-engine, rear-drive. Transmission: automatic. Standard Final Drive Ratio: 3.54:1. Steering: Recirculating ball with standard power assist. Suspension (front): independent; wishbones with coil springs. Suspension (rear): independent, with transverse leaf spring. Brakes: hydraulic, front/rear discs. Body Construction: steel unibody.

OPTIONS

E-TYPE: Radio. A detachable hardtop for the roadster ($252).

3.8 MK II: Automatic transmission and power steering: ($150). Power steering ($120).

MARK X: Air conditioning ($595)

PERFORMANCE

E-TYPE: Top Speed: 150 mph. Acceleration (0-60 mph): 6.5-7.0 seconds. Acceleration (quarter-mile): 14.8-15.3 seconds at 93-97 mph. Fuel Mileage: 19.1-21.3 mpg.

3.8 MK II: Top Speed: 115-118 mph. Acceleration (0-60 mph): 8.5-9.2 seconds with manual transmission. Acceleration (0-60 mph): 10.8 seconds with automatic transmission. Acceleration (quarter-mile): 17.6 seconds with manual transmission.

Acceleration (quarter-mile): 17.2 seconds with automatic transmission. Fuel Mileage: (manual transmission) 15-19 mpg. Fuel Mileage: (automatic transmission) 14-17 mpg.

MARK X: Top Speed: 120 mph. Acceleration (0-60 mph): 10.6 seconds. Acceleration (quarter-mile): 17.2 seconds at 80 mph. Fuel Mileage: 14-17 mpg.

CALENDAR YEAR SALES (U.S.): A total of 3,669 Jaguars were exported to the U.S. during the year ending July 1965. In calendar-year 1965, Jaguar sales to U.S. buyers, including tourist deliveries, totaled 3,993 cars.

MANUFACTURER: Jaguar Cars Ltd., Coventry, England.

DISTRIBUTOR: Jaguar Cars Inc., New York City. Johannes Eerdmans was president of Jaguar Cars, Inc., headquartered at 32 East 57th St., New York City. Jaguar Cars, Inc. was a national subsidiary of Jaguar Cars Limited of Coventry, England. Regional distributors were located across the United States.

HISTORY: The 1965 Jaguar 3.8 sedan was introduced September 1, 1964. Other 1965 Jaguar models were introduced to the U.S. market on October 15, 1964. At the end of calendar year 1965, Jaguar had 280 retail outlets in the United States.

A 1966 Jaguar XK-E (E-type) goes racing. *Bob Harrington*

1966

E-TYPE 4.2 — SIX — Writer Henry Manney described the 1966 E-Type Jaguar as "Of extremely seductive configuration and with a semi-monocoque chassis borrowed from the competition D." All E-Types carried the 4.2-litre engine and a standard four-speed manual gearbox. The steering column adjusted for both reach and height. Standard equipment included a hand choke, a battery, a jack, a tool kit, leather seats, imitation leather trim, carpets and a fresh air heater and demister with two-speed fan.

E-TYPE 2+2 COUPE 4.2 — SIX — Jaguar added a longer 2+2 coupe to the model lineup this year. It carried the 4.2-litre engine and a standard four-speed manual gearbox, but a Borg-Warner automatic transmission became available. The 2+2 rode a longer wheelbase and had a taller roof line.

3.8 MK II SEDAN — SIX — Vinyl replaced leather in 1966. New side grilles replaced the former fog lamps. Standard equipment included power steering, an adjustable steering column, door armrests and pockets, full instrumentation, an automatic choke, an overdrive switch and light, folding tables in the seat backs, twin fog lights and a self-dimming rearview mirror.

3.8 S-TYPE SEDAN — SIX — The slightly larger and more luxurious S-Type mixed family comfort with sports

car character. The 3.8S had slim bumpers, a different wheel-opening shape, a different roof line and independent rear suspension with coil springs.

4.2 MARK X — SIX — Standard equipment on the largest Jaguar sedan included variable-ratio power steering, Borg-Warner dual-range automatic transmission, a limited-slip differential and built-in walnut tables. The "Mark X" designation was not always used from 1966 on. Standard equipment included a 12-volt battery, leather interior trim, pile carpeting, a screw-pillar jack and twin 20-gallon fuel tanks.

I.D. DATA: The serial number for the E-Type is stamped on the right frame cross member, above the shock absorber mounting. For the 3.8 series, it is on the hood latch channel ahead of the radiator. For the 4.2 Mark X it is atop the right front wheel inner panel. The prefix indicates the make and model (and possibly whether car is a U.S. model). The suffix may indicate whether car is equipped with overdrive or automatic transmission, and if left-hand drive (for export). The numerical sequence is the production serial number. The engine number is stamped on the right side of the block, above the oil filter; and at the front of the cylinder head (suffix /8 or /9 indicates compression ratio). Engine and chassis numbers also appear on a brass plate on the firewall. Starting serial number: (E-Type 2+2) 1E.75001 or 1R.40001.

MODEL	BODY TYPE & SEATING	ENGINE TYPE/CID	P.O.E. PRICE	WEIGHT (LBS.)	PRODUCTION TOTAL
E-Type					
E-Type	2d Roadster-2P	I6/258	$5,384	2,464	**Note 1**
E-Type	2d Coupe-2P	I6/258	$5,580	2,520	**Note 1**
E-Type	2d Coupe-2+2P	I6/258	$6,070	N/A	**Note 1**
3.8 Mk II					
3.8 Mk II	4d Sedan-5P	I6/231	$5,272	3,136	**Note 2**
3.8 Type S					
3.8 "S"	4d Sedan-5P	I6/231	$5,786	3,440	**Note 3**
4.2 Mk X					
4.2 Mk X	4d Sedan-6P	I6/258	$6,990	3,920	**Note 4**

Note 1: A total of approximately 22,922 E-Types were produced from 1965 through 1968 (9,550 roadsters, 7,772 fixed-head coupes, and 5,600 2+2 coupes).

Note 2: A total of 30,070 3.8 Mark II sedans were produced from 1960 through 1967.

Note 3: A total of 15,070 3.8S sedans were produced from 1964 through 1968.

Note 4: A total of 5,119 Mark X sedans with the 4.2-litre engine were produced in 1965 and 1966 (2,291 for exports), plus 18 limousines.

Richard Dance Collection

1966 Jaguar 3.8 litre saloon

ENGINES

BASE SIX 3.8 MK II, BASE SIX 3.8 S-Type: Inline, dual overhead-cam six-cylinder. Cast-iron block and aluminum head. Displacement: 230.6 cid (3781 cc). Bore & Stroke: 3.425 x 4.17 in. (87 x 106 mm). Compression Ratio: 8.0:1. Brake Horsepower: 225 at 5500 rpm. Torque: 245 lbs.-ft. at 3000 rpm. Seven main bearings. Solid valve lifters. Two S.U. side-draft carburetors. Lucas ignition.

BASE SIX E-Type, BASE SIX E-TYPE 2+2, BASE SIX 4.2 MK X: Inline, dual overhead-cam six-cylinder. Cast-iron block and aluminum head. Displacement: 258.4 cid (4235 cc). Bore & Stroke: 3.625 x 4.17 in. (92.1 x 106 mm). Compression Ratio: 9.0:1. Brake Horsepower: 265 at 5400 rpm. Torque: 283 lbs.-ft. at 4000 rpm. Seven main bearings. Solid valve lifters. Three S.U. side-draft carburetors. Lucas ignition.

CHASSIS

E-TYPE: Wheelbase: 96 in. Overall Length: 175.3 in. Height: 48.0 in. (roadster 52.5 in.) Width: 65.25 in. Front Tread: 50.0 in. Rear Tread: 50.0 in. Wheel Type: steel disc. Standard Tires: 6.40 x 15.

E-TYPE 2+2: Wheelbase: 105 in. Overall Length: 184.5 in. Height: 50.0 in. (roadster 52.5 in.) Width: 65.25 in. Front Tread: 50.0 in. Rear Tread: 50.0 in. Wheel Type: steel disc. Standard Tires: 6.40 x 15.

3.8 MK II: Wheelbase: 107.4 in. Overall Length: 180.75 in. Height: 57.5 in. Width: 66.75 in. Front Tread: 55.0 in. Rear Tread: 53.4 in. Wheel Type: steel disc. Standard Tires: 205R x 14.

3.8 S-Type: Wheelbase: 107.4 in. Overall Length: 187.75 in. Height: 54.5 in. Width: 66.75 in. Front Tread: 55.25 in. Rear Tread: 54.25 in. Wheel Type: steel disc. Standard Tires: 6.40 x 15.

MARK X: Wheelbase: 120 in. Overall Length: 202.0 in. Height: 54.5 in. Width: 76.0 in. Front Tread: 58.0 in. Rear Tread: 58.0 in. Wheel Type: steel disc. Standard Tires: 205R x 14.

TECHNICAL

E-TYPE: Layout: front-engine, rear-drive. Transmission: four-speed manual with overdrive. Standard Final Drive Ratio: 3.31:1. Steering: Rack-and-pinion. Suspension (front): wishbones and torsion bars with anti-roll bar. Suspension (rear): independent with lower wishbones, coil springs and anti-roll bar. Brakes: hydraulic, front/rear discs. Body Construction: steel unibody. Fuel tank: 17 gallons (U.S.)

E-TYPE 2+2: Layout: front-engine, rear-drive. Transmission: four-speed manual with overdrive. Standard Final Drive Ratio: 3.31:1. Steering: Rack-and-pinion. Suspension (front):

wishbones and torsion bars with anti-roll bar. Suspension (rear): independent with lower wishbones, coil springs and anti-roll bar. Brakes: hydraulic, front/rear discs. Body Construction: steel unibody. Fuel tank: 17 gallons (U.S.)

3.8 MK II: Layout: front-engine, rear-drive. Transmission: four-speed manual with overdrive. Standard Final Drive Ratio: 3.54:1. Steering: Re-circulating ball. Suspension (front): rigid axle with trailing radius arms, transverse linkage bar and semi-elliptic leaf springs Suspension (rear): independent with coil springs. Brakes: hydraulic, front/rear discs. Body Construction: steel unibody.

3.8 MK S-TYPE: Layout: front-engine, rear-drive. Transmission: four-speed manual with overdrive. Standard Final Drive Ratio: 3.77:1. Steering: Re-circulating ball. Suspension (front): independent; wishbones with coil springs. Suspension (rear): independent with coil springs. Brakes: hydraulic, front/rear discs. Body Construction: steel unibody.

MARK X: Layout: front-engine, rear-drive. Transmission: automatic. Standard Final Drive Ratio: 3.54:1. Steering: Re-circulating ball with standard power assist. Suspension (front): independent; wishbones with coil springs. Suspension (rear): independent, with transverse leaf spring. Brakes: hydraulic, front/rear discs. Body Construction: steel unibody.

OPTIONS

E-TYPE: Radio. A detachable hardtop for the roadster ($252).

E-TYPE 2+2: Automatic transmission: ($345).

3.8 Mk II: Automatic transmission and power steering: ($147). Power steering ($120).

MARK X: Air conditioning ($595).

PERFORMANCE

E-TYPE: Top Speed: 150 mph. Acceleration (0-60 mph): 6.5 seconds. Acceleration (quarter-mile): 15.0 seconds at 98 mph. Fuel Mileage: 16 to 22 mpg.

E-TYPE 2+2: Top Speed: 139 mph. Acceleration (0-60 mph): 7.4 seconds. Acceleration (quarter-mile): 15.4 seconds at 93 to 97 mph. Fuel Mileage: 19.5 mpg.

1966 Jaguar Mark X saloon *Phil Hall Collection*

1966 Jaguar E-type (XK-E) roadster *Dan Lyons*

3.8 MK II: Top Speed: 115 to 118 mph. Acceleration (0-60 mph): 8.5 to 9.2 seconds with manual transmission. Acceleration (0-60 mph): 10.8 seconds with automatic transmission. Acceleration (quarter-mile): 17.6 seconds with manual transmission. Acceleration (quarter-mile): 17.2 seconds with automatic transmission. Fuel Mileage: (manual transmission) 15 to 19 mpg. Fuel Mileage: (automatic transmission) 14 to 17 mpg.

3.8 S-Type: Top Speed: 116 to 117 mph. Acceleration (0-60 mph): 11.8 seconds with automatic transmission. Acceleration (quarter-mile): 18.3 seconds with automatic transmission. Fuel Mileage: (automatic transmission) 15.3 mpg.

MARK X: Top Speed: 120 mph. Acceleration (0-60 mph): 10.4 seconds. Acceleration (quarter-mile): 17.4 seconds. Fuel Mileage: 16 mpg.

CALENDAR YEAR SALES (U.S.): Approximately 23,000 Jaguars and Daimlers were produced during 1966. In calendar-year 1966, Jaguar sales to U.S. buyers, including tourist deliveries, totaled 4,635 cars. Jaguar had the 16th highest sales total among companies importing cars into the U.S.

MANUFACTURER: (Early) Jaguar Companies, Ltd., Coventry, England; (Late) British Motor Corporation (BMC), England.

DISTRIBUTOR: (Early) Jaguar Cars Inc., New York City. (Late) British Motor Corporation/Hambro, Inc., Ridgefield, N.J.

HISTORY: Introduced to U.S. market on September 1, 1965. *Car and Driver* called the E-Type 4.2 "a delightful, multi-purpose two-seater which is equally at home in city traffic, on country roads and at racing circuits," though "no faster than the 3.8." The Jaguar Group of Companies (including Jaguar Cars, Inc. of the United States) merged with British Motor Corporation on July 11, 1966. The U.S. distributor became British Motor Corp./Hambro, Inc., headquartered in Ridgefield, N.J., yet Jaguar's U.S. sales were still reported separately from other BMC makes.

1967

E-Type — SIX — No major change was evident on the E-Type convertible or coupe. The 4.2-litre twin-cam six-cylinder engine developed 265 hp. A four-speed manual gearbox was standard. A dual-range Borg-Warner automatic transmission was optional. Wire wheels were available. Instruments included a 160-mph speedometer and tachometer. Standard equipment included a hand choke, a jack, a tool kit, leather seats, imitation leather trim, carpets and a fresh air heater and demister with two-speed fan.

E-Type — SIX — The 2+2 rode a nine-inch longer wheelbase than the coupe and roadster and had hinged rear quarter windows, and the backs of its rear seats slid forward to enlarge the luggage platform.

340 — SIX — Jaguar's compact sedan was now called the 340 (for its 3.4-litre engine). It had a considerably smaller price tag than the 3.8 Mk II. The wheelbase was the same as the Mk II. Separate front seats were upholstered Ambla leather cloth vinyl. Standard equipment included all-wheel disc brakes, and a four-speed manual gearbox. A Borg-Warner automatic transmission was optional.

420 — SIX — This new version of the Jaguar sedan was on the 107.4-inch wheelbase. It mixed the body dimensions of the former 3.8 S-Type sedan with the powerplant of the E-Type sports car. That engine was reduced in horsepower with one less carburetor. The front-end appearance was similar to the new 420G. "Varamatic" power steering was standard and the four-wheel disc brake system had separate circuits for the front and rear. An independent rear suspension featured coil springs. The 420 used a four-speed manual transmission with overdrive. Options included an automatic transmission.

420G — SIX — The new 420G Grand Saloon had the same body dimensions and engine specifications as the Mark X. It included an improved aluminized exhaust system, restyled front seats, new body chrome and a padded dashboard. A dual-range Borg-Warner automatic transmission was standard equipment. Production lasted into 1970, although the 420G was not imported to the U.S. for a long time.

I.D. DATA: The serial number for the E-Type is stamped on the right frame cross member, above the shock absorber mounting. For the 340/420 series, it is on the hood latch channel ahead of the radiator. For the 420G, it is atop the right front wheel inner panel. The prefix indicates make and model (and possibly whether car is a U.S. model). The suffix may indicate whether car is equipped with overdrive or automatic transmission, and if left-hand drive (for export). The numerical sequence is the production serial number. The engine number is stamped on the right side of the block, above the oil filter; and at the front of the cylinder head (suffix /8 or /9 indicates compression ratio). Engine and chassis numbers also appear on a brass plate on the firewall. Starting serial number: (420) 1F.25001 or (420G) G1D.77001.

ENGINES

BASE SIX 340: Inline, dual overhead-cam six-cylinder. Cast-iron block and aluminum head. Displacement: 210 cid (3442 cc). Bore & Stroke: 3.27 x 4.17 in. (83 x 106 mm). Compression Ratio: 8.0:1. Brake Horsepower: 210 at 5500 rpm. Torque: 282 lbs.-ft. at 3750 rpm. Seven main bearings. Solid valve lifters. Two S.U. sidedraft carburetors.

BASE SIX 420: Inline, dual overhead-cam six-cylinder. Cast-iron block and aluminum head. Displacement: 258.4 cid (4235 cc). Bore & Stroke: 3.625 x 4.17 in. (92.1 x 106 mm). Compression Ratio: 8.0:1. Brake Horsepower: 246 at 5500 rpm. Torque: 283 lbs.-ft. at 4000 rpm. Seven main bearings. Solid valve lifters. Two S.U. sidedraft carburetors.

BASE SIX E-TYPE, BASE SIX E-TYPE 2+2, BASE SIX 420G: Inline, dual overhead-cam six-cylinder. Cast-iron block and aluminum head. Displacement: 258.4 cid (4235 cc). Bore & Stroke: 3.625 x 4.17 in. (92.1 x 106 mm). Compression Ratio: 9.0:1. Brake Horsepower: 265 at 5400 rpm. Torque: 283 lbs.-ft. at 4000 rpm. Seven main bearings. Solid valve lifters. Three S.U. sidedraft carburetors.

CHASSIS

E-TYPE: Wheelbase: 96 in. Overall Length: 175.3 in. Height: 48.0 in. (roadster 52.5 in.) Width: 65.25 in. Front Tread: 50.0 in. Rear Tread: 50.0 in. Wheel Type: steel disc. Standard Tires: 6.40 x 15.

E-TYPE 2+2: Wheelbase: 105 in. Overall Length: 184.5 in. Height: 50.0 in. (roadster 52.5 in.) Width: 65.25 in. Front Tread: 50.0 in. Rear Tread: 50.0 in. Wheel Type: steel disc. Standard Tires: 6.40 x 15.

340: Wheelbase: 107.4 in. Overall Length: 180.75 in. Height: 57.5 in. Width: 66.75 in. Front Tread: 55.0 in. Rear Tread: 53.4 in. Wheel Type: steel disc. Standard Tires: 6.40 x 15.

420: Wheelbase: 107.4 in. Overall Length: 187.75 in. Height: 54.5 in. Width: 66.75 in. Front Tread: 55.25 in. Rear Tread: 54.25 in. Wheel Type: steel disc. Standard Tires: 185R x 15.

420G: Wheelbase: 120 in. Overall Length: 202.0 in. Height: 54.5 in. Width: 76.3 in. Front Tread: 58.0 in. Rear Tread: 58.0 in. Wheel Type: steel disc. Standard Tires: 205R x 14.

TECHNICAL

E-TYPE: Layout: front-engine, rear-drive. Transmission: four-speed manual. Standard Final Drive Ratio: 3.07:1. Steering: Rack-and-pinion. Suspension (front): wishbones and torsion bars with anti-roll bar. Suspension (rear): independent with lower wishbones, coil springs and anti-roll bar. Brakes: hydraulic, front/rear discs. Body Construction: integral steel, with front tubular frame. Fuel tank: 17 gallons (U.S.)

E-TYPE 2+2: Layout: front-engine, rear-drive. Transmission: four-speed manual with overdrive. Standard Final Drive Ratio: 3.31:1. Steering: Rack-and-pinion. Suspension (front): wishbones and torsion bars with anti-roll bar. Suspension (rear): independent with lower wishbones, coil springs and anti-roll bar. Brakes: hydraulic, front/rear discs. Body Construction: integral steel, with front tubular frame. Fuel tank: 17 gallons (U.S.).

340: Layout: front-engine, rear-drive. Transmission: four-speed manual. Standard Final Drive Ratio: 3.54:1. Steering: Re-circulating ball. Suspension (front): wishbones and torsion bars with anti-roll bar. Suspension (rear): rigid axle, trailing radius arms, transverse linkage bar and semi-elliptic leaf springs. Brakes: hydraulic, front/rear discs. Body Construction: steel unibody.

420: Layout: front-engine, rear-drive. Transmission: four-speed manual. Standard Final Drive Ratio: 3.77:1. Steering: Re-circulating ball. Suspension (front): wishbones and torsion bars with anti-roll bar. Suspension (rear): independent with coil springs. Brakes: hydraulic, front/rear discs. Body Construction: steel unibody.

420G: Layout: front-engine, rear-drive. Transmission: automatic. Standard Final Drive Ratio: 3.54:1. Steering: Re-circulating ball with standard power assist. Suspension (front): wishbones and torsion bars with anti-roll bar. Suspension (rear): independent, with transverse leaf spring. Brakes: hydraulic, front/rear discs. Body Construction: steel unibody.

OPTIONS

E-TYPE: Radio. A detachable hardtop for the roadster ($252).

E-TYPE 2+2: Automatic transmission: ($397).

The "instrument fascia" of the 1967 Jaguar 420 saloon.

Model	Body Type & Seating	Engine Type/CID	P.O.E. Price	Weight (LBS.)	Production Total
E-Type					
E-Type	2d Roadster-2P	I6/258	$5,384	2,464	**Note 1**
E-Type	2d Coupe-2P	I6/258	$5,580	2,520	**Note 1**
E-Type	2d Coupe-2+2P	I6/258	$5,870	2,744	**Note 1**
340					
340	4d Sedan-4/5P	I6/210	$4,490	3,080	N/A
420					
420	4d Sedan-5P	I6/258	$5,786	3,440	**Note 2**
420G					
420G	4d Sedan-5/6P	I6/258	$6,990	3,920	**Note 3**

Note 1: A total of approximately 22,922 E-Types were produced from 1965 through 1968 (9,550 roadsters, 7,772 fixed-head coupes, and 5,600 2+2 coupes).

Note 2: A total of 9,600 420 sedans were produced in 1967 and 1968.

Note 3: A total of 5,739 420G sedans were produced from 1967 through 1970 (2,304 for export), plus 24 limousines (10 for export).

1967 Jaguar 420 G saloon.

Phil Hall Collection

340: Automatic transmission: ($233).

420: Automatic transmission and power steering: ($147). Power steering ($120).

PERFORMANCE

E-TYPE: Top Speed: 140 to 152 mph. Acceleration (0-60 mph): 7.2 to 8.0 seconds with manual transmission. Acceleration (quarter-mile): 15.0 seconds at 98 mph. Fuel Mileage: 14 to 20 mpg.

E-TYPE 2+2: Top Speed: 139 mph. Acceleration (0-60 mph): 7.2 to 8.0 seconds with manual transmission. Acceleration (quarter-mile): 15.4 seconds at 93 to 97 mph. Fuel Mileage: 19.5 mpg.

340: Top Speed: 110 mph. Acceleration (0-60 mph): 13.00 seconds with manual transmission. Acceleration (0-60 mph): 10.8 seconds with automatic transmission. Acceleration (quarter-mile): 17.6 seconds with manual transmission. Acceleration (quarter-mile): 17.2 seconds with automatic transmission. Fuel Mileage: (manual transmission) 15-19 mpg. Fuel Mileage: (automatic transmission) 17 to 25 mpg.

420: Top Speed: 122.5 mph. Acceleration (0-60 mph): 10.4 seconds with automatic transmission. Acceleration (quarter-mile): 17.4 seconds. Fuel Mileage: (automatic transmission) 15.0 mpg.

420G: Top Speed: 125 mph. Acceleration (0-60 mph): 10.4 seconds. Acceleration (quarter-mile): 17.4 seconds.

CALENDAR YEAR SALES (U.S.): One source indicates that 6,033 Jaguars were sold by U.S. dealers during model year 1967. In calendar-year 1967, Jaguar sales to U.S. buyers, including tourist deliveries, totaled 5,839 cars.

MANUFACTURER: Jaguar Cars Ltd., Coventry, England.

DISTRIBUTOR: British Motor Holdings, USA, Inc., Ridgefield, New Jersey. Graham W. Whitehead, president. The holding company known as British Motor Holdings became British Leyland Motors, Inc. of Leonia, New Jersey.

HISTORY: One of the Jaguar companies was Daimler, a British carmaker since 1897. Jaguar purchased it from bankruptcy in 1960. The Daimler Sovereign was nearly identical to the new Jaguar 420. Jaguar was the 15th largest importer of cars into the U.S. in 1968. A merger with British Leyland created the largest British car complex in history, called the "General Motors of England." Jaguar became united with Standard-Triumph, Rover, Austin, MG and Jaguar. The first two brands formed one division and Jaguar, MG and Austin formed the other.

1968

E-TYPE — SIX — The only Jaguars available in the U.S. for the 1968 model year were the E-Type sports cars. The 340/420 sedans were not marketed here. The E-Type's horsepower rating was lowered. Bumpers that could be certified to meet new U.S. safety requirements were new this year. The cockpit was restyled.

E-TYPE 2+2 — SIX — The 2+2 again rode a nine-inch longer wheelbase than the coupe and roadster. It had hinged rear quarter windows and the backs of its rear seats slid forward to enlarge the luggage platform. The 2+2's high roofline was not a favorite of sports car enthusiasts, but this car gave the family man who wanted a sporty ride a product that could fill both needs.

I.D. DATA: The serial number for the E-Type is stamped on the right frame cross member, above the shock absorber mounting. The prefix indicates the make and model (and possibly whether the car is a U.S. model). The suffix may indicate whether the car is equipped with overdrive or automatic transmission, and if it is left-hand drive (for export). The numerical sequence is the production serial number. The engine number is stamped on the right side of the block, above the oil filter; and at the front of the cylinder head (suffix /8 or /9 indicates compression ratio). The engine and chassis numbers also appear on a brass plate on the firewall.

ENGINE

BASE SIX: Inline, dual overhead-cam six-cylinder. Cast-iron block and aluminum head. Displacement: 258.4 cid (4235 cc). Bore & Stroke: 3.625 x 4.17 in. (92.1 x 106 mm). Compression Ratio: 9.0:1. Brake Horsepower: 246 at 5500 rpm. Torque: 263 lbs.-ft. at 3000 rpm. Seven main bearings. Solid valve lifters. Three S.U. sidedraft carburetors.

CHASSIS

E-TYPE: Wheelbase: 96 in. Overall Length: 175.3 in. Height: 48.0 in. (roadster 52.5 in.) Width: 65.25 in. Front Tread: 50.0 in. Rear Tread: 50.0 in. Wheel Type: steel disc. Standard Tires: 6.40 x 15 or 185R x 15.

E-TYPE 2+2: Wheelbase: 105 in. Overall Length: 184.5 in. Height: 50.0 in. (roadster 52.5 in.) Width: 65.25 in. Front Tread: 50.0 in. Rear Tread: 50.0 in. Wheel Type: steel disc. Standard Tires: 6.40 x 15 or 185R x 15.

TECHNICAL

E-TYPE: Layout: front-engine, rear-drive. Transmission: four-speed manual. Standard Final Drive Ratio: 3.07:1. Steering: Rack-and-pinion. Suspension (front): wishbones and torsion bars with anti-roll bar. Suspension (rear): independent

Model	Body Type & Seating	Engine Type/CID	P.O.E. Price	Weight (Lbs.)	Production Total
E-Type					
E-Type	2d Roadster-2P	I6/258	$5,372	2,464	**Note 1**
E-Type	2d Coupe-2P	I6/258	$5,559	2,520	**Note 1**
E-Type	2d Coupe-2+2P	I6/258	$5,739	2,744	**Note 1**

Note 1: A total of approximately 22,922 E-Types were produced from 1965-1968 (9,550 roadsters, 7,772 fixed-head coupes and 5,600 2+2 coupes).

The 1968 Jaguar XK-E 4.2-litre coupe and roadster in a park setting. *Richard Dance Collection*

with lower wishbones, trailing lower radius arms, coil springs and anti-roll bar. Brakes: hydraulic, front/rear discs. Body Construction: integral steel, with front tubular frame. Fuel tank: 17 gallons (U.S.)

E-TYPE 2+2: Layout: front-engine, rear-drive. Transmission: four-speed manual with overdrive. Standard Final Drive Ratio: 3.31:1. Steering: Rack-and-pinion. Suspension (front): wishbones and torsion bars with anti-roll bar. Suspension (rear): independent with lower wishbones, trailing lower radius arms, coil springs and anti-roll bar. Brakes: hydraulic, front/rear discs. Body Construction: integral steel, with front tubular frame. Fuel tank: 17 gallons (U.S.)

OPTIONS

E-TYPE: Radio. A detachable hardtop for the roadster ($252).

E-TYPE 2+2: Automatic transmission: ($238).

PERFORMANCE

E-TYPE: Top Speed: 140 to 152 mph. Acceleration (0-60 mph): 7.2 to 8.0 seconds with manual transmission. Acceleration (quarter-mile): 15.0 seconds at 98 mph. Fuel Mileage: 14 to 20 mpg.

E-TYPE 2+2: Top Speed: 139 mph. Acceleration (0-60 mph): 7.2 to 8.0 seconds with manual transmission. Acceleration (quarter-mile): 15.4 seconds at 93 to 97 mph. Fuel Mileage: 19.5 mpg.

CALENDAR YEAR SALES (U.S.): In calendar-year 1968, Jaguar sales to U.S. buyers, including tourist deliveries, totaled 5,179 cars.

ADDITIONAL MODELS: A total of 2,630 type 340 sedans were produced in 1968, as well as final 3.8S models.

MANUFACTURER: Jaguar Cars Ltd., Coventry, England.

DISTRIBUTORS (JAGUAR): British Leyland Motors, Inc., 600 Willow Tree Road, Leonia, New Jersey, Austin-MG Jaguar Division. Graham E. Whitehead was president of British Leyland Motors, Inc. Regional distributors of Austin, MG and Jaguar cars in the U.S. included B & K Distributors, Inc., Minneapolis, Minnesota; British Motor Car Distributors, Ltd., San Francisco, California; Continental Car Distributors, Ltd., St. Louis, Missouri; Falvey Motor Sales, Detroit, Michigan; Great Lakes Car Distributors, Inc., Elk Grove Village, Illinois; Charles H. Hornburg, Jr., Inc., Los Angeles, California (Jaguar only); Jaguar-Daimler, Inc., New York, New York (Jaguar only); Overseas Motor Corporation, Ft. Worth, Texas; Roosevelt Automobile Company, Englewood Cliffs, New Jersey (Jaguar only) and Royston Distributors, Inc., Philadelphia, Pennsylvania. (Note: Six other British-Leyland distributors handled Austin and MG only). The Rover-Triumph Division was separate. British Leyland had a grand total of 1,180 dealers nationwide in 1968. All dealers combined delivered a total of 60,286 British Leyland cars.

HISTORY: On New Year's Day in 1968, Sir William Lyons relinquished his title as managing director of the Jaguar Group. He remained chairman and chief executive. British

Motor Holdings and Leyland merged on January 19, 1968. British Leyland Motor Company, the U.S. distributor, began operations on May 14, 1968. Jaguar's new XJ sedan and the second-series E-Type debuted during 1968. The importation of Jaguar sedans was prevented in 1968, because of U.S. emissions regulations. A different (XJ) series of sedans would appear for the 1969 model year.

Phil Hall Collection

1968 Jaguar 3.8-litre S saloon

Andrew Morland

1968 Daimler V-8 250 saloon

1968 Jaguar E-type (XK-E) 2 + 2 coupe *Dan Lyons*

1969

E-TYPE SERIES II — SIX — A second series of Jaguar's sports cars arrived in 1969. The Series II E-Type had safety features that had formerly appeared only on U.S. models. The new model had larger parking lights and signal lights. The headlights sat farther forward than before. The front air intake also was larger and sat behind a full-width bumper. The taillights grew larger and were moved below the back bumper. New side clearance lights were seen. The 2+2's windshield adopted a steeper rake angle, accomplished by moving its base forward. The 258-cid twin-cam six-cylinder engine imported to the U.S. was rated 246 hp with revised carburetion and emissions control equipment. Girling four-wheel disc brakes replaced the former Dunlop units.

E-TYPE 2+2 — SIX — The 2+2 again rode a nine-inch longer wheelbase. It had hinged rear quarter windows and the rear seat backs slid forward for added luggage space. The 2+2 provided family men with a sporty-car option.

XJ — SIX — The XJ sedan was the last design by company co-founder William Lyons. It shared few parts with earlier models. A new four-door sedan debuted this year. The XJ6 had a 108.9-inch wheelbase and a new front-end look. The rather large grille was rectangular in shape and made up of horizontal strips. Quad round headlights were installed. The parking and signal lights were mounted immediately below each headlight. The XJ used the same engine as the E-Type sports car. Standard

equipment included power steering and four-wheel disc brakes. Options included air conditioning, power windows, automatic transmission and a heated back window. A 2.8-litre version also was produced, but U.S. showrooms normally got only the 4.2-litre engine.

I.D. DATA: The serial number for the E-Type is stamped on right frame cross member, above the shock absorber mounting. For the XJ, it's on the inner fender panel within the engine compartment. The prefix indicates the make and model (and possibly whether car is a U.S. model). The suffix may indicate whether the car is equipped with overdrive or automatic transmission, and if left-hand drive (for export) is used. The numerical sequence is the production serial number. The engine number is stamped on the right side of the block, above the oil filter; and at the front of the cylinder head (suffix /8 or /9 indicates compression ratio). The engine and chassis numbers also appear on a brass plate on the firewall. Starting serial number: (E-Type roadster) 1R7001; (E-Type coupe) 1R25001; (E-Type 2+2) 1R40001; (XJ) 1L50001. Starting engine number: (XJ) 7L1001.

ENGINES

BASE SIX E-TYPE, BASE SIX E-TYPE 2+2: Inline, dual overhead-cam six-cylinder. Cast-iron block and aluminum head. Displacement: 258.4 cid (4235 cc). Bore & Stroke: 3.625

MODEL	BODY TYPE & SEATING	ENGINE TYPE/ CID	P.O.E. PRICE	WEIGHT (LBS.)	PRODUCTION TOTAL
E-Type Series II					
E-Type	2d Roadster-2P	I6/258	$5,534	2,912	**Note 1**
E-Type	2d Coupe-2P	I6/258	$5,725	2,912	**Note 1**
E-Type	2d Coupe-2+2P	I6/258	$5,907	3,024	**Note 1**
XJ					
XJ	4d Sedan-5P	I6/258	$6,270	3,556	8,085

Note 1: Approximately 18,820 Series II E-Types were produced from 1968 through 1970 (8,630 roadsters, 4,860 fixed-head coupes, and 5,330 2+2 coupes).

Phil Hall Collection

The new 1969 Jaguar Series I 4.2-litre XJ6 saloon. *Jaguar Heritage—North America*

x 4.17 in. (92.1 x 106 mm). Compression Ratio: 9.0:1. Brake Horsepower: 245 at 5500 rpm. Seven main bearings. Solid valve lifters. Two carburetors.

BASE SIX XJ: Inline, dual overhead-cam six-cylinder. Cast-iron block and aluminum head. Displacement: 258.4 cid (4235 cc). Bore & Stroke: 3.625 x 4.17 in. (92.1 x 106 mm). Compression Ratio: 8.0:1. Brake Horsepower: 240 at 5500 rpm. Seven main bearings. Solid valve lifters. Two carburetors.

CHASSIS

E-TYPE: Wheelbase: 96 in. Overall Length: 175.3 in. Height: 48.0 in. (roadster 52.5 in.) Width: 65.25 in. Front Tread: 50.0 in. Rear Tread: 50.0 in. Wheel Type: steel disc. Standard Tires: 185R x 15.

E-TYPE 2+2: Wheelbase: 105 in. Overall Length: 184.4 in. Height: 50.1 in. Width: 65.25 in. Front Tread: 50.0 in. Rear Tread: 50.0 in. Wheel Type: steel disc. Standard Tires: 185R x 15.

XJ6: Wheelbase: 108.9 in. Overall Length: 189.6 in. Height: 52.8 in. Width: 69.6 in. Front Tread: 58.0 in. Rear Tread: 58.6 in. Wheel Type: steel disc. Standard Tires: 195R x 15.

TECHNICAL

E-TYPE: Layout: front-engine, rear-drive. Transmission: four-speed manual. Standard Final Drive Ratio: 3.07:1. Steering: Rack-and-pinion. Suspension (front): wishbones and torsion bars with anti-roll bar. Suspension (rear): independent with lower wishbones, trailing lower radius arms, coil springs and anti-roll bar. Brakes: hydraulic, front/rear discs. Body Construction: integral steel, with front tubular frame. Fuel tank: 17 gallons (U.S.)

E-TYPE 2+2: Layout: front-engine, rear-drive. Transmission: four-speed manual with overdrive. Standard Final Drive Ratio: 3.31:1. Steering: Rack-and-pinion. Suspension (front): wishbones and torsion bars with anti-roll bar. Suspension (rear): independent with lower wishbones, trailing lower radius arms, coil springs and anti-roll bar. Brakes: hydraulic, front/rear discs. Body Construction: integral steel, with front tubular frame. Fuel tank: 17 gallons (U.S.)

XJ6: Layout: front-engine, rear-drive. Transmission: automatic (in U.S.). Standard Final Drive Ratio: 3.54:1. Steering: rack-and-pinion. Suspension (front): wishbones and coil springs. Suspension (rear): independent with lower wishbones, trailing lower radius arms, coil springs and anti-roll bar. Brakes: front/rear disc. Body Construction: integral steel, with sub frame.

OPTIONS

E-TYPE: Air conditioning. Automatic transmission ($195).

E-TYPE: Air conditioning ($482). Wire wheels ($132). Power steering ($160). Automatic transmission, 2+2 coupe ($238).

PERFORMANCE

E-TYPE: Top Speed: 138 mph (about 120 mph in U.S. form). Acceleration (0-60 mph): 7.2 to 8.0 seconds. Acceleration (quarter-mile): 15.5 to 15.7 seconds at 88 to 89 mph.

E-TYPE 2+2: Top Speed: 136 mph. Acceleration (0-60 mph): 8.0 to 8.1 seconds with manual transmission. Acceleration (quarter-mile): 15.8. Fuel Mileage: 19.5 mpg.

XJ: Top Speed; 124 mph. Acceleration (0-60 mph): 9.0 seconds. Acceleration (quarter-mile): 17 seconds at 85 mph.

CALENDAR YEAR SALES (U.S.): In calendar-year 1969, Jaguar sales to U.S. buyers, including tourist deliveries, totaled 5,700 cars.

MANUFACTURER: Jaguar Cars Ltd., Coventry, England. Regional distributors of Austin, MG and Jaguar cars in the U.S. were located throughout the country (see 1968). Six British-Leyland distributors handled Austin and MG only. The Rover-Triumph Division was also separate.

DISTRIBUTOR: British Leyland Motors, Inc., Leonia, New Jersey.

1969 Jaguar E-type (XK-E) 2 + 2 coupe *Andrew Morland*

1969 Jaguar E-type (XK-E) 2 + 2 coupe *Andrew Morland*

1970 Jaguar XK-E Series II roadster *Tom Glatch*

1970

E-TYPE SERIES II — 4.2 SIX — Production of the sports-car models continued with little change. As before, a roadster (convertible), two-seat coupe, and 2+2 coupe were available. Closed models featured a large window in the luggage (hatch) door, and hinged rear quarter windows. Inside were leatherette door panels, leather-upholstered bucket seats that adjusted for reach and rake, padded visors, a grab handle, glove compartment, and map light. The 2+2's fully upholstered back seat held two children. Wide-spoke 15-inch wheels had center-lock quick-change hubs and wore Dunlop high-performance tires. Girling four-wheel disc brakes had power assist. Front and rear wraparound bumpers contained overriders (guards). The convertible had a large back window in its folding top.

E-TYPE 2+2 — SIX — The 2+2 again rode a nine-inch longer wheelbase. It had hinged rear quarter windows and the rear seat backs slid forward for added luggage space. The 2+2 provided families with a sporty-car option.

XJ — SIX — The Jaguar sedan continued with little change after its 1969 debut. Power steering and a Borg-Warner automatic transmission were standard on U.S. market cars.

I.D. DATA: The serial number for the E-Type is stamped on the right frame cross member, above the shock absorber mounting. For the XJ, it's on the inner fender panel within the engine compartment. The prefix indicates make and model (and possibly whether the car is a U.S. model). The suffix may indicate whether the car is equipped with overdrive or automatic transmission, and if it's left-hand drive (for export). The numerical sequence is the production serial number. The engine number is stamped on the right side of the block, above the oil filter; and at the front of the cylinder head (suffix /8 or /9 indicates compression ratio). The engine and chassis numbers also appear on a brass plate on the firewall. Starting serial number: (E-Type roadster) 1R11052; (E-Type coupe) 1R27051; (E-Type 2+2) 1R42850; (XJ) 1L53203.

ENGINE

BASE SIX E-TYPE, BASE SIX E-TYPE 2+2: Inline, dual overhead-cam six-cylinder. Cast-iron block and aluminum head. Displacement: 258.4 cid (4235 cc). Bore & Stroke: 3.625 x 4.17 in. (92.1 x 106 mm). Compression Ratio: 9.0:1. Brake Horsepower: 246 at 5500 rpm. Torque: 263 lbs.-ft. at 3000 rpm. Seven main bearings. Solid valve lifters. Two Zenith carburetors.

BASE SIX XJ6: Inline, dual overhead-cam six-cylinder. Cast-iron block and aluminum head. Displacement: 258.4 cid (4235 cc). Bore & Stroke: 3.625 x 4.17 in. (92.1 x 106 mm). Compression Ratio: 9.0:1. Brake Horsepower: 240 at 5500 rpm. Torque: 263 lbs.-ft. at 3000 rpm. Seven main bearings. Solid valve lifters. Two Zenith carburetors.

CHASSIS

E-TYPE: Wheelbase: 96 in. Overall Length: 175.3 in. Height: 48.0 in. (roadster 52.5 in.) Width: 65.25 in. Front Tread: 50.0 in. Rear Tread: 50.0 in. Wheel Type: steel disc. Standard Tires: 185R x 15.

E-TYPE 2+2: Wheelbase: 105 in. Overall Length: 184.4 in. Height: 50.1 in. Width: 65.25 in. Front Tread: 50.0 in. Rear Tread: 50.0 in. Wheel Type: steel disc. Standard Tires: 185R x 15.

XJ6: Wheelbase: 108.9 in. Overall Length: 189.6 in. Height:

MODEL	BODY TYPE & SEATING	ENGINE TYPE/CID	P.O.E. PRICE	WEIGHT (LBS.)	PRODUCTION TOTAL
E-Type Series II					
E-Type	2d Roadster-2P	I6/258	$5,534	2,912	**Note 1**
E-Type	2d Coupe-2P	I6/258	$5,725	2,912	**Note 1**
E-Type	2d Coupe-2+2P	I6/258	$5,907	3,136	**Note 1**
XJ6					
XJ6	4d Sedan-5P	I6/258	$6,585	3,556	17,525

Note 1: Approximately 18,820 Series II E-Types were produced from 1968 through 1970 (8,630 roadsters, 4,860 fixed-head coupes, and 5,330 2+2 coupes).

Note 2: Figure shown does not include 2,695 equivalent Daimlers built in 1970.

Note 3: 2+2 coupe with automatic transmission was priced at $6,145.

52.9 in. Width: 69.6 in. Front Tread: 58.0 in. Rear Tread: 58.6 in. Wheel Type: steel disc. Standard Tires: 195R x 15.

TECHNICAL

E-TYPE: Layout: front-engine, rear-drive. Transmission: four-speed manual. Steering: Rack-and-pinion. Suspension (front): wishbones and torsion bars with anti-roll bar. Suspension (rear): independent with lower wishbones, trailing lower radius arms, coil springs and anti-roll bar. Brakes: hydraulic, front/rear discs. Body Construction: integral steel, with front tubular frame. Fuel tank: 17 gallons (U.S.)

E-TYPE 2+2: Layout: front-engine, rear-drive. Transmission: four-speed manual with overdrive. Steering: Rack-and-pinion. Suspension (front): wishbones and torsion bars with anti-roll bar. Suspension (rear): independent with lower wishbones, trailing lower radius arms, coil springs and anti-roll bar. Brakes: hydraulic, front/rear discs. Body Construction: integral steel, with front tubular frame. Fuel tank: 17 gallons (U.S.)

XJ6: Layout: front-engine, rear-drive. Transmission: automatic (in U.S.). Steering: rack-and-pinion. Suspension (front): wishbones and coil springs. Suspension (rear): independent with lower wishbones, trailing lower radius arms, coil springs and anti-roll bar. Brakes: front/rear disc. Body Construction: integral steel, with sub frame.

OPTIONS: Air conditioning: E-Type ($482); XJ ($530). Power steering: E-Type ($160). Wire wheels: E-Type ($165). Disc wheels: E-Type 2+2, XJ ($77). Hardtop: E-Type roadster ($180). Power windows: XJ ($146). Heated rear window: XJ ($48). Whitewall tires: E-Type ($27); XJ ($36).

OPTIONS

E-TYPE: Air conditioning ($482). Power steering ($160). Automatic transmission ($195). Wire wheels: E-Type ($165). Whitewall tires ($27). Detachable hardtop for roadster ($180).

E-TYPE: Air conditioning ($482). Wire wheels ($132). Power steering ($160). Automatic transmission, 2+2 coupe ($238). Wire wheels: E-Type ($165). Disc wheels ($77). Whitewall tires ($27).

XJ6: Air conditioning ($530). Disc wheels ($77). Power windows ($146). Heated rear window ($48). Whitewall tires: XJ ($36).

PERFORMANCE

E-TYPE: Top Speed: about 130 mph. Acceleration (0-60 mph): 7.5 seconds. Fuel mileage: 14 to 16 mpg.

The 1970 Jaguar ad "Domesticated but Not Declawed"

E-TYPE 2+2: Top Speed: 136 mph. Acceleration (0-60 mph): 8.7 seconds. Fuel Mileage: 15 mpg.

XJ: Top Speed: 120 mph. Acceleration (0-60 mph): 8.7 seconds. Fuel mileage: 14 to 18 mpg.

CALENDAR YEAR SALES (U.S.): In calendar-year 1970, Jaguar sales to U.S. buyers, including tourist deliveries, totaled 6,732 cars.

MANUFACTURER: Jaguar Cars Ltd., Coventry, England.

DISTRIBUTOR: British Leyland Motors, Leonia, New Jersey.

HISTORY: The 1970 models were introduced to the U.S. market on December 1, 1969. Graham W. Whitehead was again president of British Leyland, Inc., in the U.S. All British-Leyland brands gained ground in 1970 with a total of 1,117 dealers selling 69,430 cars. Jaguar introduced the new XJ6 and in the spring brought out a new V-12 model. Jaguar sold 6,732 cars in the U.S. and 70 percent had air conditioning, 29 percent had automatic transmission and 88 percent were two-door models.

1971 Jaguar XK-E (E-type) Series III roadster *Richard Dance Collection*

1971

E-TYPE SERIES II — 4.2 SIX — The 1971 model year began with little change in the Jaguar sports cars. Power for the roadster and coupe again came from the familiar 4.2-litre twin-cam six, producing 246 hp with twin Zenith carburetors.

E-TYPE 2+2 SERIES II — 4.2 SIX — The 2+2 was longer, higher and more accommodating than the coupe and roadster because it had seating for four.

E-TYPE — SERIES III — V-12 — Beneath the hood of the Series III E-Type lay Jaguar's first all-new engine since the debut of the XK-120 sports car in the early postwar years. The all-new aluminum V-12 was available in a coupe or a convertible. An enlarged hood bulge suggested the power within. The wheel openings grew taller and were highlighted by marked flares that housed wider tires. The formerly plain oval grille now contained a crosshatch insert. The roadster was dropped, and the remaining bodies now rode the same 105-inch wheelbase. Trunk lids displayed "E-Type" lettering. The combustion chambers in the new engine were formed into the piston tops, which worked with flat cylinder heads. The increased weight and U.S. emissions changes diminished the power boost. The brake rotors were now vented. E-Types destined for the U.S. wore large black bumper guards.

XJ — SIX — Jaguar's sedan entered its third season with little change. As before, power steering and an automatic transmission were standard on U.S. models. Under the hood once again was the same six-cylinder engine used in the E-Type series, but with compression dropped to 8.0:1.

I.D. DATA: The serial number for the E-Type is stamped on right frame cross member, above the shock absorber mounting; for XJ, on inner fender panel within engine compartment. The prefix indicates make and model (and possibly whether car is a U.S. model). Suffix may indicate whether car is equipped with overdrive or automatic transmission, and if left-hand drive (for export). The numerical sequence is the production serial number. The engine number is stamped on the right side of the block, above the oil filter; and at the front of the cylinder head (suffix /8 or /9 indicates compression ratio). Engine and chassis numbers also appear on a brass plate on the firewall. Starting serial number: (E-Type roadster) 2R13716; (E-Type coupe) 2R28084; (E-Type V-12 convertible) 1S20001; (E-Type V-12 coupe) 1S700001; (XJ) 1L55686. Starting engine number: (E-Type V-12) 7S1001.

ENGINES

BASE SIX E-TYPE SERIES II 4.2: Inline, dual overhead-cam six-cylinder. Cast-iron block and aluminum head. Displacement: 258.4 cid (4235 cc). Bore & Stroke: 3.625 x 4.17 in. (92.1 x 106 mm). Compression Ratio: 9.0:1. Brake Horsepower: 246 at 5500 rpm. Torque: 263 lbs.-ft. at 3000 rpm. Seven main bearings. Solid valve lifters. Two Zenith carburetors.

BASE SIX XJ6: Inline, dual overhead-cam six-cylinder. Cast-iron block and aluminum head. Displacement: 258.4 cid (4235 cc). Bore & Stroke: 3.625 x 4.17 in. (92.1 x 106 mm). Compression Ratio: 8.0:1. Brake Horsepower: 240 at 5500 rpm. Torque: 263 lbs.-ft. at 3000 rpm. Seven main bearings. Solid valve lifters. Two Zenith carburetors.

BASE E-TYPE SERIES III V-12: 60-degree, overhead-cam "vee" type 12-cylinder. Aluminum block and heads. Displacement: 326 cid (5343 cc). Bore & Stroke: 3.54 x 2.77 in. (90 x 70 mm). Compression Ratio: 9.0:1. Brake Horsepower: 314 (gross) at 6200 rpm (272 DIN at 5850, or 250 SAE net at 6000 rpm). Torque: 349 lbs.-ft. (gross) at 3800 rpm (304 DIN at 3600, or 283 SAE at 3500 rpm). Seven main bearings. Solid valve lifters. Four Zenith carburetors.

CHASSIS

E-TYPE SERIES II: Wheelbase: 96 in. Overall Length: 175.4 in. Height: 48.1 in. (roadster 52.5 in.) Width: 65.25 in. Front Tread: 50.0 in. Rear Tread: 50.0 in. Wheel Type: steel disc. Standard Tires: E70VR-15.

E-TYPE 2+2 SERIES II: Wheelbase: 105 in. Overall Length: 184.4 in. Height: 50.1 in. Width: 65.25 in. Front Tread: 50.0 in. Rear Tread: 50.0 in. Wheel Type: steel disc. Standard Tires: E70VR-15.

E-TYPE SERIES III: Wheelbase: 105 in. Overall Length: 184.4 in. Height: 51.3 in. Width: 66.1 in. Front Tread: 54.3 in. Rear Tread: 53.0 in. Wheel Type: steel disc. Standard Tires: 6.00 x 15.

XJ6: Wheelbase: 108.9 in. Overall Length: 189.6 in. Height: 52.9 in. Width: 69.8 in. Front Tread: 58.0 in. Rear Tread: 58.3 in. Wheel Type: steel disc. Standard Tires: E70VR-15.

TECHNICAL

E-TYPE: Layout: front-engine, rear-drive. Transmission: four-speed manual. Steering: Rack-and-pinion. Suspension (front): wishbones and torsion bars with anti-roll bar. Suspension (rear): independent with lower wishbones, trailing lower radius arms, coil springs and anti-roll bar. Brakes: hydraulic, front/rear discs. Body Construction: integral steel, with front tubular frame. Fuel tank: 17 gallons (U.S.)

E-TYPE 2+2: Layout: front-engine, rear-drive. Transmission: four-speed manual with overdrive. Steering: Rack-and-pinion. Suspension (front): wishbones and torsion bars with anti-roll bar. Suspension (rear): independent with lower wishbones, trailing lower radius arms, coil springs and anti-roll bar. Brakes: hydraulic, front/rear discs. Body Construction: integral steel, with front tubular frame. Fuel tank: 17 gallons (U.S.).

XJ6: Layout: front-engine, rear-drive. Transmission: automatic (in U.S.). Steering: rack-and-pinion. Suspension (front): wishbones and coil springs. Suspension (rear): independent with lower wishbones, trailing lower radius arms, coil springs and anti-roll bar. Brakes: front/rear disc. Body Construction: integral steel, with sub frame.

OPTIONS

E-TYPE: Air conditioning ($482). Power steering ($160). Automatic transmission ($195). Wire wheels: E-Type ($165). Whitewall tires ($27). Detachable hardtop for roadster ($200). Heated rear window in coupe ($44).

1971 XK-E (E-type) Series III V-12 roadster *Jaguar Heritage—North America*

Model	Body Type & Seating	Engine Type/CID	P.O.E. Price	Weight (lbs.)	Production Total
E-Type					
Series II (Six)					
E-Type	2d Roadster-2P	I6/258	$5,734	2,966	**Note 1**
E-Type	2d Coupe-2P	I6/258	$5,925	2,966	**Note 1**
E-Type 2+2					
Series II (Six)					
E-Type	2d Coupe-2+2P	I6/258	N/A	3,136	**Note 1**
E-Type					
Series III (V-12)					
E-Type	2d Convertible-2P	V-12/326	$6,950	3,435	**Note 2**
E-Type	2d Coupe-2+2P	V-12/326	$7,325	3,435	**Note 2**
XJ6					
XJ6	4d Sedan-5P	I6/258	$7,260	3,703	**23,546** **Note 3**

Note 1: Approximately 18,820 Series II E-Types were produced from 1968-1970 (8,630 roadsters, 4,860 fixed-head coupes, and 5,330 2+2 coupes).

Note 2: A total of 15,290 Series III E-Types were produced from 1971 through 1975 (7,990 convertibles and 7,300 2+2 coupes).

Note 3: Figure shown does not include 5,158 equivalent Daimlers built in 1971.

Note 4: Series III E-Type came with the same open body as the Series II, but was by this time more commonly referred to as a convertible rather than a roadster.

1971 Jaguar XJ6 sedan *Richard Dance Collection*

XJ6: Air conditioning ($530). Disc wheels ($77). Power windows ($146). Heated rear window ($48). Whitewall tires: XJ ($36).

PERFORMANCE

E-TYPE SERIES II: Top Speed: about 130 mph. Acceleration (0-60 mph): 7.5 seconds. Fuel mileage: 16 mpg.

E-TYPE 2 + 2 SERIES II: Top Speed: about 125 mph. Acceleration (0-60 mph): 8.7 seconds. Fuel mileage: 14 mpg.

E-TYPE SERIES III: Top Speed: 136 mph. Acceleration (0-60 mph): 7.5 seconds.

XJ: Top Speed: 120 mph. Acceleration (0-60 mph): 8.7 seconds. Fuel mileage: 14 to 18 mpg.

CALENDAR YEAR SALES (U.S.): In calendar-year 1971, Jaguar sales to U.S. buyers, including tourist deliveries, totaled 5,614 cars.

MANUFACTURER: Jaguar Cars Ltd., Coventry, England.

DISTRIBUTOR: British Leyland Motors, Leonia, New Jersey.

HISTORY: The 1971 models were introduced to the U.S. market on October 1, 1970 (E-Type V-12 in March 1971). The new V-12 engine had been meant for racing, then for a new sedan. Instead, it went into the Jaguar sports car when only Ferrari and Lamborghini offered a production V-12 powerplant. British Leyland, Inc. had 1,053 dealers in the U.S. and 301 of them handled the Jaguar line. Jaguar sold 5,614 cars in the U.S. In August 1971, the U.S. government dropped an imported goods surcharge that had hampered imported car sales.

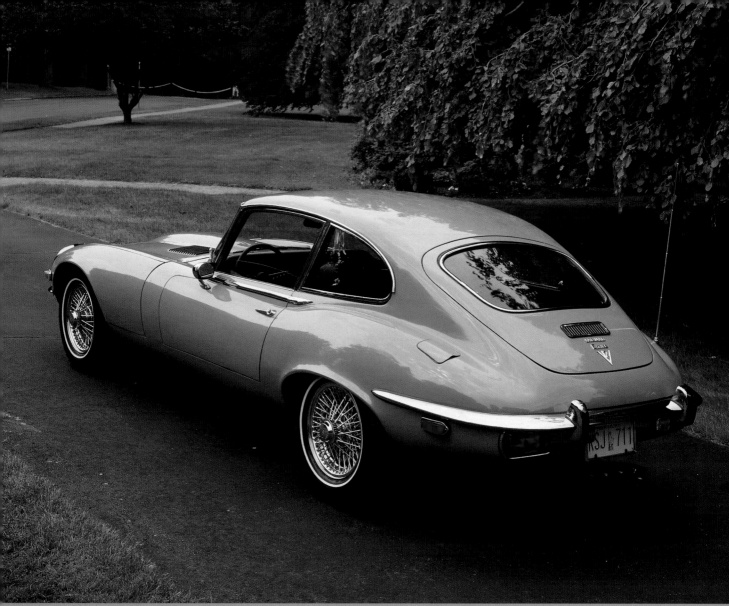

1972

E-TYPE SERIES III — V-12 — Six-cylinder E-Types faded out of the U.S. market as the V-12 engine, introduced in March 1971, gained a foothold. Little change was evident this year.

XJ6 — SIX — Changes were minimal on the Jaguar six-cylinder sedan. A GM air-conditioner compressor replaced the former York unit. An automatic transmission was standard. Published engine ratings for XJ6 sedans sold in the U.S. dropped sharply during this period, as a result of reduced compression ratios and detuning required to meet emissions standards. There was also a switch to SAE net horsepower and torque, which made all power ratings look much lower.

I.D. DATA: Serial number for E-Type is stamped on right frame cross member, above the shock absorber mounting; for XJ, on inner fender panel within engine compartment. Prefix indicates make and model (and possibly whether car is a U.S. model). Suffix may indicate whether car is equipped with overdrive or automatic transmission, and if left-hand drive (for export). Numerical sequence is the production serial number. Engine number is stamped on the right side of the block, above the oil filter; and at the front of the cylinder head (suffix /8 or /9 indicates compression ratio). Engine and chassis numbers also appear on a brass plate on the firewall. Serial number range: (E-Type convertible) 1S20103 to 1S20168; (E-Type coupe) 1S72335 to 1S72660; (XJ6) 1L64124 to 1L64774.

ENGINES

BASE SIX XJ6: Inline, dual overhead-cam six-cylinder. Cast-iron block and aluminum head. Displacement: 258.4 cid (4235 cc). Bore & Stroke: 3.625 x 4.17 in. (92.1 x 106 mm). Compression Ratio: 8.0:1. Brake Horsepower: 186 (gross), 157 (net) at 4500 rpm in U.S. form. Torque: 240 (gross) lbs.-ft. at 3750 rpm. Seven main bearings. Solid valve lifters. Two Zenith-Stromberg 175CD2SE carburetors.

Model	Body Type & Seating	Engine Type/ CID	P.O.E. Price	Weight (lbs.)	Production Total
E-Type Series III					
E-Type	2d Convertible-2P	V-12/326	$7,338	3,435	**Note 1**
E-Type	2d Coupe-2+2P	V-12/326	$7,732	3,435	**Note 1**
XJ6					
XJ6	4d Sedan-5P	I6/258	$7,683	3,528	14,885

Note 1: A total of 15,290 Series III E-Types were produced from 1971 through 1975 (7,990 convertibles and 7,300 2+2 coupes).

Note 2: Figure shown does not include 3,206 equivalent Daimlers built in 1972 (or 3,703 early V-12 sedans).

BASE V-12 E-TYPE SERIES III: 60-degree, overhead-cam "vee" type 12-cylinder. Aluminum block and heads. Displacement: 326 cid (5343 cc). Bore & Stroke: 3.54 x 2.77 in. (90 x 70 mm). Compression Ratio: 9.0:1. Brake Horsepower: 250 (SAE net) at 6000 rpm. Torque: 283 lbs.-ft. at 3500 rpm. Seven main bearings. Solid valve lifters. Four Zenith-Stromberg 175CD2SE carburetors.

CHASSIS

E-TYPE SERIES III: Wheelbase: 105 in. Overall Length: 184.4 in. Height: 51.3 in. Width: 66.1 in. Front Tread: 54.3 in. Rear Tread: 53.0 in. Wheel Type: steel disc. Standard Tires: 6.00 x 15.

XJ6: Wheelbase: 108.9 in. Overall Length: 189.6 in. Height: 52.9 in. Width: 69.75 in. Front Tread: 58.0 in. Rear Tread: 58.6 in. Wheel Type: steel disc. Standard Tires: 195R-15.

TECHNICAL

E-TYPE: Layout: front-engine, rear-drive. Transmission: four-speed manual. Standard final drive ratio: 3.54:1. Steering: Rack-and-pinion. Suspension (front): wishbones and torsion bars with anti-roll bar. Suspension (rear): independent with lower wishbones, trailing lower radius arms, coil springs and anti-roll bar. Brakes: hydraulic, front/rear discs. Body Construction: integral steel, with front tubular frame. Fuel tank: 17 gallons (U.S.)

XJ6: Layout: front-engine, rear-drive. Transmission: automatic. Standard final drive ratio: 3.54:1. Steering: rack-and-pinion. Suspension (front): wishbones, lower trailing links, coil springs and anti-roll bar. Suspension (rear): independent with lower wishbones, trailing lower radius arms, coil springs and anti-roll bar. Brakes: front/rear disc. Body Construction: integral steel, with sub frame.

OPTIONS

E-TYPE SERIES III: Air conditioning ($482). Power steering ($160). Automatic transmission ($261). Wire wheels: ($165). Chrome disc wheels ($77). Whitewall tires ($27). Detachable hardtop for roadster ($200). Heated rear window in coupe ($44).

XJ6: Heated rear window ($48).

PERFORMANCE

E-TYPE SERIES III: Top Speed: 135 mph. Acceleration (0-60 mph): 7.4 seconds. Acceleration (quarter mile): 15.4 seconds.

XJ: Top Speed: 122 mph. Acceleration (0-60 mph): 10.7

To a world filled with compromise, we make no contribution.

Which may suggest why the Jaguar XJ6 was selected as one of the world's ten best cars by Road & Track.

All cars begin as an idea. The Jaguar XJ6 began as an almost impossible idea. It was to design a sedan that would set new standards of comfort and luxury, road-holding and ride, steering and braking, performance and safety, while maintaining the standard of value traditionally associated with Jaguar.

In building the Jaguar XJ6, we held fast to that idea without compromise.

A few particulars. The XJ6 is powered by a 4.2 litre twin-overhead camshaft engine that was described by a prominent automotive publication as "almost faultless".

Motor Trend described its handling in one word: "superb".

That characteristic derives from the engineering that went into the Jaguar XJ6. A fully-independent 4-wheel suspension system designed to negotiate the ruts and bumps of English country roads.

And power-assisted rack-and-pinion steering. Caliper-type disc brakes front and rear, also power-assisted.

In naming the Jaguar XJ6 as one of the world's ten best cars of 1971, *Road & Track* wrote, "When we first drove the XJ6

we said it was 'uncannily swift, gloriously silent and safe as houses.' We still like that description. It was also one of the best-handling sedans in the world as well..."

Jaguar XJ6: an idea that became reality without compromise.

For the name of your nearest Jaguar dealer and for information about overseas delivery, dial (800) 631-1972 except in New Jersey where the number is (800) 962-2803. Calls are toll-free.

BRITISH LEYLAND MOTORS INC., LEONIA, NEW JERSEY 07605

Jaguar Heritage—North America

1972 Jaguar XJ6 ad

seconds. Acceleration (quarter mile): 17.1 seconds. Fuel mileage: 15 mpg.

CALENDAR YEAR SALES (U.S.): In calendar-year 1972, Jaguar sales to U.S. buyers, including tourist deliveries, totaled 5,122 cars.

MANUFACTURER: (Early) Jaguar Cars Ltd. Coventry, England; (Late) British Leyland UK Ltd.

DISTRIBUTOR: British Leyland Motors, Leonia, New Jersey.

HISTORY: The 1972 models were introduced to the U.S. market on December 13, 1971. By this time, British Leyland was down to 899 dealers in the U.S. Only a fraction of those dealers (probably 300 or slightly less) sold Jaguars. Fifty years after first forming SS Cars, Ltd., Sir William Lyons retired. The power and bureaucracy of British Leyland had taken control and Jaguar was faltering. British Leyland sales in the U.S. dropped to 61,661. Jaguar represented about 8 percent of the whole company, down from 8.5 percent in 1971. The new XJ-12 was announced for March 1972 delivery as a '73 model.

1973

E-TYPE SERIES III — V-12 — Production of the 12-cylinder coupe and convertible continued with little change. Standard equipment included power rack-and-pinion steering, an adjustable steering column, power disc brakes, wraparound bumpers with overriders, dual exhausts, windshield washers, heater/defroster, reclining bucket seats with adjustable headrests, leather upholstery and a padded dashboard.

XJ6 — SIX — A switch to larger front-bumper overriders was the major change this year in Jaguar's six-cylinder four-door sedan. Standard equipment included a Borg-Warner three-speed automatic transmission, air conditioning, power windows, tinted glass, rear defroster and whitewall tires on chrome turbo wheels.

XJ12 — V-12 — A 12-cylinder version of Jaguar's sedan debuted in the U.S. this year. Standard equipment was similar to the XJ6, but with the same engine as the E-Type. Leather reclining seats were standard; an AM/FM stereo radio was the sole option. For the U.S. market, the V-12's compression ratio dwindled from 9.0:1 to 7.8:1 during this period, with a corresponding fall in horsepower and torque.

I.D. DATA: The serial number is on the upper left of the dashboard, visible through the windshield. The prefix indicates the make and model (and possibly whether car is a U.S. model). The suffix may indicate whether the car is equipped with overdrive or automatic transmission, and if it is left-hand drive (for export). Numerical sequence is the production serial number.

Starting serial number: (E-Type convertible) UD1S21029; (E-Type coupe) UD1S73856; (XJ6) US1L69908BW.

ENGINES

BASE SIX XJ6: Inline, dual-overhead-cam six-cylinder. Cast-iron block and aluminum head. Displacement: 258.4 cid (4235 cc). Bore & Stroke: 3.625 x 4.17 in. (92.1 x 106 mm). Compression Ratio: 7.5:1. Brake Horsepower: 162 (net) at 4750 rpm. Torque: 213 lbs.-ft. at 3000 rpm. Seven main bearings. Solid valve lifters. Two Zenith-Stromberg 175CD2SE carburetors.

BASE V-12 E-TYPE: 60-degree, overhead-cam "vee" type 12-cylinder. Aluminum block and heads. Displacement: 326 cid (5343 cc). Bore & Stroke: 3.54 x 2.77 in. (90 x 70 mm). Compression Ratio: 7.8:1. Brake Horsepower: 244 (net) at 5250 rpm. Torque: 285 lbs.-ft. at 3500 rpm. Seven main bearings. Four Zenith-Stromberg 175CD2SE carburetors. Mark II electronic system.

BASE V-12 XJ12: 60-degree, overhead-cam "vee" type 12-cylinder. Aluminum block and heads. Displacement: 326 cid (5343 cc). Bore & Stroke: 3.54 x 2.77 in. (90 x 70 mm). Compression Ratio: 7.8:1. Brake Horsepower: 244 (net) at 5250 rpm. Torque: 285 lbs.-ft. at 3500 rpm. Seven main bearings. Four Zenith-Stromberg 175CD2SE carburetors. Mark II electronic system.

Model	Body Type & Seating	Engine Type / CID	P.O.E. Price	Weight (Lbs.)	Production Total
E-Type Series III					
E-Type	2d Convertible-2P	V-12/326	$8,475	3,462	**Note 1**
E-Type	2d Coupe-2+2P	V-12/326	$8,920	3,466	**Note 1**
XJ6/12					
XJ6	4d Sedan-5P	I6/258	$9,500	3,769	**14,850 Note 2**
XJ12	4d Sedan-5P	V-12/326	$11,025	3,881	**2,894 Note 2**

Note 1: Approximately 15,200 Series III E-Types were produced from 1971 through 1975 (7,990 convertibles and 7,300 2+2 coupes).

Note 2: Figures shown do not include equivalent Daimlers (3,206 six-cylinder and 809 12-cylinder) or early Series II models (1,656 Series II XJ6 and 168 Series II XJ12).

CHASSIS

E-TYPE SERIES III: Wheelbase: 105 in. Overall Length: 184.4 in. Height: 51.0 in. Width: 66.1 in. Front Tread: 54.3 in. Rear Tread: 53.0 in. Wheel Type: steel disc. Standard Tires: E70VR15.

XJ6: Wheelbase: 108.9 in. Overall Length: 189.6 in. Height: 52.9 in. Width: 69.75 in. Front Tread: 58.0 in. Rear Tread: 58.6 in. Wheel Type: steel disc. Standard Tires: 195R15.

XJ12: Wheelbase: 108.9 in. Overall Length: 189.6 in. Height: 52.9 in. Width: 69.75 in. Front Tread: 58.0 in. Rear Tread: 58.6 in. Wheel Type: steel disc. Standard Tires: 205/70VR15.

TECHNICAL

E-TYPE: Layout: front-engine, rear-drive. Transmission: four-speed manual. Standard final drive ratio: 3.54:1. Steering: Rack-and-pinion. Suspension (front): wishbones and torsion bars with anti-roll bar. Suspension (rear): independent with lower wishbones, trailing lower radius arms, coil springs and anti-roll bar. Brakes: hydraulic, front/rear discs. Body Construction: integral steel, with front tubular frame. Fuel tank: 17 gallons (U.S.).

XJ6: Layout: front-engine, rear-drive. Transmission: automatic. Standard final drive ratio: 3.54:1. Steering: rack-and-pinion. Suspension (front): wishbones, lower trailing links, coil springs and anti-roll bar. Suspension (rear): independent with lower wishbones, trailing lower radius arms, coil springs and anti-roll bar. Brakes: front/rear disc. Body Construction: integral steel, with sub frame.

XJ12: Layout: front-engine, rear-drive. Transmission: automatic. Standard final drive ratio: 3.31:1. Steering: rack-and-pinion. Suspension (front): wishbones, lower trailing links, coil springs and anti-roll bar. Suspension (rear): independent with lower wishbones, trailing lower radius arms, coil springs and anti-roll bar. Brakes: front/rear disc. Body Construction: integral steel, with sub frame.

OPTIONS

E-TYPE SERIES III: Automatic transmission ($269). Air conditioning ($521). Chrome wire wheels ($275). Chrome turbo disc wheels ($133). Whitewall tires ($45). Detachable hardtop for roadster ($363). Heated rear window in coupe ($58). AM/FM stereo radio ($170).

XJ6: Heated rear window ($48).

XJ12: Chrome wire wheels ($276). Air conditioning ($530).

PERFORMANCE

E-TYPE SERIES III: Top Speed: 135 mph. Acceleration (0-60 mph): 6.8 seconds. Acceleration (quarter mile): 15.4 seconds. Fuel mileage: 14 to 18 mpg.

XJ6: Top Speed: 115 mph. Acceleration (0-60 mph): 10.7 seconds. Acceleration (quarter mile): 17.1 seconds. Fuel mileage: 15 mpg.

XJ12: Top Speed: 140 mph. Acceleration (0-60 mph): 8.5 seconds. Fuel mileage: 10 to 12 mpg.

CALENDAR YEAR SALES (U.S.): In calendar-year 1973, Jaguar sales to U.S. buyers, including tourist deliveries, totaled 6,767 cars.

MANUFACTURER: British Leyland UK Ltd., Coventry, England.

DISTRIBUTOR: British Leyland Motors, Leonia, New Jersey.

HISTORY: A longer-wheelbase XJ-L sedan was available in England in 1973, but did not reach the U.S. market until the 1974 model year. The short-wheelbase 1973 XJ-12 was a one-year offering here combining the 108.9-inch (1968-1974) wheelbase with the V-12 engine. British Leyland Motors sold the largest number of cars it had sold in the U.S. since 1970 – 65,948 versus 65,924. Deliveries were 6.5 percent above the 61,661 delivered here in 1972. Out of the corporation's marques – Austin, Jaguar, Land Rover, MG and Triumph, only Triumph did not gain in sales. British Leyland was able to bump its dealer count up to 1,468 – a significant increase that did not last. Jaguar's 6,767 sales in the U.S. represented a larger 103 percent of British Leyland's calendar-year deliveries.

1973 Jaguar E-type (XK-E) Series III V-12 coupe
Andrew Morland

Dan Lyons

1973 Jaguar E-type (XK-E) roadster

Dan Lyons

1973 Jaguar E-type (XK-E) roadster

1974 Jaguar XJ6 Series II sedan *Jaguar Heritage—North America*

1974

E-TYPE SERIES III — V-12 — For its final year in the Jaguar lineup, the E-Type's detuned V-12 used a 7.8:1 compression ratio in U.S. market cars. The convertible was the only model this year. Standard equipment included leather-faced semi-reclining bucket seats with ambla panels on non-wear surfaces, ambla interior trim, and Dunlop E70VR15 SP Sport whitewall tires on ventilated chrome disc wheels. Body colors this year were: British Racing Green, Azure Blue, Dark Blue, Fern Grey, Greensand, Old English White, Pale Primrose, Sable, Signal Red, Silver Grey, Regency Red and Turquoise.

XJ6 — SERIES II — SIX — A longer-wheelbase XJ6L Series II arrived in 1974. Its lengthened body added some four inches to the rear of the front door. All four-door XJs were "L" versions. Leftover short-wheelbase six-cylinder sedans may have been sold and registered in 1974. A shallow front grille held a new rubber bumper. Inside, the "second-tier" instruments sat ahead of the driver. The headlight-on and windshield wiper controls were moved to stalks attached to the steering column. A different Borg-Warner automatic transmission was installed, along with a new type of padded steering wheel. Automatic climate control air conditioning was installed. Standard equipment included tinted glass, power windows, fully-reclining leather-faced front seats with adjustable head restraints, leather-faced rear seats, deep-pile carpeting, and a locking glovebox. Sedan colors were: British Racing Green, Fern Grey, Dark Blue, Greensand, Old English White, Pale Primrose, Sable, Signal Red, Silver Grey, Regency Red and Turquoise. Standard Dunlop E70VR15 Sport white sidewall tires were mounted on chrome disc wheels.

XJ12L/XJ12C — SERIES II — V-12 — The 12-cylinder version of Jaguar's new long-wheelbase sedan adopted the same rubber front bumper as the XJ6L, but other changes were minimal. This XJ12L was the first long-wheelbase sedan to appear in Jaguar's 1974 U.S. sales brochure. A limited-production XJ12C pillarless two-door coupe on the shorter wheelbase was a late-in-the-year arrival. The XK-E engine was used. Standard equipment was similar to that of the XJ6, but with larger SP (Sport) tires. An electrically-heated rear window was standard equipment.

I.D. DATA: The serial number is on the upper left side of the dashboard, visible through the windshield. The prefix indicates the make and model. The suffix may indicate whether the car is equipped with overdrive or automatic transmission, and if it is left-hand drive (for export). The numerical sequence is the production serial number.

ENGINES

BASE SIX XJ6 SERIES II: Inline, dual-overhead-cam six-cylinder. Cast-iron block and aluminum head. Displacement: 258.4 cid (4235 cc). Bore & Stroke: 3.625 x 4.17 in. (92.1 x 106 mm). Compression Ratio: 7.5:1. Brake Horsepower: 162 (net) at 4750 rpm. Torque: 213 lbs.-ft. at 3000 rpm. Seven main bearings. Solid valve lifters. Two Zenith-Stromberg 175CD2SE carburetors.

BASE V-12 E-TYPE SERIES III: 60-degree, overhead-cam "vee" type 12-cylinder. Aluminum block and heads.

Model	Body Type & Seating	Engine Type/CID	P.O.E. Price	Weight (lbs.)	Production Total
E (E-Type)					
E-Type	2d Convertible-2P	V-12/326	$9,200	3,375	**Note 1**
XJ6					
XJ6L	4d Sedan-5P	I6/258	$11,500	4,053	**Note 2**
XJ12					
XJ12C	2d Coupe-5P	V-12/326	N/A	N/A	**Note 3**
XJ12L	4d Sedan-5P	V-12/326	$13,000	4,277	**Note 3**

Note 1: Approximately 15,200 Series III E-Types were produced from 1971 through 1975 (7,990 convertibles and 7,300 2+2 coupes).

Note 2: Approximately 18,270 XJ6 Jaguars (and 4,282 six-cylinder Daimlers) were produced in 1974.

Note 3: Approximately 4,744 XJ12 Jaguars (and 1,560 V-12 Daimlers) were produced in 1974.

1974 Jaguar XJ12L sedan *Phil Hall Collection*

Displacement: 326 cid (5343 cc). Bore & Stroke: 3.54 x 2.77 in. (90 x 70 mm). Compression Ratio: 7.8:1. Brake Horsepower: 244 (net) at 5250 rpm. Torque: 285 lbs.-ft. at 3500 rpm. Seven main bearings. Four Zenith-Stromberg 175CD2SE carburetors. Mark II electronic system.

BASE V-12 XJ12 SERIES II: 60-degree, overhead-cam "vee" type 12-cylinder. Aluminum block and heads. Displacement: 326 cid (5343 cc). Bore & Stroke: 3.54 x 2.77 in. (90 x 70 mm). Compression Ratio: 7.8:1. Brake Horsepower: 244 (net) at 5250 rpm. Torque: 285 lbs.-ft. at 3500 rpm. Seven main bearings. Four Zenith-Stromberg 175CD2SE carburetors. Mark II electronic system.

CHASSIS

E-TYPE SERIES III: Wheelbase: 105 in. Overall Length: 189.6 in. Height: 48.4 in. Width: 66.1 in. Front Tread: 54.4 in. Rear Tread: 52.75 in. Wheel Type: steel disc. Standard Tires: Dunlop E70VR15 SP Sport.

XJ6L SERIES II: Wheelbase: 112.8 in. Overall Length: 191.0 in. Height: 54.1 in. Width: 69.75 in. Front Tread: 58.0 in. Rear Tread: 58.6 in. Wheel Type: steel disc. Standard Tires: Dunlop E70VR15 SP Sport

XJ12C SERIES II: Wheelbase: 108.9 in. Overall Length: 194.8 in. Height: 54.1 in. Width: 69.75 in. Front Tread: 58.0 in. Rear Tread: 58.6 in. Wheel Type: steel disc. Standard Tires: Dunlop 205/70VR15 SP Sport.

XJ12L SERIES II: Wheelbase: 112.8 in. Overall Length:

198.8 in. Height: 54.1 in. Width: 69.75 in. Front Tread: 58.0 in. Rear Tread: 58.6 in. Wheel Type: steel disc. Standard Tires: Dunlop 205/70VR15 SP Sport.

TECHNICAL

E-TYPE: Layout: front-engine, rear-drive. Transmission: four-speed manual. Overall E-Type gear ratios: (1st) 10.38:1; (2nd) 6.74:1; (3rd) 4.91:1; (4th) 3.54:1. Standard final drive ratio: 3.54:1. Steering: Rack-and-pinion. Suspension (front): wishbones and torsion bars with anti-roll bar. Suspension (rear): independent with lower wishbones, trailing lower radius arms, coil springs and anti-roll bar. Brakes: hydraulic, front/ rear discs. Body Construction: integral steel, with front tubular frame. Fuel tank: 17 gallons (U.S.)

XJ6 SERIES II: Layout: front-engine, rear-drive. Transmission: automatic. Standard final drive ratio: 3.31:1. Steering: rack-and-pinion. Suspension (front): wishbones, lower trailing links, coil springs and anti-roll bar. Suspension (rear): independent with lower wishbones, trailing lower radius arms, coil springs and anti-roll bar. Brakes: front/rear disc. Body Construction: integral steel, with sub frame.

XJ12 SERIES II: Layout: front-engine, rear-drive. Transmission: automatic. Standard final drive ratio: 3.31:1. Steering: rack-and-pinion. Suspension (front): wishbones, lower trailing links, coil springs and anti-roll bar. Suspension (rear): independent with lower wishbones, trailing lower radius arms, coil springs and anti-roll bar. Brakes: front/rear disc. Body Construction: integral steel, with sub frame.

OPTIONS

E-TYPE SERIES III: Automatic transmission ($269). Air conditioning ($521). Chrome wire wheels ($275). Chrome turbo disc wheels ($133). Whitewall tires ($45). Detachable hardtop for roadster ($363). AM/FM stereo radio ($170).

XJ6 SERIES II: Heated rear window ($48).

XJ12 SERIES II: Chrome wire wheels ($276). Air conditioning ($530).

PERFORMANCE

E-TYPE SERIES III: Top Speed: 135 mph. Acceleration (0-60 mph): 6.8 seconds. Acceleration (quarter mile): 15.4 seconds. Fuel mileage: 14 to 18 mpg.

XJ6 SERIES II: Top Speed: 115 mph. Acceleration (0-60 mph): 10.7 seconds. Acceleration (quarter mile): 17.1 seconds. Fuel mileage: 15 mpg.

XJ12 SERIES II: Top Speed: 140 mph. Acceleration (0-60 mph): 8.5 seconds. Fuel mileage: 10 to 12 mpg.

CALENDAR YEAR SALES (U.S.): In calendar-year 1974, Jaguar sales to U.S. buyers, including tourist deliveries, totaled 5,299 cars.

MANUFACTURER: British Leyland UK, Ltd., Coventry, England.

DISTRIBUTOR: British Leyland Motors, Leonia, New Jersey.

HISTORY: The final E-Type coupes were built at the end of the 1973 model year, while the last convertibles came off the line in mid-1974. The last E-Type was built in England in September with registration number HDU 555N. It is now housed at the Jaguar-Daimler Heritage Trust Museum at Browns Lane, Coventry. Reduction to a three-day work week in Great Britain early in 1974 limited shipments of Jaguars to the U.S. The reduction was due to a coal workers' strike and the international energy crisis. British Leyland dropped back to 812 retail outlets in the U.S. and sales here dropped 16 percent to 54,851 cars. Jaguar accounted for 9.7 percent of British Leyland's U.S. business. British Leyland had little regard for the unique Jaguar brand and the marque's rich heritage.

1974 Jaguar E-type (XK-E) V-12 Commemorative Edition roadster *Andrew Morland*

THE MAGNIFICENT WORLD OF JAGUAR.

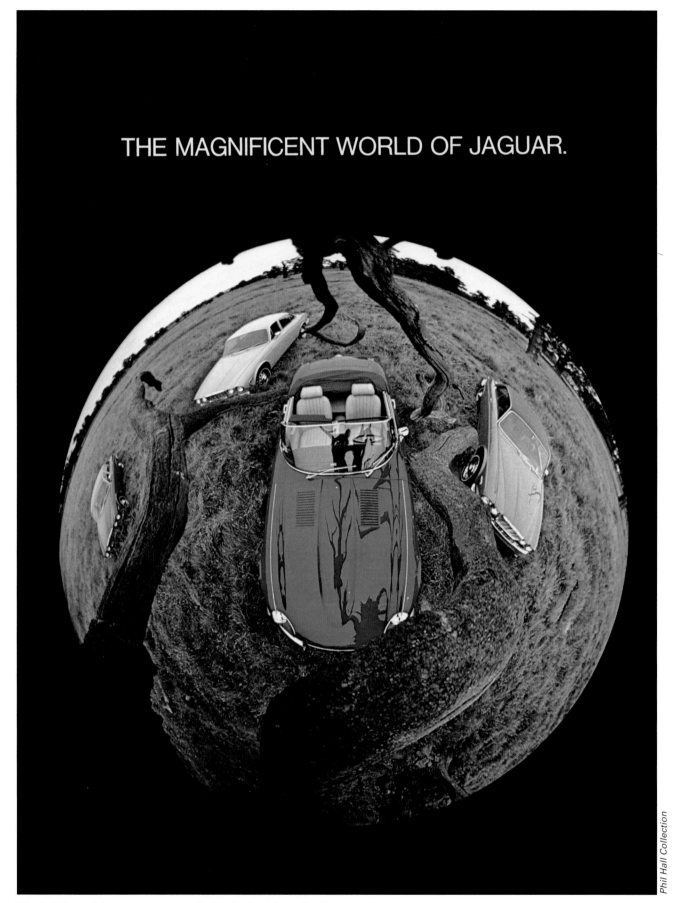

The full line of Jaguars was creatively displayed on the 1974 catalog.

1975 Jaguar XJ-S coupe Phil Hall Collection

1975

XJ6 SERIES II — SIX — An XJ6C coupe replaced the former short-wheelbase, six-cylinder sedan. Except for its shorter stance, vinyl top covering and shorter roofline, it was identical to the XJ6L. Product changes were otherwise minimal. The six got an automatic choke. Sixty percent of the Jaguars made this year were six-cylinder cars. Standard equipment included automatic transmission, power disc brakes, radial-ply tires, AM/FM radio, tinted glass, air conditioning, bucket seats, a clock and a rear window defogger.

XJ12 SERIES II — V-12 — Product changes in the V-12 models were also minimal. Electronic fuel injection replaced carburetors on the V-12 engine. Standard equipment included automatic transmission, power disc brakes, radial-ply tires, AM/FM radio, tinted glass, air conditioning, bucket seats, a clock and a rear window defogger.

I.D. DATA: The serial number is on the "A" (windshield) pillar. The prefix indicates the make and model (and possibly whether car is a U.S. model). The suffix may indicate whether the car is equipped with overdrive or automatic transmission, and if it is left-hand drive (for export). The numerical sequence is the production serial number. The starting serial number: (XJ6C) UF2J50045BW; (XJ6L) UF2T54779; (XJ12C) UF2G50060BW; (XJ12L) UF2R53930BW.

ENGINES

BASE SIX XJ6 SERIES II: Inline, dual-overhead-cam six-cylinder. Cast-iron block and aluminum head. Displacement: 258.4 cid (4235 cc). Bore & Stroke: 3.625 x 4.17 in. (92.1 x 106 mm). Compression Ratio: 7.5:1. Brake Horsepower: 162 (net) at 4750 rpm. Torque: 213 lbs.-ft. at 3000 rpm. Seven main bearings. Solid valve lifters. Two Zenith-Stromberg 175CD2SE carburetors.

BASE V-12 XJ12 SERIES II: 60-degree, overhead-cam "vee" type 12-cylinder. Aluminum block and heads. Displacement: 326 cid (5343 cc). Bore & Stroke: 3.54 x 2.77 in. (90 x 70 mm). Compression Ratio: 7.8:1. Brake Horsepower: 244 (net) at 5250 rpm. Torque: 285 lbs.-ft. at 3500 rpm. Seven main bearings. Four Zenith-Stromberg 175CD2SE carburetors. Mark II electronic system.

CHASSIS

XJ6C SERIES II: Wheelbase: 108.9 in. Overall Length: 191.0 in. Height: 55.0 in. Width: 69.75 in. Front Tread: 58.0 in. Rear Tread: 58.6 in. Wheel Type: steel disc. Standard Tires: Dunlop E70VR15 SP Sport.

XJ6L SERIES II: Wheelbase: 112.8 in. Overall Length: 200.5 in. Height: 54.1 in. Width: 69.75 in. Front Tread: 58.0 in. Rear Tread: 58.6 in. Wheel Type: steel disc. Standard Tires: Dunlop E70VR15 SP Sport.

XJ12C SERIES II: Wheelbase: 108.9 in. Overall Length: 194.7 in. Height: 55.0 in. Width: 69.75 in. Front Tread: 58.0 in. Rear Tread: 58.6 in. Wheel Type: steel disc. Standard Tires: Dunlop 205/70VR15 SP Sport.

Model	Body Type & Seating	Engine Type/ CID	P.O.E. Price	Weight (Lbs.)	Production Total
XJ6 Series II					
XJ6C	2d Coupe-5P	I6/258	$13,750	4,022	1,968
XJ6L	4d Sedan-5P	I6/258	$13,100	4,053	14,229
XJ12 Series II					
XJ12C	2d Coupe-5P	V12/326	$15,650	4,005	493
XJ12L	4d Sedan-5P	V12/326	$14,900	4,277	2,239

Note 1: Production figures shown are approximate and do not include Daimler totals. Body Style Note: Jaguar literature initially referred to two-door models as sedans rather than coupes.

XJ12L SERIES II: Wheelbase: 112.8 in. Overall Length: 200.5 in. Height: 55.0 in. Width: 69.75 in. Front Tread: 58.0 in. Rear Tread: 58.6 in. Wheel Type: steel disc. Standard Tires: Dunlop 205/70VR15 SP Sport.

TECHNICAL

XJ6 SERIES II: Layout: front-engine, rear-drive. Transmission: automatic. Standard final drive ratio: 3.31:1. Steering: rack-and-pinion. Suspension (front): wishbones, lower trailing links, coil springs and anti-roll bar. Suspension (rear): independent with lower wishbones, trailing lower radius arms, coil springs and anti-roll bar. Brakes: front/rear disc. Body Construction: integral steel, with sub frame.

XJ12 SERIES II: Layout: front-engine, rear-drive. Transmission: automatic. Standard final drive ratio: 3.31:1. Steering: rack-and-pinion. Suspension (front): wishbones, lower trailing links, coil springs and anti-roll bar. Suspension (rear): independent with lower wishbones, trailing lower radius arms, coil springs and anti-roll bar. Brakes: front/rear disc. Body Construction: integral steel, with sub frame.

OPTIONS

XJ6 SERIES II: Heated rear window ($48).

XJ12 SERIES II: Chrome wire wheels ($276).

PERFORMANCE

XJ6 SERIES II: Top Speed: 115 mph. Acceleration (0-60 mph): 10.7 seconds. Acceleration (quarter mile): 17.1 seconds. Fuel mileage: 15 mpg.

XJ12 SERIES II: Top Speed: 140 mph. Acceleration (0-60 mph): 8.5 seconds. Fuel mileage: 10 to 12 mpg.

CALENDAR YEAR SALES (U.S.): In calendar-year 1975, Jaguar sales to U.S. buyers, including tourist deliveries, totaled 6,799 cars.

MANUFACTURER: Leyland Cars, Great Britain.

DISTRIBUTOR: British Leyland Motors, Leonia, New Jersey.

HISTORY: Leyland Cars succeeded the faltering Jaguar/Leyland association this year. In December 1974, an investigation team began compiling an assessment of the British Leyland. In April 1975 the team made some important recommendations that included the disbanding of Jaguar's management team and eliminating the position of chief executive of Jaguar. This provoked the immediate resignation of managing director Geoffrey Robinson, who fundamentally disagreed with Sir Don Ryder's conclusions. Robinson felt, correctly, that such moves would destroy much of Jaguar's individuality and identity. The managers of British-Leyland did not realize Jaguar's sales potential and the need to preserve its individuality. Though the British Leyland dealer count in the U.S. dropped to just 681 retail outlets, 1975 was the best sales year in history for the "British General Motors." Deliveries of 70,839 cars were 30.7 percent ahead of 1974 and 2.8 percent higher than the British Leyland record set in 1970.

1975 Jaguar XJ12L sedan *Phil Hall Collection*

The XJ was advertised as "The uncommon luxury car, built to handle and respond like a sports car" and "...probably the best sedan available anywhere in the world." Jaguar sales increased from 5,299 in 1974 to 6,799 in 1975, probably because more of the company's U.S. sales outlets were selling the full range of brands. By 1975, 28 percent of British Leyland dealers here were selling all five marques, compared to just two percent as recently as 1973. Jaguar's 6,799 sales in the U.S. represented 9.60 percent of British Leyland business, a slight drop from 1974's 9.78 percent.

1975 Jaguar XJ-S coupe *Phil Hall Collection*

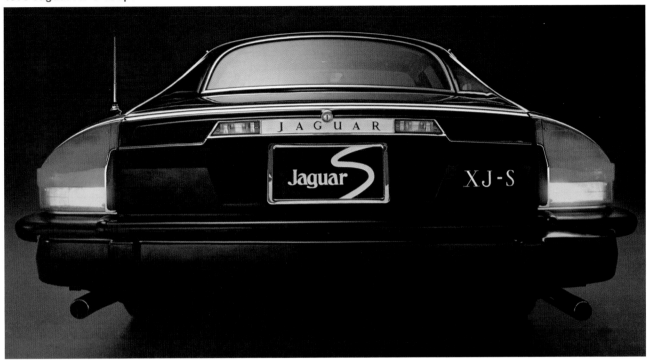

1975 Jaguar XJ-S coupe *Phil Hall Collection*

1976 Jaguar XJ12C coupe *Phil Hall Collection*

1976

XJ-S — V-12 — The all-new Jaguar XJ-S sports car debuted in 1976, powered by the fuel-injected 5.3-liter V-12 nestled into what was basically the XK-E frame and supported by an XK-E type suspension. Jaguar promoted the 2+2 coupe as "a new breed of cat." Styling features included a low-sweeping hood, smooth sides and rounded corners. Quad round headlights sat in oval housings at the ends of a squat, wide, rectangular grille. A black rubber front bumper held amber park/signal lights. The side marker lights were located just ahead of the front wheels. The rear roof pillars extended back towards the rear of the car, in a gentle curve, to create a "flying buttress" effect. There were spoilers under the front and rear bumpers. A Borg-Warner Model 12 three-speed automatic transmission was used. Standard equipment included air conditioning with automatic temperature control, an AM/FM stereo radio with eight-track tape player, power windows, tinted glass, fully-reclining leather-faced front seats, a heated rear window and a remote-control rearview mirror. All instruments sat in a nacelle just ahead of the driver. Standard colors were: British Racing Green, Regency Red, Silver Grey, Greensand, Signal Red, Dark Blue, Fern Grey, Old English White, Squadron Blue, Carriage Brown and Yellow Gold.

XJ6 SERIES II — SIX — Little change was evident in the six-cylinder model, offered with either short (coupe) or long (sedan) wheelbase. Standard equipment included automatic transmission, power steering, power disc brakes, radial-ply tires, reclining bucket seats, air conditioning, an AM/FM stereo radio, tinted glass, a clock, a rear window defogger and styled wheels. This year 57.7 percent of Jaguars sold in the U.S. had the six.

XJ12 — SERIES II — V-12 — The XJ12 also came in two- and four-door models again this year. Standard equipment included automatic transmission, power steering, power disc brakes, radial-ply tires, reclining bucket seats, air conditioning, an AM/FM stereo radio, tinted glass, a clock, a rear window defogger and styled wheels.

I.D. DATA: Serial number is on the "A" (windshield) pillar. Prefix indicates make and model. Suffix may indicate whether car is equipped with overdrive or automatic transmission, and if left-hand drive (for export). Numerical sequence is the production serial number. Starting serial number: (XJ-S) UF2W500002BW or UG2W50168BW; (XJ6C) UG2J51369BW; (XJ6L) UG2T56746BW; (XJ12C) UG2G50426BW; (XJ12L) UG2R54264BW.

ENGINES

BASE SIX XJ6: Inline, dual-overhead-cam six-cylinder. Cast-iron block and aluminum head. Displacement: 258.4 cid (4235 cc). Bore & Stroke: 3.625 x 4.17 in. (92.1 x 106 mm). Compression Ratio: 7.5:1. Brake Horsepower: 162 at 4750 rpm. Torque: 225 lbs.-ft. at 2500 rpm. Seven main bearings. Solid valve lifters. Two Zenith-Stromberg 175CD2SE carburetors.

BASE V-12 XJ12: 60-degree, overhead-cam "vee" type 12-cylinder. Aluminum block and head. Displacement: 326 cid (5343 cc). Bore & Stroke: 3.54 x 2.77 in. (90 x 70 mm). Compression Ratio: 8.0:1. Brake Horsepower: 244 at 4500/5250 rpm. Torque: 269 lbs.-ft. at 4500 rpm. Seven main bearings. Electronic fuel injection.

Model	Body Type & Seating	Engine Type/ CID	P.O.E. Price	Weight (lbs.)	Prod. Total
XJ-S					
GT	2d Coupe-2+2P	V12/326	$19,000	3,935	4,020
XJ6 Series II					
XJ6C	2d Coupe-5P	I6/258	$14,850	4,024	2,659
XJ6L	4d Sedan-5P	I6/258	$14,100	4,068	15,440
XJ12 Series II					
XJ12C	2d Coupe-5P	V12/326	$16,850	4,220	979
XJ12L	4d Sedan-5P	V12/326	$16,100	4,334	3,283

BASE V-12 XJ-S: 60-degree, overhead-cam "vee" type 12-cylinder. Aluminum block and head. Displacement: 326 cid (5343 cc). Bore & Stroke: 3.54 x 2.77 in. (90 x 70 mm). Compression Ratio: 8.0:1. Brake Horsepower: 244 at 4500/5250 rpm. Torque: 269 lbs.-ft. at 4500 rpm. Seven main bearings. Bosch electronic fuel injection.

CHASSIS

XJ6C SERIES II: Wheelbase: 108.8 in. Overall Length: 191.0 in. Height: 55.0 in. Width: 69.75 in. Front Tread: 58.0 in. Rear Tread: 58.6 in. Wheel Type: steel disc. Standard Tires: Dunlop E70VR15 SP Sport.

XJ6L SERIES II: Wheelbase: 112.8 in. Overall Length: 200.5 in. Height: 54.1 in. Width: 69.75 in. Front Tread: 58.0 in. Rear Tread: 58.6 in. Wheel Type: steel disc. Standard Tires: Dunlop E70VR15 SP Sport.

XJ12C SERIES II: Wheelbase: 108.8 in. Overall Length: 194.7 in. Height: 55.0 in. Width: 69.75 in. Front Tread: 58.0 in. Rear Tread: 58.6 in. Wheel Type: steel disc. Standard Tires: Dunlop 205/70VR15 SP Sport.

XJ12L SERIES II: Wheelbase: 112.8 in. Overall Length: 200.5 in. Height: 55.0 in. Width: 69.75 in. Front Tread: 58.0 in. Rear Tread: 58.6 in. Wheel Type: steel disc. Standard Tires: Dunlop 205/70VR15 SP Sport.

XJ-S: Wheelbase: 102.0 in. Overall Length: 192.25 in. Height: 47.8 in. Width: 70.62 in. Front Tread: 58.6 in. Rear Tread: 58.65 in. Wheel Type: steel disc. Standard Tires: Dunlop 205/70VR15 Sports Super Steel-belted-radial whitewalls.

TECHNICAL

XJ6 SERIES II: Layout: front-engine, rear-drive. Transmission: automatic. Standard final drive ratio: 3.31:1. Steering: rack-and-pinion. Suspension (front): wishbones, lower trailing links, coil springs and anti-roll bar. Suspension (rear): independent with lower wishbones, trailing lower radius arms, coil springs and anti-roll bar. Brakes: front/rear disc. Body Construction: integral steel, with sub frame.

XJ12 SERIES II: Layout: front-engine, rear-drive.

1976 Jaguar XJ6 sedan

Phil Hall Collection

1976 Jaguar XJ12 sedan

Phil Hall Collection

Transmission: automatic. Standard final drive ratio: 3.54:1. Steering: rack-and-pinion. Suspension (front): wishbones, lower trailing links, coil springs and anti-roll bar. Suspension (rear): independent with lower wishbones, trailing lower radius arms, coil springs and anti-roll bar. Brakes: front/rear disc. Body Construction: integral steel, with sub frame.

XJ-S: Layout: front-engine, rear-drive. Transmission: automatic. Standard final drive ratio: 3.07:1. Steering: rack-and-pinion. Suspension (front): semi-trailing wishbones with coil springs and anti-roll bar Suspension (rear): independent with lower wishbones, trailing lower radius arms, coil springs and anti-roll bar. Brakes: front/rear disc. Body Construction: integral steel, with sub frame.

OPTIONS

XJ6 SERIES II: Heated rear window ($48). Vinyl top.

XJ12 SERIES II: Chrome wire wheels ($276). Vinyl top.

PERFORMANCE

XJ6C SERIES II: Acceleration (0-60 mph): 11.9 seconds. Acceleration (quarter mile): 18.2 seconds at 77 mph.

XJ12 SERIES II: Top Speed: 140 mph. Acceleration (0-60 mph): 8.5 seconds. Fuel mileage: 10 to 12 mpg.

XJ-S: Top Speed: 150 mph. Acceleration (0-60 mph): 8.9 seconds. Acceleration (quarter mile): 15.9 seconds.

CALENDAR YEAR SALES (U.S.): In calendar-year 1976, Jaguar sales to U.S. buyers, including tourist deliveries, totaled 7,382 cars.

MANUFACTURER: Leyland Cars, Great Britain.

DISTRIBUTOR: British Leyland Motors Inc., 600 Willow Tree Rd., Leonia, New Jersey.

HISTORY: The new Jaguar XJ-S took five Category I victories in its first Trans Am racing season. Jaguar advertised, "It may be the best-handling four-passenger car in the world." Some sources say that the XJ-S was the last Jaguar designed by Sir William Lyons, but according to Roger Hicks in his *Jaguar Illustrated History* the XJ-S was the first Jaguar styled without the scrutiny of Sir William. The 1976 Jaguar model year was unusually long and lasted 15 months, allowing Jaguar to switch to a model year basis. British Leyland had just 512 dealers in the United States this year. British Leyland sales in America dropped eight percent to 65,164 cars.

1977 Jaguar XJ-S *Richard Dance Collection*

1977

XJ-S — V-12 — Production of the new 2+2 coupe, introduced for 1976, continued with little change. A four-speed manual gearbox became available, but not on U.S. models. Standard colors were: British Racing Green, Regency Red, Silver Grey, Greensand, Signal Red, Dark Blue, Fern Grey, Old English White, Squadron Blue, Carriage Brown, and Yellow Gold. Cast aluminum wheels were standard on the 1977 XJ-S and 20 percent of all Jaguars sold in America during the calendar year had styled aluminum wheels.

XJ6 SERIES II — SIX — Little change was evident in the six-cylinder coupe and sedan, which again carried the familiar twin-cam six-cylinder engine. Standard equipment included a three-speed automatic transmission, power steering, power disc brakes, radial-ply tires, reclining bucket seats, automatic-temperature-control air conditioning, an AM/FM stereo radio with eight-track tape player, tinted glass, a clock and a rear window defogger. This year 53.9 percent of Jaguars sold in the U.S. had the six.

XJ12 SERIES II — V-12 — No significant change was evident in the 12-cylinder version of Jaguar's sedan, but the coupe faded out of the picture. For the U.S. market, the fuel-injected engine produced 244 horsepower. Standard equipment included a three-speed automatic transmission, power steering, power disc brakes, radial-ply tires, reclining bucket seats, automatic-temperature-control air conditioning, an AM/FM stereo radio with eight-track tape player, tinted glass, a clock and a rear window defogger.

I.D. DATA: An 11-symbol serial number is on the "A" (windshield) pillar. Symbol one indicates manufacture to U.S. specs. Symbol two denotes model year; three and four, the body style. The remaining symbols make up the sequential serial number. Starting serial number: (XJ-S) UH2W52737BW; (XJ6C) UH2J52842BW; (XJ6L) UH2T63599BW; (XJ12L) UH2R56786BW.

ENGINES

BASE SIX XJ6: Inline, dual-overhead-cam six-cylinder. Cast-iron block and aluminum head. Displacement: 258.4 cid (4235 cc). Bore & Stroke: 3.625 x 4.17 in. (92.1 x 106 mm). Compression Ratio: 7.5:1. Brake Horsepower: 162 at 4750 rpm. Torque: 225 lbs.-ft. at 2500 rpm. Seven main bearings. Solid valve lifters. Two Zenith-Stromberg 175CD2SE carburetors.

Model	Body Type & Seating	Engine Type/ CID	P.O.E. Price	Weight (lbs.)	Prod. Total
XJ-S					
GT	2d Coupe-2+2P	V12/326	$20,250	3,935	3,861
XJ6 Series II					
XJ6C	2d Coupe-5P	I6/258	$15,750	4,024	1,835
XJ6L	4d Sedan-5P	I6/258	$15,000	4,068	10,956
XJ12 Series II					
XJ12C	2d Coupe-5P	V12/326	$18,000	4,235	339
XJ12L	4d Sedan-5P	V12/326	$17,250	4,334	1,913

BASE V-12 XJ12: 60-degree, overhead-cam "vee" type 12-cylinder. Aluminum block and head. Displacement: 326 cid (5343 cc). Bore & Stroke: 3.54 x 2.77 in. (90 x 70 mm). Compression Ratio: 7.8:1. Brake Horsepower: 244 at 4500/5250 rpm. Torque: 269 lbs.-ft. at 4500 rpm. Seven main bearings. Electronic fuel injection.

BASE V-12 XJ-S: 60-degree, overhead-cam "vee" type 12-cylinder. Aluminum block and head. Displacement: 326 cid (5343 cc). Bore & Stroke: 3.54 x 2.77 in. (90 x 70 mm). Compression Ratio: 8.0:1. Brake Horsepower: 244 at 4500/5250 rpm. Torque: 269 lbs.-ft. at 4500 rpm. Seven main bearings. Bosch electronic fuel injection.

CHASSIS

XJ6C SERIES II: Wheelbase: 108.8 in. Overall Length: 191.0 in. Height: 55.0 in. Width: 69.75 in. Front Tread: 58.0 in. Rear Tread: 58.6 in. Wheel Type: steel disc. Standard Tires: Dunlop ER70VR15 SP Sport.

XJ6L SERIES II: Wheelbase: 112.8 in. Overall Length: 200.5 in. Height: 54.1 in. Width: 69.75 in. Front Tread: 58.0 in. Rear Tread: 58.6 in. Wheel Type: steel disc. Standard Tires: Dunlop ER70VR15 SP Sport.

XJ12C SERIES II: Wheelbase: 108.8 in. Overall Length: 194.7 in. Height: 55.0 in. Width: 69.75 in. Front Tread: 58.0 in. Rear Tread: 58.6 in. Wheel Type: steel disc. Standard Tires: Dunlop 205/70VR15 SP Sport whitewalls.

XJ12L SERIES II: Wheelbase: 112.8 in. Overall Length: 200.5 in. Height: 55.0 in. Width: 69.75 in. Front Tread: 58.0 in. Rear Tread: 58.6 in. Wheel Type: steel disc. Standard Tires: Dunlop 205/70VR15 SP Sport whitewalls..

XJ-S: Wheelbase: 102.0 in. Overall Length: 192.25 in. Height: 47.8 in. Width: 70.62 in. Front Tread: 58.6 in. Rear Tread: 58.65 in. Wheel Type: steel disc. Standard Tires: Dunlop 205/70VR15 Sports Super steel-belted-radial whitewalls.

TECHNICAL

XJ6 SERIES II: Layout: front-engine, rear-drive. Transmission: automatic. Standard final drive ratio: 3.31:1. Steering: rack-and-pinion. Suspension (front): wishbones, lower trailing links, coil springs and anti-roll bar. Suspension (rear): independent with lower wishbones, trailing lower radius arms, coil springs and anti-roll bar. Brakes: front/rear disc. Body Construction: integral steel, with sub frame.

XJ12 SERIES II: Layout: front-engine, rear-drive. Transmission: automatic. Standard final drive ratio: 3.54:1. Steering: rack-and-pinion. Suspension (front): wishbones, lower trailing links, coil springs and anti-roll bar. Suspension (rear): independent with lower wishbones, trailing lower radius arms, coil springs and anti-roll bar. Brakes: front/rear disc. Body Construction: integral steel, with sub frame.

XJ-S: Layout: front-engine, rear-drive. Transmission: automatic. Standard final drive ratio: 3.07:1. Steering: rack-and-pinion. Suspension (front): semi-trailing wishbones with coil springs and anti-roll bar Suspension (rear): independent

1977 Jaguar XJ-S *Richard Dance Collection*

1977 Jaguar XJ12 sedan

with lower wishbones, trailing lower radius arms, coil springs and anti-roll bar. Brakes: front/rear disc. Body Construction: integral steel, with sub frame.

OPTIONS: 16.1 percent had a factory-installed vinyl roof. 80 percent had factory-installed styled steel wheels. 20 percent had factory installed styled aluminum wheels.

PERFORMANCE

XJ6 SERIES II: Top Speed: 141 mph. Acceleration (0-60 mph): 11.9 seconds. Acceleration (quarter mile): 18.2 seconds at 77 mph. Fuel mileage: 14 to 18 mpg.

XJ12 SERIES II: Top Speed: 140 mph. Acceleration (0-60 mph): 8.5 seconds. Fuel mileage: 10 to 13 mpg.

XJ-S: Top Speed: 150 mph. Acceleration (0-60 mph): 8.0 seconds. Acceleration (quarter mile): 15.9 seconds. Fuel mileage: 9 to 14 mpg.

CALENDAR YEAR SALES (U.S.): In calendar-year 1977, Jaguar sales to U.S. buyers, including tourist deliveries, totaled 4,349 cars.

MANUFACTURER: Leyland Cars, Great Britain.

DISTRIBUTOR: British Leyland Motors Inc., 600 Willow Tree Rd., Leonia, New Jersey. President: Graham W. Whitehead. Vice-President Sales: Michael H. Dale. Public Relations Manager: Michael L. Cook.

HISTORY: British Leyland had 520 dealers in the U.S. this year. British Leyland sales in America climbed five percent to 68,476 cars. Nevertheless, a comprehensive reorganization of British Leyland was up for consideration by the stockholders and other interested parties in England. The reorganization plan included a major decentralization move that would make the parent firm a holding company and set up separate marketing, manufacturing and heavy-duty divisions. Jaguars accounted for 5.36 percent of British Leyland's U.S. sales in calendar year 1977.

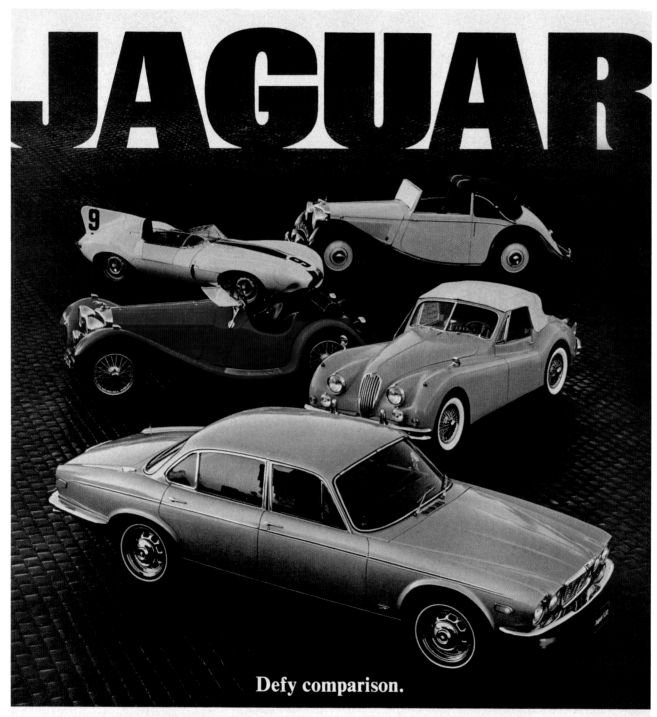

JAGUAR

Defy comparison.

Jaguars have always been defiantly individual cars. Consider the XJ12; it is literally a class of one, the only production four-door V-12 sedan in the world. And this uncompromising machine is unique in ways that extend far beyond its source of power.

The XJ12 handles with the agility and precision of all-independent suspension, rack and pinion steering and power disc brakes on all four wheels. The great smoothness and response of the electronically fuel-injected V-12 only enhance the car's remarkable all-round performance characteristics.

The inner world of this uncommon sedan is a harmony of thoughtful luxuries: hand-matched walnut veneers enrich the dashboard. Topgrain hides cover the seats. The car is totally considerate of its occupant's every wish: there are no factory options whatever. Even the thermostatically-controlled heat and air conditioning and the AM/FM stereo radio and tape deck are standard.

Still another Jaguar amenity is a remarkably thoughtful warranty: for 12 months, regardless of mileage, Jaguar will replace or repair any part of the car that is defective or that simply wears out, provided only that the car is properly maintained.

The only exceptions are the tires, which are warranted by the tire manufacturer, and spark plugs and filters, which are routine replacement items. Even then, if the plugs or filters are defective, Jaguar will pay to replace them.

In a world filled with common denominators, it is refreshing to know that Jaguar remains defiantly incomparable. For the name of the Jaguar dealer nearest you, call these numbers toll-free: (800) 447-4700, or, in Illinois, (800) 322-4400. British Leyland Motors Inc., Leonia, New Jersey 07605.

1977 Jaguar ad with an XJ12 sedan, XK 150, SS 100, D-type and Mk IV drophead

1978

XJ-S — V-12 — Production of Jaguar's 2+2 coupe continued with little change. It was again powered by Jaguar's 326-cid V-12 engine and three-speed automatic. This year 41.5 percent of Jaguars sold in the U.S. were XJ-S and XJ12 models with the V-12. Cast aluminum wheels were standard on the 1978 XJ-S and 22 percent of all Jaguars sold in America during the calendar year had styled aluminum wheels.

XJ6 — SERIES II — SIX — Jaguar's sedan continued with minimal change, until Lucas/Bosch L-Jetronic fuel injection replaced the twin carburetors in the six-cylinder engine, adding 14 hp. Only the four-door sedan was listed for sale in the U.S. Standard equipment included a three-speed automatic transmission, power steering, power disc brakes, radial-ply tires, reclining bucket seats, automatic-temperature-control air conditioning, an AM/FM stereo radio with eight-track tape player, tinted glass, a clock and a rear window defogger. This year 58.5 percent of Jaguars sold in the U.S. had the six.

XJ12 — SERIES II — V-12 — No significant change was evident in the 12-cylinder version of Jaguar's sedan. Standard equipment included a three-speed automatic transmission, power steering, power disc brakes, radial-ply tires, reclining bucket seats, automatic-temperature-control air conditioning, an AM/FM stereo radio with eight-track tape player, tinted glass, a clock and a rear window defogger. This year 41.5 percent of Jaguars sold in the U.S. were XJ-S and XJ12 models with the V-12.

I.D. DATA: An 11-symbol serial number is on the "A" (windshield) pillar. Symbol one indicates manufacture to U.S.

specs. Symbol two denotes model year; three and four, the body style. The remaining symbols make up the sequential serial number. Starting serial number: (XJ-S) UJ2W54673BW; (XJ6L) UJ2T69451BW; (XJ12L) UJ2R58421BW. Serial numbering system changed at midyear (effective in May 1978) to a 14-symbol number. Starting serial number: (XJ-S) JNVEV48C100001; (XJ6) JAVLN48C100001; (XJ12) JBVLV48C100001.

ENGINES

BASE SIX XJ6 (EARLY): Inline, dual-overhead-cam six-cylinder. Cast-iron block and aluminum head. Displacement: 258.4 cid (4235 cc). Bore & Stroke: 3.625 x 4.17 in. (92.1 x 106 mm). Compression Ratio: 7.5:1. Brake Horsepower: 162 at 4750 rpm. Torque: 225 lbs.-ft. at 2500 rpm. Seven main bearings. Solid valve lifters. Two Zenith-Stromberg 175CD2SE carburetors.

BASE SIX XJ6 (LATE): Inline, dual-overhead-cam six-cylinder. Cast-iron block and aluminum head. Displacement: 258.4 cid (4235 cc). Bore & Stroke: 3.625 x 4.17 in. (92.1 x 106 mm). Compression Ratio: 7.5:1. Brake Horsepower: 176 at 4750 rpm. Torque: 219 lbs.-ft. at 4500 rpm. Seven main bearings. Solid valve lifters. Lucas/Bosch L-Jetronic fuel injection.

BASE V-12 XJ12: 60-degree, overhead-cam "vee" type 12-cylinder. Aluminum block and head. Displacement: 326 cid (5343 cc). Bore & Stroke: 3.54 x 2.77 in. (90 x 70 mm). Compression Ratio: 7.8:1. Brake Horsepower: 244 at

Model	Body Type & Seating	Engine Type/CID	P.O.E. Price	Weight (lbs.)	Production Total
XJ-S					
GT	2d Coupe-2+2P	V12/326	$23,900	3,936	3,217
XJ6 Series II					
XJ6	4d Sedan-5P	I6/258	$19,000	4,068	15,422
XJ12 Series II					
XJ12	4d Sedan-5P	V12/326	$23,900	4,334	3,284

Note 1: Production totals shown are approximate and do not include equivalent Daimler sedans.

A 1978 Jaguar ad features both the XJ12 and XJ6 sedans.

4500/5250 rpm. Torque: 269 lbs.-ft. at 4500 rpm. Seven main bearings. Electronic fuel injection.

BASE V-12 XJ-S: 60-degree, overhead-cam "vee" type 12-cylinder. Aluminum block and head. Displacement: 326 cid (5343 cc). Bore & Stroke: 3.54 x 2.77 in. (90 x 70 mm). Compression Ratio: 8.0:1. Brake Horsepower: 244 at 4500/5250 rpm. Torque: 269 lbs.-ft. at 4500 rpm. Seven main bearings. Bosch electronic fuel injection.

CHASSIS

XJ6L SERIES II: Wheelbase: 112.8 in. Overall Length: 200.5 in. Height: 54.1 in. Width: 69.75 in. Front Tread: 58.2 in. Rear Tread: 58.9 in. Wheel Type: ventilated steel disc. Standard

Tires: Dunlop ER70VR15 SP Sport.

XJ12 SERIES II: Wheelbase: 112.8 in. Overall Length: 200.5 in. Height: 54.1 in. Width: 69.75 in. Front Tread: 58.2 in. Rear Tread: 58.9 in. Wheel Type: ventilated steel disc. Standard Tires: Dunlop 205/70VR15 SP Sport whitewalls.

XJ-S: Wheelbase: 102.0 in. Overall Length: 192.25 in. Height: 47.8 in. Width: 70.62 in. Front Tread: 58.6 in. Rear Tread: 58.65 in. Wheel Type: Cast aluminum. Standard Tires: Dunlop 205/70VR15 Sports Super steel-belted-radial whitewalls.

TECHNICAL

XJ6 SERIES II: Layout: front-engine, rear-drive.

Transmission: automatic. Standard final drive ratio: 3.31:1. Steering: rack-and-pinion. Suspension (front): wishbones, lower trailing links, coil springs and anti-roll bar. Suspension (rear): independent with lower wishbones, trailing lower radius arms, coil springs and anti-roll bar. Brakes: front/rear disc. Body Construction: integral steel, with sub frame.

XJ12 SERIES II: Layout: front-engine, rear-drive. Transmission: automatic. Standard final drive ratio: 3.54:1. Steering: rack-and-pinion. Suspension (front): wishbones, lower trailing links, coil springs and anti-roll bar. Suspension (rear): independent with lower wishbones, trailing lower radius arms, coil springs and anti-roll bar. Brakes: front/rear disc. Body Construction: integral steel, with sub frame.

XJ-S: Layout: front-engine, rear-drive. Transmission: automatic. Standard final drive ratio: 3.07:1. Steering: rack-and-pinion. Suspension (front): semi-trailing wishbones with coil springs and anti-roll bar. Suspension (rear): independent with lower wishbones, trailing lower radius arms, coil springs and anti-roll bar. Brakes: front/rear disc. Body Construction: integral steel, with sub frame.

OPTIONS: 22 percent of Jaguars sold in the U.S. had factory-installed styled aluminum wheels. 88 percent of Jaguars sold in the U.S. had factory-installed styled steel wheels.

PERFORMANCE

XJ6 SERIES II: Top Speed: 115 mph. Acceleration (0-60 mph): 11.9 seconds. Acceleration (quarter mile): 18.2 seconds at 77 mph. Fuel mileage: 13 to 18 mpg.

XJ12 SERIES II: Top Speed: 140 mph. Acceleration (0-60 mph): 9.0 seconds. Fuel mileage: 10 to 13 mpg.

XJ-S: Top Speed: 140 to 150 mph. Acceleration (0-60 mph): 8.0 seconds. Acceleration (quarter mile): 15.9 seconds. Fuel mileage: 9 to 14 mpg.

CALENDAR YEAR SALES (U.S.): In calendar-year 1978, Jaguar sales to U.S. buyers, *including tourist deliveries*, totaled 4,965 cars. The Jaguars sold in the U.S. during calendar-year 1978 were reported as 1,050 XJ-S, 2,766 XJ6, and 938 XJ12 models. Tourist deliveries for the calendar year probably accounted for the difference in the two totals.

MANUFACTURER: British Leyland UK, Ltd. (then Jaguar Rover Triumph Ltd.), Coventry, England.

DISTRIBUTOR: British Leyland Motors, Inc., (then Jaguar Rover Triumph, Inc.), 600 Willow Tree Rd., Leonia, New Jersey. President: Graham W. Whitehead. Vice president Sales: Michael H. Dale. Public Relations Manager: Michael L. Cook.

HISTORY: Jaguar Rover Triumph, Inc. was the new corporate title for British Leyland Motors Inc., following the excorporation* of the automotive division from British Leyland Ltd. The company experienced its worst year in an entire decade during 1978. Sales in the U.S. dropped 42.4 percent to just 48,068 MG, Rover, Triumph and Jaguar cars. The decline was due to economic and labor problems affecting the parent firm in England and came despite favorable monetary conditions. Japanese cars were taking customers away from the Triumph and MG sports cars. The U.S. arm's main strength seemed to be in its highest-priced cars like the Jaguar models, where sales increased a bit. The cars were sold at 597 retail outlets across the U.S. this year.

*Breaking apart from a legal corporation.

1978 Jaguar Group 44 XJS Trans Am racing car

Jaguar Heritage—North America

1979

XJ-S — V-12 — Jaguar's amazingly responsive 12-cylnder sport coupe helped the company win two Driver's Championships, plus the 1978 Manufacturer's Championship in its first two seasons of Trans Am Category I racing, yet the car was superbly luxurious, silent in motion and a pure pleasure to drive. The 1979 model had no significant change. Standard equipment included a three-speed automatic transmission, power steering, power 4-wheel disc brakes, radial-ply tires, reclining bucket seats, automatic-temperature-control air conditioning, an AM/FM sound system, tinted glass, a clock and a rear window defogger.

XJ6 SERIES II — SIX — The XJ-6 and its nearly identical twin the XJ-12 combined superb handling with uncommon luxury, leather seats, a walnut dashboard and so much that no factory options were offered. A Series III sedan debuted during the model year and reflected big improvements in quality and reliability. Standard equipment included a three-speed automatic transmission, power steering, power 4-wheel disc brakes, radial-ply tires, reclining bucket seats, automatic-temperature-control air conditioning, an AM/FM stereo radio with eight-track tape player, tinted glass, a clock and a rear window defogger. This year 67 percent of Jaguars sold in the U.S. had the six.

Note 1: A Series III XJ6 sedan arrived in the middle of calendar-year 1979. It was considered a 1980 model.

XJ12 SERIES II — V-12 — No major change was evident in the 12-cylinder version of Jaguar's four-door sedan. GM's Turbo Hydra-matic three-speed automatic transmission was standard. A Series III version debuted during the model year. Standard equipment included a three-speed automatic

transmission, power steering, power 4-wheel disc brakes, radial-ply tires, reclining bucket seats, automatic-temperature-control air conditioning, an AM/FM stereo radio with eight-track tape player, tinted glass, a clock and a rear window defogger.

Note 2: A Series III XJ12 sedan arrived in the middle of calendar-year 1979. It was considered a 1980 model.

I.D. DATA: A 14-symbol serial number is on the "A" (windshield) pillar. Symbol one indicates manufacturer. Symbol two denotes the model. Symbol three indicates a car made to U.S. specifications. Symbol four identifies the body style. Symbol five indicates engine type; six, the transmission and steering; seven, the model year; eight, the assembly plant. The remaining symbols make up the sequential serial number. Starting serial number: (XJ-S) JNVEV49C100234; (XJ6) JAVLN49C100749; (XJ12) JBVLV49C100770.

ENGINES

BASE SIX XJ6: Inline, dual-overhead-cam six-cylinder. Cast-iron block and aluminum head. Displacement: 258.4 cid (4235 cc). Bore & Stroke: 3.625 x 4.17 in. (92.1 x 106 mm). Compression Ratio: 7.5:1. Brake Horsepower: 176 at 4750 rpm. Torque: 219 lbs.-ft. at 4500 rpm. Seven main bearings. Solid valve lifters. Lucas/Bosch L-Jetronic fuel injection.

BASE V-12 XJ12: 60-degree, overhead-cam "vee" type 12-cylinder. Aluminum block and head. Displacement: 326 cid (5343 cc). Bore & Stroke: 3.54 x 2.77 in. (90 x 70 mm). Compression Ratio: 7.8:1. Brake Horsepower: 244 at 4500/5250 rpm. Torque: 269 lbs.-ft. at 4500 rpm. Seven main bearings. Electronic fuel injection.

BASE V-12 XJ-S: 60-degree, overhead-cam "vee" type 12-cylinder. Aluminum block and head. Displacement: 326 cid (5343 cc). Bore & Stroke: 3.54 x 2.77 in. (90 x 70 mm). Compression Ratio: 8.0:1. Brake Horsepower: 244 at 4500/5250 rpm. Torque: 269 lbs.-ft. at 4500 rpm. Seven main bearings. Bosch electronic fuel injection.

CHASSIS

XJ6 SERIES II: Wheelbase: 112.8 in. Overall Length: 200.5 in. Height: 54.1 in. Width: 69.75 in. Front Tread: 58.2 in. Rear Tread: 58.9 in. Wheel Type: steel wheel. Standard Tires: Dunlop ER70VR15 SP Sport.

XJ12 SERIES II: Wheelbase: 112.8 in. Overall Length: 200.5 in. Height: 54.1 in. Width: 69.75 in. Front Tread: 58.2 in. Rear Tread: 58.9 in. Wheel Type: styled steel. Standard Tires: Dunlop 205/70VR15 steel-belted whitewalls.

XJ-S: Wheelbase: 102.0 in. Overall Length: 192.25 in. Height: 47.8 in. Width: 70.62 in. Front Tread: 58.6 in. Rear Tread: 58.65 in. Wheel Type: styled steel. Standard Tires: Dunlop 205/70VR15 Sports Super steel-belted-radial whitewalls.

TECHNICAL

XJ6 SERIES II: Layout: front-engine, rear-drive. Transmission: automatic. Standard final drive ratio: 3.31:1. Steering: rack-and-pinion. Suspension (front): wishbones, lower trailing links, coil springs and anti-roll bar. Suspension (rear): independent with lower wishbones, trailing lower radius arms, coil springs and anti-roll bar. Brakes: front/rear disc. Body Construction: integral steel, with sub frame.

XJ12 SERIES II: Layout: front-engine, rear-drive. Transmission: automatic. Standard final drive ratio: 3.31:1. Steering: rack-and-pinion. Suspension (front): wishbones, lower trailing links, coil springs and anti-roll bar. Suspension (rear): independent with lower wishbones, trailing lower radius arms, coil springs and anti-roll bar. Brakes: front/rear disc. Body Construction: integral steel, with sub frame.

XJ-S: Layout: front-engine, rear-drive. Transmission: automatic. Standard final drive ratio: 3.31:1. Steering: rack-and-pinion. Suspension (front): semi-trailing wishbones with coil springs and anti-roll bar. Suspension (rear): independent with lower wishbones, trailing lower radius arms, coil springs and anti-roll bar. Brakes: front/rear disc. Body Construction: integral steel, with sub frame.

OPTIONS: 0.5 percent of Jaguars sold in the U.S. had wheel covers. 95 percent of Jaguars sold in the U.S. had factory-installed styled steel wheels. 67 percent of Jaguars sold in the U.S. had the inline six.

PERFORMANCE

XJ6 SERIES II: Top Speed: 116 mph. Acceleration (0-60 mph): 9.6 seconds. Acceleration (quarter mile): 17.7 seconds at 77 mph. Fuel mileage: 17 mpg.

XJ12 SERIES II: Top Speed: 140 mph. Acceleration (0-60 mph): 9.0 seconds. Fuel mileage: 10-13 mpg.

XJ-S: Top Speed: 140 to 150 mph. Acceleration (0-60 mph): 8.0 seconds. Acceleration (quarter mile): 15.9 seconds. Fuel mileage: 10 mpg.

CALENDAR YEAR SALES (U.S.): In calendar-year 1979, Jaguar sales to U.S. buyers, including tourist deliveries, totaled 3,551 cars (695 XJ-S, 2,313 XJ6, and 543 XJ12).

MANUFACTURER: British Leyland, Ltd., 41/46 Piccadilly, London, England.

1979 Jaguar Series III XJ12 5.3 sedan

Model	Body Type & Seating	Engine Type/ CID	P.O.E. Price	Weight (lbs.)	Production Total
XJ-S					
GT	2d Coupe-2+2P	V12/326	$25,000	3,936	2,414
XJ6 Series II					
XJ6	4d Sedan-5P	I6/258	$20,000	4,068	**Note 3**
XJ12 Series II					
XJ12	4d Sedan-5P	V12/326	$22,000	4,334	**Note 4**

Note 3: About 1,528 Series II and 6,146 Series III XJ6 sedans were produced in 1979 (not including Daimlers).

Note 4: About 429 Series II and 155 Series III XJ12 sedans were produced in 1979 (not including Daimlers).

1979 Jaguar Series III XJ6 4.2 sedan

1979 Jaguar Series III XJ6 4.2 sedan

DISTRIBUTOR: Jaguar Rover Triumph Inc., 600 Willow Tree Rd., Leonia, New Jersey. President: Graham W. Whitehead. Vice president Sales: Michael H. Dale.

HISTORY: Jaguar Rover Triumph, Inc. continued to struggle in the U.S. market with an aging product line and supply problems that stemmed from production trouble overseas. The company sold only 42,306 cars in the U.S., the worst performance in a decade. New product launches and supplies of current models were held back due to problems that the parent firm, British Leyland, Ltd., was having in England. There were frequent reorganizations, strikes and political turmoil. British Leyland was having problems competing in the modern world marketplace and Jaguar was suffering because of it. In the U.S., Jaguar-Rover-Triumph, Inc. had decided to concentrate on sport models and high-priced Jaguar luxury cars. The company based at Nuffield House, 41/46 Piccadilly in London, had worldwide sales of $6,578,000,000 and lost $257,000,000. Percy Plant became Jaguar's new chairman – for a short while.

1980

XJ-S — V-12 — Once again, Jaguar's 2+2 sports coupe continued with no significant change except for new body colors. Standard colors this year were: Atlantis Blue metallic, Brazilia Brown metallic, Cotswold Yellow, Damson Red, Racing Green metallic, Sebring Red, and Tudor White. Standard equipment included a three-speed automatic transmission, power steering, power 4-wheel disc brakes, radial-ply tires, reclining bucket seats, automatic-temperature-control air conditioning, an AM/FM sound system, tinted glass, a clock, a rear window defogger and styled aluminum wheels.

XJ6 — SERIES III — SIX — The Series III arrived in mid-1979 as a 1980 model. Changes included a taller roof line and a slightly larger rear window. The rear roof pillars were slightly narrower, while the windshield grew larger. Wraparound bumpers were added both front and rear, while the restyled taillights incorporated both back-up lights and stop lights. It takes an expert to tell a Series III from a Series II, yet the new model reflected substantial improvements in quality and reliability. All Series III XJ sedans were fuel-injected and featured improved trim and components. A Series III is probably the best Jaguar for all-around "daily driver" use for most people. Mechanical changes were minimal. The XJ6 sedan was powered by a fuel-injected version of the familiar twin-cam engine. It was hooked to the Borg-Warner three-speed automatic transmission. A five-speed manual gearbox (identical to that used in the Rover 3500) became available. Cruise control was a new option. Body colors were the same as for the XJ-S, except for Sebring Red. Standard equipment included an AM/FM stereo with cassette player, power steering, power 4-wheel disc brakes, automatic-temperature air conditioning, power windows, tinted glass, a clock, a heated rear window and power mirrors. This year 85 percent of Jaguars sold in the U.S. had the six.

I.D. DATA: A 14-symbol serial number is on the "A" (windshield) pillar. Symbol one indicates the manufacturer. Symbol two denotes the model. Symbol three indicates a car made to U.S. specifications. Symbol four identifies the body style. Symbol five indicates the engine type; six, the transmission and steering; seven, the model year; and eight, the assembly plant. The remaining symbols make up the sequential serial number. Starting serial number: (XJ6) JAVLN4AC310676. Serial number prefix: (XJ-S) JNVEV.

ENGINES

BASE SIX XJ6: Inline, dual-overhead-cam six-cylinder. Cast-iron block and aluminum head. Displacement: 258.4 cid (4235 cc). Bore & Stroke: 3.625 x 4.17 in. (92.1 x 106 mm). Compression Ratio: 7.5:1. Brake Horsepower: 176 at 4750 rpm. Torque: 219 lbs.-ft. at 4500 rpm. Seven main bearings. Solid valve lifters. Lucas/Bosch L-Jetronic fuel injection.

BASE V-12 XJ-S: 60-degree, overhead-cam "vee" type 12-cylinder. Aluminum block and head. Displacement: 326 cid (5343 cc). Bore & Stroke: 3.54 x 2.77 in. (90 x 70 mm). Compression Ratio: 7.8:1. Brake Horsepower: 244 at 4500/5250 rpm. Torque: 269 lbs.-ft. at 4500 rpm. Seven main bearings. Bosch electronic fuel injection.

CHASSIS

XJ6 SERIES III: Wheelbase: 112.8 in. Overall Length: 199.5 in. Height: 54.0 in. Width: 69.75 in. Front Tread: 58.3 in. Rear Tread: 58.9 in. Wheel Type: ventilated chrome disc. Standard Tires: Dunlop ER70VR15 SP Sport.

Model	Body Type & Seating	Engine Type/CID	P.O.E. Price	Weight (LBS.)	Production Total
XJ-S					
GT	2d Coupe-2+2P	V12/326	$30,000	3,936	1,131
XJ6 Series III					
XJ6	4d Sedan-5P	I6/258	$25,000	4,075	9,836

Note 1: The XJ12 was dropped from the U.S. market this year, though it remained in production (and some were sold during the model year).

Note 2: A total of 814 Jaguar XJ12 sedans were also produced in England this year, plus 604 12-cylinder Daimlers.

1980 Jaguar Series III XJ6 4.2 sedan

XJ-S: Wheelbase: 102.0 in. Overall Length: 192.25 in. Height: 47.8 in. Width: 70.62 in. Front Tread: 58.6 in. Rear Tread: 58.65 in. Wheel Type: cast aluminum alloy. Standard Tires: Dunlop 205/70VR15 Sports Super steel-belted-radial whitewalls.

TECHNICAL

XJ6 SERIES III: Layout: front-engine, rear-drive. Transmission: Borg-Warner automatic. Standard final drive ratio: 3.31:1 or 3.07:1. Steering: power rack-and-pinion. Suspension (front): ""anti-dive" with coil springs and anti-roll bar. Suspension (rear): independent with lower wishbones, trailing lower radius arms and coil springs. Brakes: front/rear disc. Body Construction: integral steel, with sub frame.

XJ-S: Layout: front-engine, rear-drive. Transmission: Turbo-Hydra-Matic 400. Standard final drive ratio: 3.31:1 or 3.07:1. Steering: power rack-and-pinion. Suspension (front): ""anti-dive" with coil springs and anti-roll bar. Suspension (rear): independent with lower wishbones, trailing lower radius arms, coil springs and anti-roll bar. Brakes: front/rear disc. Body Construction: integral steel, with sub frame.

PERFORMANCE

XJ6 SERIES III: Top Speed: 115 mph. Acceleration (0-60 mph): 9.6 seconds. Acceleration (quarter mile) 17.9 seconds. Fuel mileage: 14 mpg.

XJ-S: Top Speed: 140 to 150 mph. Acceleration (0-60 mph): 8.0 seconds. Acceleration (quarter mile) 15.9 seconds. Fuel mileage: 10 mpg.

CALENDAR YEAR SALES (U.S.): In calendar-year 1980, Jaguar sales to U.S. buyers, including tourist deliveries, totaled 2,951 cars. The U.S. calendar-year sales of 2,951 units included 2,275 XJ6 models, 420 XJ-S models and 256 XJ12 models.

MANUFACTURER: British Leyland, Ltd., 41/46 Piccadilly, London, England.

DISTRIBUTOR: Jaguar Rover Triumph Inc., Leonia, New Jersey.

HISTORY: U.S. sales of Jaguar Rover Triumph cars fell 24.5 percent to just 31,949 units. The company had 408 retail outlets in the U.S. as of January 1, 1980. By year's end, 10 of them would leave or go under. Jaguar represented 8.4 percent of all British Jaguar Rover Triumph sales in the U.S. (5.5 percent for the XJ6, 1.6 percent for the XJ-S and 1.3 percent for the XJ12. In England, British Leyland Ltd. reported worldwide sales of $6,500,000,000 and a bigger-than-ever loss of $1,200,000,000. The company produced 548,000 vehicles and sold 56,906 cars in the U.S. A bitter labor strike at the Jaguar facility on Browns Road, Coventry, led to the issuing of an ultimatum: "Return to work or lose your jobs" by Sir Michael Edwarde. Also this year, Jaguar got a full-time chairman. John Eagan, who assumed the job, was an expert in agricultural equipment parts.

A racing version of the XJ-S Jaguar in action. *Bob Harrington*

1981

XJ-S — V-12 — Jaguar's 2+2 sports coupe was not officially listed for sale in the U.S. this year, though a small number were sold. Standard equipment included a three-speed automatic transmission, power steering, power 4-wheel disc brakes, radial-ply tires, reclining bucket seats, automatic-temperature-control air conditioning, an AM/FM sound system, tinted glass, a clock, a rear window defogger and styled aluminum wheels.

XJ6 SERIES III — SIX — Production of the restyled six-cylinder sedan, introduced for the 1980 model year, continued with little change. Standard equipment included an AM/FM stereo with cassette player, power steering, power 4-wheel disc brakes, automatic-temperature air conditioning, power windows, tinted glass, a clock, a heated rear window and power mirrors. This year 85 percent of Jaguars sold in the U.S. had the six.

I.D. DATA: A 17-symbol Vehicle Identification Number is on the upper left of the instrument panel, visible through the windshield. Symbols 1 through 3 identify the manufacturer, make, and vehicle type. Symbol four indicates model; five, vehicle class; six, body style; seven, engine. Symbol eight denotes transmission type, followed by a check digit. Symbol 10 indicates model year ("B" = 1981); symbol 11, the assembly plant. The final six digits form the sequential serial number. The starting serial number is: (XJ6) SAJAV134()BC320092.

ENGINES

BASE SIX XJ6: Inline, dual-overhead-cam six-cylinder.

Cast-iron block and aluminum head. Displacement: 258.4 cid (4235 cc). Bore & Stroke: 3.625 x 4.17 in. (92.1 x 106 mm). Compression Ratio: 7.8:1. Brake Horsepower: 176 at 4750 rpm. Torque: 219 lbs.-ft. at 2500 rpm. Seven main bearings. Solid valve lifters. Electronic fuel injection.

BASE V-12 XJ-S: 60-degree, overhead-cam, vee-type 12-cylinder. Aluminum block and head. Displacement: 326 cid (5343 cc). Bore & Stroke: 3.54 x 2.77 in. (90 x 70 mm). Compression Ratio: 7.8:1. Brake Horsepower: 244 at 5250 rpm. Torque: 269 lbs.-ft. at 4500 rpm. Seven main bearings. Electronic fuel injection.

CHASSIS

XJ6 SERIES III: Wheelbase: 112.8 in. Overall Length: 199.5 in. Height: 54.0 in. Width: 69.75 in. Front Tread: 58.3 in. Rear Tread: 58.9 in. Wheel Type: ventilated chrome disc. Standard Tires: Dunlop ER70VR15 SP Sport

XJ-S: Wheelbase: 102.0 in. Overall Length: 192.25 in. Height: 47.8 in. Width: 70.62 in. Front Tread: 58.6 in. Rear Tread: 58.65 in. Wheel Type: cast aluminum alloy. Standard Tires: Dunlop 205/70VR15 Sports Super steel-belted-radial whitewalls.

TECHNICAL

XJ6 SERIES III: Layout: front-engine, rear-drive. Transmission: Borg-Warner automatic. Standard final drive

Model	Body Type & Seating	Engine Type/CID	P.O.E. Price	Weight (lbs.)	Production Total
XJ-S					
GT	2d Coupe-2+2P	V12/326	N/A	N/A	1,252
XJ6					
XJ6	4d Sedan-5P	I6/258	$27,500	4,060	10,216

Note 1: Figures shown are approximate and do not include equivalent Daimler sedans. A total of 457 XJ12 Jaguars also were produced (plus 415 12-cylinder Daimlers).

1981 Jaguar Series III XJ6 sedan

ratio: 3.07:1. Steering: power rack-and-pinion. Suspension (front): "anti-dive" with coil springs and anti-roll bar. Suspension (rear): independent with lower wishbones, trailing lower radius arms and coil springs. Brakes: front/rear disc. Body Construction: integral steel, with sub frame.

XJ-S: Layout: front-engine, rear-drive. Transmission: Turbo-Hydra-Matic 400. Standard final drive ratio: 3.31:1 or 3.07:1. Steering: power rack-and-pinion. Suspension (front): "anti-dive" with coil springs and anti-roll bar. Suspension (rear): independent with lower wishbones, trailing lower radius arms, coil springs and anti-roll bar. Brakes: front/rear disc. Body Construction: integral steel, with sub frame.

OPTIONS: No factory options offered.

PERFORMANCE

XJ6 SERIES III: Top Speed: 116 mph. Acceleration (0-60 mph): 9.6 seconds. Acceleration (quarter mile) 17.7 seconds at 77 mph. Fuel mileage: 17 mpg.

XJ12 SERIES II: Top Speed: 140 mph. Acceleration (0-60 mph): 9.0 seconds. Fuel mileage: 10 to 13 mpg.

XJ-S: Top Speed: 140 to 150 mph. Acceleration (0-60 mph): 8.0 seconds. Acceleration (quarter mile) 15.9 seconds. Fuel mileage: 10 mpg.

CALENDAR YEAR SALES (U.S.): Either 4,688 or 4,695 Jaguars were sold in the U.S. during 1981 (both figures appear in sources). This included 232 XJ-S models.

MANUFACTURER: British Leyland, Ltd., London, England.

DISTRIBUTOR: Jaguar Rover Triumph, Inc., Leonia, New Jersey.

HISTORY: Total U.S. sales for Jaguar Triumph Rover, Inc. were 18,921 and included 9,759 Triumphs, 4,688 Jaguars, 3,700 MGs and 774 Rovers. In October 1980, British Leyland, Ltd. announced that it was halting production of MGs. By September of 1981, Triumph was also gone. Jaguar and Rover survived. In England, British Leyland, Ltd. reported a loss of $900,000,000. Graham W. Whitehead continued as president and Michael H. Dale continued as vice president of sales and service.

The striking Group 44 Jaguar XJR-5 racer from 1982. *Jaguar Heritage—North America*

1982

XJ-S — V-12 — Jaguar's 12-cylinder coupe continued with little change, except for the adoption of a high-swirl, high-compression cylinder head. That gave it the name HE (for "High Efficiency"). The 326-cid (5.3-litre) engine came only with a three-speed automatic transmission. Standard equipment included four-wheel power disc brakes, power steering, radial tires, reclining front seats, automatic-temperature-control air conditioning, tinted glass and styled aluminum wheels.

XJ6 SERIES III — SIX — Production of Jaguar's basic sedan continued with little change. The engine was again the familiar twin-cam 4.2-litre six with electronic fuel injection. It was hooked to three-speed automatic transmission. Standard equipment included four-wheel power disc brakes, power steering, power sunroof, power windows and door mirrors, tinted glass, cruise control, automatic-temperature air conditioning, a 25-watt AM/FM digital stereo radio with scan tuning and cassette player, a power antenna, central locking, an electric rear-window defroster, a power driver's seat, radial tires, styled wheels (90 percent had aluminum wheels), an adjustable steering column, reclining front seats, and leather upholstery.

XJ6 VANDEN PLAS — SIX — A new luxury edition of the six-cylinder four-door sedan added such extra equipment as full leather upholstery, woven throw rugs, wood-veneer dash applique', rear-compartment reading lamps, rear center armrest with built-in storage compartment, and special body emblems.

Standard equipment also included four-wheel power disc brakes, power steering, power sunroof, power windows and door mirrors, tinted glass, cruise control, automatic-temperature air conditioning, a 25-watt AM/FM digital stereo radio with scan tuning and cassette player, a power antenna, central locking, an electric rear-window defroster, a power driver's seat, radial tires, styled wheels (90 percent had aluminum wheels), an adjustable steering column, reclining front seats, and leather upholstery.

I.D. DATA: A 17-symbol Vehicle Identification Number is on the top left of the instrument panel, visible through the windshield. Symbols one though three indicate origin and make. Symbol four denotes model; symbol five, the restraint system; symbol six, the body style ("1" = four-door sedan; "5" = two-door coupe). Symbol seven is the engine code; symbol eight, the steering and transmission code. Next is a check digit, followed by a letter indicating model year (C = 1982). Symbol 11 (letter C) identifies the assembly plant, followed by a six-digit sequential production number. The starting serial numbers are: (XJ-S) SAJNV5()()()CC105233 (XJ6) SAJAV1()()()CC105233; (Vanden Plas) SAJAY1()()()CC105233.

ENGINES

BASE SIX XJ6 SERIES III: Inline, dual overhead-cam six-cylinder. Cast-iron block and aluminum head. Displacement: 258 cid (4235 cc). Bore & Stroke: 3.63 x 4.17 in. (92 x 106

Model	Body Type & Seating	Engine Type/CID	P.O.E. Price	Weight (lbs.)	Production Total
XJ-S					
HE	2d Coupe-2+2P	V12/326	$32,100	4,075	3,348
XJ6 Series III					
III	4d Sedan-5P	I6/258	$29,500		**Note 1**
Vanden Plas	4d Sedan-5P	I6/258	$32,000	4,075	**Note 1**

Note 1: Combined production (in England) was approximately 14,422 six-cylinder cars.

Note 2: A total of 518 Jaguar XJ12 sedans also were produced, plus 835 12-cylinder Daimlers.

mm). Compression Ratio: 8.1:1. Brake Horsepower: 176 at 4750 rpm. Torque: 219 lbs.-ft. at 2500 rpm. Seven main bearings. Thimble tappets. Electronic fuel injection.

BASE SIX XJ6 VANDEN PLAS: Inline, dual overhead-cam six-cylinder. Cast-iron block and aluminum head. Displacement: 258 cid (4235 cc). Bore & Stroke: 3.63 x 4.17 in. (92 x 106 mm). Compression Ratio: 8.1:1. Brake Horsepower: 176 at 4750 rpm. Torque: 219 lbs.-ft. at 2500 rpm. Seven main bearings. Thimble tappets. Electronic fuel injection.

BASE V-12 XJ-S: 60-degree, "vee" type overhead-cam twelve-cylinder. Aluminum block and heads. Displacement: 326 cid (5343 cc). Bore & Stroke: 3.54 x 2.76 in. (90 x 70 mm). Compression Ratio: 11.5:1. Brake Horsepower: 262 at 5000 rpm. Torque: 290 lbs.-ft. at 3000 rpm. Seven main bearings. Thimble tappets. Electronic fuel injection.

CHASSIS

XJ6 SERIES III: Wheelbase: 112.8 in. Overall Length: 199.6 in. Height: 54.2 in. Width: 69.6 in. Front Tread: 58.3 in. Rear Tread: 58.9 in. Wheel Type: ventilated chrome disc. Standard Tires: 205/70VR15.

XJ6 VANDEN PLAS: Wheelbase: 112.8 in. Overall Length: 199.6 in. Height: 52.8 in. Width: 69.6 in. Front Tread: 58.3 in. Rear Tread: 58.9 in. Wheel Type: ventilated chrome disc. Standard Tires: 205/70VR15.

XJ-S: Wheelbase: 102.0 in. Overall Length: 191.3 in. Height: 49.6 in. Width: 70.6 in. Front Tread: 58.6 in. Rear Tread: 59.2 in. Wheel Type: cast aluminum alloy. Standard Tires: Dunlop 215/70VR15 Sports Super steel-belted-radial whitewalls.

TECHNICAL

XJ6 SERIES III: Layout: front-engine, rear-drive. Transmission: Borg-Warner automatic. Standard final drive ratio: 2.88:1. Steering: power rack-and-pinion. Suspension (front): "anti-dive" with coil springs and anti-roll bar. Suspension (rear): independent with lower wishbones, trailing lower radius arms and coil springs. Brakes: front/rear disc. Body Construction: steel unibody. Fuel Tank: 23.6 gallons.

XJ6 VANDEN PLAS: Layout: front-engine, rear-drive. Transmission: Borg-Warner automatic. Standard final drive ratio: 2.88:1. Steering: power rack-and-pinion. Suspension (front): "anti-dive" with coil springs and anti-roll bar. Suspension (rear): independent with lower wishbones, trailing

The 1982 Jaguar XJ-S interior.

lower radius arms and coil springs. Brakes: front/rear disc. Body Construction: steel unibody. Fuel Tank: 23.6 gallons.

XJ-S: Layout: front-engine, rear-drive. Transmission: Turbo-Hydra-Matic 400. Standard final drive ratio: 2.881. Steering: power rack-and-pinion. Suspension (front): "anti-dive" with coil springs and anti-roll bar. Suspension (rear): independent with lower wishbones, trailing lower radius arms, coil springs and anti-roll bar. Body Construction: steel unibody. Fuel Tank: 24 gallons.

PERFORMANCE

XJ6 SERIES III: Top Speed: 116 mph. Acceleration (0-60 mph): 9.6 seconds. Acceleration (quarter mile) 17.7 seconds at 77 mph. Fuel mileage: 17 mpg.

XJ-S: Top Speed: 140 to 150 mph. Acceleration (0-60 mph): 8.0 seconds. Acceleration (quarter mile): 15.9 seconds. Fuel mileage: 10 mpg.

CALENDAR YEAR SALES (U.S.): A total of 10,349 Jaguars were sold in the U.S. during calendar year 1982. The total included 8,940 XJ6 sedans and 1,409 XJ-S coupes.

OWNER: BL Plc., 35-38 Portman Sq., London, England.

MANUFACTURER: Jaguar Cars Ltd., Coventry, England.

DISTRIBUTOR: Jaguar Cars, Inc., 600 Willow Tree Road, Leonia, New Jersey.

HISTORY: Jaguar celebrated its 60th year in business in 1982. The 1982 models were introduced to U.S. buyers in October, 1981. In England, British Leyland, Ltd. became BL Plc. The U.S. branch was renamed Jaguar Cars Incorporated. With Triumph and Rover discontinued, the company's 330 U.S. dealers concentrated on Jaguar sales and increased them by 120 percent over 1981. The figure was even 40 percent better than the previous high set in 1976. In England, BL Plc. reported sales of $4,608,000,000, which was lower than 1981's total of $5,451,100,000. However, the company cut its losses from $644,480,000 in 1981 to just $344,000,000 in 1982. Production of all BL products fell from 517,000 units in 1981 to 514,000 in 1982. Graham W. Whitehead continued as president, Michael H. Dale continued as vice president of sales and service and Mike Cook continued as public relations manager.

1982 Jaguar Vanden Plas sedan

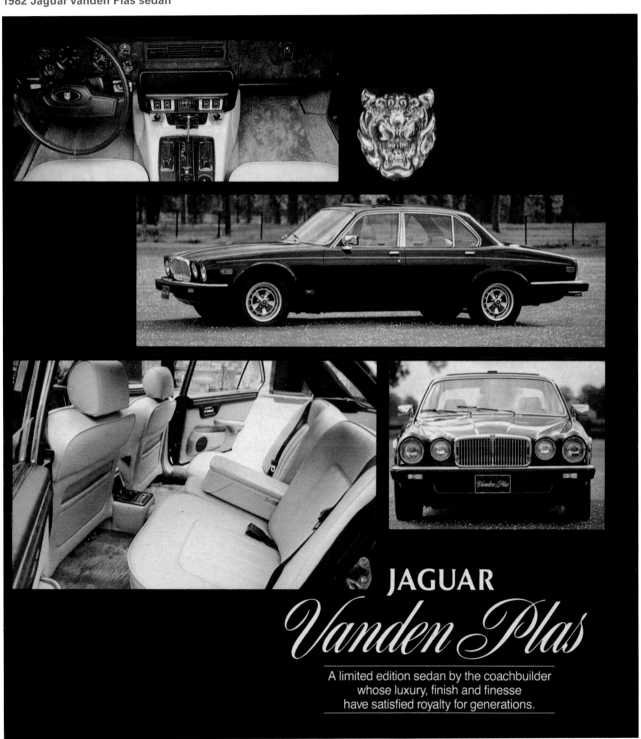

JAGUAR
Vanden Plas

A limited edition sedan by the coachbuilder
whose luxury, finish and finesse
have satisfied royalty for generations.

1983

XJ-S — V-12 — A revised version of the 12-cylinder coupe was anticipated during the 1983 model year, but did not arrive. Instead, this was a carryover model with details little changed from 1982. The V-12 engine continued with its high-swirl cylinder head. Standard equipment was similar to 1982. Standard equipment included an AM/FM radio with cassette, an adjustable steering column, cruise control, power windows, power door locks, a digital clock, a rear window defogger, 4-wheel power disc brakes, power steering, radial tires, reclining front seats, automatic temperature control air conditioning, tinted glass and aluminum styled wheels.

XJ6 - SERIES III — SIX — Production of Jaguar's basic sedan continued with little change. The engine was again the familiar twin-cam 4.2-litre six with electronic fuel injection. It was hooked to a three-speed automatic transmission. Standard equipment included an AM/FM radio with cassette, an adjustable steering column, cruise control, power windows, power door locks, a digital clock, a rear window defogger, 4-wheel power disc brakes, power steering, radial tires, reclining front seats, automatic temperature control air conditioning, tinted glass, aluminum styled wheels and a sunroof.

XJ6 VANDEN PLAS — SIX — The luxurious Vanden Plas included all of the XJ6 features plus extra equipment including full leather upholstery, woven throw rugs, a wood-veneer dash applique', rear-compartment reading lamps, a rear center armrest with built-in storage compartment, and special body emblems.

I.D. DATA: A 17-symbol Vehicle Identification Number is on the top left of the instrument panel, visible through the windshield. Symbols one through three indicate origin and make. Symbol four denotes the model; symbol five, the restraint system; symbol six, the body style ("1" = four-door sedan; "5" = two-door coupe). Symbol seven is the engine code; symbol eight, the steering and transmission code. Next is a check digit, followed by a letter indicating model year (D = 1983). Symbol 11 (letter C)

identifies the assembly plant, followed by a six-digit sequential production number. The starting serial numbers are: (XJ-S) SAJNV5()4()DC000001; (XJ6) SAJAV1()4()DC000001; (Vanden Plas) SAJAY1()4()DC000001.

ENGINES

BASE SIX XJ6 SERIES III: Inline, dual overhead-cam six-cylinder. Cast-iron block and aluminum head. Displacement: 258 cid (4235 cc). Bore & Stroke: 3.63 x 4.17 in. (92 x 106 mm). Compression Ratio: 8.1:1. Brake Horsepower: 176 at 4750 rpm. Torque: 219 lbs.-ft. at 2500 rpm. Seven main bearings. Thimble tappets. Electronic fuel injection.

BASE SIX XJ6 VANDEN PLAS: Inline, dual overhead-cam six-cylinder. Cast-iron block and aluminum head. Displacement: 258 cid (4235 cc). Bore & Stroke: 3.63 x 4.17 in. (92 x 106 mm). Compression Ratio: 8.1:1. Brake Horsepower: 176 at 4750 rpm. Torque: 219 lbs.-ft. at 2500 rpm. Seven main bearings. Thimble tappets. Electronic fuel injection.

BASE V-12 XJ-S: 60-degree, "vee" type overhead-cam twelve-cylinder. Aluminum block and heads. Displacement: 326 cid (5343 cc). Bore & Stroke: 3.54 x 2.76 in. (90 x 70 mm). Compression Ratio: 11.5:1. Brake Horsepower: 262 at 5000 rpm. Torque: 290 lbs.-ft. at 3000 rpm. Seven main bearings. Thimble tappets. Electronic fuel injection.

CHASSIS

XJ6 SERIES III: Wheelbase: 112.8 in. Overall Length: 199.6 in. Height: 52.8 in. Width: 69.6 in. Front Tread: 58.3 in. Rear Tread: 58.9 in. Wheel Type: ventilated chrome disc. Standard Tires: 205/70VR15.

XJ6 VANDEN PLAS: Wheelbase: 112.8 in. Overall Length: 199.6 in. Height: 52.8 in. Width: 69.6 in. Front Tread: 58.3 in. Rear Tread: 58.9 in. Wheel Type: ventilated chrome disc.

Standard Tires: 205/70VR15.

XJ-S: Wheelbase: 102.0 in. Overall Length: 191.7 in. Height: 47.8 in. Width: 70.6 in. Front Tread: 58.6 in. Rear Tread: 59.2 in. Wheel Type: cast aluminum alloy. Standard Tires: Dunlop 215/70VR15.

TECHNICAL

XJ6 SERIES III: Layout: front-engine, rear-drive. Transmission: Borg-Warner automatic. Standard final drive ratio: 2.88:1. Steering: power rack-and-pinion. Suspension (front): "anti-dive" with coil springs and anti-roll bar. Suspension (rear): independent with lower wishbones, trailing lower radius arms and coil springs. Brakes: front/rear disc. Body Construction: steel unibody. Fuel Tank: 23.6 gallons.

XJ6 VANDEN PLAS: Layout: front-engine, rear-drive. Transmission: Borg-Warner automatic. Standard final drive ratio: 2.88:1. Steering: power rack-and-pinion. Suspension (front): "anti-dive" with coil springs and anti-roll bar. Suspension (rear): independent with lower wishbones, trailing lower radius arms and coil springs. Brakes: front/rear disc. Body Construction: steel unibody. Fuel Tank: 23.6 gallons.

XJ-S: Layout: front-engine, rear-drive. Transmission: Turbo-Hydra-Matic 400. Standard final drive ratio: 2.88:1. Steering: power rack-and-pinion. Suspension (front): "anti-dive" with coil springs and anti-roll bar. Suspension (rear): independent with lower wishbones, trailing lower radius arms, coil springs and anti-roll bar. Body Construction: steel unibody. Fuel Tank: 24 gallons.

PERFORMANCE

XJ6 SERIES III: Top Speed: 116 mph. Acceleration (0-60 mph): 9.6 seconds. Acceleration (quarter mile) 17.7 seconds at 77 mph. Fuel mileage: 17 mpg.

XJ-S: Top Speed: 140 to 150 mph. Acceleration (0-60 mph):

1983 Jaguar Series III XJ6 sedan

IT JUST KEEPS GETTING BETTER AND BETTER: INTRODUCING THE MAGNIFICENT JAGUAR FOR '83

Model	Body Type & Seating	Engine Type/CID	P.O.E. Price	Weight (lbs.)	Production Total
XJ-S					
HE	2d Coupe-2+2P	V12/326	$34,000	3,950	4,457
XJ6 Series III					
III	4d Sedan-5P	I6/258	$30,500	4,066	**Note 1**
XJ6 Vanden Plas					
Vanden Plas	4d Sedan-5P	I6/258	$33,500	4,066	**Note 1**

Note 1: Combined production (in England) was approximately 17,412 six-cylinder cars.
Note 2: A total of 341 Jaguar XJ12 sedans also were produced.
Note 3: Jaguar also produced 3,206 Daimler sixes and 1,668 Daimler 12s.

Jaguar promoted its stylish XJ-S coupe in 1983 advertising.

8.0 seconds. Acceleration (quarter mile) 15.9 seconds. Fuel mileage: 10 mpg.

CALENDAR YEAR SALES (U.S.): A total of 15,815 Jaguars were sold in the U.S. during calendar year 1983. The total included 13,110 XJ6 sedans and 2,705 XJ-S coupes.

OWNER: BL Plc., 35-38 Portman Sq., London, England.

MANUFACTURER: Jaguar Cars Ltd., Coventry, England.

DISTRIBUTOR: Jaguar Cars, Inc., 600 Willow Tree Road, Leonia, New Jersey.

HISTORY: Introduced in U.S. market in November, 1982. A cabriolet version of the XJ-S became available in Europe late in 1983, but would not arrive in the U.S. market until the 1987 model year. The company's U.S. dealer count had dropped to 205 outlets by the beginning of 1983, but Jaguar sales in the "States" were up 53 percent and set a record for the second year in a row. That was 33 percent above the 21,800 cars sold worldwide in 1982. "Home Market" sales in England were 7,050, which made Jaguar the leading luxury car maker in the United Kingdom. Graham W. Whitehead continued as president, Michael H. Dale continued as vice president of sales and service and Mike Cook continued as public relations manager.

1984 Jaguar Series III XJ6 sedan

1984

XJ-S — V-12 — Except for the addition of halogen headlights and new body color choices, the Jaguar coupe was a carryover from 1983. A total of 10 colors now were offered. As before, the 326-cid (5.3-litre) V-12 engine drove a General Motor THM-400 80 three-speed automatic transmission. Standard equipment included power four-wheel disc brakes, power steering and all the features listed with the XJ6 sedan, plus full leather interior trim, leather-bound steering wheel, and burl-elm instrument panel applique' and door inserts.

XJ6 — SERIES III — SIX — Halogen headlights went on the six-cylinder four-door sedan which was again offered in base and Vanden Plas editions. Product changes were otherwise minimal. Both models wore 205/70VR15 Pirelli P5 tires. The bodies of the base model came in 10 colors, while the Vanden Plas had a choice of five (versus just two in the prior year). The drivetrain was the same as in 1983: a 4.2-litre Inline six hooked to GM's THM-400 80 three-speed automatic transmission. As before, the interior featured wood dashboard trim and leather-faced seats. Standard equipment also included power four-wheel disc brakes, power steering, a power sunroof, cruise control, automatic air conditioning, an AM/FM stereo radio with cassette player and power antenna, tinted glass, central door locking, intermittent wipers, power windows and mirrors, an electric rear-window defroster, a power driver's seat and an adjustable steering column.

XJ6 VANDEN PLAS — SIX — The more posh Vanden Plas added rear-compartment reading lamps, woven throw rugs, a wood-veneer dash applique', rear center armrest with storage compartment, full leather upholstery, and special body emblems.

I.D. DATA: A 17-symbol Vehicle Identification Number is on the top left of the instrument panel, visible through the windshield. Symbols 1 through 3 indicate origin and make. Symbol four denotes model; symbol five, the restraint system; symbol six, the body style ("1" = four-door sedan; "5" = two-door coupe). Symbol seven is the engine code; symbol eight, the steering and transmission code. Next is a check digit, followed by a letter indicating model year (E = 1984). Symbol 11 (letter C) identifies the assembly plant, followed by a six-digit sequential production number. The starting serial numbers are: (XJ-S) SAJNV5()4()EC000001; (XJ6) SAJAV1()4()EC000001; (Vanden Plas) SAJAY1()4()EC000001.

ENGINE

BASE SIX XJ6: Inline, dual overhead-cam six-cylinder. Cast-iron block and aluminum head. Displacement: 258 cid (4235 cc). Bore & Stroke: 3.63 x 4.17 in. (92 x 106 mm). Compression Ratio: 8.1:1. Brake Horsepower: 176 at 4750 rpm. Torque: 219 lbs.-ft. at 2500 rpm. Seven main bearings. Thimble tappets. Electronic fuel injection.

Model	Body Type & Seating	Engine Type/CID	P.O.E. Price	Weight (lbs.)	Production Total
XJ-S					
HE	2d Coupe-2+2P	V12/326	$34,700	3,950	5,813
XJ6 Series III					
III	4d Sedan-5P	I6/258	$31,100	4,066	Note 1
XJ6 Vanden Plas					
Vanden Plas	4d Sedan-5P	I6/258	$34,200	4,066	Note 1

Note 1: Combined production (in England) was approximately 19,578 six-cylinder Jaguars.
Note 2: A total of 1,509 Jaguar XJ12 sedans also were produced.
Note 3: Jaguar also produced 3,206 Daimler sixes and 1,005 Daimler 12s.

1984 Jaguar XJ-S coupe

BASE SIX XJ6 VANDEN PLAS: Inline, dual overhead-cam six-cylinder. Cast-iron block and aluminum head. Displacement: 258 cid (4235 cc). Bore & Stroke: 3.63 x 4.17 in. (92 x 106 mm). Compression Ratio: 8.1:1. Brake Horsepower: 176 at 4750 rpm. Torque: 219 lbs.-ft. at 2500 rpm. Seven main bearings. Thimble tappets. Electronic fuel injection.

BASE V-12 XJ-S: 60-degree, "vee" type overhead-cam twelve-cylinder. Aluminum block and heads. Displacement: 326 cid (5343 cc). Bore & Stroke: 3.54 x 2.76 in. (90 x 70 mm). Compression Ratio: 11.5:1. Brake Horsepower: 262 at 5000 rpm. Torque: 290 lbs.-ft. at 3000 rpm. Seven main bearings. Thimble tappets. Electronic fuel injection.

CHASSIS

XJ6 SERIES III: Wheelbase: 112.8 in. Overall Length: 199.6 in. Height: 52.8 in. Width: 69.6 in. Front Tread: 58.3 in. Rear Tread: 58.9 in. Wheel Type: ventilated chrome disc. Standard Tires: 205/70VR15.

XJ6 VANDEN PLAS: Wheelbase: 112.8 in. Overall Length: 199.6 in. Height: 52.8 in. Width: 69.6 in. Front Tread: 58.3 in. Rear Tread: 58.9 in. Wheel Type: ventilated chrome disc. Standard Tires: 205/70VR15.

XJ-S: Wheelbase: 102.0 in. Overall Length: 191.7 in. Height: 47.8 in. Width: 70.6 in. Front Tread: 58.6 in. Rear Tread: 59.2 in. Wheel Type: cast aluminum alloy. Standard Tires: Dunlop 215/70VR15.

TECHNICAL

XJ6 SERIES III: Layout: front-engine, rear-drive. Transmission: Borg-Warner automatic. Standard final drive ratio: 2.88:1. Steering: power rack-and-pinion. Suspension (front): "anti-dive" with coil springs and anti-roll bar. Suspension (rear): independent with lower wishbones, trailing lower radius arms and coil springs. Brakes: front/rear disc. Body Construction: steel unibody. Fuel Tank: 23.6 gallons.

XJ6 VANDEN PLAS: Layout: front-engine, rear-drive. Transmission: Borg-Warner automatic. Standard final drive ratio: 2.88:1. Steering: power rack-and-pinion. Suspension (front): "anti-dive" with coil springs and anti-roll bar. Suspension (rear): independent with lower wishbones, trailing lower radius arms and coil springs. Brakes: front/rear disc. Body Construction: steel unibody. Fuel Tank: 23.6 gallons.

XJ-S: Layout: front-engine, rear-drive. Transmission: Turbo-Hydra-Matic 400. Standard final drive ratio: 2.88:1. Steering:

power rack-and-pinion. Suspension (front): "anti-dive" with coil springs and anti-roll bar. Suspension (rear): independent with lower wishbones, trailing lower radius arms, coil springs and anti-roll bar. Body Construction: steel unibody. Fuel Tank: 24 gallons.

PERFORMANCE

XJ6 SERIES III: Top Speed: 116 mph. Acceleration (0-60 mph): 9.6 seconds. Acceleration (quarter mile): 17.7 seconds at 77 mph. Fuel mileage: 17 mpg.

XJ-S: Top Speed: 140-150 mph. Acceleration (0-60 mph): 8.0 seconds. Acceleration (quarter mile): 15.9 seconds. Fuel mileage: 10 mpg.

CALENDAR YEAR SALES (U.S.): A total of 18,044 Jaguars were sold in the U.S. during 1984. The total included 14,564 XJ6 sedans and 3,480 XJ-S coupes.

OWNER: BL Plc., 35-38 Portman Sq., London, England; then Jaguar PLC, Browns Lane, Allesley, Coventry, England

MANUFACTURER: Jaguar PLC, Browns Lane, Allesley, Coventry, England.

DISTRIBUTOR: Jaguar Cars, Inc., 600 Willow Tree Road, Leonia, New Jersey.

HISTORY: Introduced in U.S. market in October 1983. The company's U.S. dealer count dropped to 190. Graham W. Whitehead continued as president, Michael H. Dale continued as vice president of sales and service and Mike Cook continued as public relations manager. In August, Jaguar Cars, Ltd. was spun off from BL PLC (a British government-owned entity) to become a stock company called Jaguar PLC. Public reaction was a strong demand for shares in Jaguar. In fact, demand for the shares was over-subscribed within a half-hour of the initial public offering on the London Stock Exchange. Underlying the change was the fact that Jaguar returned to profitability with worldwide sales of 32,956 cars in calendar-year 1984. That was a 15 percent increase. U.S. sales, up 14 percent, were another record. Home Market sales were also a record, as were deliveries in West Germany and Canada. Jaguar PLC had sales of $919,400,000 and earned a profit of $61,800,000. The "new" company had about 9,500 employees.

1984 Jaguar XJ-S coupe

1985

XJ-S — V-12 — Appearance and standard equipment for the HE (High Efficiency) coupe were similar to 1984. Standard equipment included the V-12 engine, automatic transmission, power four-wheel disc brakes, power steering, automatic temperature control air conditioning, tinted glass, styled aluminum wheels, a radio and cassette, an adjustable steering column, cruise control, power windows, power door locks, a digital clock, a rear window defogger, a rear window wiper, full leather interior trim, a leather-bound steering wheel, a burl-elm instrument panel applique' and burl-elm door inserts.

XJ6 — SERIES III — SIX — Standard equipment included the I6 engine, automatic transmission, power four-wheel disc brakes, power steering, automatic temperature control air conditioning, tinted glass, styled aluminum wheels, a 40-watt stereo radio and cassette player, an adjustable steering column, a trip computer, cruise control, power windows, power door locks, a digital clock, a rear window defogger and a rear window wiper.

XJ6 VANDEN PLAS — SIX — The six-cylinder Vanden Plas sedan added rear-compartment reading lamps, woven throw rugs, a wood-veneer dash applique', rear center armrest with storage compartment, full leather upholstery, and special body emblems.

I.D. DATA: A 17-symbol Vehicle Identification Number is on the top left of the instrument panel, visible through the windshield. Symbols 1 through 3 indicate origin and make. Symbol four denotes the model; symbol five, the restraint system; symbol six, the body style ("1" = four-door sedan; "5" = two-door coupe). Symbol seven is the engine code; and symbol eight, the steering and transmission code. Next is a check digit, followed by a letter indicating model year (F = 1985). Symbol 11 (letter C) identifies the assembly plant, followed by a six-digit sequential production number. Starting serial numbers are: (XJ-S) SAJNV5()4()FC000001; (XJ6) SAJAV1()4()FC000001; (Vanden Plas) SAJAY1()4()FC000001.

ENGINE

BASE SIX XJ6: Inline, dual overhead-cam six-cylinder. Cast-iron block and aluminum head. Displacement: 258 cid (4235 cc). Bore & Stroke: 3.63 x 4.17 in. (92 x 106 mm). Compression Ratio: 8.1:1. Brake Horsepower: 176 at 4750 rpm. Torque: 219 lbs.-ft. at 2500 rpm. Seven main bearings. Thimble tappets. Electronic fuel injection.

BASE SIX XJ6 VANDEN PLAS: Inline, dual overhead-cam six-cylinder. Cast-iron block and aluminum head. Displacement: 258 cid (4235 cc). Bore & Stroke: 3.63 x 4.17 in. (92 x 106 mm). Compression Ratio: 8.1:1. Brake Horsepower:

176 at 4750 rpm. Torque: 219 lbs.-ft. at 2500 rpm. Seven main bearings. Thimble tappets. Electronic fuel injection.

BASE V-12 XJ-S: 60-degree, "vee" type overhead-cam twelve-cylinder. Aluminum block and heads. Displacement: 326 cid (5343 cc). Bore & Stroke: 3.54 x 2.76 in. (90 x 70 mm). Compression Ratio: 11.5:1. Brake Horsepower: 262 at 5000 rpm. Torque: 290 lbs.-ft. at 3000 rpm. Seven main bearings. Thimble tappets. Electronic fuel injection.

CHASSIS

XJ6 SERIES III: Wheelbase: 113 in. Overall Length: 199.6 in. Height: 52.8 in. Width: 69.6 in. Front Tread: 58.3 in. Rear Tread: 58.9 in. Wheel Type: ventilated chrome disc. Standard Tires: 215/70VR15 Pirelli P5.

XJ6 VANDEN PLAS: Wheelbase: 112.8 in. Overall Length: 199.6 in. Height: 52.8 in. Width: 69.6 in. Front Tread: 58.3 in. Rear Tread: 58.9 in. Wheel Type: ventilated chrome disc. Standard Tires: 205/70VR15.

XJ-S: Wheelbase: 102.0 in. Overall Length: 191.7 in. Height: 47.8 in. Width: 70.6 in. Front Tread: 58.6 in. Rear Tread: 59.2 in. Wheel Type: cast aluminum alloy. Standard Tires: Dunlop 215/70VR15.

TECHNICAL

XJ6 SERIES III: Layout: front-engine, rear-drive. Transmission: Borg-Warner automatic. Standard final drive ratio: 2.88:1. Steering: power rack-and-pinion. Suspension (front): "anti-dive" with coil springs and anti-roll bar. Suspension (rear): independent with lower wishbones, trailing lower radius arms and coil springs. Brakes: front/rear disc. Body Construction: steel unibody. Fuel Tank: 23.6 gallons.

XJ6 VANDEN PLAS: Layout: front-engine, rear-drive.

Transmission: Borg-Warner automatic. Standard final drive ratio: 2.88:1. Steering: power rack-and-pinion. Suspension (front): "anti-dive" with coil springs and anti-roll bar. Suspension (rear): independent with lower wishbones, trailing lower radius arms and coil springs. Brakes: front/rear disc. Body Construction: steel unibody. Fuel Tank: 23.6 gallons.

XJ-S: Layout: front-engine, rear-drive. Transmission: Turbo-Hydra-Matic 400. Standard final drive ratio: 2.881. Steering: power rack-and-pinion. Suspension (front): ""anti-dive" with coil springs and anti-roll bar. Suspension (rear): independent with lower wishbones, trailing lower radius arms, coil springs and anti-roll bar. Body Construction: steel unibody. Fuel Tank: 24 gallons.

PERFORMANCE

XJ6 SERIES III: Top Speed: 116 mph. Acceleration (0-60 mph): 9.6 seconds. Acceleration (quarter mile): 17.7 seconds at 77 mph. Fuel mileage: 17 mpg.

XJ-S: Top Speed: 140 to 150 mph. Acceleration (0-60 mph): 8.0 seconds. Acceleration (quarter mile): 15.9 seconds. Fuel mileage: 10 mpg.

CALENDAR YEAR SALES (U.S.): A total of 20,528 Jaguars were sold in the U.S. during 1985. The total included 16,744 XJ6 sedans and 3,784 XJ-S coupes.

MANUFACTURER: Jaguar PLC, Coventry, England.

DISTRIBUTOR: Jaguar Cars, Inc., 600 Willow Tree Road, Leonia, New Jersey.

HISTORY: Introduced in the U.S. in September, 1984. A new all-alloy AJ6 (Advanced Jaguar) six-cylinder engine, as introduced in Europe for the 1984 model year, was expected in U.S. models, along with a new cabriolet (convertible) body style.

The Group 44 Jaguar XJR-7 shows its racing prowess. *Bob Harrington*

Model	Body Type & Seating	Engine Type/CID	P.O.E. Price	Weight (lbs.)	Production Total
XJ-S HE					
XJ-S	2d Coupe-2+2P	V12/326	$36,000	3,980	N/A
XJ6 Series III					
XJ6	4d Sedan-5P	I6/258	$32,250	4,075	N/A
XJ6 Vanden Plas					
VDP	4d Sedan-5P	I6/258	$35,550	4,081	N/A

1985 Jaguar Series III XJ6 sedan

As offered in Europe, the new 3.6-litre six, which would replace the long-lived XK-derived inline six-cylinder engine, produced 225 hp and 240 lbs.-ft. of torque, using 9.6:1 compression. The convertible would not arrive until the 1987 model year, the new engine a year later. Jaguar ranked among the top five car models in J.D. Power's Consumer Satisfaction Index for two years in a row, a dramatic change for a company whose products had formerly suffered quality problems. Still, the company's U.S. dealer count dropped to 173. Jaguar PLC had sales of $1,082,400,000 and earned a profit of $127,000,000. Jaguar PLC had 10,200 employees. Graham W. Whitehead continued as president, Michael H. Dale continued as vice president of sales and service and Mike Cook continued as public relations manager of Jaguar Cars, Inc. in New Jersey.

In England, Sir William Lyons passed away. From his partnership with William Walmsley in 1922 through his official retirement in 1972 and well beyond that date, Sir William was the heart and soul of Jaguar. One could almost have put his image on the cars in place of the Jaguar head. Knighted in 1956, he was always known for putting his own touches on the cars he built. He was also frugal and had a stubborn streak. When owners questioned design features, said the Jag-Lovers Web site, "...the answer is always that's the way Lyons wanted it to be." When a New York XK-140 owner questioned why his heater didn't work well in cold weather Lyons answered "Young man, you just put on an overcoat." He earned his place among other icons of the automotive world.

THE TWO MOST EXCITING ENGINES IN THE WORLD.

THE JAGUAR V-12

In the luxurious street version Jaguar XJ-S an electronic ignition system unleashes the only production V-12 engine in America. The fuel injected aluminum alloy Jaguar V-12 develops 262 HP for a top speed of 139 mph. At normal cruising speed the car has immense reserves of torque for passing or evasive maneuvers. *Road & Track* (May 1984) voted it "Best sports/GT car over $25,000." In its unique blending of exhilarating performance, creature comforts, silence and smoothness, the Jaguar S-type is perhaps the most seductive GT machine in the world.

THE JAGUAR V-12

Jaguars have blazed a trail of glory on the world's legendary tracks from LeMans to Sebring to Daytona. Today, the XJR-5 prototype carries forth this proud heritage. With a modified Jaguar V-12 engine the prototype develops 600 HP for a top speed of over 230 mph. Four victories for the XJR-5 in its first full season of IMSA racing have added to the Jaguar legend. Thus far in 1984, Jaguars have run at eight IMSA GT events. The results: XJR-5s have finished in the top three 10 times including a 1-2 sweep of the Miami Grand Prix.

JAGUAR
A BLENDING OF ART AND MACHINE

Jaguar's XJ-S coupe and Group 44 racer together in a 1985 ad.

1986

XJ-S — V-12 — Appearance and standard equipment for the Jaguar's coupe were similar to 1985. New body colors included British Racing Green. A power sunroof joined the options list. It was priced at $1,300. Though ostensibly a four-seater, even Jaguar described the V-12 coupe's back seat as "occasional seating for two." Standard equipment included the V-12 engine, automatic transmission, power four-wheel disc brakes, power steering, automatic temperature control air conditioning, tinted glass, styled aluminum wheels, a radio and cassette, an adjustable steering column, cruise control, power windows, power door locks, a digital clock, a rear window defogger, a rear window wiper, full leather interior trim, a leather-bound steering wheel, a burl-elm instrument panel applique' and burl-elm door inserts.

XJ6 SERIES III — SIX — British Racing Green was one of the new color choices for the Jaguar six-cylinder sedan. A walnut finish was added to the center console of the base sedan, while the Vanden Plas added rear-seat headrests. Otherwise, appearance and equipment were similar to 1985. Standard equipment included the I6 engine, automatic transmission, power four-wheel disc brakes, power steering, automatic temperature control air conditioning, tinted glass, styled aluminum wheels, a 40-watt stereo radio and cassette player, an adjustable steering column, a trip computer, cruise control, power windows, power door locks, a digital clock, a rear window defogger and a rear window wiper.

XJ6 VANDEN PLAS — SIX — The six-cylinder Vanden Plas sedan added rear-compartment reading lamps, woven throw rugs, a wood-veneer dash applique', rear center armrest with storage compartment, full leather upholstery, and special body emblems.

I.D. DATA: A 17-symbol Vehicle Identification Number is on the top left of the instrument panel, visible through the windshield. Symbols 1 through 3 indicate origin and make. Symbol four denotes the model; symbol five, the restraint system; symbol six, the body style ("1" = four-door sedan; "5" = two-door coupe). Symbol seven is the engine code; symbol eight, the steering and transmission code. Next is a check digit, followed by a letter indicating model year (G = 1986). Symbol 11 (letter C) identifies the assembly plant, followed by a six-digit sequential production number. Starting serial numbers are: (XJ-S) SAJNV5()4()GC000001; (XJ6) SAJAV1()4()GC000001; (Vanden Plas) SAJAY1()4()GC000001.

ENGINE

BASE SIX XJ6: Inline, dual overhead-cam six-cylinder. Cast-iron block and aluminum head. Displacement: 258 cid (4235 cc). Bore & Stroke: 3.63 x 4.17 in. (92 x 106 mm). Compression Ratio: 8.1:1. Brake Horsepower: 176 at 4750 rpm. Torque: 219 lbs.-ft. at 2500 rpm. Seven main bearings. Thimble tappets. Electronic fuel injection.

BASE SIX XJ6 VANDEN PLAS: Inline, dual overhead-cam six-cylinder. Cast-iron block and aluminum head. Displacement: 258 cid (4235 cc). Bore & Stroke: 3.63 x 4.17 in. (92 x 106 mm). Compression Ratio: 8.1:1. Brake Horsepower: 176 at 4750 rpm. Torque: 219 lbs.-ft. at 2500 rpm. Seven main bearings. Thimble tappets. Electronic fuel injection.

Model	Body Type & Seating	Engine Type/ CID	P.O.E. Price	Weight (lbs.)	Prod. Total
XJ-S HE					
XJ-S	2d Coupe-2+2P	V12/326	$36,000	3,980	N/A
XJ6 Series III					
Series III	4d Sedan-5P	I6/258	$32,250	4,064	N/A
XJ6 Vanden Plas					
Vanden Plas	4d Sedan-5P	I6/258	$35,550	4,074	N/A

BASE V-12 XJ-S: 60-degree, "vee" type overhead-cam twelve-cylinder. Aluminum block and heads. Displacement: 326 cid (5343 cc). Bore & Stroke: 3.54 x 2.76 in. (90 x 70 mm). Compression Ratio: 11.5:1. Brake Horsepower: 262 at 5000 rpm. Torque: 290 lbs.-ft. at 3000 rpm. Seven main bearings. Thimble tappets. Electronic fuel injection.

CHASSIS

XJ6 SERIES III: Wheelbase: 113 in. Overall Length: 199.6 in. Height: 52.8 in. Width: 69.6 in. Front Tread: 58.3 in. Rear Tread: 58.9 in. Wheel Type: ventilated chrome disc. Standard Tires: 215/70VR15 Pirelli P5.

XJ6 VANDEN PLAS: Wheelbase: 113 in. Overall Length: 199.6 in. Height: 52.8 in. Width: 69.6 in. Front Tread: 58.3 in. Rear Tread: 58.9 in. Wheel Type: ventilated chrome disc. Standard Tires: 205/70VR15.

XJ-S: Wheelbase: 102.0 in. Overall Length: 191.7 in. Height: 47.8 in. Width: 70.6 in. Front Tread: 58.6 in. Rear Tread: 59.2 in. Wheel Type: cast aluminum alloy. Standard Tires: Dunlop 215/70VR15.

TECHNICAL

XJ6 SERIES III: Layout: front-engine, rear-drive. Transmission: Borg-Warner automatic. Standard final drive ratio: 2.88:1. Steering: power rack-and-pinion. Suspension (front): "anti-dive" with coil springs and anti-roll bar. Suspension (rear): independent; lower control arms, longitudinal links, coil springs and anti-roll bar. Brakes: front/rear disc. Body Construction: steel unibody. Fuel Tank: 23.6 gallons.

XJ6 VANDEN PLAS: Layout: front-engine, rear-drive. Transmission: Borg-Warner automatic. Standard final drive ratio: 2.88:1. Steering: power rack-and-pinion. Suspension (front): "anti-dive" with coil springs and anti-roll bar. Suspension (rear): independent; lower control arms, longitudinal links, coil springs and anti-roll bar. Brakes: front/rear disc. Body Construction: steel unibody. Fuel Tank: 23.6 gallons.

XJ-S: Layout: front-engine, rear-drive. Transmission: Turbo-Hydra-Matic 400. Standard final drive ratio: 2.881. Steering: power rack-and-pinion. Suspension (front): "anti-dive" with coil springs and anti-roll bar. Suspension (rear): independent; lower control arms, longitudinal links, coil springs and anti-roll bar. Body Construction: steel unibody. Fuel Tank: 24 gallons.

OPTIONS: Power sunroof: XJ-S ($1,300). A sun roof was installed in 19,639 of the 24,464 Jaguars sold in the U.S. during calendar-year 1986.

PERFORMANCE

XJ6 SERIES III: Top Speed: 116 mph. Acceleration (0-60 mph): 9.6 seconds. Acceleration (quarter mile): 17.7 seconds at 77 mph. Fuel mileage: 17 mpg.

XJ-S: Top Speed: 140 to 150 mph. Acceleration (0-60 mph): 8.0 seconds. Acceleration (quarter mile): 15.9 seconds. Fuel mileage: 10 mpg.

CALENDAR YEAR SALES (U.S.): A total of 24,464 Jaguars were sold in the U.S. during calendar-year 1986. The total included 19,579 XJ6 sedans and 4,885 XJ-S coupes.

MANUFACTURER: Jaguar PLC, Coventry, England.

DISTRIBUTOR: Jaguar Cars, Inc., 600 Willow Tree Road, Leonia, New Jersey.

HISTORY: Introduced in the U.S. in October 1985. Graham W. Whitehead continued as president, Michael H. Dale continued as vice president of sales and service and Mike Cook continued as public relations manager of Jaguar Cars, Inc. in New Jersey. This was Jaguar's fifth consecutive year of sales increases and the total for the calendar year was up 19 percent from 1985. Sales of the Series II XJ6 sedan were a record and increased 17 percent over 1985. XJ-S sales were also a record. Jaguar PLC, the British parent firm, had sales of $1,339,000,000 and earned a profit of $134,500,000. Worldwide sales were again a record at 41,256 cars, up eight percent for the year. Jaguar PLC had 10,200 employees.

1986 Jaguar XJ-S coupe *Dan Lyons*

1986 Jaguar XJ-S coupe

The XJ-S coupe and XJ-SC cabriolet together in a 1986 ad.

The 1987 Jaguar XJ-S coupe with (bottom to top) an SS 100, XK 120 and D-type.

1987

XJ-S — V-12 — Appearance and standard equipment for Jaguar's coupe were similar to 1986. Standard equipment included the V-12 engine, automatic transmission, power four-wheel disc brakes, power steering, automatic-temperature-control air conditioning, tinted glass, styled aluminum wheels, a radio and cassette, an adjustable steering column, cruise control, a rear window defogger, a rear window wiper, full leather interior trim, a leather-bound steering wheel, and a burl-elm instrument panel applique'.

XJ-SC — V-12 — At Jaguar, the big news for 1987 was the arrival of a new XJ-SC two-seat cabriolet to join the original V-12 coupe. It debuted in the U.S. in the spring of 1986. The new model had removable Targa roof panels and a manually-operated folding rear-quarter top. It was based on a modified standard coupe. For 1987, a removable hardtop section was offered. The "hardtop" had heated rear glass and could be mounted in place of the standard folding soft top. The cabriolet included full rear luggage-area carpeting. A manual override was added to the climate-control system.

XJ-S HESS & EISENHART — V-12 — Hess & Eisenhart, based in Ohio, was a builder of high-quality "professional cars" such as presidential limousines, funeral cars and ambulances. In 1987, the firm started converting XJ-S coupes into true open touring cars without the "roll cage" structure of the factory-

built, Targa-style Cabriolet. Standard equipment was similar to that of the coupe.

XJ6 — SIX — Prices jumped sharply, yet standard equipment included the I6 engine, automatic transmission, power four-wheel disc brakes, power steering, automatic-temperature-control air conditioning, tinted glass, a digital clock, cruise control, delay windshield wipers, and a rear window defogger, dual remote-control OSRV mirrors, styled aluminum wheels, a radio and a cassette player.

XJ6 VANDEN PLAS — SIX — The Vanden Plas edition came with all XJ6 equipment, plus a special wood-veneer dash applique', full leather upholstery, rear center armrest, and rear reading lamps.

I.D. DATA: A 17-symbol Vehicle Identification Number is on the top left of the instrument panel, visible through the windshield. Symbols one through three indicate origin and make. Symbol four denotes model; symbol five, the restraint system; symbol six, the body style ("1" = four-door sedan; "5" = two-door coupe; "3" = cabriolet). Symbol seven is the engine code; symbol eight, the steering and transmission code. Next is a check digit, followed by a letter indicating model year (H = 1987). Symbol 11 (letter C) identifies the assembly plant, followed by a six-digit sequential production number. Starting serial numbers

MODEL	BODY TYPE & SEATING	ENGINE TYPE/CID	P.O.E. PRICE	WEIGHT (LBS.)	PRODUCTION TOTAL
XJ-S					
XJ-S	2d Coupe-2+2P	V12/326	$39,700	3,980	N/A
XJ-SC Cabriolet					
XJ-SC	2d Cabriolet-2P	V12/326	$44,250	4,040	N/A
XJ-S Hess & Eisenhart Convertible					
XJ-SC	2d Convertible-2P	V12/326	$46,950	4,040	N/A
XJ6 Series III					
XJ6	4d Sedan-5P	I6/258	$36,300	4,,064	N/A
XJ6 Vanden Plas					
Vanden Plas	4d Sedan-5P	I6/258	$40,100	4,074	N/A

The beautiful profile of the 1987 Jaguar XJ6 sedan.

are: (XJ-S coupe) SAJNV5()4()HC000001; (XJ-S cabriolet) SAJNV3()4()HC000001; (XJ6) SAJAV1()4()HC000001; (Vanden Plas) SAJAY1()4()HC000001.

ENGINE

BASE SIX XJ6: Inline, dual overhead-cam six-cylinder. Cast-iron block and aluminum head. Displacement: 258 cid (4235 cc). Bore & Stroke: 3.63 x 4.17 in. (92 x 106 mm). Compression Ratio: 8.1:1. Brake Horsepower: 176 at 4750 rpm. Torque: 219 lbs.-ft. at 2500 rpm. Seven main bearings. Thimble tappets. Electronic fuel injection.

BASE SIX XJ6 VANDEN PLAS: Inline, dual overhead-cam six-cylinder. Cast-iron block and aluminum head. Displacement: 258 cid (4235 cc). Bore & Stroke: 3.63 x 4.17 in. (92 x 106 mm). Compression Ratio: 8.1:1. Brake Horsepower: 176 at 4750 rpm. Torque: 219 lbs.-ft. at 2500 rpm. Seven main bearings. Thimble tappets. Electronic fuel injection.

BASE V-12 XJ-SC CABRIOLET AND XJ-S CONVERTIBLE: 60-degree, "vee" type overhead-cam twelve-cylinder. Aluminum block and heads. Displacement: 326 cid (5343 cc). Bore & Stroke: 3.54 x 2.76 in. (90 x 70 mm). Compression Ratio: 11.5:1. Brake Horsepower: 252 at 5000 rpm.. Seven main bearings. Thimble tappets. Electronic fuel injection.

BASE V-12 XJ-S COUPE: 60-degree, "vee" type overhead-cam twelve-cylinder. Aluminum block and heads. Displacement: 326 cid (5343 cc). Bore & Stroke: 3.54 x 2.76 in. (90 x 70 mm). Compression Ratio: 11.5:1. Brake Horsepower: 262 at 5000 rpm. Torque: 290 lbs.-ft. at 3000 rpm. Seven main bearings. Thimble tappets. Electronic fuel injection.

CHASSIS

XJ6 SERIES III: Wheelbase: 113 in. Overall Length: 199.6 in. Height: 52.8 in. Width: 69.6 in. Front Tread: 58.3 in. Rear Tread: 58.9 in. Wheel Type: ventilated chrome disc. Standard Tires: 215/70VR15 Pirelli P5.

XJ6 VANDEN PLAS: Wheelbase: 113 in. Overall Length: 199.6 in. Height: 52.8 in. Width: 69.6 in. Front Tread: 58.3

in. Rear Tread: 58.9 in. Wheel Type: ventilated chrome disc. Standard Tires: 205/70VR15.

XJ-SC CABRIOLET AND XJ-S CONVERTIBLE:
Wheelbase: 102.0 in. Overall Length: 191.7 in. Height: 47.8 in. Width: 70.6 in. Front Tread: 58.6 in. Rear Tread: 59.2 in. Wheel Type: cast aluminum alloy. Standard Tires: Dunlop 215/70VR15.

XJ-S COUPE:
Wheelbase: 102.0 in. Overall Length: 191.7 in. Height: 47.8 in. Width: 70.6 in. Front Tread: 58.6 in. Rear Tread: 59.2 in. Wheel Type: cast aluminum alloy. Standard Tires: Dunlop 215/70VR15.

TECHNICAL

XJ6 SERIES III: Layout: front-engine, rear-drive. Transmission: Borg-Warner automatic. Standard final drive ratio: 2.88:1:1. Steering: power rack-and-pinion. Suspension (front): "anti-dive" with coil springs and anti-roll bar. Suspension (rear): independent; lower control arms, longitudinal links, coil springs and anti-roll bar. Brakes: front/rear disc. Body Construction: steel unibody. Fuel Tank: 23.6 gallons.

XJ6 VANDEN PLAS: Layout: front-engine, rear-drive. Transmission: Borg-Warner automatic. Standard final drive ratio: 2.88:1:1. Steering: power rack-and-pinion. Suspension (front): "anti-dive" with coil springs and anti-roll bar. Suspension (rear): independent; lower control arms, longitudinal links, coil springs and anti-roll bar. Brakes: front/rear disc. Body Construction: steel unibody. Fuel Tank: 23.6 gallons.

XJ-S (ALL): Layout: front-engine, rear-drive. Transmission: Turbo-Hydra-Matic 400. Standard final drive ratio: 2.88:1:1. Steering: power rack-and-pinion. Suspension (front): "anti-dive" with coil springs and anti-roll bar. Suspension (rear): independent; lower control arms, longitudinal links, coil springs and anti-roll bar. Body Construction: steel unibody. Fuel Tank: 24 gallons.

OPTIONS: Rear window defogger for XJ-S (installed in 83 percent of cars sold in the U.S.)

PERFORMANCE

XJ6 SERIES III: Top Speed: 116 mph. Acceleration (0-60 mph): 9.6 seconds. Acceleration (quarter mile): 17.7 seconds at 77 mph. Fuel mileage: 17 mpg.

XJ-S: Top Speed: 140 to 150 mph. Acceleration (0-60 mph): 8.0 seconds. Acceleration (quarter mile): 15.9 seconds. Fuel mileage: 10 mpg.

CALENDAR YEAR SALES (U.S.): A total of 22,919 Jaguars were sold in the U.S. during calendar year 1987. The total included 17,271 XJ6 sedans and 5,648 XJ-S coupes, convertibles and cabriolets.

MANUFACTURER: Jaguar PLC, Browns Lane, Allesley, Coventry, England.

DISTRIBUTOR: Jaguar Cars, Inc., 600 Willow Tree Road, Leonia, New Jersey.

HISTORY: The 1987 Jaguars were introduced in September 1986. A true convertible (converted by Hess & Eisenhardt) was announced and priced at $46,950. After five "up" years in a row, Jaguar sales declined in 1987. The company blamed supply restraints following the release of an all-new XJ6. U.S. sales for the calendar year were 22,919. Sales of the XJ6 (both new and old) declined 12 percent while the XJ-S enjoyed a 10 percent sales increase. Jaguar PLC, the British parent firm, had sales of $1,822,000,000 and earned a profit of $111,454,500.

1987 Jaguar XJ-SC cabriolet

Dan Lyons

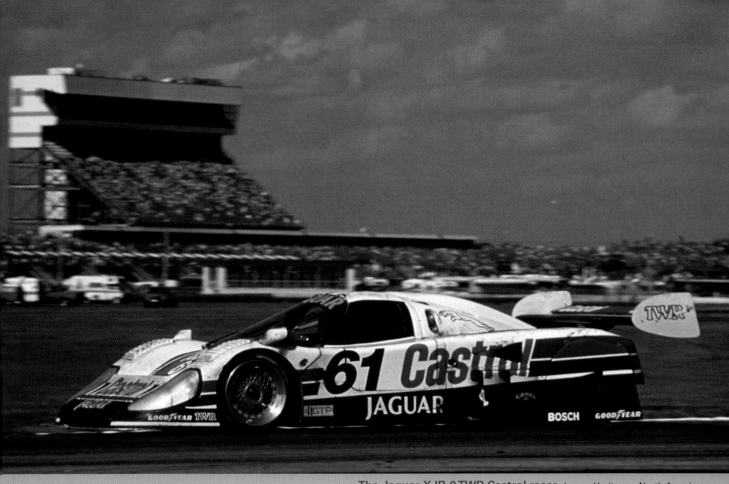

1988

XJ-S — V-12 — The XJ-S coupe had a new center console with wood veneer trim, heated front-seat cushions, and electrically-adjustable lumbar support for the driver's seat. Other standard equipment included the V-12 engine, three-speed automatic transmission, power four-wheel disc brakes, automatic-temperature-control air conditioning, tinted glass, styled aluminum wheels, a radio and cassette, a digital clock, and a rear window defogger. The V-12 in all XJ-S models had 10 additional horsepower.

XJ-SC — V-12 — The XJ-SC Targa-style cabriolet also got a new center console with wood veneer trim, heated front-seat cushions, and electrically-adjustable lumbar support for the driver's seat. Standard equipment was similar to that of the coupe.

XJ-S HESS & EISENHART — V-12 — In addition to the Targa-style XJ-SC cabriolet, Jaguar's 12-cylinder model offered the full-fledged convertible conversion by Hess & Eisenhart, the Cincinnati, Ohio, custom body builder. It had a power top and was available only on special order.

XJ6 (XJ-40) — SIX — This new "XJ-40" model did not share any components with earlier XJ-S. The new XJ6 was shorter, wider, taller and lighter. Replacing the twin-cam six was a new 3.6-liter aluminum six with four valves per cylinder and multi-point fuel injection. It had a new ZF four-speed automatic with overdrive fourth gear. The fully-independent suspension was modified. An 4-wheel disc anti-lock braking system was added. Standard equipment included an electronic AM/FM stereo radio with cassette player, automatic-temperature-control air conditioning, and leather-faced seats.

XJ6 (XJ-40) VANDEN PLAS — SIX — A Vanden Plas edition of the XJ sedan was again offered. It included fold-down burl walnut picnic tables on the front seatbacks, headlight washers, heated front seats, a limited-slip differential, full leather upholstery, a special wood-veneer dash applique', special body emblems, a rear center armrest with a built-in storage compartment and rear reading lamps.

I.D. DATA: A 17-symbol Vehicle Identification Number is on the top left of the instrument panel, visible through the windshield. Symbols 1 through 3 indicate origin and make. Symbol four denotes model; symbol five, the restraint system; symbol six, the body style ("1" = four-door sedan; "5" = two-door coupe; "3" = cabriolet). Symbol seven is the engine code; symbol eight, the steering and transmission code. Next is a check digit, followed by a letter indicating model year (J = 1988). Symbol 11 (letter C) identifies the assembly plant, followed by a six-digit sequential production number. Starting serial numbers are: (XJ-S coupe/convertible) SAJNV5()4()JC000001; (XJ-S cabriolet)

SAJNA3()4()JC000001; (XJ6) SAJHV1()4()JC000001; (Vanden Plas) SAJKV1()4()JC000001.

ENGINES

BASE SIX XJ6: Inline, dual overhead-cam six-cylinder. Aluminum block and head. Displacement: 219 cid (3590 cc). Bore & Stroke: 3.58 x 3.62 in. (91 x 92 mm). Compression Ratio: 8.2:1. Brake Horsepower: 181 at 4750 rpm. Torque: 221 lbs.-ft. at 3750 rpm. Port fuel injection.

BASE V-12 XJ-S: 60-degree, "vee" type overhead-cam twelve-cylinder. Aluminum block and heads. Displacement: 326 cid (5343 cc). Bore & Stroke: 3.54 x 2.76 in. (90 x 70 mm). Compression Ratio: 11.5:1. Brake Horsepower: 262 at 5000 rpm. Torque: 290 lbs.-ft. at 3000 rpm. Seven main bearings. Thimble tappets. Port fuel injection.

BASE SIX XJ6 VANDEN PLAS: Inline, dual overhead-cam six-cylinder. Aluminum block and head. Displacement: 219 cid (3590 cc). Bore & Stroke: 3.58 x 3.62 in. (91 x 92 mm). Compression Ratio: 8.2:1. Brake Horsepower: 181 at 4750 rpm. Torque: 221 lbs.-ft. at 3750 rpm. Port fuel injection.

BASE V-12 XJ-S COUPE: 60-degree, "vee" type overhead-cam twelve-cylinder. Aluminum block and heads. Displacement: 326 cid (5343 cc). Bore & Stroke: 3.54 x 2.76 in. (90 x 70 mm). Compression Ratio: 11.5:1. Brake Horsepower: 262 at 5000 rpm. Torque: 290 lbs.-ft. at 3000 rpm. Seven main bearings. Thimble tappets. Electronic fuel injection.

BASE V-12 XJ-SC CABRIOLET AND XJ-S

CONVERTIBLE: 60-degree, "vee" type overhead-cam twelve-cylinder. Aluminum block and heads. Displacement: 326 cid (5343 cc). Bore & Stroke: 3.54 x 2.76 in. (90 x 70 mm). Compression Ratio: 11.5:1. Brake Horsepower: 252 at 5000 rpm. Seven main bearings. Thimble tappets. Electronic fuel injection.

CHASSIS

XJ6 SERIES III: Wheelbase: 113 in. Overall Length: 196.4 in. Wheelbase: 113 in. Overall Length: 196.4 in. Height: 54.3 in. Width: 78.9 in. Front Tread: 59.1 in. Rear Tread: 59.0 in. Wheel Type: ventilated chrome disc. Standard Tires: 205/70VR15 Pirelli P5.

XJ6 VANDEN PLAS: Wheelbase: 113 in. Overall Length: 196.4 in. Height: 54.3 in. Width: 78.9 in. Front Tread: 59.1 in. Rear Tread: 59.0 in. Wheel Type: ventilated chrome disc. Standard Tires: 205/70VR15 Pirelli P5.

XJ-S (ALL): Wheelbase: 102.0 in. Overall Length: 191.7 in. Height: 47.8 in. Width: 70.6 in. Front Tread: 58.6 in. Rear Tread: 59.2 in. Wheel Type: cast aluminum alloy. Standard Tires: 205/70VR15 Pirelli P5.

TECHNICAL

XJ6 SERIES III: Layout: front-engine, rear-drive. Transmission: Borg-Warner automatic. Standard final drive ratio: 2.88:1:1. Steering: power rack-and-pinion. Suspension (front): upper/lower control arms with coil springs and anti-roll bar. Suspension (rear): Independent with lower control arms,

1988 Jaguar XJ6 sedan with sunroof

Model	Body Type & Seating	Engine Type/CID	P.O.E. Price	Weight (lbs.)	Production Total
XJ-S	2d Coupe-2+2P	V12/326	$41,500	4,040	N/A
XJ-SC Cabriolet					
XJ-SC	2d Cabriolet-2P	V12/326	$47,450	4,040	N/A
XJ-S Hess & Eisenhart Convertible					
XJ-S	2d Convertible-2+2P	V12/326	$49,000	4,250	N/A
XJ6					
XJ6	4d Sedan-5P	I6/219	$40,500	3,903	N/A
XJ6 (XJ-40) Vanden Plas					
Vanden Plas	4d Sedan-5P	I6/219	$44,500	3,960	N/A

The futuristic 1988 Jaguar XJ 220 prototype

The 1988 Jaguar XJ-SC cabriolet with its unique top open.

ride-leveling struts and coil springs. Brakes: front/rear disc. Body Construction: steel unibody. Fuel Tank: 23.2 gallons.

XJ6 VANDEN PLAS: Layout: front-engine, rear-drive. Transmission: Borg-Warner automatic. Standard final drive ratio: 2.88:1.1. Steering: power rack-and-pinion. Suspension (front): upper/lower control arms with coil springs and anti-roll bar. Suspension (rear): Independent with lower control arms, ride-leveling struts and coil springs. Brakes: front/rear disc. Body Construction: steel unibody. Fuel Tank: 23.2 gallons.

XJ-S (ALL): Layout: front-engine, rear-drive. Transmission: Turbo-Hydra-Matic 400. Standard final drive ratio: 2.88:11. Steering: power rack-and-pinion. Suspension (front): upper/lower control arms with coil springs and anti-roll bar. Suspension (rear): Independent with coil springs. Brakes: front/rear disc. Body Construction: steel unibody. Fuel Tank: 24 gallons.

OPTIONS: Rear window defogger for XJ-S (installed in 57.4 percent of cars sold in U.S.).

PERFORMANCE

XJ6: Acceleration (0-60 mph): 10.4 seconds.

XJ-S: Top Speed: 140 to 150 mph. Acceleration (0-60 mph): 8.0 seconds. Acceleration (quarter mile): 15.9 seconds. Fuel mileage: 10 mpg.

CALENDAR YEAR SALES (U.S.): A total of 20,727

Jaguars were sold in the U.S. during calendar year 1988. The total included 15,944 XJ6 sedans and 4,783 XJ-S coupes, convertibles and cabriolets.

MANUFACTURER: Jaguar PLC, Browns Lane, Allesley, Coventry, England.

DISTRIBUTOR: Jaguar Cars, Inc., 600 Willow Tree Road, Leonia, New Jersey.

HISTORY: A soft luxury-car market pushed Jaguar's U.S. sales volume down another nine percent to 21,000 units. Sales of the XJ6 were down nine percent to 16,000 and sales of the XJ-S were also down nine percent to 5,000. Demand for Jaguars in other parts of the world remained strong. Jaguar Cars PLC built a record 51,939 Jaguars and Daimlers in Coventry, England, an eight percent increase and the first time annual production exceeded 50,000 units. The year resulted in a financial loss, because the U.S. dollar declined against the British pound. A limited-edition 1988 Jaguar XJR-S was planned to commemorate Jaguar's return to international motor sports competition.

A rare 1989 Jaguar V-12 Rouge coupe *Bob Harrington*

1989

XJ-S COUPE — V-12 — A price hike was the major change for Jaguar's 12-cylinder models in 1989. Both models got a new anti-lock braking system developed jointly by Jaguar and the Alfred Teves Company. Other new items included electrically-heated seats with power lumbar adjustment, a new steering wheel and 235/60VR15 Pirelli P600 tires on new alloy wheels. Standard equipment included the carryover V-12, a three-speed automatic transmission, and an AM/FM stereo with cassette player. A limited-production "Collection Rouge" coupe, offered in Signal Red, was released in 1989 as a 1990 model. The first 213 of these cars sold in the U.S. were included in 1989 calendar-year production figures. The Rouge coupe cost $3,000 more than the standard four-seat coupe.

XJ-S CONVERTIBLE — V-12 — A new XJ-S convertible replaced the former Targa-style model. The two-passenger convertible was built in Jaguar's own plant. The new convertible had a power top and heated glass back window, plus a locking luggage compartment. Other features were similar to the coupe.

XJ6 (XJ-40) — SIX — A shorter final-drive ratio (3.58:1 rather than the former 2.88:1:1) and more powerful engine were the major changes for the Jaguar six-cylinder sedan. The revised engine got a compression boost to 9.6:1, for output of 195 hp (versus 181 hp in 1988). Jaguar claimed the engine changes did not harm fuel mileage significantly, but premium gas was required. Bosch anti-lock braking and a self-leveling suspension were standard. Other standard equipment included

power front bucket seats (with leather facings), power door locks (with infrared remote control), heated power mirrors and fog lamps. On the dashboard were LED gauges and an electronically-tuned AM/FM stereo with channel-19 CB monitor.

XJ6 (XJ-40) VANDEN PLAS — SIX — The posh Vanden Plas model added headlight washers, a limited-slip differential, heated front seats, walnut picnic tables (on seatbacks), full leather seat trim, rear reading lamps and a rear storage armrest. The Majestic version, which came only in Regency Red body color, included a magnolia leather interior, diamond-polished alloy wheels and an alarm system. The Majestic sedan was released late in 1989 as a 1990 model.

Note 1: The Majestic and Vanden Plas names were long associated with Daimler in England. The Majestic Major line were stately sedans that competed with Bentley. Vanden Plas was the Daimler coachbuilder.

I.D. DATA: A 17-symbol Vehicle Identification Number is on the top left of the instrument panel, visible through the windshield. Symbols one through three indicate the origin and make. Symbol four denotes the model; symbol five, the restraint system; symbol six, the body style ("1"= four-door sedan; "5" = two-door coupe; "4" = convertible). Symbol seven is the engine code and symbol eight is the steering and transmission code. Next is a check digit, followed by a letter indicating model year (K = 1989). Symbol 11 (letter C) identifies the assembly plant, followed by a six-digit sequential production number. The starting serial numbers are: (XJ-S coupe) SAJNA5()4()JC000001;

Model	Body Type & Seating	Engine Type/ CID	P.O.E. Price	Weight (lbs.)	Production Total
XJ-S Coupe					
XJ-S	2d Coupe-2+2P	V12/326	$47,000	4,015	N/A
XJ-S Convertible					
XJ-S	2d Convertible-2P	V12/326	$56,000	4,190	N/A
XJ6 Series III					
XJ6	4d Sedan-5P	I6/219	$43,500	3,903	N/A
XJ6 Vanden Plas					
Vanden Plas	4d Sedan-5P	I6/219	$47,500	3,960	N/A

Note 2: For the calendar year Jaguar PLC produced 48,138 Jaguar and Daimler cars for the worldwide market, a steep decline from the record 51,839 made in 1988.

(XJ-S convertible) SAJNV4()4()JC000001; (XJ6 and XJ-40)) SAJHY1()4()KC000001; (Vanden Plas) SAJKY1()4()KC000001.

ENGINES

BASE SIX XJ6: Inline, dual overhead-cam six-cylinder (24-valve). Aluminum block and head. Displacement: 219 cid (3590 cc). Bore & Stroke: 3.58 x 3.62 in. (91 x 92 mm). Compression Ratio: 9.6:1. Brake Horsepower: 195 at 5000 rpm. Torque: 232 lbs.-ft. at 4000 rpm. Port fuel injection.

BASE SIX XJ6 VANDEN PLAS: Inline, dual overhead-cam six-cylinder (24-valve). Aluminum block and head. Displacement: 219 cid (3590 cc). Bore & Stroke: 3.58 x 3.62 in. (91 x 92 mm). Compression Ratio: 9.6:1. Brake Horsepower: 195 at 5000 rpm. Torque: 232 lbs.-ft. at 4000 rpm. Port fuel injection.

BASE V-12 XJ-S: 60-degree, "vee" type overhead-cam twelve-cylinder. Aluminum block and heads. Displacement: 326 cid (5343 cc). Bore & Stroke: 3.54 x 2.76 in. (90 x 70 mm). Compression Ratio: 11.5:1. Brake Horsepower: 262 at 5000 rpm. Torque: 290 lbs.-ft. at 3000 rpm. Seven main bearings. Thimble tappets. Port fuel injection.

CHASSIS

XJ6 SERIES III: Wheelbase: 113 in. Overall Length: 196.4 in. Height: 54.3 in. Width: 78.9 in. Front Tread: 59.1 in. Rear

The Jaguar XJ 220 prototype with (top to bottom) the XJ 13 prototype, the D-type, and the C-type.

Jaguar Heritage – North America

Tread: 59.0 in. Wheel Type: ventilated chrome disc. Standard Tires: 205/70VR15 Pirelli P5.

XJ6 VANDEN PLAS: Wheelbase: 113 in. Overall Length: 196.4 in. Height: 54.3 in. Width: 78.9 in. Front Tread: 59.1 in. Rear Tread: 59.0 in. Wheel Type: ventilated chrome disc. Standard Tires: 205/70VR15 Pirelli P5.

XJ-S (ALL): Wheelbase: 102.0 in. Overall Length: 191.7 in. Height: 47.8 in. Width: 70.6 in. Front Tread: 58.6 in. Rear Tread: 59.2 in. Wheel Type: cast aluminum alloy. Standard Tires: Pirelli P600 235/60VR15.

TECHNICAL

XJ6 SERIES III: Layout: front-engine, rear-drive. Transmission: Borg-Warner automatic. Standard final drive ratio: 3.58:1. Steering: rack-and-pinion, power-assisted. Brakes: front/rear disc. Suspension (front): upper/lower control arms with coil springs and anti-roll bar. Suspension (rear): independent with lower control arms, ride-leveling struts and coil springs. Body Construction: steel unibody. Fuel Tank: 23.2 gallons.

XJ6 VANDEN PLAS: Layout: front-engine, rear-drive. Transmission: Borg-Warner automatic. Standard final drive ratio: 3.58:1. Steering: rack-and-pinion, power-assisted. Brakes: front/rear disc. Suspension (front): upper/lower control arms with coil springs and anti-roll bar. Suspension (rear): independent with lower control arms, ride-leveling struts and coil springs. Body Construction: steel unibody. Fuel Tank: 23.2 gallons.

XJ-S (ALL): Layout: front-engine, rear-drive. Transmission: Turbo-Hydra-Matic 400. Standard final drive ratio: 2.88:1:1. Steering: rack-and-pinion, power-assisted. Brakes: front/rear disc. Suspension (front): upper/lower control arms with coil springs and anti-roll bar. Suspension (rear): independent with coil springs. Body Construction: steel unibody. Fuel Tank: 24 gallons.

PERFORMANCE

XJ6: Acceleration (0-60 mph): 9.6 seconds.

XJ-S: Top Speed: 140 to 150 mph. Acceleration (0-60 mph): 8.0 seconds. Acceleration (quarter mile) 15.9 seconds. Fuel mileage: 10 mpg.

CALENDAR YEAR SALES AND TOURIST DELIVERIES (U.S.): Jaguar's sales and tourist deliveries for calendar-year 1989 totaled 18,967 cars. The total included 10,126 XJ6 Series III sedans, 3,966 Vanden Plas sedans, 417 Majestic sedans, 213 Rouge coupes, 1,688 XJ-S coupes and 2,557 XJ-S-SC convertibles.

MODEL YEAR SALES AND TOURIST DELIVERIES (U.S.): Jaguar's model year sales in the U.S. were 19,461 cars and included 15,140 XJ6 models and 4,321 XJ-S models.

MANUFACTURER: Jaguar PLC, Browns Lane, Allesley, Coventry, England.

DISTRIBUTOR: Jaguar Cars, Inc., 555 MacArthur Blvd., Mahwah, New Jersey.

HISTORY: On November 1, 1989, Ford Motor Company approached Jaguar and offered a proposal that was accepted after a lengthy debate. The agreement stated that Ford recognized the integrity of the Jaguar marques and stipulated that Jaguar would stay a separate legal entity with self-sustaining finances and its own board of directors. On December 1, the Jaguar board recommended acceptance of the offer from Ford. The deal was closed on February 28, 1990 and Jaguar was removed from the London Stock Exchange listings. It was announced that Ford's help with research and development would move up the launch date of a new XJ-S. Ford's purchase of Jaguar changed the XJR-S super car project. The program was first delayed and later cancelled. Still later, the decision was made to produce 50 coupes and 50 convertibles as 1993 models for the U.S. market. The company also had plans to bring the new XJ220 to the U.S. The delivery of the first of these exotic super cars in North America was expected to take place in 1992. The 1989 Jaguar production models were introduced to the U.S. market in September 1988. Jaguar Cars, Inc., now at Mahwah, New Jersey, saw U.S. sales drop 8.4 percent to 18,967. The sales of XJ6 models slipped nine percent to 15,944 and XJ-S sales fell seven percent to 4,458.

1989 Jaguar XJ6 sedan

A 1989 Pirelli ad features an XJ-S convertible in real Jaguar colors.

1990 Jaguar Sovereign sedan *Andrew Morland*

1990

XJ-S COUPE — V-12 — The 1990 XJ-S coupe looked similar to the 1989 model. A driver's-side airbag became standard in the 12-cylinder coupe for 1990. The 262-hp V-12 was again coupled to the three-speed automatic transmission. Standard equipment included a trip computer.

XJ-S COLLECTION ROUGE COUPE — V-12 — The limited-production "Collection Rouge" coupe, which arrived in the fall of 1989 as a 1990 model, was continued. It came only in Signal Red and cost $3,000 more than the standard four-seat coupe. It included a Magnolia leather interior.

XJ-S CONVERTIBLE — V-12 — The 1990 XJ-S convertible looked similar to the 1989 model. A driver's-side airbag became standard equipment. The convertible included a power top and heated glass back window. Other features were similar to those of the coupe.

XJ6 (XJ-40) — SIX — A larger and more powerful "AJ6" engine became standard, boosting horsepower from 195 to 223. That increase was claimed to cut 0 to 60 mph acceleration down to 8.6 seconds. A Teves anti-lock braking system replaced the former Girling/Bosch version.

XJ6 (XJ-40) SOVEREIGN — SIX — The Sovereign upgrade model added hydraulic ride control, a power sunroof, burl walnut inlays and rear head restraints.

XJ6 (XJ-40) VANDEN PLAS —SIX — The posh Vanden Plas added headlight washers with heated nozzles, heated front seats, leather-covered seatbacks, fog lamps, and rear reading lights.

XJ6 (XJ-40) VANDEN PLAS MAJESTIC —SIX — The Majestic, which came only in Regency Red body color, included a Magnolia leather interior, diamond-polished alloy wheels, and an alarm system.

I.D. DATA: A 17-symbol Vehicle Identification Number is on the top left of the instrument panel, visible through the windshield. Symbols one through three indicate the origin and make. Symbol four denotes the model; symbol five, the restraint system; symbol six, the body style ("1" = four-door sedan; "5" = two-door coupe). Symbol seven is the engine code; symbol eight, the steering and transmission code. Next is a check digit, followed by a letter indicating model year (L = 1990). Symbol 11 (letter C) identifies the assembly plant, followed by a six-digit sequential production number. Starting serial number: (XJ-S coupe) SAJNW5()4()JC000001; (XJ-S convertible) SAJNW4()4()JC000001; (XJ6) SAJFY1()4()LC000001; (Sovereign) SAJHY1()4()LC000001; (Vanden Plas) SAJKY1()4()LC000001; (Majestic) SAJMY1()4()LC000001.

ENGINES

BASE SIX XJ6 AND XJ6 SOVEREIGN: Inline, dual overhead-cam six-cylinder (AJ6 24-valve). Aluminum block and head. Displacement: 243 cid (3980 cc). Bore & Stroke: 3.58 x 4.015 in. (91 x 102 mm). Compression Ratio: 9.6:1. Brake Horsepower: 223 at 4750 rpm. Torque: 278 lbs.-ft. at 3650 rpm. Port fuel injection.

BASE SIX XJ6 VANDEN PLAS and VANDEN PLAS MAJESTIC: Inline, dual overhead-cam six-cylinder (AJ6 24-valve). Aluminum block and head. Displacement: 243 cid (3980 cc). Bore & Stroke: 3.58 x 4.015 in. (91 x 102 mm). Compression Ratio: 9.6:1. Brake Horsepower: 223 at 4750 rpm. Torque: 278 lbs.-ft. at 3650 rpm. Port fuel injection.

BASE V-12 XJ-S COUPE and XJ-S CONVERTIBLE:

60-degree, "vee" type overhead-cam twelve-cylinder. Aluminum block and heads. Displacement: 326 cid (5343 cc). Bore & Stroke: 3.54 x 2.76 in. (90 x 70 mm). Compression Ratio: 11.5:1. Brake Horsepower: 262 at 5000 rpm. Torque: 290 lbs.-ft. at 3000 rpm. Seven main bearings. Thimble tappets. Port fuel injection.

BASE V-12 XJ-S COLLECTION ROUGE COUPE: 60-degree, "vee" type overhead-cam twelve-cylinder. Aluminum block and heads. Displacement: 326 cid (5343 cc). Bore & Stroke: 3.54 x 2.76 in. (90 x 70 mm). Compression Ratio: 11.5:1. Brake Horsepower: 262 at 5000 rpm. Torque: 290 lbs.-ft. at 3000 rpm. Seven main bearings. Thimble tappets. Port fuel injection.

CHASSIS

XJ6: Wheelbase: 113 in. Overall Length: 196.4 in. Height: 54.3 in. Width: 78.9 in. Front Tread: 59.1 in. Rear Tread: 59.0 in. Wheel Type: ventilated chrome disc. Standard Tires: 205/70VR15 Pirelli P5.

XJ6 SOVEREIGN: Wheelbase: 113 in. Overall Length: 196.4 in. Height: 54.3 in. Width: 78.9 in. Front Tread: 59.1 in. Rear Tread: 59.0 in. Wheel Type: ventilated chrome disc. Standard Tires: 205/70VR15 Pirelli P5.

XJ6 VANDEN PLAS: Wheelbase: 113 in. Overall Length: 196.4 in. Height: 54.3 in. Width: 78.9 in. Front Tread: 59.1 in. Rear Tread: 59.0 in. Wheel Type: ventilated chrome disc. Standard Tires: 205/70VR15 Pirelli P5.

XJ6 VANDEN PLAS MAJESTIC: Wheelbase: 113 in. Overall Length: 196.4 in. Height: 54.3 in. Width: 78.9 in. Front Tread: 59.1 in. Rear Tread: 59.0 in. Wheel Type: ventilated chrome disc. Standard Tires: 205/70VR15 Pirelli P5.

XJ-S COUPE: Wheelbase: 102.0 in. Overall Length: 191.7 in. Height: 47.8 in. Width: 70.6 in. Front Tread: 58.6 in. Rear Tread: 59.2 in. Wheel Type: cast aluminum alloy. Standard Tires: Pirelli P600 235/60VR15.

XJ-S ROUGE COUPE: Wheelbase: 102.0 in. Overall Length: 191.7 in. Height: 47.8 in. Width: 70.6 in. Front Tread: 58.6 in. Rear Tread: 59.2 in. Wheel Type: cast aluminum alloy. Standard Tires: Pirelli P600 235/60VR15.

XJ-S CONVERTIBLE: Wheelbase: 102.0 in. Overall Length: 191.7 in. Height: 47.8 in. Width: 70.6 in. Front Tread: 58.6 in. Rear Tread: 59.2 in. Wheel Type: cast aluminum alloy. Standard Tires: Pirelli P600 235/60VR15.

TECHNICAL

XJ6 COUPE: Layout: front-engine, rear-drive. Transmission: Automatic. Standard final drive ratio: 3.59:1. Steering: rack-and-pinion, power-assisted. Brakes: front/rear disc. Suspension (front): upper/lower control arms with coil springs and anti-roll bar. Suspension (rear): independent with lower control arms, ride-leveling struts and coil springs. Body Construction: steel unibody. Fuel Tank: 23.2 gallons.

XJ6 SOVEREIGN: Layout: front-engine, rear-drive. Transmission: Automatic. Standard final drive ratio: 3.59:1. Steering: rack-and-pinion, power-assisted. Brakes: front/rear disc. Suspension (front): upper/lower control arms with coil springs and anti-roll bar. Suspension (rear): independent with lower control arms, ride-leveling struts and coil springs. Body Construction: steel unibody. Fuel Tank: 23.2 gallons.

XJ6 VANDEN PLAS: Layout: front-engine, rear-drive. Transmission: Automatic. Standard final drive ratio: 3.58:1. Steering: rack-and-pinion, power-assisted. Brakes: front/rear disc. Suspension (front): upper/lower control arms with coil springs and anti-roll bar. Suspension (rear): independent with lower control arms, ride-leveling struts and coil springs. Body Construction: steel unibody. Fuel Tank: 23.2 gallons.

XJ6 VANDEN PLAS MAJESTIC: Layout: front-engine, rear-drive. Transmission: Automatic. Standard final drive ratio: 3.58:1. Steering: rack-and-pinion, power-assisted. Brakes: front/rear disc. Suspension (front): upper/lower control

1990 Jaguar XJ-S convertible

MODEL	BODY TYPE & SEATING	ENGINE TYPE/CID	P.O.E. PRICE	WEIGHT (LBS.)	PRODUCTION TOTAL
XJ-S Coupe					
XJ-S	2d Coupe-4P	V12/326	$48,000	4,015	N/A
XJ-S Convertible					
XJ-S	2d Convertible-2P	V12/326	$57,000	4,190	N/A
XJ-S Collection Rouge					
XJ-S	2d Coupe-4P	V12/326	$51,000	4,015	N/A
XJ6 Series III					
XJ6	4d Sedan-5P	I6/243	$39,700	3,903	N/A
XJ6 Sovereign					
Sovereign	4d Sedan-5P	I6/243	$43,000	3,980	N/A
Vanden Plas					
Vanden Plas	4d Sedan-5pI6/243	I6/243	$48,000	3,975	N/A
Vanden Plas Majestic					
Majestic	4d Sedan-5P	I6/243	$53,000	3,980	N/A

Note 1: For the calendar year Jaguar PLC produced 41,891 Jaguar and Daimler cars for the worldwide market, a decline from the 48,138 made in 1989.

arms with coil springs and anti-roll bar. Suspension (rear): independent with lower control arms, ride-leveling struts and coil springs. Body Construction: steel unibody. Fuel Tank: 23.2 gallons.

XJ-S COUPE: Layout: front-engine, rear-drive. Transmission: Turbo-Hydra-Matic 400. Standard final drive ratio: 2.88:1. Steering: rack-and-pinion, power-assisted. Brakes: front/rear disc. Suspension (front): upper/lower control arms with coil springs and anti-roll bar. Suspension (rear): independent with coil springs. Body Construction: steel unibody. Fuel Tank: 24 gallons.

XJ-S ROUGE COUPE: Layout: front-engine, rear-drive. Transmission: Turbo-Hydra-Matic 400. Standard final drive ratio: 2.88:1. Steering: rack-and-pinion, power-assisted. Brakes: front/rear disc. Suspension (front): upper/lower control arms with coil springs and anti-roll bar. Suspension (rear): independent with coil springs. Body Construction: steel unibody. Fuel Tank: 24 gallons.

XJ-S CONVERTIBLE: Layout: front-engine, rear-drive. Transmission: Turbo-Hydra-Matic 400. Standard final drive

ratio: 2.88:1. Steering: rack-and-pinion, power-assisted. Brakes: front/rear disc. Suspension (front): upper/lower control arms with coil springs and anti-roll bar. Suspension (rear): independent with coil springs. Body Construction: steel unibody. Fuel Tank: 21.6 gallons.

PERFORMANCE

XJ-S: Top Speed: 140 to 150 mph. Acceleration (0-60 mph): 8.0 seconds. Acceleration (quarter mile) 15.9 seconds. Fuel mileage: 10 mpg.

CALENDAR YEAR SALES AND TOURIST DELIVERIES (U.S.): Jaguar's U.S. retail sales and tourist deliveries for calendar-year 1990 totaled 18,728 cars. The total included 3,364 XJ6 Series III sedans, 7,223 Sovereign sedans, 2,868 Vanden Plas sedans, 558 Majestic sedans, 145 Collection Rouge coupes, 1,513 XJ-S coupes and 3,057 XJ-S-SC convertibles.

MODEL YEAR SALES AND TOURIST DELIVERIES (U.S.): Jaguar's U.S. retail sales and tourist deliveries for the model year 1990 totaled 19,176 cars. This total included 3,779 XJ6 sedans, 7,191 Sovereign sedans, 2,632 Vanden Plas sedans, 783 Vanden Plas Majestic sedans, 1,487 XJ-S coupes, 276 XJ-S Collection Rouge coupes and 3,028 XJ-SC convertibles.

MANUFACTURER: Jaguar PLC, Browns Lane, Allesley, Coventry, England.

DISTRIBUTOR: Jaguar Cars, Inc., 555 MacArthur Blvd., Mahwah, New Jersey.

HISTORY: A worldwide economic slide during 1990 resulted in declining Jaguar sales. Jaguar's XJ220 super car headed towards real world production in 1991. The XJ220 featured an aluminum and magnesium alloy body that was bonded to a unitized aluminum "tub" type frame. Jaguar regained the Worlds Sports Car Championship with the revolutionary XJR-14 totally dominating the series. Jaguar XJR-12's finished second, third and fourth at the 1991 Le Mans.

1990 Jaguar sedans: (top to bottom) XJ6, Sovereign, Vanden Plas and Vanden Plas Majestic
Richard Dance Collection

THE JAGUAR XJ-S

The 1990 XJ-S coupe with a C-type and a D-type in Jaguar literature.

Phil Hall Collection

Jaguar sedans from left to right, the XJ6, Sovereign and Vanden Plas.

1991

XJ6 (XJ-40) — SIX — The 1991 XJ series adjusted shock-absorber settings for a softer ride, added a more efficient fuel pump and upgraded the sound system. Standard features included 4-wheel power disc ABS brakes and automatic-temperature-control air conditioning.

XJ6 (XJ-40) SOVEREIGN — SIX — The Sovereign upgrade was the most popular version of the XJ6, though sales were down from calendar year 1990. The package added hydraulic ride control, a power sunroof, and burl walnut inlays.

XJ6 (XJ-40) VANDEN PLAS — SIX — The posh Vanden Plas outsold the base XJ6 in calendar year 1991. The Vanden Plas package added a limited-slip differential, heated front seats, folding burl walnut picnic tables (on front seatbacks), fog lamps, and rear reading lights.

XJ6 (XJ-40) VANDEN PLAS MAJESTIC — SIX —- The Majestic came only in Regency Red body and featured a magnolia leather interior, diamond-polished alloy wheels and an alarm system. U.S. calendar year sales show that 20 were sold in calendar-year 1991.

XJ-S — V-12 — Adding two new interior colors, Magnolia and Doeskin, helped Jaguar highlight a new palette of colors called the "Classic Collection." Standard features included 4-wheel power disc ABS brakes and automatic-temperature-control air conditioning.

XJ-S COLLECTION ROUGE COUPE — V-12 — The limited-production "Collection Rouge" coupe came only in Signal Red and cost $3,000 more than the standard four-seat coupe. U.S. calendar year sales show that two (2) were sold in calendar-year 1991.

XJ-S CONVERTIBLE — V-12 — The 1991 convertible included all coupe equipment plus a power top, a heated glass back window and a locking luggage compartment behind the seats.

I.D. DATA: The Vehicle Identification Number is located on the top left-hand surface of the instrument panel and is visible through the windshield. The VIN has 17 symbols. The first three symbols indicate the origin and make: SAJ=British Jaguar. The fourth symbol designates the model. The fifth symbol designates the specification and restraint system. The sixth symbol designates the body style. The fourth, fifth and sixth symbols are referred to in some sources as the model number: FY1-XJ6 sedan, HY1=XJ6 Sovereign, KY1=XJ6 Vanden Plas, TW5=XJ-S coupe, TW4=XJ-S convertible. The seventh symbol is the engine code. The eighth symbol indicates the type of transmission and steering system and is a 4. The ninth character is the check digit. The 10th symbol indicates the model year: M=1991. The 11th symbol indicates the assembly plant: C=Browns Lane, England. The last six symbols are the sequential production numbers.

ENGINES

BASE SIX XJ6, XJ6 SOVEREIGN and XJ6 VANDEN PLAS: Inline, dual overhead-cam six-cylinder (AJ6 24-valve). Aluminum block and head. Displacement: 243 cid (3980 cc). Bore & Stroke: 3.58 x 4.015 in. (91 x 102 mm). Compression Ratio: 9.6:1. Brake Horsepower: 223 at 4750 rpm. Torque: 278 lbs.-ft. at 3650 rpm. Port fuel injection.

BASE V-12 XJ-S COUPE and CONVERTIBLE: 60-degree, "vee" type overhead-cam twelve-cylinder. Aluminum block and heads. Displacement: 326 cid (5343 cc). Bore & Stroke: 3.54 x 2.76 in. (90 x 70 mm). Compression Ratio: 11.5:1. Brake Horsepower: 263 at 5350 rpm. Torque: 290 lbs.-ft. at 3000 rpm. Seven main bearings. Thimble tappets. Port fuel injection.

CHASSIS

XJ6: Wheelbase: 113 in. Overall Length: 196.4 in. Height: 54.3 in. Width: 78.9 in. Front Tread: 59.1 in. Rear Tread:

MODEL	BODY TYPE & SEATING	ENGINE TYPE/CID	P.O.E. PRICE	WEIGHT (LBS.)	PRODUCTION TOTAL
XJ6 Sedan					
XJ6	4d Sedan-5P	I6/243	$43,000	3,935	N/A
XJ6 Sovereign					
Sovereign	4d Sedan-5P	I6/243	$47,800	3,979	
XJ6 Vanden Plas					
Vanden Plas	4d Sedan-5p	I6/243	$52,800	4,035	N/A
XJ-S Coupe					
XJ-S	2d Coupe-2+2P	V12/326	$53,000	4,050	N/A
XJ-S Convertible					
XJ-S	2d Convertible-2+2P	V12/326	$63,600	4,250	N/A

Note 1: For the calendar year Jaguar PLC produced 22,967 Jaguar and Daimler cars for the worldwide market, a decline from the 41,891 made in 1990.

1991 Jaguar Sovereign sedan

59.0 in. Wheel Type: ventilated chrome disc. Standard Tires: 205/70VR15 Pirelli P5.

XJ6 SOVEREIGN: Wheelbase: 113 in. Overall Length: 196.4 in. Height: 54.3 in. Width: 78.9 in. Front Tread: 59.1 in. Rear Tread: 59.0 in. Wheel Type: ventilated chrome disc. Standard Tires: 205/70VR15 Pirelli P5.

XJ6 VANDEN PLAS: Wheelbase: 113 in. Overall Length: 196.4 in. Height: 54.3 in. Width: 78.9 in. Front Tread: 59.1 in. Rear Tread: 59.0 in. Wheel Type: ventilated chrome disc. Standard Tires: 205/70VR15 Pirelli P5.

XJ-S COUPE: Wheelbase: 102.0 in. Overall Length: 191.7 in. Height: 47.8 in. Width: 70.6 in. Front Tread: 58.6 in. Rear Tread: 59.2 in. Wheel Type: cast aluminum alloy. Standard Tires: Pirelli P600 235/60VR15.

XJ-S CONVERTIBLE: Wheelbase: 102.0 in. Overall Length: 191.7 in. Height: 47.8 in. Width: 70.6 in. Front Tread: 58.6 in. Rear Tread: 59.2 in. Wheel Type: cast aluminum alloy. Standard Tires: Pirelli P600 235/60VR15

TECHNICAL

XJ6 COUPE: Layout: front-engine, rear-drive. Transmission: Automatic. Standard final drive ratio: 3.59:1. Steering: rack-

and-pinion, power-assisted. Brakes: front/rear disc. Suspension (front): upper/lower control arms with coil springs and anti-roll bar. Suspension (rear): independent with lower control arms, ride-leveling struts and coil springs. Body Construction: steel unibody. Fuel Tank: 23.2 gallons.

XJ6 SOVEREIGN: Layout: front-engine, rear-drive. Transmission: Automatic. Standard final drive ratio: 3.59:1. Steering: rack-and-pinion, power-assisted. Brakes: front/rear disc. Suspension (front): upper/lower control arms with coil springs and anti-roll bar. Suspension (rear): independent with lower control arms, ride-leveling struts and coil springs. Body Construction: steel unibody. Fuel Tank: 23.2 gallons.

XJ6 VANDEN PLAS: Layout: front-engine, rear-drive. Transmission: Automatic. Standard final drive ratio: 3.58:1. Steering: rack-and-pinion, power-assisted. Brakes: front/rear disc. Suspension (front): upper/lower control arms with coil springs and anti-roll bar. Suspension (rear): independent with lower control arms, ride-leveling struts and coil springs. Body Construction: steel unibody. Fuel Tank: 23.2 gallons.

XJ-S COUPE: Layout: front-engine, rear-drive. Transmission: Turbo-Hydra-Matic 400. Standard final drive ratio: 2.88:1. Steering: rack-and-pinion, power-assisted. Brakes: front/rear disc. Suspension (front): upper/lower control arms with coil springs and anti-roll bar. Suspension (rear): independent with coil springs. Body Construction: steel unibody. Fuel Tank: 24 gallons.

XJ-S CONVERTIBLE: Layout: front-engine, rear-drive. Transmission: Turbo-Hydra-Matic 400. Standard final drive ratio: 2.88:1. Steering: rack-and-pinion, power-assisted. Brakes: front/rear disc. Suspension (front): upper/lower control arms with coil springs and anti-roll bar. Suspension (rear): independent with coil springs. Body Construction: steel unibody. Fuel Tank: 21.6 gallons.

OPTIONS: None

PERFORMANCE

XJ6 SOVEREIGN: Top Speed: 140 to 150 mph. Acceleration (0-60 mph): 9.0 seconds. Acceleration (quarter mile) 16.8 seconds. Fuel mileage: 17 to 22 mpg.

XJ-S CONVERTIBLE: Top Speed: 140 to 150 mph. Acceleration (0-60 mph): 10.3 seconds. Acceleration (quarter mile) 17.7 seconds. Fuel mileage: 12 to 16 mpg.

CALENDAR YEAR SALES AND TOURIST DELIVERIES (U.S.): Jaguar's U.S. retail sales and tourist deliveries for calendar-year 1991 totaled 9,376 cars. The total included 478 XJ6 Series sedans, 4,520 Sovereign sedans, 1,620 Vanden Plas sedans, 20 Majestic sedans, 2 Collection Rouge coupes, 1,007 XJ-S coupes and 1,729 XJ-S-SC convertibles.

MODEL YEAR SALES AND TOURIST DELIVERIES (U.S.): Jaguar's U.S. retail sales and tourist deliveries for model year 1991 totaled 11,780 cars. This total included 1,031 XJ6 sedans, 5,237 Sovereign sedans, 2,194 Vanden Plas sedans, 37 Vanden Plas Majestic sedans, 1,064 XJ-S coupes, 10 XJ-S Collection Rouge coupes and 2,117 XJ-SC convertibles.

MANUFACTURER: Jaguar Cars Ltd., Browns Lane, Allesley, Coventry, England.

DISTRIBUTOR: Jaguar Cars, Inc., 555 MacArthur Blvd., Mahwah, New Jersey.

HISTORY: Jaguar Cars, Ltd., was now the business name of the English parent company. In New Jersey, the name Jaguar Cars, Inc. continued to be used. The 1990 Jaguar coupes and convertibles were introduced to the U.S. market in October 1990. There were many exciting new developments to enhance the product range. The most significant came in May 1991 with a substantial face-lift to the "early 1992" XJ-S models that incorporated body styling changes, a redesigned interior, improved feature and equipment levels and the AJ6 4.0-liter engine in place of the 3.6-liter version.

1991 Jaguar XJ6 sedan

1991 Jaguar Vanden Plas sedan

1992 Jaguar Vanden Plas Majestic sedan

1992

XJ6 (XJ-40) SEDAN — SIX — All four XJ models shared the same mechanicals but differed in luxury features. Standard features included a four-speed automatic transmission, 4-wheel power disc ABS brakes, automatic-temperature-control air conditioning, and a premium sound system.

XJ6 (XJ-40) SOVEREIGN — SIX — Standard equipment for the Sovereign model was the same as on the sedan, plus hydraulic ride control, a power sunroof, burl walnut inlays and rear head restraints.

XJ6 (XJ-40) VANDEN PLAS— SIX — The Vanden Plas package added a limited-slip differential, headlight washers with heated nozzles, heated front seats, folding burl walnut picnic tables (on front seatbacks), leather-covered seatbacks, fog lamps, and rear reading lights.

XJ6 (XJ-40) VANDEN PLAS MAJESTIC — SIX — The top-of-the-line Majestic returned, cloaked in a Black Cherry metallic paint with contrasting Oyster metallic rear panel and wheels. It also had unique hood and upper side chrome trim, and special badges. Autolux leather combined with Wilton carpets to create one of the most luxurious cars available in 1992.

XJ-S COUPE — V-12 — Revisions included wrap-around neutral-density taillights, flared rocker panels, a new grille,

and front chrome trim. Inside, a new instrument panel, sport seats, and a new computer added to the lush interior. Standard features included ABS brakes, automatic-temperature-control air conditioning, a power sunroof, a driver's side air bag and a premium sound system.

XJ-S CONVERTIBLE — V-12 — Product revisions for 1992 included the same wrap-around neutral-density taillights, flared rocker panels, new grille, a new instrument panel and sport seats, and a new computer. In addition, the ragtop included a power top, and a heated glass back window.

I.D. DATA: The Vehicle Identification Number is located on the top left-hand surface of the instrument panel and is visible through the windshield. The VIN has 17 symbols. The first three symbols indicate the origin and make: SAJ=British Jaguar. The fourth symbol designates the model. The fifth symbol designates the specification and restraint system. The sixth symbol designates the body style. The fourth, fifth and sixth symbols are referred to in some sources as the model number: FY1=XJ6 sedan, HY1=XJ6 Sovereign, KY1=XJ6 Vanden Plas, MY1=XJ6 Majestic, NW5=XJ-S coupe, NW4=XJ-S convertible. The seventh symbol is the engine code. The eighth symbol indicates the type of transmission and steering system. The ninth character is the check digit. The 10th symbol indicates the model year: N=1992. The 11th symbol indicates the assembly plant: C=Browns Lane, England. The last six symbols are the sequential production number.

ENGINES

BASE SIX XJ6: Inline, dual overhead-cam six-cylinder (AJ6 24-valve). Aluminum block and head. Displacement: 243 cid (3980 cc). Bore & Stroke: 3.58 x 4.015 in. (91 x 102 mm). Compression Ratio: 9.6:1. Brake Horsepower: 223 at 4750 rpm. Torque: 278 lbs.-ft. at 3650 rpm. Port fuel injection.

BASE SIX XJ6 SOVEREIGN: Inline, dual overhead-cam six-cylinder (AJ6 24-valve). Aluminum block and head. Displacement: 243 cid (3980 cc). Bore & Stroke: 3.58 x 4.015 in. (91 x 102 mm). Compression Ratio: 9.6:1. Brake Horsepower: 223 at 4750 rpm. Torque: 278 lbs.-ft. at 3650 rpm. Port fuel injection.

BASE SIX XJ6 VANDEN PLAS: Inline, dual overhead-cam six-cylinder (AJ6 24-valve). Aluminum block and head. Displacement: 243 cid (3980 cc). Bore & Stroke: 3.58 x 4.015 in. (91 x 102 mm). Compression Ratio: 9.6:1. Brake Horsepower: 223 at 4750 rpm. Torque: 278 lbs.-ft. at 3650 rpm. Port fuel injection.

BASE V-12 XJ-S COUPE: 60-degree, "vee" type overhead-cam twelve-cylinder. Aluminum block and heads. Displacement: 326 cid (5343 cc). Bore & Stroke: 3.54 x 2.76 in. (90 x 70 mm). Compression Ratio: 11.5:1. Brake Horsepower: 263 at 5350 rpm. Torque: 290 lbs.-ft. at 3000 rpm. Seven main bearings. Thimble tappets. Port fuel injection.

BASE V-12 XJ-S CONVERTIBLE: 60-degree, "vee" type overhead-cam twelve-cylinder. Aluminum block and heads. Displacement: 326 cid (5343 cc). Bore & Stroke: 3.54 x 2.76 in. (90 x 70 mm). Compression Ratio: 11.5:1. Brake Horsepower: 263 at 5350 rpm. Torque: 290 lbs.-ft. at 3000 rpm. Seven main bearings. Thimble tappets. Port fuel injection.

CHASSIS

XJ6: Wheelbase: 113 in. Overall Length: 196.4 in. Height: 54.3 in. Width: 78.9 in. Front Tread: 59.1 in. Rear Tread: 59.0 in. Wheel Type: ventilated chrome disc. Standard Tires: 205/70VR15 Pirelli P5.

XJ6 SOVEREIGN: Wheelbase: 113 in. Overall Length: 196.4 in. Height: 54.3 in. Width: 78.9 in. Front Tread: 59.1 in. Rear Tread: 59.0 in. Wheel Type: ventilated chrome disc. Standard Tires: 205/70VR15 Pirelli P5.

XJ6 VANDEN PLAS: Wheelbase: 113 in. Overall Length: 196.4 in. Height: 54.3 in. Width: 78.9 in. Front Tread: 59.1 in. Rear Tread: 59.0 in. Wheel Type: ventilated chrome disc. Standard Tires: 205/70VR15 Pirelli P5.

XJ-S COUPE: Wheelbase: 102.0 in. Overall Length: 191.7 in. Height: 48.6 in. Width: 70.6 in. Front Tread: 58.6 in. Rear Tread: 59.2 in. Wheel Type: cast aluminum alloy. Standard Tires: Pirelli P600 235/60VR15.

XJ-S CONVERTIBLE: Wheelbase: 102.0 in. Overall Length: 191.7 in. Height: 48.6 in. Width: 70.6 in. Front Tread: 58.6 in. Rear Tread: 59.2 in. Wheel Type: cast aluminum alloy. Standard Tires: Pirelli P600 235/60VR15.

TECHNICAL

XJ6 COUPE: Layout: front-engine, rear-drive. Transmission: Automatic. Standard final drive ratio: 3.59:1. Steering: rack-and-pinion, power-assisted. Brakes: front/rear disc. Suspension (front): upper/lower control arms with coil springs and anti-roll bar. Suspension (rear): independent with lower control arms, ride-leveling struts and coil springs. Body Construction: steel unibody. Fuel Tank: 23.2 gallons.

XJ6 SOVEREIGN and VANDEN PLAS: Layout: front-engine, rear-drive. Transmission: Automatic. Standard final drive ratio: 3.59:1. Steering: rack-and-pinion, power-assisted. Brakes: front/rear disc. Suspension (front): upper/lower control arms with coil springs and anti-roll bar. Suspension (rear): independent with lower control arms, ride-leveling struts and coil springs. Body Construction: steel unibody. Fuel Tank: 23.2 gallons.

1992 Jaguar SJ-S convertible *Jaguar Heritage - North America*

MODEL	BODY TYPE & SEATING	ENGINE TYPE/ CID	P.O.E. PRICE	WEIGHT (LBS.)	PRODUCTION TOTAL
XJ6 Sedan					
XJ6	4d Sedan-5P	I6/243	$44,500	3,935	N/A
XJ6 Sovereign					
Sovereign	4d Sedan-5P	I6/243	$49,500	3,979	N/A
XJ6 Vanden Plas					
Vanden Plas	4d Sedan-5p	I6/243	$54,500	4,035	N/A
XJ6 Vanden Plas Majestic					
Majestic	4d Sedan-5P	I6/243	$49,500	4,035	N/A
XJ-S Coupe					
XJ-S	2d Coupe-2+2P	V12/326	$60,500	3,970	N/A
XJ-S Convertible					
XJ-S	2d Convertible-2+2P	V12/326	$58,900	4,149	N/A

Note 1: For the calendar year Jaguar Ltd. produced 15,981 Jaguars and 4,620 Daimlers for the worldwide market.

The Jaguar V-12 racer, circa 1992.

XJ-S COUPE: Layout: front-engine, rear-drive. Transmission: Turbo-Hydra-Matic 400. Standard final drive ratio: 2.88:1. Steering: rack-and-pinion, power-assisted. Brakes: front/rear disc. Suspension (front): upper/lower control arms with coil springs and anti-roll bar. Suspension (rear): independent with coil springs. Body Construction: steel unibody. Fuel Tank: 24 gallons.

XJ-S CONVERTIBLE: Layout: front-engine, rear-drive. Transmission: Turbo-Hydra-Matic 400. Standard final drive ratio: 2.88:1. Steering: rack-and-pinion, power-assisted. Brakes: front/rear disc. Suspension (front): upper/lower control arms with coil springs and anti-roll bar. Suspension (rear): independent with coil springs. Body Construction: steel unibody. Fuel Tank: 21.6 gallons.

PERFORMANCE

XJ6 SOVEREIGN: Top Speed: 140 to 150 mph. Acceleration (0-60 mph): 8.3 seconds. Acceleration (quarter mile) 16.8 seconds. Fuel mileage: 17 to 22 mpg.

XJ-S CONVERTIBLE: Top Speed: 140 to 150 mph. Acceleration (0-60 mph): 10.3 seconds. Acceleration (quarter mile) 16.3 seconds. Fuel mileage: 13 to 18 mpg.

CALENDAR YEAR SALES AND TOURIST DELIVERIES (U.S.): Jaguar's U.S. retail sales and tourist deliveries for calendar-year 1992 totaled 8,681 cars. The total included 1,925 XJ6 sedans, 2,707 Sovereign sedans, 1,744 Vanden Plas sedans, 247 Vanden Plas Majestic sedans, 702 XJ-S coupes and 1,356 XJ-S-SC convertibles.

MODEL YEAR SALES AND TOURIST DELIVERIES (U.S.): Jaguar's U.S. retail sales and tourist deliveries for model year 1992 totaled 8,612 cars. This total included 939 XJ6 sedans, 3,663 Sovereign sedans, 1,655 Vanden Plas sedans, 225 Vanden Plas Majestic sedans, 777 XJ-S coupes and 1,353 XJ-SC convertibles.

MANUFACTURER: Jaguar Cars, Ltd., Browns Lane, Allesley, Coventry, England.

DISTRIBUTOR: Jaguar Cars, Inc., 555 MacArthur Boulevard, Mahwah, New Jersey.

HISTORY: Introduced in September 1991. Jaguar celebrated its 70th anniversary in September 1992. Jaguar's Nick Scheele said, "Sir William Lyons believed in providing his customers with distinctive, exciting products which offered world class performance, ride and handling at a value for money price. Our aim for the future is to ... produce new products which are unmistakably Jaguar and are worthy of their heritage." New Jaguar "Insignia" models were launched late in 1992 for 1993 and created more individual and distinctive Jaguar and Daimler cars.

From a heritage of inspired design and engineering, comes the best Jaguar ever built.

They are some of the most coveted automobiles of all time. The 1961 E-type. The 1954 XK-140. The 1936 SS-100—automobiles that created the indelible tradition of Jaguar design and engineering excellence. Today, that tradition is carried forward by the 1992 XJS.

Through the years, Jaguar has pioneered technological innovations such as monocoque construction, four-wheel disc brakes, and fully independent suspension—achievements reflected today in the best sporting Jaguar ever built.

Now, computers and robotics are part of a highly advanced manufacturing process. New quality assurance procedures and sophisticated electronic controls exist side-by-side with the time-honored art of handcrafting wood and leather.

For its owner, the reward is a car of sensuous beauty and enviable performance. Its interior is an environment of unparalleled luxury and convenience. Race-bred handling and agile response create a relationship between driver and car at once confident and exhilirating.

And for 1992, even Jaguar's warranty has been enhanced, to four years/50,000 miles. For the nearest dealer, who can provide details on the limited warranty and Jaguar Royal Charter Care, call 1-800-4-JAGUAR.

J A G U A R

A   B L E N D I N G   O F   A R T   A N D   M A C H I N E

Jaguar Heritage—North America

1992 Jaguar XJ-S convertible

A 1922 Swallow Sidecar stands next to the XJ 220 in 1993. *Jaguar Heritage—North America*

1993

XJ6 (XJ-40) — SIX — The Sovereign trim level became the XJ6. A new body-colored front spoiler improved aerodynamic performance. Other new features included a CFC-free air conditioning system.

XJ6 (XJ-40) VANDEN PLAS — SIX — Standard equipment was the same as on the XJ6 sedan, plus special metallic paint, unique chrome trim and special badges, and Autolux leather upholstery.

XJ-12 (XJ-40) — SIX — A new 301-hp late-year model was fashioned from an XJ6 sedan modified to house an all-new 6.0-liter 24-valve V-12 engine. Records indicate 512 of these cars were sold as 1993 model-year units, although the XJ-12 is often considered a 1994 model.

XJ-S (4.0 LITER) COUPE — SIX — This year the Jaguar XJ-S coupe came with the 4.0-liter inline six under the bonnet. The XJ-S got a new four-speed electronic ZF automatic transmission.

XJ-S (4.0 LITER) CONVERTIBLE — SIX — The Jaguar XJ-S convertible also used the 4.0-liter six. A stainless steel strut assembly increased the torsional rigidity of the convertible body shell by 25 percent.

XJ-S-R (6.0 LITER) COUPE — V-12 — Since 1988, Tom Walkinshaw Racing's JaguarSport group had been turning out the XJ-S-R (racing). In 1993, 50 coupes and 50 convertibles were built for the U.S. market with Bilstein gas-pressurized shock absorbers, and heavy-duty suspension.

XJ-S-R (6.0 LITER) CONVERTIBLE — V-12 — Special features of the XJ-S-R convertible were similar to those for the coupe. The open car came with a power top and a heated glass back window.

I.D. DATA: The Vehicle Identification Number is located on the top left-hand surface of the instrument panel and is visible through the windshield. The VIN has 17 symbols. The first three symbols indicate the origin and make: SAJ=British Jaguar. The fourth symbol designates the model. The fifth symbol designates the specification and restraint system. The sixth symbol designates the body style. The fourth, fifth and sixth symbols are referred to in some sources as the model number: HW1-XJ6 sedan, KW1=XJ6 Vanden Plas, NW5=XJ-S coupe, NW4=XJ-S convertible. The seventh symbol is the engine code. The eighth symbol indicates the type of transmission and steering system. The ninth character is the check digit. The 10th symbol indicates the model year: P=1993. The 11th symbol indicates the assembly plant: C=Browns Lane, England. The last six symbols are the sequential production number.

Model	Body Type & Seating	Engine Type/CID	P.O.E. Price	Weight (lbs.)	Production Total
XJ6 Sovereign Sedan					
XJ6 Sovereign	4d Sedan-5P	I6/243	$50,330	4,024	N/A
XJ6 Vanden Plas Sedan					
VDP	4d Sedan -5P	I6/243	$57,330	4,035	N/A
XJ-S Coupe					
4.0L	2d Coupe-2+2P	I6/243	$50,330	3,725	N/A
XJ-S Convertible					
4.0L	2d Convertible-2+2P	I6/243	$57,330	3,950	N/A
XJ-S-R Coupe					
6.0L	2d Coupe-2+2P	V12/366	$50,330	4,025	50
XJ-S-R Convertible					
6.0L	2d Convertible-2+2P	V12/366	$73,000	4,200	50
XJ-12 Sedan					
6.0L	2d Coupe-2+2P	V12/366	$80,100	3,970	N/A

Note 1: For the calendar year Jaguar Ltd. produced 24,883 Jaguars and 4,684 Daimlers for the worldwide market.

ENGINES

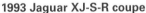

BASE SIX XJ6 and VANDEN PLAS: Inline, dual overhead-cam six-cylinder (AJ6 24-valve). Aluminum block and head. Displacement: 243 cid (3980 cc). Bore & Stroke: 3.58 x 4.015 in. (91 x 102 mm). Compression Ratio: 9.5:1. Brake Horsepower: 223 at 4750 rpm. Torque: 278 lbs.-ft. at 3650 rpm. Port fuel injection.

BASE SIX XJ-S COUPE and XJ-S CONVERTIBLE: Inline, dual overhead-cam six-cylinder (AJ6 24-valve). Aluminum block and head. Displacement: 243 cid (3980 cc). Bore & Stroke: 3.58 x 4.015 in. (91 x 102 mm). Compression Ratio: 9.5:1. Brake Horsepower: 219 at 4750 rpm. Torque: 278 lbs.-ft. at 3650 rpm. Port fuel injection.

BASE SIX XJ-S-R COUPE and XJ-S-R CONVERTIBLE: 60-degree, "vee" type overhead-cam twelve-cylinder. Aluminum block and heads. Displacement: 366 cid (5993 cc). Bore & Stroke: 3.54 x 3.10 in. (90 x 78.5 mm). Compression Ratio: 11.0:1. Brake Horsepower: 318 at 5200 rpm. Torque: 339 lb-ft. at 3750 rpm. Seven main bearings. Thimble tappets. Port fuel injection.

BASE V-12 XJ-12 SEDAN: 60-degree, "vee" type overhead-cam twelve-cylinder. Aluminum block and heads. Displacement: 366 cid (5993 cc). Bore & Stroke: 3.54 x 3.10 in. (90 x 78.5 mm). Compression Ratio: 11.0:1. Brake Horsepower: 301 at 5350 rpm. Torque: 339 lb-ft. at 3750 rpm. Seven main bearings. Thimble tappets. Port fuel injection.

CHASSIS

XJ6: Wheelbase: 113 in. Overall Length: 196.4 in. Height: 54.1 in. Width: 78.9 in. Front Tread: 59.1 in. Rear Tread: 59.0 in. Wheel Type: ventilated chrome disc. Standard Tires: 205/70VR15 Pirelli P5.

XJ6 VANDEN PLAS: Wheelbase: 113 in. Overall Length:

1993 Jaguar XJ-S-R coupe

1993 Jaguar XJ-S convertible

196.4 in. Height: 54.1 in. Width: 78.9 in. Front Tread: 59.1 in. Rear Tread: 59.0 in. Wheel Type: ventilated chrome disc. Standard Tires: 205/70VR15 Pirelli P5.

XJ-S COUPE: Wheelbase: 102.0 in. Overall Length: 191.7 in. Height: 48.6 in. Width: 70.6 in. Front Tread: 58.6 in. Rear Tread: 59.2 in. Wheel Type: cast aluminum alloy. Standard Tires: Pirelli P600 235/60VR15.

XJ-S CONVERTIBLE: Wheelbase: 102.0 in. Overall Length: 191.7 in. Height: 48.6 in. Width: 70.6 in. Front Tread: 58.6 in. Rear Tread: 59.2 in. Wheel Type: cast aluminum alloy. Standard Tires: Pirelli P600 235/60VR15.

XJ-S-R COUPE: Wheelbase: 102.0 in. Overall Length: 191.7 in. Height: 48.6 in. Width: 70.6 in. Front Tread: 58.6 in. Rear Tread: 59.2 in. Wheel Type: 16 x 8 JaguarSport cast aluminum alloy. Standard Tires: Goodyear Eagle 225/50ZR-16 (front), Goodyear Eagle 245/55ZR-16 (rear).

XJ-S-R CONVERTIBLE: Wheelbase: 102.0 in. Overall Length: 191.7 in. Height: 48.6 in. Width: 70.6 in. Front Tread: 58.6 in. Rear Tread: 59.2 in. Wheel Type: 16 x 8 JaguarSport cast aluminum alloy. Standard Tires: Goodyear Eagle 225/50ZR-16 (front), Goodyear Eagle 245/55ZR-16 (rear).

XJ-12 SEDAN: Wheelbase: 113 in. Overall Length: 196.4 in. Height: 54.1 in. Width: 78.9 in. Front Tread: 59.1 in. Rear Tread: 59.0 in.

TECHNICAL

XJ6: Layout: front-engine, rear-drive. Transmission: Four-speed automatic. Standard final drive ratio: 3.59:1. Steering: rack-and-pinion, power-assisted. Brakes: front/rear disc. Suspension (front): upper/lower control arms with coil springs and anti-roll bar. Suspension (rear): independent with lower control arms, ride-leveling struts and coil springs. Body Construction: steel unibody. Fuel Tank: 23.2 gallons.

XJ6 VANDEN PLAS: Layout: front-engine, rear-drive. Transmission: Four-speed automatic. Standard final drive ratio: 3.58:1. Steering: rack-and-pinion, power-assisted. Brakes: front/rear disc. Suspension (front): upper/lower control arms with coil springs and anti-roll bar. Suspension (rear): independent with lower control arms, ride-leveling struts and coil springs. Body Construction: steel unibody. Fuel Tank: 23.2 gallons.

XJ-S COUPE: Layout: front-engine, rear-drive. Transmission: Automatic. Standard final drive ratio: 2.88:1. Steering: rack-and-pinion, power-assisted. Brakes: front/rear disc. Suspension (front): upper/lower control arms with coil springs and anti-roll bar. Suspension (rear): independent with coil springs. Body Construction: steel unibody. Fuel Tank: 24 gallons.

XJ-S CONVERTIBLE: Layout: front-engine, rear-drive. Transmission: Automatic. Standard final drive ratio: 2.88:1. Steering: rack-and-pinion, power-assisted. Brakes: front/rear disc. Suspension (front): upper/lower control arms with coil springs and anti-roll bar. Suspension (rear): independent with coil springs. Body Construction: steel unibody. Fuel Tank: 21.6 gallons.

XJ-S-R COUPE: Layout: front-engine, rear-drive. Transmission: Three-speed automatic. Standard final drive ratio: 2.88:1. Steering: rack-and-pinion, power-assisted. Brakes: 11.1-in. vented front disc/10.3-in. inboard rear disc.

Suspension (front): upper/lower A-arms, coil springs, tube shocks and anti-roll bar. Suspension (rear): lower A-arms, fixed half shafts acting as upper links, trailing arms, dual coil springs and dual tube shocks. Body Construction: steel unibody. Fuel Tank: 23.6 gallons.

XJ-S-R CONVERTIBLE: Layout: front-engine, rear-drive. Transmission: Three-speed automatic. Standard final drive ratio: 2.88:1. Steering: rack-and-pinion, power-assisted. Brakes: 11.1-in. vented front disc/10.3-in. inboard rear disc. Suspension (front): upper/lower A-arms, coil springs, tube shocks and anti-roll bar. Suspension (rear): lower A-arms, fixed half shafts acting as upper links, trailing arms, dual coil springs and dual tube shocks. Body Construction: steel unibody. Fuel Tank: 21.6 gallons.

XJ-12 SEDAN: Layout: front-engine, rear-drive. Transmission: Four-speed automatic. Standard final drive ratio: 3.59:1. Steering: rack-and-pinion, power-assisted. Brakes: front/rear disc. Suspension (front): upper/lower control arms with coil springs and anti-roll bar. Suspension (rear): independent with lower control arms, ride-leveling struts and coil springs. Body Construction: steel unibody. Fuel Tank: 23.2 gallons.

PERFORMANCE

XJ6: Acceleration (0-60 mph): 8.3 seconds. Acceleration (quarter mile) 16.8 seconds. Fuel mileage: 17 to 22 mpg.

XJ-S: Acceleration (0-60 mph): 7.8 seconds. Acceleration (quarter mile) 16.3 seconds. Fuel mileage: 17 to 23 mpg.

XJ-S-R: Top speed: 167 mph. Acceleration (0-60 mph): 7.0 seconds. Acceleration (quarter mile): 15.2 seconds at 96.0 mph. Fuel mileage: 12 to 16 mpg.

XJ-12: Acceleration (0-60 mph): 7.5 seconds. Acceleration (quarter mile) 15.9 seconds. Fuel mileage: 12 to 16 mpg.

CALENDAR YEAR SALES AND TOURIST DELIVERIES (U.S.): Jaguar's U.S. retail sales and tourist deliveries for calendar-year 1993 totaled 12,734 cars. The total included 7,134 XJ6 sedans, 37 Sovereign sedans, 1,838 Vanden Plas sedans, 3 Vanden Plas Majestic sedans, 756 XJ-12 sedans, 890 XJ-S coupes and 2,076 XJ-S convertibles.

MODEL YEAR SALES AND TOURIST DELIVERIES (U.S.): Jaguar's U.S. retail sales and tourist deliveries for model year 1993 totaled 11,090 cars. This included 5,922 XJ6 sedans, 150 Sovereign sedans, 1,759 Vanden Plas sedans, 39 Vanden Plas Majestic sedans, 512 XJ-12s, 954 XJ-S coupes and 1,764 XJ-S convertibles.

MANUFACTURER: Jaguar Cars, Ltd., Browns Lane, Allesley, Coventry, England.

DISTRIBUTOR: Jaguar Cars, Inc., 555 MacArthur Boulevard, Mahwah, New Jersey.

HISTORY: The XJ-12 sedan and its Daimler Double Six cousin used a more powerful, refined, and economical 6.0-liter 318-hp V-12. The XJ6 earned the title "Safest Car in Britain" in a government survey. During 1993, Jaguars went on sale in Russia and Eastern Block countries and Inchcape Pacific was made Jaguar's China distributor. In 1993, limited number XJR-S 6.0-litre models were sold only in the U.S. market and all are very collectible.

1993 Jaguar Vanden Plas sedan

1994

XJ6 (XJ-40) SEDAN — SIX — Jaguar offered a flagship sedan with power that set it above the masses. Standard features included 4-wheel power disc ABS brakes, automatic temperature control CFC-free air conditioning, 12-way power memory seats, a power sunroof, and an 80-watt Alpine stereo.

XJ6 (XJ-40) VANDEN PLAS — SIX — Standard equipment on the Vanden Plas model was the same as on the XJ6 sedan, plus special metallic paint with a contrasting rear panel and wheels, unique hood and upper side chrome trim, special badges, Autolux leather upholstery and Wilton carpets.

XJ-12 (XJ-40) SEDAN — V-12 — Standard features included a V-12, 4-wheel power disc ABS brakes, automatic temperature control CFC-free air conditioning, a power sunroof and a premium stereo system with CD player. A driver's side airbag was installed in 30 percent of 892 cars.

XJ-S 4.0-LITER COUPE — SIX — Standard features included a six-cylinder engine, 4-wheel power disc ABS brakes, automatic-temperature-control air conditioning, and a premium sound system. Eighty percent had a limited-slip differential.

XJ-S 4.0-LITER CONVERTIBLE — SIX — The six-cylinder convertible included a stainless steel strut assembly under the front end of the car to increase the torsional rigidity of the convertible body shell by 25 percent. Standard features included a power top and a heated glass back window.

XJ-S 6.0-LITER COUPE — V-12 — The V-12 was used in 18.4 percent of the XJ-S model, including coupes. The 6.0-liter coupe had standard equipment similar to that of the 4.0-liter coupe.

XJ-S 6.0-LITER CONVERTIBLE — V-12 — The V-12 was used in 18.4 percent of the XJ-S models made in the calendar year. The 6.0-liter convertible had standard equipment similar to the 4.0-liter convertible.

I.D. DATA: The Vehicle Identification Number is located on the top left-hand surface of the instrument panel and is visible through the windshield. The VIN has 17 symbols. The first three symbols indicate the origin and make: SAJ=British Jaguar. The fourth symbol designates the model. The fifth symbol designates the specification and restraint system. The sixth symbol designates the body style. The fourth, fifth and sixth symbols are referred to in some sources as the model number: HX1=XJ6 sedan, KX1=XJ6 Vanden Plas, MX1-XJ-12 NX5=XJ-S coupe, NX5=XJ-12 coupe, NX2=XJ-S6 convertible, NX2=XJ-12 convertible. The seventh symbol is the engine code. The eighth symbol indicates the type of transmission and steering system. The ninth character is the check digit. The 10th symbol indicates the model year: R=1994. The 11th symbol indicates the assembly plant: C=Browns Lane, England. The last six symbols are the sequential production number.

ENGINES

BASE SIX XJ6 and XJ6 VANDEN PLAS: Inline, dual overhead-cam six-cylinder (AJ6 24-valve). Aluminum block and head. Displacement: 243 cid (3980 cc). Bore & Stroke: 3.58 x 4.015 in. (91 x 102 mm). Compression Ratio: 9.5:1. Brake Horsepower: 223 at 4750 rpm. Torque: 278 lbs.-ft. at 3650 rpm. Port fuel injection.

BASE SIX XJ-S 4.0-LITER COUPE and 4.0-LITER CONVERTIBLE: Inline, dual overhead-cam six-cylinder (AJ6 24-valve). Aluminum block and head. Displacement: 243 cid (3980 cc). Bore & Stroke: 3.58 x 4.015 in. (91 x 102 mm). Compression Ratio: 9.5:1. Brake Horsepower: 219 at 4750 rpm. Torque: 278 lbs.-ft. at 3650 rpm. Port fuel injection.

BASE SIX XJ-S-R 6.0-LITER COUPE and 6.0-LITER CONVERTIBLE: 60-degree, "vee" type overhead-cam twelve-cylinder. Aluminum block and heads. Displacement: 366 cid (5993 cc). Bore & Stroke: 3.54 x 3.10 in. (90 x 78.5 mm). Compression Ratio: 11.0:1. Brake Horsepower: 301 at 5350 rpm. Seven main bearings. Thimble tappets. Port fuel injection.

BASE 6.0-LITER V-12 XJ-12 SEDAN: 60-degree, "vee" type overhead-cam twelve-cylinder. Aluminum block and heads. Displacement: 366 cid (5993 cc). Bore & Stroke: 3.54 x 3.10 in. (90 x 78.5 mm). Compression Ratio: 11.0:1. Brake Horsepower: 301 at 5350 rpm. Seven main bearings. Thimble tappets. Port fuel injection.

CHASSIS

XJ6: Wheelbase: 113 in. Overall Length: 196.5 in. Height: 54.3 in. Width: 78.9 in. Front Tread: 59.1 in. Rear Tread: 59.0 in. Wheel Type: ventilated chrome disc.

XJ6 VANDEN PLAS: Wheelbase: 113 in. Overall Length: 195.4 in. Height: 54.3 in. Width: 78.9 in. Front Tread: 59.1 in. Rear Tread: 59.0 in. Wheel Type: ventilated chrome disc.

XJ-S 4.0-LITER COUPE: Wheelbase: 102.0 in. Overall Length: 191.7 in. Height: 48.7 in. Width: 70.6 in. Front Tread: 58.6 in. Rear Tread: 59.2 in. Wheel Type: cast aluminum alloy.

XJ-S 4.0-LITER CONVERTIBLE: Wheelbase: 102.0 in. Overall Length: 191.7 in. Height: 48.7 in. Width: 70.6 in. Front Tread: 58.6 in. Rear Tread: 59.2 in. Wheel Type: cast aluminum alloy.

XJ-S 6.0-LITER COUPE: Wheelbase: 102.0 in. Overall Length: 191.7 in. Height: 48.7 in. Width: 70.6 in. Front Tread: 58.6 in. Rear Tread: 59.2 in. Wheel Type: cast aluminum alloy.

XJ-S 6.0-LITER CONVERTIBLE: Wheelbase: 102.0 in. Overall Length: 191.7 in. Height: 48.7 in. Width: 70.6 in. Front Tread: 58.6 in. Rear Tread: 59.2 in. Wheel Type: cast aluminum alloy.

XJ-12 SEDAN: Wheelbase: 113 in. Overall Length: 196.4 in. Height: 54.1 in. Width: 79.3 in. Front Tread: 59.1 in. Rear Tread: 59.0 in.

TECHNICAL

XJ6: Layout: front-engine, rear-drive. Transmission: Four-speed automatic. Standard final drive ratio: 3.59:1. Steering:

1994 Jaguar XJ-S coupe and convertible *Phil Hall Collection*

The most deeply civilized supercar on the world's roads today.

MODEL	BODY TYPE & SEATING	ENGINE TYPE/CID	P.O.E. PRICE	WEIGHT (LBS.)	PRODUCTION TOTAL
XJ6 Sedan					
XJ6 SXJ6	4d Sedan-5P	I6/243	$52,330	4,075	N/A
XJ6 Vanden Plas Sedan					
Vanden Plas	4d Sedan-5P	I6/243	$59,980	4,105	N/A
XJ-12 Sedan					
XJ-12	4d Sedan-5P	V12/366	$72,330	4,445	N/A
XJ-S 4.0-Litre Coupe					
4.0	2d Coupe-2+2P	I6/243	$52,530	3,805	N/A
XJ-S 4.0-Litre Convertible					
4.0	2d Convertible-2+2P	I6/243	$60,530	3,980	N/A
XJ-S 6.0-Litre Coupe					
6.0	2d Coupe-2+2P	V12/366	$70,530	4,053	N/A
XJ-S 6.0-Litre Convertible					
6.0	2d Convertible-2+2P	V12/366	$80,530	4,306	N/A

Note 1: For the calendar year Jaguar Ltd. produced 25,940 Jaguars and 5,489 Daimlers for the worldwide market.

rack-and-pinion, power-assisted. Brakes: front/rear disc. Suspension (front): upper/lower control arms with coil springs and anti-roll bar. Suspension (rear): independent with lower control arms, ride-leveling struts and coil springs. Body Construction: steel unibody. Fuel Tank: 23.2 gallons.

XJ6 VANDEN PLAS: Layout: front-engine, rear-drive. Transmission: Four-speed automatic. Standard final drive ratio: 3.58:1. Steering: rack-and-pinion, power-assisted. Brakes: front/rear disc. Suspension (front): upper/lower control arms with coil springs and anti-roll bar. Suspension (rear): independent with lower control arms, ride-leveling struts and coil springs. Body Construction: steel unibody. Fuel Tank: 23.2 gallons.

XJ-S 4.0-LITER COUPE: Layout: front-engine, rear-drive. Transmission: Automatic. Standard final drive ratio: 2.88:1. Steering: rack-and-pinion, power-assisted. Brakes: front/rear disc. Suspension (front): upper/lower control arms with coil springs and anti-roll bar. Suspension (rear): independent with coil springs. Body Construction: steel unibody. Fuel Tank: 24 gallons.

XJ-S 4.0-LITER CONVERTIBLE: Layout: front-engine, rear-drive. Transmission: Automatic. Standard final drive ratio: 2.88:1. Steering: rack-and-pinion, power-assisted. Brakes: front/rear disc. Suspension (front): upper/lower control arms with coil springs and anti-roll bar. Suspension (rear): independent with coil springs. Body Construction: steel unibody. Fuel Tank: 21.6 gallons.

1994 XJ6 and XJ12 sedans *Phil Hall Collection*

XJ6
4.0L Sedan

XJ12
6.0L Sedan

1994 Jaguar XJ6 sedan *Phil Hall Collection*

XJ-S 6.0-LITER COUPE: Layout: front-engine, rear-drive. Transmission: Automatic. Standard final drive ratio: 2.88:1. Steering: rack-and-pinion, power-assisted. Brakes: front/rear disc. Suspension (front): upper/lower control arms with coil springs and anti-roll bar. Suspension (rear): independent with coil springs. Body Construction: steel unibody. Fuel Tank: 24 gallons.

XJ-S 6.0-LITER CONVERTIBLE: Layout: front-engine, rear-drive. Transmission: Automatic. Standard final drive ratio: 2.88:1. Steering: rack-and-pinion, power-assisted. Brakes: front/rear disc. Suspension (front): upper/lower control arms with coil springs and anti-roll bar. Suspension (rear): independent with coil springs. Body Construction: steel unibody. Fuel Tank: 21.6 gallons.

XJ-12 SEDAN: Layout: front-engine, rear-drive. Transmission: Four-speed automatic. Standard final drive ratio: 3.59:1. Steering: rack-and-pinion, power-assisted. Brakes: front/rear disc. Suspension (front): upper/lower control arms with coil springs and anti-roll bar. Suspension (rear): independent with lower control arms, ride-leveling struts and coil springs. Body Construction: steel unibody. Fuel Tank: 23.2 gallons.

PERFORMANCE

XJ6: Acceleration (0-60 mph): 8.3 seconds. Acceleration (quarter mile): 16.8 seconds. Fuel mileage: 17 to 22 mpg.

XJ-S: Acceleration (0-60 mph): 7.8 seconds. Acceleration (quarter mile): 15.9 seconds. Fuel mileage: 17 to 23 mpg.

XJ-12: Acceleration (0-60 mph): 7.5 seconds. Acceleration (quarter mile): 15.9 seconds. Fuel mileage: 12 to 16 mpg.

CALENDAR YEAR SALES AND TOURIST DELIVERIES (U.S.): Jaguar's U.S. retail sales and tourist deliveries for calendar-year 1994 totaled 15,195 cars. The total included 7,160 XJ6 sedans, 2,712 Vanden Plas sedans, 160 XJR sedans, 871 XJ-12 sedans, 726 XJ-S coupes and 3,566 XJ-S convertibles.

MODEL YEAR SALES AND TOURIST DELIVERIES (U.S.): Jaguar's U.S. retail sales and tourist deliveries for model year 1994 totaled 14,913 cars. This total included 7,776 XJ6 sedans, 2,551 Vanden Plas sedans, 2 XJR sedans, 863 XJ-12s, 800 XJ-S coupes and 3,221 XJ-S convertibles.

MANUFACTURER: Jaguar Cars, PLC, Browns Lane, Allesley, Coventry, England.

DISTRIBUTOR: Jaguar Cars, Inc., 555 MacArthur Boulevard, Mahwah, New Jersey.

HISTORY: The XJ-12 was introduced in April of 1993. The XJ6 started production in September of 1993. Other models started in June of 1993.

1995 Jaguar XJ6 (also called X300) sedan *Jaguar Heritage—North America*

1995

XJ6 SEDAN — SIX — The new XJ Series debuted at the Paris Motor Show in October 1994 and Jaguar launched a new, world-class quality car, simultaneously in every one of its markets around the globe. The new XJ Series was the first product program to be delivered by Jaguar since its acquisition by Ford.

XJ6 VANDEN PLAS LUXURY SEDAN — SIX — The luxurious Vanden Plas model included premium leather interior trim, burl walnut interior trim, and a Luxury package of options. In April, long-wheelbase Vanden Plas sedans started leaving the assembly lines for availability in all markets by June.

XJR SUPERCHARGED SPORT SEDAN — SIX — Standard equipment included a supercharged DOHC inline six, and the Luxury and All-Weather packages.

XJ12 SEDAN — V-12 — Standard equipment included power 4-wheel ABS brakes, an AM/FM stereo cassette system and a 6-disc CD changer, and the Luxury package and All-Weather packages.

XJ-S 4.0-LITER COUPE — SIX — Standard equipment included power rack-and-pinion steering, power 4-wheel ABS brakes, and automatic-temperature-control air conditioning.

XJ-S 4.0-LITER CONVERTIBLE — SIX — In addition to the features of the XJ-S 4.0-liter coupe the six-cylinder XJ-S convertible had a larger fuel tank, and a power folding convertible roof.

XJ-S 6.0-LITER COUPE — V-12 — A color-keyed grille, door mirrors and headlight bezels differentiated the 6.0-litre model from the 4.0-litre model. It had Autolux leather upholstery and the All-Weather package.

XJ-S 6.0-LITER CONVERTIBLE — V-12 — The XJ-S 6.0-liter convertible included the color-keyed grille, Autolux leather upholstery, the All-Weather package, a 6-disc CD changer, and a larger fuel tank.

I.D. DATA: The Vehicle Identification Number is located on the top left-hand surface of the instrument panel and is visible through the windshield. The VIN has 17 symbols. The first three symbols indicate the origin and make: SAJ=British Jaguar. The fourth symbol designates the model. The fifth symbol designates the specification and restraint system. The sixth symbol designates the body style. The fourth, fifth and sixth symbols are referred to in some sources as the model number: HX1-XJ6 sedan, KX1=XJ6 Vanden Plas, PX1=XJR sedan, MX1-XJ12 NX5=XJ-S6 coupe, NX5=XJ12 coupe,

MODEL	BODY TYPE & SEATING	ENGINE TYPE/CID	P.O.E. PRICE	WEIGHT (LBS.)	PRODUCTION TOTAL
XJ6 Sedan					
XJ6	4d Sedan-5P	I6/243	$53,900	4,075	**Note 1**
XJ6 Vanden Plas Sedan					
Vanden Plas	4d Sedan -5P	I6/243	$62,900	4,105	**Note 1**
XJR Sport Sedan					
XJR	4d Sedan-5P	I6/243	$65,950	4,125	**Note 1**
XJ12 Sedan					
XJ12	4d Sedan-5P	V12/366	$77,700	4,445	**Note 1**
XJ-S 4.0 Coupe					
4.0	2d Coupe-2+2P	I6/243	$53,400	3,805	**Note 1**
XJ-S 4.0 Convertible					
4.0	2d Convertible-2P	I6/243	$61,550	3,980	**Note 1**
XJ-S 6.0 Coupe					
6.0	2d Coupe-2+2P	V12/366	$72,350	4,053	**Note 1**
XJ-S 6.0 Convertible					
6.0	2d Convertible-2P	V12/366	$82,550	4,306	**Note 1**

Note 1: For the calendar year Jaguar Ltd. produced 34,421 Jaguars and 6,602 Daimlers for the worldwide market.

1995 Jaguar XJS 6.0-litre 2 + 2 convertible

NX2=XJ-S6 convertible, NX2=XJ12 convertible. The seventh symbol is the engine code. The eighth symbol indicates the type of transmission and steering system. The ninth character is the check digit. The 10th symbol indicates the model year: S=1995. The 11th symbol indicates the assembly plant: C=Browns Lane, England. The last six symbols are the sequential production number.

ENGINES

BASE SIX XJ6 SEDAN and XJ6 VANDEN PLAS SEDAN: Dual-overhead-cam inline six-cylinder (24-valve). Cast-iron block and aluminum heads. Displacement: 243 cid (3980 cc). Bore & Stroke: 3.59 x 2.99 in. (91 x 76 mm). Compression Ratio: 10.0:1. Brake Horsepower: 245 at 4700 rpm. Torque: 289 lbs.-ft. at 4000 rpm. Multi-point fuel injection, twin spray injectors.

BASE SUPERCHARGED SIX XJR: Dual-overhead-cam inline six-cylinder (24-valve) with a Roots-type supercharger and intercooler. Cast-iron block and aluminum heads. Displacement: 243 cid (3980 cc). Bore & Stroke: 3.59 x 2.99 in. (91 x 76 mm). Compression Ratio: 8.5:1. Brake Horsepower: 322 at 5000 rpm. Torque: 378 lbs.-ft. at 3050 rpm. Multi-point fuel injection, twin spray injectors.

BASE V-12 XJ12: Overhead-cam "vee" type twelve-cylinder (24-valve). Aluminum block and heads. Displacement: 243 cid (3980 cc). Bore & Stroke: 3.59 x 2.99 in. (91 x 76 mm). Compression Ratio: 9.0:1. Brake Horsepower: 313 at 5350 rpm. Torque: 353 lbs.-ft. at 3750 rpm. Multi-point fuel injection, twin spray injectors.

BASE SIX XJ-S 4.0-LITER COUPE and XJ-S 4.0-LITER CONVERTIBLE: Dual-overhead-cam inline six-cylinder (24-valve). Cast-iron block and aluminum heads. Displacement: 243 cid (3980 cc). Bore & Stroke: 3.59 x 2.99 in. (91 x 76 mm). Compression Ratio: 10.0:1. Brake Horsepower: 237 at 4700 rpm. Torque: 289 lbs.-ft. at 4000 rpm. Multi-point fuel injection, twin spray injectors.

BASE V-12 XJ-S 6.0-LITER COUPE and 6.0-LITER CONVERTIBLE: Overhead-cam "vee" type twelve-cylinder (24-valve). Aluminum block and heads. Displacement: 243 cid (3980 cc). Bore & Stroke: 3.59 x 2.99 in. (91 x 76 mm). Compression Ratio: 9.0:1. Brake Horsepower: 301 at 5350 rpm.

Torque: 353 lbs.-ft. at 3750 rpm. Multi-point fuel injection, twin spray injectors.

CHASSIS

XJ6 SEDAN: Wheelbase: 113 in. Overall Length: 197.8 in. Height: 53.1 in. Width: 78.9 in. Front Tread: 59.1 in. Rear Tread: 59.0 in. Wheel Type: alloy wheels. Tires: Pirelli P4000 225/60ZR16.

XJ6 VANDEN PLAS LUXURY SEDAN: Wheelbase: (early) 113 in.; (late) 117.9 in. Overall Length: (early) 197.8 in.; (late) 202.8 in. Height: 53.5 in. Width: 78.9 in. Front Tread: 59.1 in. Rear Tread: 59.0 in. Wheel Type: alloy wheels. Tires: Pirelli P4000 225/60ZR16.

XJR SPORT SEDAN: Wheelbase: 113 in. Overall Length: 197.8 in. Height: 53.1 in. Width: 78.9 in. Front Tread: 59.1 in. Rear Tread: 59.0 in. Wheel Type: alloy wheels. Tires: Pirelli P Zero 255/45ZR17.

XJ12 SEDAN: Wheelbase: (early) 113 in.; (late) 117.9 in. Overall Length: (early) 197.8 in.; (late) 202.8 in. Height: 53.5 in. Width: 78.9 in. Front Tread: 59.1 in. Rear Tread: 59.0 in. Wheel Type: alloy wheels. Tires: Pirelli P4000 225/60ZR16.

XJ-S 4.0-LITER COUPE and 4.0 LITER CONVERTIBLE: Wheelbase: 102.0 in. Overall Length: 191.7 in. Height: 48.7 in. Width: 70.6 in. Front Tread: 59.4 in. Rear Tread: 59.4 in. Wheel Type: Sport alloy wheels. Tires: Pirelli P4000 225/60ZR16.

XJ-S 6.0-LITER COUPE and 6.0 LITER CONVERTIBLE: Wheelbase: 102.0 in. Overall Length: 191.2 in. Height: 48.7 in. Width: 70.6 in. Front Tread: 59.4 in. Rear Tread: 59.4 in. Wheel Type: Sport alloy wheels. Tires: Pirelli P4000 225/60ZR16.

TECHNICAL

XJ6 and XJ6 VANDEN PLAS: Layout: front-engine, rear-drive. Transmission: Automatic. Steering: rack-and-pinion, power-assisted. Brakes: power 4-wheel disc ABS. Suspension (front): fully independent, unequal length upper and lower wishbones, steel coil springs, telescopic dampers and anti-roll bar. Suspension (rear): fully independent wishbones with anti-squat concentric steel coil springs on Bilstein dampers. Body Construction: steel unibody. Fuel Tank: 23.1 gallons.

XJR: Layout: front-engine, rear-drive. Transmission: Automatic. Steering: Sport-Tuned speed-sensitive rack-and-pinion, power-assisted. Brakes: power 4-wheel disc ABS. Sport Suspension (front): fully independent, unequal length upper and lower wishbones, steel coil springs, telescopic dampers and anti-roll bar. Sport Suspension (rear): fully independent wishbones with anti-squat concentric steel coil springs on Bilstein dampers. Body Construction: steel unibody. Fuel Tank: 23.1 gallons.

XJ12 SEDAN: Layout: front-engine, rear-drive. Transmission: Automatic. Steering: rack-and-pinion, power-assisted. Brakes:

This 1996 ad shows the Jaguar XJ series, then and now.

power 4-wheel disc ABS. Suspension (front): fully independent, unequal length upper and lower wishbones, steel coil springs, telescopic dampers and anti-roll bar. Suspension (rear): fully independent wishbones with anti-squat concentric steel coil springs on Bilstein dampers. Body Construction: steel unibody. Fuel Tank: 23.1 gallons.

XJ-S 4.0-LITER COUPE AND 4.0-LITER CONVERTIBLE: Layout: front-engine, rear-drive. Transmission: Automatic. Steering: rack-and-pinion, power-assisted. Brakes: power 4-wheel disc ABS. Suspension (front): fully independent, upper and lower A arms, coil springs and anti-roll bar. Suspension (rear): fully independent trailing link with control arm and two coil springs and two telescopic shock absorbers per side. Body Construction: steel unibody. Fuel Tank: 24.0 gallons.

XJ-S 6.0-LITER COUPE AND 6.0-LITER CONVERTIBLE: Layout: front-engine, rear-drive. Transmission: Automatic. Steering: rack-and-pinion, power-assisted. Brakes: power 4-wheel disc ABS. Suspension (front): fully independent, upper and lower A arms, coil springs and anti-roll bar. Suspension (rear): fully independent trailing link with control arm and two coil springs and two telescopic shock absorbers per side. Body Construction: steel unibody. Fuel Tank: 24.0 gallons.

OPTIONS

XJ6: Luxury package including power sun roof and integrated 4-channel garage door and gate opener ($2,900).

XJ6 VANDEN PLAS: Autolux leather upholstery in Vanden Plas sedan only ($250). Premium sound system with CD player ($1,800).

XJR: Nonstandard color or special trim order ($2,000).

XJ12: Engine block heater ($100).

XJ-S 4.0-LITER COUPE: CD player ($800). Sport-tuned suspension ($500).

XJ-S 4.0-LITER CONVERTIBLE: All-Weather package including power headlight washers, engine block heater and heated front seats ($2,000).

XJ-S 6.0-LITER COUPE: Nonstandard color or special trim package ($2,000). Chrome wheels ($1,500)

XJ-S 6.0-LITER CONVERTIBLE: Nonstandard color or special trim package ($2,000).

PERFORMANCE

XJ6: Acceleration (0-60 mph): 8.3 seconds. Acceleration (quarter mile): 16.8 seconds. Fuel mileage: 17 to 22 mpg.

XJR: Acceleration (0-60 mph): 6.6 seconds. Acceleration (quarter mile): 14.9 seconds. Fuel mileage: 15 to 21 mpg.

XJ-S: Acceleration (0-60 mph): 7.8 seconds. Acceleration (quarter mile): 15.9 seconds. Fuel mileage: 17 to 23 mpg.

XJ12: Acceleration (0-60 mph): 7.5 seconds. Acceleration (quarter mile): 15.9 seconds. Fuel mileage: 12 to 16 mpg.

CALENDAR YEAR SALES AND TOURIST DELIVERIES (U.S.): Jaguar's U.S.. retail sales and tourist deliveries for calendar-year 1995 totaled 18,085 cars. The total included 9,120 XJ6 sedans, 3,463 Vanden Plas sedans, 557 XJR sedans, 410 XJ12 sedans, 415 XJ-S coupes and 4,120 XJ-S convertibles. Of the 4,535 total XJ-S models built, 81 percent had the 4.0-liter six installed and 19 percent had the 6.0-liter V-12.

MODEL YEAR SALES AND TOURIST DELIVERIES (U.S.): Jaguar's U.S.. retail sales and tourist deliveries for model year 1995 totaled 17,785 cars. This total included 8,344 XJ6 sedans, 3,418 Vanden Plas sedans, 619 XJR sedans, 566 XJ12s, 494 XJ-S coupes and 4,344 XJ-S convertibles.

MANUFACTURER: Jaguar Cars, PLC, Browns Lane, Allesley, Coventry England.

DISTRIBUTOR: Jaguar Cars, 555 MacArthur Boulevard, Mahwah, New Jersey.

HISTORY: Jaguar's worldwide sales for 1995 rose 45.7 percent, driven by the new XJ Series. In May, the company announced two Celebration XJ-S models to commemorate 60 years of the legendary Jaguar marque. Jaguar's product range was expanded in June with the launch the long-wheelbase XJ sedan.

1995 Jaguar XJR sedan

1996

XJ6 SEDAN — SIX — The leaping jaguar on the hood and a full-size spare were added as standard equipment. The 4L DOHC six was revised. The Luxury package was made standard equipment and the base XJ6 could now be had with the All-Weather package at extra cost.

XJ6 VANDEN PLAS LUXURY SEDAN — SIX — This year all Vanden Plas sedans were on the extended wheelbase. The extra room was all behind the "B" pillar and the roof was modified for an additional half inch of head room. The fabled tea trays adorned the backs of the front seats.

XJR SUPERCHARGED SPORT SEDAN — SIX — A quieter cabin and standard heated rear seats were XJR upgrades. Standard equipment included the All-Weather package, an AM/FM stereo cassette system, and automatic temperature and humidity control.

XJ12 SEDAN — V-12 — This year all XJ12 sedans were on the extended wheelbase. The extra room was all behind the "B" pillar, allowing for an exceptionally spacious backseat with 4-1/2 inches of added legroom. The roof was modified for an additional half inch of head room.

XJ-S 4.0-LITER CONVERTIBLE — SIX — Celebrating its 20th year of production the 1996 XJ-S became the longest running model in Jaguar history, though in its final year of production. Only 4.0-liter convertibles were sold as 1996 models.

I.D. DATA: (North America) The VIN is located on a VIN plate attached to the top left of the dash and visible through the windshield. The black painted aluminum plate is etched with the full VIN. A white painted air bag symbol is to the left of the VIN and "Jaguar Cars Ltd." is in white painted below the VIN. The VIN structure has 17 symbols. The first three symbols are the world manufacturer identifier SAJ=Jaguar. The fourth symbol indicates model: H=XJ6 (U.S..) or Sovereign (Canada), K=Vanden Plas (long wheelbase), M=XJ12, N=XJ-S, P=XJR Sport (short wheelbase). The fifth symbol indicates the restraint system: N=2 air bags (Canada), X=2 air bags (U.S..). The sixth symbol indicates body type: 1=4d sedan, 2=2d convertible 2+ 2, 5=2d coupe, 6=4d 5-seat sedan (long wheelbase). The seventh symbol indicates the engine: 1=4.0-litre supercharged, 2=4.0-litre twin canister, 3=6.0-litre V-12, 7=4.0-litre supercharged twin canister. The eighth symbol indicates type of transmission: 4=5-speed automatic LHS. The ninth symbol is a check digit. The 10th symbol indicates model year: U=1996. The 11th symbol indicates the assembly plant: C=Browns Lane, England. The last six symbols are the sequential production number.

ENGINES

BASE SIX XJ6 SEDAN and VANDEN PLAS SEDAN: Dual-overhead-cam inline six-cylinder (24-valve). Cast-iron block and aluminum heads. Displacement: 243 cid (3980 cc). Bore & Stroke: 3.59 x 2.99 in. (91 x 76 mm). Compression Ratio: 10.0:1. Brake Horsepower: 245 at 4700 rpm. Torque:

MODEL	BODY TYPE & SEATING	ENGINE TYPE/CID	P.O.E. PRICE	WEIGHT (LBS.)	PRODUCTION TOTAL
XJ6 Sedan					
XJ6	4d Sedan-5P	I6/243	$56,900	4,075	**Note 1**
XJ6 Vanden Plas Sedan					
Vanden Plas	4d Sedan-5p	I6/243	$65,000	4,105	**Note 1**
XJR Sedan					
XJR	4d Sedan-5P	I6/243	$66,850	4,125	**Note 1**
XJ12 Sedan					
XJ12	4d Sedan-5P	V12/366	$79,950	4,445	**Note 1**
XJ-S 4.0-Litre Convertible					
4.0	2d Convertible-2+2P	I6/243	$62,150	3,980	**Note 1**

Note 1: For the calendar year Jaguar Ltd. produced 32,382 Jaguars and 6,208 Daimlers for the worldwide market.

1996 Jaguar XK8 coupe *Andrew Morland*

289 lbs.-ft. at 4000 rpm. Multi-point fuel injection, twin spray injectors.

BASE SUPERCHARGED SIX XJR: Dual-overhead-cam inline six-cylinder (24-valve) with a Roots-type supercharger and intercooler. Cast-iron block and aluminum head. Displacement: 243 cid (3980 cc). Bore & Stroke: 3.59 x 2.99 in. (91 x 76 mm). Compression Ratio: 8.5:1. Brake Horsepower: 322 at 5000 rpm. Torque: 378 lbs.-ft. at 3050 rpm. Multi-point fuel injection, twin spray injectors.

BASE V-12 XJ12: Overhead-cam "vee" type twelve-cylinder (24-valve). Aluminum block and heads. Displacement: 243 cid (3980 cc). Bore & Stroke: 3.59 x 2.99 in. (91 x 76 mm). Compression Ratio: 9.0:1. Brake Horsepower: 301 at 5350 rpm. Torque: 353 lbs.-ft. at 3750 rpm. Multi-point fuel injection, twin spray injectors.

BASE SIX XJ-S 4.0-LITER CONVERTIBLE: Dual-overhead-cam inline six-cylinder (24-valve). Cast-iron block and aluminum head. Displacement: 243 cid (3980 cc). Bore & Stroke: 3.59 x 2.99 in. (91 x 76 mm). Compression Ratio: 10.0:1. Brake Horsepower: 237 at 4700 rpm. Torque: 289 lbs.-ft. at 4000 rpm. Multi-point fuel injection, twin spray injectors.

CHASSIS

XJ6 SEDAN: Wheelbase: 113 in. Overall Length: 197.8 in. Height: 53.1 in. Width: 78.9 in. Front Tread: 59.1 in. Rear Tread: 59.0 in. Wheel Type: alloy wheels. Tires: 225/60ZR16.

XJ6 VANDEN PLAS LUXURY SEDAN: Wheelbase: 117.9 in. Overall Length: 202.8 in. Height: 53.5 in. Width: 78.9 in. Front Tread: 59.1 in. Rear Tread: 59.0 in. Wheel Type: alloy wheels. Tires: 225/60ZR16.

XJR SPORT SEDAN: Wheelbase: 113 in. Overall Length: 197.8 in. Height: 53.1 in. Width: 78.9 in. Front Tread: 59.1 in. Rear Tread: 59.0 in. Wheel Type: alloy wheels. Tires: 255/45ZR17.

XJ12 SEDAN: Wheelbase: 117.9 in. Overall Length: 202.8 in. Height: 53.5 in. Width: 78.9 in. Front Tread: 59.1 in. Rear Tread: 59.0 in. Wheel Type: alloy wheels. Tires: 225/60ZR16.

XJ-S 4.0-LITER CONVERTIBLE: Wheelbase: 102.0 in. Overall Length: 191.2 in. Height: 48.7 in. Width: 70.6 in. Front Tread: 59.4 in. Rear Tread: 59.4 in. Wheel Type: Sport alloy wheels. Tires: 225/60ZR16.

TECHNICAL

XJ6: Layout: front-engine, rear-drive. Transmission: Automatic. Steering: rack-and-pinion, power-assisted. Brakes: power 4-wheel disc ABS. Suspension (front): fully independent, unequal length upper and lower wishbones, steel coil springs, telescopic dampers and anti-roll bar. Suspension (rear): fully independent wishbones with anti-squat concentric steel coil springs on Bilstein dampers. Body Construction: steel unibody. Fuel Tank: 23.1 gallons. Trunk volume: 11.1 cu. ft.

XJ6 VANDEN PLAS: Layout: front-engine, rear-drive. Transmission: Automatic. Steering: rack-and-pinion, power-assisted. Brakes: power 4-wheel disc ABS. Suspension (front): fully independent, unequal length upper and lower wishbones, steel coil springs, telescopic dampers and anti-roll bar. Suspension (rear): fully independent wishbones with anti-squat concentric steel coil springs on Bilstein dampers. Body Construction: steel unibody. Fuel Tank: 23.1 gallons. Trunk volume: 12.0 cu. ft.

XJR: Layout: front-engine, rear-drive. Transmission: Automatic. Steering: Sport-Tuned speed-sensitive rack-and-pinion, power-assisted. Brakes: power 4-wheel disc ABS. Sport Suspension (front): fully independent, unequal length upper and lower wishbones, steel coil springs, telescopic dampers and anti-roll bar. Sport Suspension (rear): fully independent wishbones with anti-squat concentric steel coil springs on Bilstein dampers. Body Construction: steel unibody. Fuel Tank: 23.1 gallons. Trunk volume: 11.1 cu. ft.

XJ12 SEDAN: Layout: front-engine, rear-drive. Transmission: Automatic. Steering: rack-and-pinion, power-assisted. Brakes: power 4-wheel disc ABS. Suspension (front): fully independent, unequal length upper and lower wishbones, steel coil springs, telescopic dampers and anti-roll bar. Suspension (rear): fully independent wishbones with anti-squat concentric steel coil springs on Bilstein dampers. Body Construction: steel unibody. Fuel Tank: 23.1 gallons. Trunk volume: 12.0 cu. ft.

XJ-S 4.0-LITER CONVERTIBLE: Layout: front-engine, rear-drive. Transmission: Automatic. Steering: rack-and-pinion,

1996 Jaguar XJR sedan

1996 Jaguar XJ12 sedan

power-assisted. Brakes: power 4-wheel disc ABS. Suspension (front): fully independent, upper and lower A arms, coil springs and anti-roll bar. Suspension (rear): fully independent trailing link with control arm and two coil springs and two telescopic shock absorbers per side. Body Construction: steel unibody. Fuel Tank: 24.0 gallons.

OPTIONS

XJ6: All-Weather package including heated front seats and traction control ($2,250). Nonstandard color or special trim order ($2,000).

XJ6 VANDEN PLAS: CD player ($800). Nonstandard color or special trim order ($2,000).

XJR: Nonstandard color or special trim order ($2,000).

XJ12: Nonstandard color or special trim order ($2,000).

XJ-S 4.0-LITER CONVERTIBLE: All-Weather package including power headlight washers, engine block heater and heated front seats ($300). Sport-tuned suspension ($500).

PERFORMANCE

XJ6: Acceleration (0-60 mph): 8.3 seconds. Acceleration (quarter mile): 16.8 seconds. Fuel mileage: 17 to 22 mpg.

XJR: Acceleration (0-60 mph): 6.6 seconds. Acceleration (quarter mile): 14.9 seconds. Fuel mileage: 15 to 21 mpg.

XJ-S: Acceleration (0-60 mph): 7.8 seconds. Acceleration (quarter mile): 15.9 seconds. Fuel mileage: 17 to 23 mpg.

XJ12: Acceleration (0-60 mph): 7.5 seconds. Acceleration (quarter mile): 15.9 seconds. Fuel mileage: 12 to 16 mpg.

CALENDAR YEAR SALES AND TOURIST DELIVERIES (U.S.): Jaguar's U.S.. retail sales and tourist deliveries for calendar-year 1996 totaled 17,878 cars. The total included 7,583 XJ6 sedans, 4,383 Vanden Plas sedans, 618 XJR sedans, 374 XJ12 sedans, 3 XJ-S coupes, 2,867 XJ-S convertibles and 2,050 (1997 year-model) XK8s.

MODEL YEAR SALES AND TOURIST DELIVERIES (U.S..): Jaguar's U.S.. retail sales and tourist deliveries for model year 1996 totaled 16,576 cars. This total included 7,654 XJ6 sedans, 4,658 Vanden Plas sedans, 515 XJR sedans, 482 XJ12s and 3,267 XJ-S convertibles.

MANUFACTURER: Jaguar Cars, Ltd., (Subsidiary of Ford Motor Company), Browns Lane, Allesley, Coventry England.

DISTRIBUTOR: Jaguar Cars, Inc., 555 MacArthur Boulevard, Mahwah, New Jersey.

HISTORY: The new XJ8 sports car – the "spiritual successor" to the fabled XK-E – was being prepared for its 1997 launch as the year wound to an end. The Museum of Modern Art in New York places an early E-Type roadster in its permanent collection only the third so honored by the museum.

1997 Jaguar XJ6 sedan

1997

XJ6 SEDAN — SIX — A black-vane grille replaced the chrome grille. All XJ6 models received a contoured rear bench seat. Standard equipment included 4-wheel power ABS disc brakes, Luxury package, a four-speed overdrive automatic transmission, and power windows.

XJ6L LONG-WHEELBASE SEDAN — SIX — A long-wheelbase sedan called the XJ6L was added to the XJ6 lineup. Standard equipment included driver and passenger air bags, Luxury package, and a four-speed overdrive automatic transmission.

XJ6 VANDEN PLAS LONG-WHEELBASE LUXURY SEDAN — SIX — The luxurious Vanden Plas model featured the Convenience package which included a universal garage door opener, and a memory seat.

XJR SUPERCHARGED SPORT SEDAN — SIX — The XJR high-performance model returned with a new 3-point center rear safety belt added. Standard features included halogen fog lamps, Luxury package, and compact 6-disc CD changer.

XK8 SPORTS COUPE — V-8 — The elegant new Jaguar XK8 had a new, state-of-the-art V-8 that made 290 hp. This car signaled to the world that Jaguar had returned to a position of prominence. Standard equipment included automatic air conditioning and a five-speed automatic transmission with overdrive.

XK8 SPORTS CONVERTIBLE — V-8 — In addition to standard features of the XK8 coupe, the convertible also had a folding top with a glass rear window.

I.D. DATA: (North America) The VIN is located on a VIN plate attached to the top left of the dash and visible through the windshield. The black painted aluminum plate is etched with the full VIN. A white painted air bag symbol is to the left of the VIN and "Jaguar Cars Ltd." Is white painted below the VIN. The VIN structure has 17 symbols. The first three symbols are the world manufacturer identifier SAJ=Jaguar. The fourth symbol indicates model: G=XK8 coupe and convertible, H=XJ6 (U.S..) or Sovereign (Canada), K=Vanden Plas (long wheelbase), P=XJR Sport (short wheelbase). The fifth symbol indicates the restraint system: N=2 air bags (Canada), X=2 air bags (U.S..). The sixth symbol indicates body type: 1=4d sedan, 2=2d convertible 2+ 2, 5=2d coupe, 6=4d 5-seat sedan (long wheelbase). The seventh symbol indicates the engine:

Model	Body Type & Seating	Engine Type/ CID	P.O.E. Price	Weight (lbs.)	Production Total
XJ6 Sedan					
XJ6	4d Sedan-5P	I6/243	$54,400	4,080	**Note 1**
XJ6L Long-Wheelbase Sedan					
XJ6L	4d Sedan-5P	I6/243	$59,400	4,110	**Note 1**
XJ6 Vanden Plas Sedan					
Vanden Plas	4d Sedan-5p	I6/243	$63,800	4,130	**Note 1**
XJR Sport Sedan					
XJR	4d Sedan-5P	I6/243	$65,300	4,125	**Note 1**
XK8 Sport Coupe					
4.0	2d Coupe-2+2P	V8/243	$64,900	3,673	**Note 1**
XK8 Sport Convertible					
4.0	2d Convertible-2+2P	V8/243	$69,900	3,867	**Note 1**

Note 1: For the calendar year Jaguar Ltd. produced 38,112 Jaguars and 5,439 Daimlers for the worldwide market.

1=4.0-litre supercharged, 2=4.0-litre twin canister, 7=4.0-litre supercharged twin canister. The eighth symbol indicates type of transmission: 4=5-speed automatic LHS, 8=manual 5-speed. The ninth symbol is a check digit. The 10th symbol indicates model year: V=1997. The 11th symbol indicates the assembly plant: C-Browns Lane, England. The last six symbols are the sequential production number.

ENGINES

BASE SIX XJ6, XJ6L and XJ6 VANDEN PLAS: Dual-overhead-cam inline six-cylinder (24-valve). Aluminum alloy block and head. Displacement: 243 cid (3980 cc). Bore & Stroke: 3.58 x 4.02 in. (91 x 102 mm). Compression Ratio: 10.0:1. Brake Horsepower: 245 at 4800 rpm. Torque: 289 lbs.- ft. at 4000 rpm. Electronic port fuel injection.

BASE SUPERCHARGED SIX XJR: Dual-overhead-cam inline six-cylinder (24-valve) with a Roots-type supercharger and intercooler. Aluminum block and head. Displacement: 243 cid (3980 cc). Bore & Stroke: 3.58 x 4.02 in. (91 x 102 mm). Compression Ratio: 8.5:1. Brake Horsepower: 322 at 5000 rpm. Torque: 378 lbs.-ft. at 3050 rpm. Electronic port fuel injection.

BASE V-8 XK8 COUPE and XK8 CONVERTIBLE: Dual-overhead-cam "vee" type eight-cylinder (32-valve). Aluminum block and heads. Displacement: 243 cid (3980 cc). Bore & Stroke: 3.39 x 3.39 in. (86 x 86 mm). Compression

1997 Jaguar XK8 convertible

1997 Jaguar XJ8 sedan

Ratio: 10.75:1. Brake Horsepower: 290 at 6100 rpm. Torque: 290 lbs.-ft. at 4200 rpm. Electronic port fuel injection.

CHASSIS

XJ6 SEDAN: Wheelbase: 113 in. Overall Length: 197.8 in. Height: 53.1 in. Width: 70.8 in. Front Tread: 59.0 in. Rear Tread: 59.0 in. Wheel Type: alloy wheels. Tires: 225/60ZR16.

XJ6L SEDAN: Wheelbase: 117.9 in. Overall Length: 202.8 in. Height: 53.5 in. Width: 70.8 in. Front Tread: 59.0 in. Rear Tread: 59.0 in. Wheel Type: alloy wheels. Tires: 225/60ZR16.

XJ6 VANDEN PLAS LUXURY SEDAN: Wheelbase: 117.9 in. Overall Length: 202.8 in. Height: 53.5 in. Width: 70.8 in. Front Tread: 59.0 in. Rear Tread: 59.0 in. Wheel Type: alloy wheels. Tires: 225/60ZR16.

XJR SPORT SEDAN: Wheelbase: 113 in. Overall Length: 197.8 in. Height: 53.1 in. Width: 70.8 in. Front Tread: 59.0 in. Rear Tread: 59.0 in. Wheel Type: alloy wheels. Tires: 255/45ZR17.

XK8 COUPE: Wheelbase: 101.9 in. Overall Length: 187.4 in. Height: 51.0 in. Width: 72.0 in. Front Tread: 59.0 in. Rear Tread: 59.0 in. Wheel Type: alloy wheels. Tires: 245/50ZR17.

XK8 CONVERTIBLE: Wheelbase: 101.9 in. Overall Length: 187.4 in. Height: 51.4 in. Width: 72.0 in. Front Tread: 59.0 in. Rear Tread: 59.0 in. Wheel Type: alloy wheels. Tires: 245/50ZR17.

TECHNICAL

XJ6: Layout: front-engine, rear-drive. Transmission: Four-speed automatic. Steering: rack-and-pinion, power-assisted. Brakes: power 4-wheel disc ABS. Suspension (front): fully independent, unequal length upper and lower wishbones, steel coil springs, telescopic dampers and anti-roll bar. Suspension (rear): fully independent wishbones with anti-squat concentric steel coil springs on Bilstein dampers. Body Construction: steel unibody. Fuel Tank: 23.1 gallons. Trunk volume: 11.1 cu. ft.

XJ6L and XJ6 VANDEN PLAS: Layout: front-engine, rear-drive. Transmission: Four-speed automatic. Steering: rack-and-pinion, power-assisted. Brakes: power 4-wheel disc ABS. Suspension (front): fully independent, unequal length upper and lower wishbones, steel coil springs, telescopic dampers and anti-roll bar. Suspension (rear): fully independent wishbones with anti-squat concentric steel coil springs on Bilstein dampers. Body Construction: steel unibody. Fuel Tank: 23.1 gallons. Trunk volume: 12.0 cu. ft.

XJR: Layout: front-engine, rear-drive. Transmission: Four-speed automatic. Steering: Sport-Tuned speed-sensitive rack-and-pinion, power-assisted. Brakes: power 4-wheel disc ABS. Sport Suspension (front): fully independent, unequal length upper and lower wishbones, steel coil springs, telescopic dampers and anti-roll bar. Sport Suspension (rear): fully independent wishbones with anti-squat concentric steel coil springs on Bilstein dampers. Body Construction: steel unibody. Fuel Tank: 23.1 gallons. Trunk volume: 11.1 cu. ft.

XJ8 COUPE and XJ8 CONVERTIBLE: Layout: front-engine, rear-drive. Transmission: Five-speed automatic. Steering: rack-and-pinion, power-assisted. Brakes: power 4-wheel disc ABS. Suspension (front): fully independent, unequal length upper and lower wishbones, steel coil springs, telescopic dampers and anti-roll bar. Suspension (rear): fully independent wishbones with anti-squat concentric steel coil springs on Bilstein dampers. Body Construction: steel unibody. Fuel Tank: 23.1 gallons.

OPTIONS

XJ6: All-Weather package including heated front and rear seats and traction control ($2,000). CD changer ($800). Premium sound system with CD player ($1,800).

XJ6L: Convenience package including an automatic remote-control day-night mirror, a memory seat and memorized steering wheel adjustments ($350). Nonstandard color paint ($1,000).

XJ6 VANDEN PLAS: CD changer ($800). California, New York, Massachusetts emissions ($30). Nonstandard color paint ($1,000). Chrome wheels ($1,000).

XJR: Gas guzzler tax ($2,100). California emissions ($30). Nonstandard color paint ($1,000).

XK8 COUPE: All-Weather package including heated front and rear seats and traction control ($2,000). CD changer ($800). Premium sound system with CD player ($1,800).

XK8 CONVERTIBLE: CD changer ($800). Nonstandard color paint ($1,000). Premium sound system with CD player ($1,800). Chrome wheels ($1,000).

PERFORMANCE

XJ6: Acceleration (0-60 mph): 8.3 seconds. Acceleration (quarter mile): 16.8 seconds. Fuel mileage: 17 to 22 mpg.

XJR: Acceleration (0-60 mph): 6.6 seconds. Acceleration (quarter mile): 14.9 seconds. Fuel mileage: 15 to 21 mpg.

XK8 (COUPE): Acceleration (0-60 mph): 6.5 seconds. Acceleration (quarter mile): 15.2 seconds. Fuel mileage: 17 to 25 mpg.

XK8 (CONVERTIBLE): Acceleration (0-60 mph): 6.7 seconds. Acceleration (quarter mile): 15.5 seconds. Fuel mileage: 17 to 24 mpg.

CALENDAR YEAR SALES AND TOURIST DELIVERIES (U.S.): Jaguar's U.S.. retail sales and tourist deliveries for calendar-year 1997 totaled 19,503 cars. The total included 8,598 XJ6/XJ6L sedans, 3,174 Vanden Plas sedans, 768 XJR sedans, 48 XJ12 sedans, 51 XJ-S convertibles and 6,864 XK8s.

MODEL YEAR SALES AND TOURIST DELIVERIES (U.S..): Jaguar's U.S. retail sales and tourist deliveries for model year 1997 totaled 19,197 cars. This total included 7,797 XJ6 sedans, 2,908 Vanden Plas sedans, 635 XJR sedans, 110 XJ12s, 354 XJ-S convertibles and 7,393 XK8s.

MANUFACTURER: Jaguar Cars, Ltd., (Subsidiary of Ford Motor Company), Browns Lane, Allesley, Coventry England.

DISTRIBUTOR: Jaguar Cars, 555 MacArthur Boulevard, Mahwah, New Jersey.

HISTORY: Jaguar kept the production of its two new cars, the S-Type and the "Baby Jag" (X400), in England. The British government committed to giving Ford $70.1 million to produce the X400 at Ford's Halewood plant. Building the 2001 S-Type in England meant retaining 2,900 jobs there. Jaguar U.S. sales rose just over nine percent. A new XJ8 line was due out in 1998.

1997 Jaguar XKR sedan

The pleasure is all yours. Experience the supercharged 322hp, 4.0-litre, 24-valve engine and uniquely calibrated, racing-inspired suspension. Truly, a defiantly individualistic approach to luxury. For more information, call 1-800-4-JAGUAR or visit www.jaguarcars.com/us.

JAGUAR
A new breed of Jaguar

The famed Jaguar "leaper" in motion on a highway.

1998

XJ8 SEDAN — V-8 — The XJ8 succeeded the XJ6. Jaguar dropped the XK8 sports car's 4.0-liter V-8 into the sedan. The XK8's five-speed ZF automatic transmission was also used. Automatic stability control (ASC) was standard. Changes included a beefing up of the chassis to handle the "torquey" V-8.

XJ8L LONG-WHEELBASE SEDAN — V-8 — The XJ8 was offered in the long-wheelbase sedan version, which included the same array of standard equipment as the standard wheelbase model.

XJ8 VANDEN PLAS — V-8 — Standard equipment on the upscale version of the new XJ8 included dual front air bags, new side-mounted air bags mounted in the front seat, automatic-temperature-control air conditioning, 4-wheel power ABS disc brakes, and cruise control among its many features.

XJR SPORT SEDAN — V-8 — Standard equipment on the sports-performance version of the new XJ8 included dual front and new side-mounted air bags, a supercharged DOHC V-8 engine with intercooler, and a power-operated tilt-and-slide sun roof.

XK8 SPORTS COUPE — V-8 — The XK8 enhancements included an engine immobilizer system. Standard equipment included automatic-temperature-control air conditioning, a DOHC V-8 engine, a five-speed ECT automatic transmission with Normal and Sport modes, and Connolly leather upholstery.

XK8 SPORTS CONVERTIBLE — V-8 — Standard equipment on the open-bodied sports car included all features found on the coupe plus a power convertible top with a glass rear window.

I.D. DATA: (North America) The VIN is located on a VIN plate attached to the top left of the dash and visible through the windshield. The black painted aluminum plate is etched with the full VIN. A white painted air bag symbol is to the left of the VIN and "Jaguar Cars Ltd." Is white painted below the VIN. The VIN structure has 17 symbols. The first three symbols are the world manufacturer identifier SAJ=Jaguar. The fourth symbol indicates model: G=XK8 coupe and convertible, H=XJ6 (U.S..) or Sovereign (Canada), H=XJ8/XJ8L, K=Vanden Plas (long wheelbase), P=XJR Sport (short wheelbase). The fifth symbol indicates the restraint system: N=2 air bags (Canada), X=2 air bags (U.S..). The sixth symbol indicates body type: 1=4d sedan, 2=2d convertible 2+ 2, 4=2d convertible, 5=2d coupe, 6=4d 5-seat sedan (long wheelbase), 7=4d 4-seat sedan (long wheelbase). The seventh symbol indicates the engine: 1=4.0-litre supercharged, 2=4.0-litre twin canister, 8=4.0-litre supercharged twin canister, 9=4.0-litre twin canister (Mexico). The eighth symbol indicates type of transmission: 4=5-speed

Model	Body Type & Seating	Engine Type/ CID	P.O.E. Price	Weight (lbs.)	Production Total
XJ8 Sedan					
XJ8	4d Sedan-5P	V8/243	$54,750	3996	**Note 1**
Long-Wheelbase Sedan					
XJ8L	4d Sedan-5P	V8/243	$59,750	4044	**Note 1**
XJ					
Vanden Plas Sedan					
Vanden Plas	4d Sedan-5p	V8/243	$63,800	4048	**Note 1**
XJR Sedan					
XJR	4d Sedan-5P	V8/243	$67,400	4075	**Note 1**
XK8 Coupe					
4.0	2d Coupe-2+2P	V8/243	$64,900	3673	**Note 1**
XK8 Convertible					
4.0	2d Convertible-2+2P	V8/243	$69,900	3867	**Note 1**

Note 1: For the calendar year Jaguar Ltd. produced 43,173 Jaguars and 6,852 Daimlers for the worldwide market.

, X K 8   C O N V E R T I B L E

1998 Jaguar XK8 convertible

automatic LHS. The ninth symbol is a check digit. The 10th symbol indicates model year: W=1998. The 11th symbol indicates the assembly plant: C-Browns Lane, England. The last six symbols are the sequential production number.

ENGINES

BASE V-8 XJ8, XJ8L and XJ8 VANDEN PLAS: Dual-overhead-cam "vee" type eight-cylinder (32-valve). Aluminum block and heads. Displacement: 243 cid (3980 cc). Bore & Stroke: 3.39 x 3.39 in. (86 x 86 mm). Compression Ratio: 10.75:1. Brake Horsepower: 290 at 6100 rpm. Torque: 290 lbs.-ft. at 4200 rpm. Electronic sequential port fuel injection.

BASE V-8 XJR: Dual-overhead-cam "vee" type eight-cylinder (32-valve) with a Roots-type supercharger and intercooler. Aluminum block and head. Displacement: 243 cid (3980 cc).

Bore & Stroke: 3.39 x 3.39 in. (86 x 86 mm). Compression Ratio: 9.0:1. Brake Horsepower: 370 at 6150 rpm. Torque: 387 lbs.-ft. at 3600 rpm. Electronic sequential port fuel injection.

BASE V-8 XK8 COUPE and XK8 CONVERTIBLE: Dual-overhead-cam "vee" type eight-cylinder (32-valve). Aluminum block and heads. Displacement: 243 cid (3980 cc). Bore & Stroke: 3.39 x 3.39 in. (86 x 86 mm). Compression Ratio: 10.75:1. Brake Horsepower: 290 at 6100 rpm. Torque: 290 lbs.-ft. at 4200 rpm. Electronic sequential port fuel injection.

CHASSIS

XJ8 SEDAN: Wheelbase: 113 in. Overall Length: 197.8 in. Height: 52.7 in. Width: 70.8 in. Front Tread: 59.1 in. Rear Tread: 59.0 in. Wheel Type: alloy wheels. Tires: 225/60ZR16.

XJ8L SEDAN: Wheelbase: 117.9 in. Overall Length: 202.7 in. Height: 52.7 in. Width: 70.8 in. Front Tread: 59.1 in. Rear Tread: 59.0 in. Wheel Type: alloy wheels. Tires: 225/60ZR16.

XJ8 VANDEN PLAS LUXURY SEDAN: Wheelbase: 117.9 in. Overall Length: 202.7 in. Height: 53.2 in. Width: 70.8 in. Front Tread: 59.0 in. Rear Tread: 59.0 in. Wheel Type: alloy wheels. Tires: 225/60ZR16.

XJR SPORT SEDAN: Wheelbase: 113 in. Overall Length: 197.8 in. Height: 52.7 in. Width: 70.8 in. Front Tread: 59.1 in. Rear Tread: 59.0 in. Wheel Type: alloy wheels. Tires: 255/45ZR17.

XK8 COUPE: Wheelbase: 101.9 in. Overall Length: 187.4 in. Height: 51.0 in. Width: 72.0 in. Front Tread: 59.2 in. Rear Tread: 59.0 in. Wheel Type: alloy wheels. Tires: 245/50ZR17.

XK8 CONVERTIBLE: Wheelbase: 101.9 in. Overall Length: 187.4 in. Height: 51.4 in. Width: 72.0 in. Front Tread: 59.2 in. Rear Tread: 59.0 in. Wheel Type: alloy wheels. Tires: 245/50ZR17.

TECHNICAL

XJ8: Layout: front-engine, rear-drive. Transmission: Five-speed automatic. Steering: rack-and-pinion, power-assisted. Brakes: power 4-wheel disc ABS. Suspension (front): fully independent, unequal length upper and lower wishbones, steel coil springs, telescopic dampers and anti-roll bar. Suspension (rear): fully independent wishbones with anti-squat concentric steel coil springs on Bilstein dampers. Body Construction: steel unibody. Fuel Tank: 23.1 gallons. Trunk volume: 11.1 cu. ft.

XJ8L and XJ8 VANDEN PLAS: Layout: front-engine, rear-drive. Transmission: Five-speed automatic. Steering: rack-and-pinion, power-assisted. Brakes: power 4-wheel disc ABS. Suspension (front): fully independent, unequal length upper and lower wishbones, steel coil springs, telescopic dampers and anti-roll bar. Suspension (rear): fully independent wishbones with anti-squat concentric steel coil springs on Bilstein dampers. Body Construction: steel unibody. Fuel Tank: 23.1 gallons. Trunk volume: 12.0 cu. ft.

XJR: Layout: front-engine, rear-drive. Transmission: Five-speed automatic. Steering: Sport-Tuned speed-sensitive rack-and-pinion, power-assisted. Brakes: power 4-wheel disc ABS. Sport Suspension (front): fully independent, unequal length upper and lower wishbones, steel coil springs, telescopic dampers and anti-roll bar. Sport Suspension (rear): fully independent wishbones with anti-squat concentric steel coil springs on Bilstein dampers. Body Construction: steel unibody. Fuel Tank: 23.1 gallons. Trunk volume: 11.1 cu. ft.

XJ8 COUPE and XJ8 CONVERTIBLE: Layout: front-engine, rear-drive. Transmission: Five-speed automatic. Steering: rack-and-pinion, power-assisted. Brakes: power 4-wheel disc ABS. Suspension (front): fully independent,

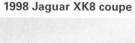

1998 Jaguar XK8 coupe

unequal length upper and lower wishbones, steel coil springs, telescopic dampers and anti-roll bar. Suspension (rear): fully independent wishbones with anti-squat concentric steel coil springs on Bilstein dampers. Body Construction: steel unibody. Fuel Tank: 23.1 gallons.

OPTIONS

XJ8: All-Weather package including heated front and rear seats and traction control ($2,000).

XJ8L: Harmon Kardon audio system including 6-disc CD auto-changer ($1,800).

XJ8 VANDEN PLAS: 6-disc CD auto-changer ($800, but standard with Harmon Kardon audio system).

XJR: Convenience package delete, including a universal garage door opener, a memory seat and memorized steering wheel adjustments ($350 credit).

XK8 COUPE: Premium sound system with CD player ($1800). Chrome wheels ($1,000).

XK8 CONVERTIBLE: All-Weather package including heated front and rear seats and traction control ($2,000). Chrome wheels ($1,000).

PERFORMANCE

XJR: Acceleration (0-60 mph): 6.7 seconds. Acceleration (quarter mile): 13.7 seconds. Fuel mileage: 15-21 mpg.

XK8 (COUPE): Acceleration (0-60 mph): 6.5 seconds. Acceleration (quarter mile): 15.2 seconds. Fuel mileage: 17 to 25 mpg.

XK8 (CONVERTIBLE): Acceleration (0-60 mph): 6.7 seconds. Acceleration (quarter mile): 15.5 seconds. Fuel mileage: 17 to 24 mpg.

CALENDAR YEAR SALES AND TOURIST DELIVERIES (U.S.): Jaguar's U.S.. retail sales and tourist deliveries for calendar-year 1998 totaled 22,503 cars. The total included 10,191 XJ8/XJ8L sedans, 4,789 Vanden Plas sedans, 1,662 XJR sedans and 6,864 XK8s.

MODEL YEAR SALES AND TOURIST DELIVERIES (U.S..): Jaguar's U.S.. retail sales and tourist deliveries for model year 1998 totaled 22,192 cars. This total included 10,075 XJ6 sedans, 4,753 Vanden Plas sedans, 1,479 XJR sedans, 1 XJ12, 1 XJ-S convertible and 5,883 XK8s.

MANUFACTURER: Jaguar Cars, Ltd., (Subsidiary of Ford Motor Company), Browns Lane, Allesley, Coventry, England.

DISTRIBUTOR: Jaguar Cars, 555 MacArthur Boulevard, Mahwah, New Jersey.

HISTORY: At the 1998 Paris Salon, Jaguar unveiled the XK180 concept car, created to commemorate the 50th anniversary of the Jaguar XK sports car. A second XK180 was built for the North American International Auto Show in Detroit in January 1999.

1998 Jaguar XJ8L sedan

1999

XJ8 — V-8 — There were not a lot of changes for the new V-8-powered Jaguar sedans. The 4.0-litre V-8 engine received a number of internal changes including dual-tipped platinum spark plugs, air-assist fuel injectors and a revised electronic throttle and engine management system.

XK8 — V-8 — The XK8's 4.0-litre V-8 engine also had dual-tipped platinum spark plugs, air-assist fuel injectors and a revised electronic throttle and engine management system. Two new paint colors, were called Phoenix (Signal) Red and Alpine (light) Green. A beige convertible top was offered for the first time.

I.D. DATA: (North America) The VIN is located on a VIN plate attached to the top left of the dash and visible through the windshield. The black painted aluminum plate is etched with the full VIN. A white painted air bag symbol is to the left of the VIN and "Jaguar Cars Ltd. Is white painted below the VIN. The VIN structure has 17 symbols. The first three symbols are the world manufacturer identifier SAJ=Jaguar. The fourth symbol indicates model: G=XK8 coupe and convertible, H=XJ8/XJ8L, K=Vanden Plas (long wheelbase), P=XJR Sport (short wheelbase). The fifth symbol indicates the restraint system: D=depowered air bags and side bags (U.S..), E=depowered air bags without side air bags (U.S..), F=depowered air bags and side bags (Canada), G=depowered air bags without side air bags (Canada), N=2 air bags (Canada), P=depowered air bags and side air bags (Mexico), S=full power air bags (Mexico), T=depowered air bags (Mexico), X=2 air bags (U.S..). The sixth symbol indicates body type: 1=4d sedan, 2=2d convertible 2+ 2, 5=2d coupe, 6=4d 5-seat sedan (long wheelbase). The seventh symbol indicates the engine: 0=4.0-litre emissions L, twin canister, 8=4.0-litre supercharged twin canister, 5=4.0-litre emissions C, twin canister. The eighth symbol indicates type of transmission: 4=5-speed automatic LHS. The ninth symbol is a check digit. The 10th symbol indicates model year: X=1999. The 11th symbol indicates the assembly plant: C-Browns Lane, England. The last six symbols are the sequential production number.

ENGINES

BASE V-8 XJ8 and XK8: Dual-overhead-cam "vee" type eight-cylinder (32-valve). Aluminum block and heads. Displacement: 243 cid (3980 cc). Bore & Stroke: 3.39 x 3.39 in. (86 x 86 mm). Compression Ratio: 10.75:1. Brake Horsepower: 290 at 6100 rpm. Torque: 290 lbs.-ft. at 4200 rpm. Electronic sequential port fuel injection.

BASE XJR SUPERCHARGED V-8: Dual-overhead-cam "vee" type eight-cylinder (32-valve) with a Roots-type supercharger and intercooler. Aluminum block and head. Displacement: 243 cid (3980 cc). Bore & Stroke: 3.39 x 3.39 in. (86 x 86 mm). Compression Ratio: 9.0:1. Brake Horsepower: 370 at 6150 rpm. Torque: 387 lbs.-ft. at 3600 rpm. Electronic sequential port fuel injection.

Model	Body Type & Seating	Engine Type/CID	P.O.E. Price	Weight (Lbs.)	Production Total
XJ-Sedan					
XJ8	4d Sedan -5P	V8/243	$55,200	3,938	**Note 1**
XJ8L	4d Sedan -5P	V8/243	$60,250	3,967	**Note 1**
Vanden Plas	4d Sedan-5p	V8/243	$64,300	3,993	**Note 1**
XJR	4d Sedan-5P	V8/243	$68,450	4,026	**Note 1**
XK8					
4.0	2d Coupe-2+2P	V8/243	$65,750	3,709	**Note 1**
4.0	2d Convertible-2+2P	V8/243	$70,750	3,943	**Note 1**

Note 1: U.K. passenger car production figures for calendar year 1999 were: (S-Type) 52,996, (XK8 and XKR) 11,419, (Sedans) 16,900. Jaguar also produced 5,002 Daimlers giving the company a production total of 86,317 cars.

The 1999 Jaguar XK8 dash is inviting to potential drivers.

CHASSIS

XJ: Wheelbase: 113 in. Overall length: 197.8 in. Height: 52.7 in. Width: 70.8 in. Front Tread: 59.2 in. Rear Tread: 59.0 in.

XJR: Wheelbase: 113 in. Overall length: 197.8 in. Height: 52.7 in. Width: 70.8 in. Front Tread: 59.2 in. Rear Tread: 59.0 in.

VANDEN PLAS: 117.9 in. Overall length: 202.7 in. Height: 53.2 in. Width: 70.8 in. Front Tread: 59.2 in. Rear Tread: 59.0 in.

XJ8L: 117.9 in. Overall length: 202.7 in. Height: 53.2 in. Width: 72.0 in. Front Tread: 59.2 in. Rear Tread: 59.0 in.

XK8: 101.9 in. Overall length: 187.4 in. Height: (coupe) 51.0 in.; (convertible) 51.4 in. Width: 72.0 in. Front Tread: 59.2 in. Rear Tread: 59.0 in.

TECHNICAL

XJ: Layout: front-engine, rear-drive. Transmission: five-speed manual. Steering: rack-and-pinion. Brakes: front disc/rear disc. Body Construction: steel unibody.

XJR: Layout: front-engine, rear-drive. Transmission: five-speed manual. Steering: rack-and-pinion. Brakes: front disc/rear disc. Body Construction: steel unibody.

VANDEN PLAS: Layout: front-engine, rear-drive. Transmission: five-speed manual. Steering: rack-and-pinion. Brakes: front disc/rear disc. Body Construction: steel unibody.

XJ8L: Layout: front-engine, rear-drive. Transmission: five-speed manual. Steering: rack-and-pinion. Brakes: front disc/rear disc. Body Construction: steel unibody.

XK8: Layout: front-engine, rear-drive. Transmission: automatic in XK8. Steering: rack-and-pinion. Brakes: front disc/rear disc. Body Construction: steel unibody.

PERFORMANCE

XJR: Acceleration (0-60 mph): 6.7 seconds. Acceleration (quarter mile): 13.7 seconds. EPA Fuel Economy City/Highway miles per gallon: (XJR VDP SC) 15/21.

XJ8L: Fuel Economy City/Highway miles per gallon: (XJ8, XJ8L) 17/24.

XK8: Acceleration 0-60 mph: (coupe) 6.5 seconds, (convertible) 6.7 seconds. Acceleration quarter mile: (coupe) 15.2 seconds; (Convertible) 15.5 seconds. EPA Fuel Economy City/Highway miles per gallon: 17/24.

XKR: Acceleration (0-60 mph): 6.9 seconds. Acceleration (quarter mile): 13.9 seconds. EPA Fuel Economy City/Highway miles per gallon: 16/23.

SALES/PRODUCTION: U.K. passenger Jaguar/Daimler production for calendar year 1999 was 86,317 cars. Model year production for the U.S.. market was 19,498 cars as follows: (XJ8) 7,366, (XK8) 6,154, (Vanden Plas) 4,438, (XJR) 1,540. U.S.. sales of cars registered as 1999 models included: (S-Type) 8,999, (Vanden Plas) 4,521, (XJ6) 8,617, (XJR) 1,760 and (XK8) 5,705. Calendar year sales for the U.S.. market were: (S-Type) 15,541, (Vanden Plas) 4,438, (XJ6) 7,366, (XJR) 1,540, (XK8) 6,154.

MANUFACTURER: Jaguar Cars, Ltd., Browns Lane, Allesley, Coventry, England.

DISTRIBUTOR: Jaguar Cars, Inc., Mahwah, New Jersey.

HISTORY: In the fall of 1999, big changes to company operations took place. Dr. Wolfgang Reitzle – an ex-BMW executive – became chairman of Jaguar and president of PAG, formed earlier in 1999. Beasley and his PR department worked quickly to dispel any notion that Jaguar's individuality or future were threatened. Stuart Dyble, head of Jaguar's communications department, stressed that product committees, program teams and engineering personnel would remain pure Jaguar. Over the years, PAG would pour enormous amounts of money into Jaguar improving its facilities, products and sales, but not the bottom line.

1999 Jaguar XJ8 sedan

The beautiful Jaguar XK 180 concept vehicle.

2000

S-TYPE — SIX/V-8 — Introduced in May 1999 as Jaguar's first offering of the 2000 model year, the S-Type was a key component in Jaguar's plans to increase its worldwide production by 200 percent. Based upon the same platform as the Lincoln LS, the S-Type brought Jaguar luxury and elegance to a segment of the market they had been absent from for decades. Assembled in a new plant at Castle Bromwich, near Birmingham, England, the S-Type was named in honor of the 3.8 S-Type of the 1960s. Its long list of available features included Satellite Navigation, Dynamic Stability Control, Computer Active Technology Suspension and the industry's first application of voice-activated heater, telephone and radio controls.

XJ8 — V-8 — New standard equipment for the Jaguar XJ/Vanden Plas models included all-speed traction control, rain-sensing windshield wipers, child seat tether anchors and Gen II front air bags. The ABS braking system was upgraded and the brake booster was modified to provide a more positive feel. The XJR's power plant was put into the luxurious XJ8 Vanden Plas sedan. The supercharged Vanden Plas offered both sports car performance and limited-edition luxury.

XK8/XKR — V-8 — All XK8 coupes and convertibles received full-range traction control, rain-sensing windshield wipers and larger-diameter front brake rotors. The XKR was easily distinguished by its wire-mesh grille, functional hood louvers, a small rear deck lid spoiler and 18-inch alloy wheels. A supercharged Jaguar engine made the XKR the fastest-accelerating Jaguar since the X-220.

I.D. DATA: (North America) The VIN is located on a VIN plate attached to the top left of the dash and visible through the windshield. The black painted aluminum plate is etched with the full VIN. A white painted air bag symbol is to the left of the VIN and "Jaguar Cars Ltd." is white painted below the VIN. The VIN structure has 17 symbols. The first three symbols are the world manufacturer identifier SAJ=Jaguar. The fourth symbol indicates the market and air bag system (starting in 2000 all Jaguar sedans have driver and passenger front air bags and front seat side airbags): F, B=Canada, P,R=Mexico, D,J=U.S.A. The fifth symbol indicates transmission and steering: A=automatic transmission left-hand steering (LHS). The sixth and seventh symbols indicate body type: 01=S-Type 4-door sedan, 14=XJ8 4d sedan, 15=XJR 4-door sedan, 23=XJ8L 4d sedan, 24=Vanden Plas 4d sedan, 25=Vanden Plas supercharged, 41=XK8/XKR coupe, 42=XK8/XKR convertible. The eighth symbol indicates emissions control system: B=XKR, XJR/Vanden Plas supercharged, C=S-Type V-6, XJ8, XJ8L, Vanden Plas, XK8, D=S-Type V-8. The ninth symbol is a check digit. The 10th symbol indicates model year: Y=2000. The 11th symbol indicates model line and assembly plant: F=3.0-litre S-Type V-6, Castle Bromwich, England, G=4.0-litre S-Type V-8, Castle Bromwich, England, L=4.0-litre sedan, Browns Lane, England,

M=4.0-litre supercharges, Browns Lane, England, N=4.0-litre XK8, Browns Lane, England, P=XKR supercharged, Browns Lane, England. The 12th symbol indicates the model: A, B, C=XK8, F, G, H=XJ Sedan, L, M, N= S-Type. The last five symbols are the sequential production number.

ENGINES

BASE V-6 3.0 S-Type: Dual-overhead-cam "vee" type six-cylinder (32-valve). Aluminum block and heads. Displacement: 181 cid (2967 cc). Bore & Stroke: 3.50 x 3.13 in. (89 x 79.5 mm). Compression Ratio: 10.5:1. Brake Horsepower: 249 at 6810 rpm. Torque: 221 lbs.-ft. at 4520 rpm. Electronic sequential port fuel injection.

BASE V-8 XJ8 and V-8 XK8: Dual-overhead-cam "vee" type eight-cylinder (32-valve). Aluminum block and heads. Displacement: 243 cid (3980 cc). Bore & Stroke: 3.39 x 3.39 in. (86 x 86 mm). Compression Ratio: 10.75:1. Brake Horsepower: 290 at 6100 rpm. Torque: 290 lbs.-ft. at 4200 rpm. Electronic sequential port fuel injection.

BASE V-8 4.0 S-TYPE: Dual-overhead-cam "vee" type eight-cylinder (32-valve). Aluminum block and heads. Displacement: 243 cid (3980 cc). Bore & Stroke: 3.39 x 3.39 in. (86 x 86 mm). Compression Ratio: 10.75:1. Brake Horsepower: 281 at 6100 rpm. Torque: 287 lbs.-ft. at 4300 rpm. Electronic sequential port fuel injection.

BASE XJR SUPERCHARGED V-8, XJ8 and VANDEN PLAS SUPERCHARGED V-8: Dual-overhead-cam "vee" type eight-cylinder (32-valve) with a Roots-type supercharger and intercooler. Aluminum block and heads. Displacement: 243 cid (3980 cc). Bore & Stroke: 3.39 x 3.39 in. (86 x 86 mm). Compression Ratio: 9.0:1. Brake Horsepower: 370 at 6150 rpm. Torque: 387 lbs.-ft. at 3600 rpm. Electronic sequential port fuel injection.

CHASSIS

S-TYPE: Wheelbase: 114.5 in. Overall length: 191.3 in. Height: 55.7 in. Width: 71.6 in. Front Tread: 60.5 in. Rear Tread: 60.8 in.

XJ: Wheelbase: 113 in. Overall length: 197.8 in. Height: 52.7 in. Width: 70.8 in. Front Tread: 59.1 in. Rear Tread: 59.0 in.

XJR: Wheelbase: 113 in. Overall length: 197.8 in. Height: 52.7 in. Width: 70.8 in. Front Tread: 59.1 in. Rear Tread: 59.0 in.

VANDEN PLAS: 117.9 in. Overall length: 202.7 in. Height: 53.2 in. Width: 70.8 in. Front Tread: 59.1 in. Rear Tread: 59.0 in.

XJ8L: 117.9 in. Overall length: 202.7 in. Height: 53.2 in. Width: 70.8 in. Front Tread: 59.1 in. Rear Tread: 59.0 in.

XK8: 101.9 in. Overall length: 187.4 in. Height: (coupe) 51.0 in., (convertible) 51.4 in. Width: 72.0 in. Front Tread: 59.2 in. Rear Tread: 59.0 in.

2000 Jaguar XJR sedan

Model	Body Type & Seating	Engine Type/CID	P.O.E. Price	Weight (lbs.)	Production Total
S-Type					
3.0	4d Sedan-5P	V8/181	$42,500	3,650	**Note 1**
4.0L	4d Sedan-5P	V8/243	$48,000	3,770	**Note 1**
XJ-Sedan					
XJ8	4d Sedan-5P	V8/243	$55,650	3,946	**Note 1**
XJ8L	4d Sedan-5P	V8/243	$60,700	3,988	**Note 1**
Vanden Plas	4d Sedan-5P	V8/243	$64,750	4,010	**Note 1**
XJR	4d Sedan-5P	V8/243	$68,550	4,050	**Note**
XK8					
XK8	2d Coupe-2+2P	V8/243	$66,200	3,726	**Note 1**
XK8	2d Convertible-2+2P	V8/243	$71,200	3,962	**Note 1**
XKR	2d Coupe-2+2P	V8/243	$76,800	3,785	**Note 1**
XKR	2d Convertible-2+2P	V8/243	$81,800	4,021	**Note 1**

Note 1: U.K. passenger car production figures listed the following Jaguar totals for 2000: (S-Type) 53,521, (XK8 and XKR) 12,238, (Sedans) 17,911. Jaguar also produced 5,174 Daimlers giving a total production of 88,844 cars.

The impressive 2000 Jaguar XKR coupe in motion.

XKR: 101.9 in. Overall length: 187.4 in. Height: (coupe) 50.3., (convertible) 50.7 in. Width: 72.0 in. Front Tread: (59.2 in. Rear Tread: 58.6 in.

TECHNICAL

S-TYPE: Layout: front-engine, rear-drive. Transmission: five-speed manual. Steering: rack-and-pinion. Brakes: front disc/rear disc. Body Construction: steel unibody.

XJ: Layout: front-engine, rear-drive. Transmission: five-speed manual. Steering: rack-and-pinion. Brakes: front disc/rear disc. Body Construction: steel unibody.

XJR: Layout: front-engine, rear-drive. Transmission: five-speed manual. Steering: rack-and-pinion. Brakes: front disc/rear disc. Body Construction: steel unibody.

VANDEN PLAS: Layout: front-engine, rear-drive. Transmission: five-speed manual. Steering: rack-and-pinion. Brakes: front disc/rear disc. Body Construction: steel unibody.

XJ8L: Layout: front-engine, rear-drive. Transmission: five-speed manual. Steering: rack-and-pinion. Brakes: front disc/rear disc. Body Construction: steel unibody.

XK8: Layout: front-engine, rear-drive. Transmission: automatic in XK8. Steering: rack-and-pinion. Brakes: front disc/rear disc. Body Construction: steel unibody.

XKR: Layout: front-engine, rear-drive. Transmission: automatic in XK8. Steering: rack-and-pinion. Brakes: front disc/rear disc. Body Construction: steel unibody.

PERFORMANCE

S-TYPE: Acceleration 0-60 mph: (S-Type 3.0) 8.0 seconds; (S-Type 4.0) 6.5 seconds. Acceleration quarter mile: (S-Type 3.0) 15.9 seconds; (S-Type 4.0) 15.0 seconds. EPA Fuel Economy City/Highway miles per gallon: (S-Type 3.0) 18/26; (S-Type 4.0) 17/23.

XJR: Acceleration (0-60 mph): 6.7 seconds. Acceleration (quarter mile): 13.7 seconds. EPA Fuel Economy City/Highway miles per gallon: (XJR VDP SC) 16/21.

XJ8L: Fuel Economy City/Highway miles per gallon: (XJ8, XJ8L) 17/24.

XK8: Acceleration (0-60 mph): 6.5 seconds. Acceleration quarter mile: (coupe) 15.2 seconds, (Convertible) 15.5 seconds. EPA Fuel Economy City/Highway miles per gallon: (coupe) 17/25, (convertible) 16/22.

XKR: Acceleration (0-60 mph): 6.9 seconds. Acceleration (quarter mile): 13.9 seconds. EPA Fuel Economy City/Highway miles per gallon: 16/23.

SALES/PRODUCTION: Calendar year production of Jaguars in England for 2000 included 53,521 S-Types, 12,238 XK8/XKR models and 17,911 sedans. The company also produced 5,174 Jaguars. Jaguar production was included as part of the Ford Group in England. Model year sales for the U.S. market included 24,507 S-Types, 7,155 XJ8/XJ6 models, 6,729 XK8s, 3,944 Vanden Plas models and 1,393 XJRs for a total of 43,728 cars.

MANUFACTURER: Jaguar Cars, Ltd., Browns Lane, Allesley, Coventry, England.

DISTRIBUTOR: Jaguar Cars, Inc., Mahwah, New Jersey.

HISTORY: In the 2000 calendar year, the Jaguar brand was part of the Ford Group of automotive brands. U.S. consumers purchased or leased 4,339,031 new cars and trucks from Ford, Mercury, Lincoln, Jaguar, Volvo, and Land Rover dealers, breaking the company's record of 4,163,369 vehicles set the previous season. At the end of calendar year 2000, Jaguar Cars had 141 retail outlets in the United States. Jaguar set a new U.S. sales record in 2000 as 43,728 customers elected to experience what Jaguar called "the art of performance."

2000 Jaguar S-type sedan

The striking 2001 Jaguar F-type concept vehicle.

2001

S-TYPE — SIX/V-8 — Sales were proceeding as planned, and the S-Type nearly doubled the number of new Jaguars delivered worldwide. The 4.0 received new "Sprint" 10-spoke 16-inch alloy wheels. All body side moldings were eliminated from all S-Types. Reverse Park Control provided rear bumper sonar for object detection.

XJ8 — V-8 — Reverse Park Control was also standard on all XJs. A six-disc CD changer was also standard in all XJs. The Vanden Plas got a new alloy wheel design and a 320-watt Alpine Audiophile Sound system. The XJR got heated rear seats, and the Vanden Plas Supercharged received a satellite navigation system as standard equipment.

XK8 — V-8 — To enhance their performance image, Jaguar offered a selection of high performance components for their cars and introduced the Silverstone limited edition models of the XK8 coupe and convertible. They were equipped with BBS modular wheels, ultra-low profile tires, and aluminum four-piston caliper Brembo brakes. A Platinum coat of paint and unique interior appointments distinguished the Silverstone edition XK8. All XKs received de-powered front and side airbags and front seats with separate head restraints. The front fog lights were fitted in a more flush fashion.

I.D. DATA: (North America) The VIN is located on a VIN plate attached to the top left of the dash and visible through the windshield. The black painted aluminum plate is etched with the full VIN. A white painted air bag symbol is to the left of the VIN and "Jaguar Cars Ltd." is white painted below the VIN. The VIN structure has 17 symbols. The first three symbols are the world manufacturer identifier SAJ=Jaguar. The fourth symbol indicates the market and air bag system (in 2001 all Jaguar sedans have driver and passenger front air bags and front seat side airbags): F=Canada, P=Mexico, D=U.S.A. The fifth symbol indicates transmission and steering: A=automatic transmission left-hand steering (LHS). The sixth and seventh symbols indicate body type: 01=S-Type 4-door sedan, 14=XJ8 4d sedan, 15=XJR 4-door sedan, 23=XJ8L 4d sedan, 24=Vanden Plas 4d sedan, 25=Vanden Plas supercharged, 41=XK8/XKR coupe, 42=XK8/XKR convertible. The eighth symbol indicates emissions control system: B=XKR, XJR/Vanden Plas supercharged, C=S-Type V-6, XJ8, XJ8L, Vanden Plas, XK8, D=X-Type 2.5-litre, G=Mexico V-8 normally aspirated, K=Mexico V-8 supercharged, N=U.S. and Canada S-Type 3.0-litre, P=U.S. and Canada S-Type 4.0-litre, R=Mexico 3.0-litre S-Type, S=Mexico 4.0-litre S-Type. The ninth symbol is a check digit. The 10th symbol indicates model year: 1=2001. The 11th symbol indicates model line and assembly plant: F=3.0-litre S-Type V-6, Castle Bromwich, England, G=4.0-litre S-Type V-8, Castle Bromwich, England, L=4.0-litre sedan, Browns Lane, England, M=4.0-litre supercharges, Browns Lane, England, N=4.0-litre XK8, Browns Lane, England, P=XKR supercharged, Browns Lane, England. The 12th symbol indicates the model: A, B, C=XK, F, G, H=XJ Sedan, L, M, N= S-Type. The last five symbols are the sequential production number.

ENGINES

BASE 3.0-LITRE V-6 S-TYPE: Dual-overhead-cam "vee" type six-cylinder (32-valve). Aluminum block and heads. Displacement: 181 cid (2967 cc). Bore & Stroke: 3.50 x 3.13 in. (89 x 79.5 mm). Compression Ratio: 10.5:1. Brake Horsepower: 240 at 6100 rpm. Torque: 220 lbs.-ft. at 4520 rpm. Electronic sequential port fuel injection.

BASE V-8 XJ8, XK8: Dual-overhead-cam "vee" type eight-cylinder (32-valve). Aluminum block and heads. Displacement: 243 cid (3980 cc). Bore & Stroke: 3.39 x 3.39 in. (86 x 86 mm). Compression Ratio: 10.75:1. Brake Horsepower: 290 at 6100 rpm. Torque: 290 lbs.-ft. at 4200 rpm. Electronic sequential port fuel injection (4.0 S-Type) same as 3996 cc V-8 above except Brake Horsepower: 281 at 61000. Torque: 287 at 4300 rpm.

BASE SUPERCHARGED V-8 XJR, VANDEN PLAS, XK8 SILVERSTONE: Dual-overhead-cam "vee" type eight-cylinder (32-valve) with a Roots-type supercharger and intercooler. Aluminum block and head. Displacement: 243 cid (3980 cc). Bore & Stroke: 3.39 x 3.39 in. (86 x 86 mm). Compression Ratio: 9.0:1. Brake Horsepower: 370 at 6150 rpm. Torque: 387 lbs.-ft. at 3600 rpm. Electronic sequential port fuel injection.

CHASSIS

S-TYPE: Wheelbase: 114.5 in. Overall length: 191.3 in. Height: 55.7 in. Width: 71.6 in. Front Tread: 60.5 in. Rear Tread: 60.8 in.

XJ: Wheelbase: 113 in. Overall length: 197.8 in. Height: 52.7 in. Width: 70.8 in. Front Tread: 59.1 in. Rear Tread: 59.0 in.

XJR: Wheelbase: 113 in. Overall length: 197.8 in. Height: 52.7 in. Width: 70.8 in. Front Tread: 59.1 in. Rear Tread: 59.0 in.

VANDEN PLAS: Wheelbase: 117.9 in. Overall length: 202.7 in. Height: 53.2 in. Width: 70.8 in. Front Tread: 59.1 in. Rear Tread: 59.0 in.

XJ8L: Wheelbase: 117.9 in. Overall length: 202.7 in. Height: 53.2 in. Width: 70.8 in. Front Tread: 59.1 in. Rear Tread: 59.0 in.

XK8: Wheelbase: 101.9 in. Overall length: 187.4 in. Height: (coupe) 51.0 in.; (convertible) 51.4 in. Width: 72.0 in. Front Tread: 59.2 in. Rear Tread: 59.0 in.

XKR: Wheelbase: 101.9 in. Overall length: 187.4 in. Height: (coupe) 50.3.; (convertible) 50.7 in. Width: 72.0 in. Front Tread: (59.2 in. Rear Tread: 58.6 in.

TECHNICAL

S-TYPE: Layout: front-engine, rear-drive. Transmission: five-speed manual. Steering: rack-and-pinion. Brakes: front disc/rear disc. Body Construction: steel unibody.

Pretty in red is this 2001 Jaguar XKR coupe.

Model	Body Type & Seating	Engine Type/ CID	P.O.E. Price	Weight (lbs.)	Production Total
S-Type					
3.0	4d Sedan-5P	V8/181	$43,655	3,816	**Note 1**
4.0L	4d Sedan-5P	V8/243	$49,355	3,903	**Note 1**
XJ-Sedan					
XJ8	4d Sedan-5P	V8/243	$56,355	3,946	**Note 1**
XJ8L	4d Sedan-5P	V8/243	$62,355	3,988	**Note 1**
Vanden Plas	4d Sedan-5p	V8/243	$67,655	4,010	**Note 1**
Vanden Plas SC	4d Sedan-5p	V8/243	$83,355	4,079	**Note 1**
XJR	4d Sedan-5P	V8/243	$69.355	4,050	**Note 1**
XK8					
XK8	2d Coupe-2+2P	V8/243	$69,155	3,726	**Note 1**
XK8	2d Convertible-2+2P	V8/243	$74,155	3,962	**Note 1**
XKR					
XKR	2d Coupe-2+2P	V8/243	$80,155	3,785	**Note 1**
XKR	2d Convertible-2+2P	V8/243	$85,155	4,021	**Note 1**
XKR S	2d Coupe-2+2p	V8/243	$96,905	4,785	**Note 1**
XKR S	2d Convertible 2+2p	V8/243	$96,905	4,021	**Note 1**

Note 1: U.K. passenger car production figures listed the following Jaguar totals for 2001: (S-Type) 38,325, (XK8 and XKR) 10,738, (X-Type) 55,610, (Sedans) 13,722. Jaguar also produced 4,077 Daimlers giving total production of 122,472 cars.

This 2001 Jaguar XK8 convertible is ready for sun and fun.

XJ: Layout: front-engine, rear-drive. Transmission: five-speed manual. Steering: rack-and-pinion. Brakes: front disc/rear disc. Body Construction: steel unibody.

XJR: Layout: front-engine, rear-drive. Transmission: five-speed manual. Steering: rack-and-pinion. Brakes: front disc/rear disc. Body Construction: steel unibody.

VANDEN PLAS: Layout: front-engine, rear-drive. Transmission: five-speed manual. Steering: rack-and-pinion. Brakes: front disc/rear disc. Body Construction: steel unibody.

XJ8L: Layout: front-engine, rear-drive. Transmission: five-speed manual. Steering: rack-and-pinion. Brakes: front disc/rear disc. Body Construction: steel unibody.

XK8: Layout: front-engine, rear-drive. Transmission: automatic in XK8. Steering: rack-and-pinion. Brakes: front disc/rear disc. Body Construction: steel unibody.

XKR: Layout: front-engine, rear-drive. Transmission: automatic in XK8. Steering: rack-and-pinion. Brakes: front disc/rear disc. Body Construction: steel unibody.

PERFORMANCE

S-TYPE: Acceleration 0-60 mph: (S-Type 3.0) 8.0 seconds; (S-Type 4.0) 6.5 seconds. Acceleration quarter mile: (S-Type 3.0) 15.9 seconds; (S-Type 4.0) 15.0 seconds. EPA Fuel Economy City/Highway miles per gallon: (S-Type 3.0) 18/26; (S-Type 4.0) 17/23.

XJR: Acceleration (0-60 mph): 6.7 seconds. Acceleration (quarter mile): 13.7 seconds. EPA Fuel Economy City/Highway miles per gallon: (XJR VDP SC) 16/21.

XJ8L: Fuel Economy City/Highway miles per gallon: (XJ8, XJ8L) 17/24.

XK8: Acceleration (0-60 mph): 6.5 seconds. Acceleration (quarter mile): (coupe) 15.2 seconds; (convertible) 15.5 seconds. EPA Fuel Economy City/Highway miles per gallon: (coupe) 17/25; (convertible) 16/22.

XKR: Acceleration (0-60 mph): 6.9 seconds. Acceleration (quarter mile): 13.9 seconds. EPA Fuel Economy City/Highway miles per gallon: 16/23.

SALES/PRODUCTION: Jaguar production totals in England for calendar-year 2001 were: (S-Type) 38,325, (XK8 and XKR) 10,738, (X-Type) 55,610, (sedans) 13,722. Jaguar also produced 4,077 Daimlers giving total production of 122,472 cars. Jaguar's U.S. market new car sales for calendar-year 2001 were 36,917 units and included: (S-Type) 20,045, (Vanden Plas) 3,591, (XJ6/XJ8) 5,914, (XJR) 1,249, (XK8) 6,118. Jaguar's U.S. market new car sales for calendar-year 2001 were 44,532 and included: (S-Type) 19,548, (Vanden Plas) 3,162, (X-Type) 9,765, (XJ6/XJ8) 5,850, (XJR) 1,070, (XK8) 5,137.

MANUFACTURER: Jaguar Cars, Ltd., Browns Lane, Coventry, England.

DISTRIBUTOR: Aston Martin, Jaguar, Land Rover of North America, Irvine, California.

HISTORY: In the 2001 calendar year, the Jaguar brand was part of the Ford Group of automotive brands. U.S. consumers purchased or leased 4,095,215 new cars and trucks from Ford, Mercury, Lincoln, Jaguar, Volvo, and Land Rover dealers, breaking the company's record of 4,339,031 vehicles set the previous season. At the end of calendar year 2001, Jaguar Cars had 148 retail outlets in the United States. Jaguar set a new U.S. sales record in 2001 as 44,539 customers purchased Jaguars.

2001 Jaguar XJR sedan *Phil Hall Collection*

An array of 2002 Jaguar X-type sedans.

2002

X-TYPE — V-6 — Jaguar's mid-size four-door sedan and first-ever all-wheel-drive car had a sloping roof and a center-divided "electric shaver" grille. It came in 2.5- and 3.0-litre models and both all-aluminum DOHC V-6s were derived from the larger S-Type engine. The 2.5 sedan came fully equipped with hundreds of standard features. The 3.0-litre sedan included the larger 231-hp motor.

S-TYPE — SIX/V-8 — The S-Type came out of Jaguar's Birmingham, England factory, but shared many parts with the Lincoln LS built in Wixom, Michigan. The S-Type could be spotted by its aerodynamic "horse collar" grille and lamps set further apart. It came with a 3.0-litre DOHC V-6, 5-speed automatic transmission and a long list of features. The top-of-the line was the 4.0-litre sedan with a 32-valve V-8.

XJ/Vanden Plas — V-8 — Jaguar's XJ Series models were built at the home plant in Coventry, England. Several new models were added in 2002 – the XJ Sport, the XJR 100 and the Super V-8. The XJ Sport combined the standard V-8 power train with an upgraded sport suspension and 18-in. wheels. The

limited edition XKR 100 commemorated the 100th anniversary of the birth of Jaguar founder Sir William Lyons.

XK8/XKR — V-8 — Also built in Coventry, the XK8 and XKR models were the modern day XKEs with a high-tech flavor. They had a smooth, undulating cigar-shaped body with a nasty "I-mean-business" rake from rear to front. The XK8 had a V-8 and the XKR had a supercharged version. A special built-for-collectors XKR 100 also honored Sir William Lyons. Jaguar built just 300 XKR 100s for North America, 10 percent of them convertibles.

I.D. DATA: (North America) The VIN plate is attached to the top left of the dash and visible through the windshield. The black painted aluminum plate is etched with the full VIN. A white painted air bag symbol is to the left of the VIN and "Jaguar Cars Ltd." is in white below the VIN. The VIN structure has 17 symbols. The first three symbols are the world manufacturer identifier SAJ=Jaguar. The fourth symbol indicates the market and air bag system (in 2002 all Jaguar sedans have driver and passenger front air bags and front seat side airbags and the X-type also has front and rear outboard head cushion air bags): F,G=Canada, P,T=Mexico, D,E=U.S.A. The fifth symbol indicates transmission and steering: A=automatic transmission left-hand steering (LHS), B=manual transmission left-hand steering. The sixth and seventh symbols indicate body type: 01=S-Type 4-door sedan, 03=S-Type Sport 4d sedan, 12=XJ Sport, 14=XJ8 4d sedan, 15=XJR 4-door sedan, 24=Vanden Plas 4d sedan, 25=Vanden Plas supercharged, 41=XK8/XKR coupe, 42=XK8/XKR convertible, 51=X-Type 4d sedan, 53=X-Type Sport 4d sedan. The eighth symbol indicates emissions control system: B=XKR, XJR/Vanden Plas supercharged, C=XJ8, XJ Sport, Vanden Plas, XK8, X-Type 3.0-litre, D=X-Type 2.5-litre, G=Mexico V-8 normally aspirated, K=Mexico V-8 supercharged, N=U.S. and Canada S-Type 3.0-litre, P=U.S. and Canada S-Type 4.0-litre, R=Mexico 3.0-litre S-Type, S=Mexico 4.0-litre S-Type. The ninth symbol is a check digit. The 10th symbol indicates model year: 2=2002. The 11th symbol indicates model line and assembly plant: F=3.0-litre S-Type V-6, Castle Bromwich, England, G=4.0-litre S-Type V-8, Castle Bromwich, England, L=4.0-litre sedan, Browns Lane, England, M=4.0-litre supercharged, Browns Lane, England, N=4.0-litre XK8, Browns Lane, England, P=XKR supercharged, Browns Lane, England, W=3.0-litre X-Type, Halewood, England, X=2.5-litre X-Type, Halewood, England. The 12th symbol indicates the model: A=XK, C,D=X-Type, F=XJ Sedan, L, M, N= S-Type. The last five symbols are the sequential production number.

ENGINES

BASE V-6 X-TYPE 2.5: Dual-overhead-cam "vee" type six-cylinder (32-valve). Aluminum block and heads. Displacement: 151 cid/2.5 litre (2495 cc). Bore & Stroke: 81.6 x 79.5 mm. Compression Ratio: 10.3:1. Brake Horsepower: 192 at 6800 rpm. Torque: 241 Nm. at 30000 rpm. Electronic sequential port fuel injection.

BASE V-6 X-TYPE 3.0: Dual-overhead-cam "vee" type six-cylinder (32-valve). Aluminum block and heads. Displacement: 181 cid/3.0-litre (2967 cc). Bore & Stroke: 89 x 79.5 mm. Compression Ratio: 10.5:1. Brake Horsepower: 227 at 6800 rpm. Torque: 279 Nm. at 3000 rpm. Electronic sequential port fuel injection.

BASE V-6 S-TYPE 3.0: Dual-overhead-cam "vee" type six-cylinder (32-valve). Aluminum block and heads. Displacement: 181 cid/3.0-litre (2967 cc). Bore & Stroke: 89 x 79.5 mm. Compression Ratio: 10.5:1. Brake Horsepower: 235 at 6800 rpm. Torque: 293 Nm. at 4100 rpm. Electronic sequential port fuel injection.

BASE V-8 S-TYPE 4.0: Dual-overhead-cam "vee" type eight-cylinder (32-valve). Aluminum block and heads. Displacement: 243 cid/4.0-litre (3980 cc). Bore & Stroke: 3.39 x 3.39 in. (86 x 86 mm). Compression Ratio: 10.75:1. Brake Horsepower: 281 at 6100. Torque: 287 at 4300 rpm. Electronic sequential port fuel injection.

BASE V-8 XJ8/XK8 4.0: Dual-overhead-cam "vee" type eight-cylinder (32-valve). Aluminum block and heads. Displacement: 243 cid/4.0-litre (3980 cc). Bore & Stroke: 3.39 x 3.39 in. (86 x 86 mm). Compression Ratio: 10.75:1. Brake Horsepower: 290 at 6100 rpm. Torque: 290 lbs.-ft. at 4200 rpm. Electronic sequential port fuel injection.

2002 Jaguar S-type R sedan

Model	Body Type & Seating	Engine Type/CID	P.O.E. Price	Weight (lbs.)	Production Total
X-Type Series					
2.5L	4d Sedan-5P	V6/151	$29,950	3,428	**Note 1**
2.5L	4d Sedan Sport-5P	V6/151	$34,450	3,428	**Note 1**
3.0L	4d Sedan-5P	V6/181	$35,950	3,516	**Note 1**
3.0L	4d Sedan Sport-5P	V6/181	$40,450	3,516	**Note 1**
S-Type Series					
3.0	4d Sedan-5P	V8/181	$43,675	3,816	**Note 1**
3.0	4d Sedan Sport-5P	V8/181	$47,675	3,816	**Note 1**
4.0L	4d Sedan-5P	V8/243	$49,330	3,903	**Note 1**
4.0L	4d Sedan Sport-5P	V8/243	$51,330	3,903	**Note 1**
XJ/Vanden Plas Series					
XJ8	4d Sedan-5P	V8/243	$56,330	3,995	**Note 1**
XJ8	4d Sedan Sport-5P	V8/243	$59,330	3,995	**Note 1**
Vanden Plas	4d Sedan-5p	V8/243	$68,330	4,006	**Note 1**
XJR	4d Sedan-5P	V8/243	$71,830	4,063	**Note 1**
XJ Super	4d Sedan-5P	V8/243	$79,330	4,129	**Note 1**
XK8/XKR Series					
XK8	2d Coupe-2+2P	V8/243	$69,330	3,759	**Note 1**
XK8	2d Convertible-2+2P	V8/243	$74,330	3,990	**Note 1**
XKR	2d Coupe-2+2P	V8/243	$81,330	3,827	**Note 1**
XKR	2d Convertible-2+2P	V8/243	$86,330	4,039	**Note 1**

The exotic 2002 Jaguar Formula One race car.

BASE V-8 XJR, XKR, XJ SUPER: Dual-overhead-cam "vee" type eight-cylinder (32-valve) with a Roots-type supercharger and intercooler. Aluminum block and head. Displacement: 243 cid (3980 cc). Bore & Stroke: 3.39 x 3.39 in. (86 x 86 mm). Compression Ratio: 9.0:1. Brake Horsepower: 370 at 6150 rpm. Torque: 387 lbs.-ft. at 3600 rpm. Electronic sequential port fuel injection.

CHASSIS

X-TYPE: Wheelbase: 106.7 in. Overall length: 183.9 in. Width: 70.4 in. Height: 54.8 in. Tires: P205/55VR16.

S-TYPE: Wheelbase: 114.5 in. Overall length: 191.4 in. Width: 80.3 in. Height: 55.7 in. Tires: (Base) P225/55HR16, (Sport 3.0) P235/50ZR17, (Sport 4.0) P235/50ZR17.

XJ8, XJ Sport, XJR: Wheelbase: 113.0 in. Overall length: 197.8. Width: 70.8 in. Height: 52.7 in.

XJ8 Vanden Plas, XJ Super V-8: Wheelbase: 117.9 in. Overall length: 202.7. Width: 70.8 in. Height: 53.2 in.

XK8: Wheelbase: 101.9 in. Overall length: 187.4 in. Width: 72.0 in. Height: (coupe) 50.5 in., (convertible) 51 in.

XKR, XKR 100: Wheelbase: 101.9 in. Overall length: 187.4 in. Width: 72.0 in. Height: (coupe) 50.3 in., (convertible) 50.7 in.

TECHNICAL

X-TYPE 2.5, 2.5 SPORT: Layout: front-engine, rear-drive. Standard transmission: five-speed manual. Optional transmission: five speed automatic. Steering: rack-and-pinion. Brakes: 4-wheel ABS. Body Construction: steel unibody. Traction control standard.

X-TYPE 3.0, 3.0 SPORT: Layout: front-engine, rear-drive. Standard transmission: five-speed automatic. Optional transmission: five speed automatic. Steering: rack-and-pinion. Brakes: 4-wheel ABS. Body Construction: steel unibody. Traction control standard.

S-TYPE: Layout: front-engine, rear-drive. Standard transmission: six-speed automatic. Steering: rack-and-pinion. Brakes: 4-wheel ABS. Body Construction: steel unibody. Traction control standard.

XJ8, XJ8 VANDEN PLAS, XJR: Layout: front-engine, rear-drive. Standard transmission: five-speed automatic. Steering: rack-and-pinion. Brakes: 4-wheel ABS. Body Construction: steel unibody. Traction control: standard.

XK8, XKR, XKR 100: Layout: front-engine, rear-drive. Standard transmission: five-speed automatic. Steering: rack-and-pinion. Brakes: 4-wheel ABS. Body Construction: steel unibody. Stability control: standard. Traction control: standard.

SALES/PRODUCTION: Jaguar Cars produced 122,929 vehicles in England in calendar-year 2002. These were counted as part of Ford production totals in England. This total included 10,876 XJ models, 6,861 XK models, 69,059 X-Type models and 36,133 S-Type models. U.S. calendar-year sales of Jaguars included 15,965 S-Type models, 2,424 XJ8 Vanden Plas models, 33,018 X-Type models, 4,738 XJ8 and XJ6 models combined, 1,124 XJR models and 3,935 XK8 models.

MANUFACTURER: Jaguar Cars Ltd., Browns Lane, Coventry, England.

DISTRIBUTOR: Aston Martin, Jaguar, Land Rover of North America, Irvine, California.

HISTORY: In 2002, Jaguars were marketed by Aston Martin, Jaguar, and Land Rover of North America, headquartered in Irvine, California. The Jaguar brand was part of the Ford Group of automotive brands. Jaguar's U.S. sales for calendar 2002 were 61,204 units.

2002 Jaguar XJ8 SE long-wheelbase sedan

2003

X-TYPE — V-6 — Jaguar's mid-size four-door retained its center-divided "electric shaver" grille. It again came in 2.5- and 3.0-litre models. The standard equipment list included dynamic stability control, electronic brake force distribution, speed-sensitive power steering, dual-stage front airbags, side-impact airbags and curtain airbags. The 2.5 sedan, in spite of having "entry-level" luxury niche pricing (under $30,000) came fully equipped with hundreds of standard features. The 3.0 sedan included the larger 231-hp motor, a 5-speed automatic transmission and a wood-trimmed gearshift knob. During the year the "sport" versions of the X-Type were dropped.

S-TYPE — SIX/V-8 — The S-Type continued with a body that brought back memories of late-1950s Jaguar sedans, a "horse collar" grille and wide-apart front lamps. The 2003 model lineup was expanded to include a new S-Type R with a powerful supercharged engine. All S-Types had front suspension revisions and an all-new interior. A 4.2-litre engine replaced the previous 4.0-litre engine in V-8 models. A new six-speed automatic transmission was standard in the S-Type R and in V-8 models. Leather seats, bird's-eye maple interior trim, a 140-watt sound system, heated OSRV mirrors and alloy rims were standard on all five S-Types. V-8s also had added power seat adjusters, 17-inch wheels, a power moon roof, memory seats, and auto-dimming mirrors. Sport models added bigger brakes and a Computer Active Technology suspension system (with the bigger V-6 or V-8s). The S-Type R, with its supercharged 4.2, also included Brembo brakes, a special interior, a small spoiler, 18-in. wheels, performance tires, a bright mesh grille and Xenon headlights.

XJ8 — V-8 — The XJ was Jaguar's flagship sedan. It had a kind of long-nose look and came with an automatic climate control system, a 6 CD changer and a sunroof. The Sport version added a tuned suspension and performance tires. The Vanden Plas sedan was a long-wheelbase model with an upgraded interior. The XJR added the supercharged V-8, CAT's active suspension and a DVD navigation system. The Super was a blend of the "R" and the Vanden Plas. Two limited-edition versions of the XJ8 were announced. The standard wheelbase Sovereign included an Alpine stereo, further upgraded interior fittings, a chrome grille and specific alloy wheels. Jaguar also planned to build 395 XJRs with an optional R1 performance package.

XK8 — V-8 — Exterior changes to the XKR sports cars included new wheels, a few small changes in body badges and standard xenon headlights on the XKR (optional on other models). There were also some new colors including Jaguar Racing Green. Under the hood two new 4.2-liter V-8s (one supercharged) were available, both hooked to a six-speed automatic transmission.

I.D. DATA: The VIN is located on a VIN plate attached to the top left of the dash and visible through the windshield. The black painted aluminum plate is etched with the full VIN. A white painted air bag symbol is to the left of the VIN and "Jaguar Cars Ltd." is in white below the VIN. The VIN structure has 17 symbols. The first three symbols are the world manufacturer identifier SAJ=Jaguar. The fourth symbol indicates the market and air bag system. The fifth symbol indicates transmission and steering. The sixth and seventh symbols indicate body type. The eighth symbol indicates emissions control system. The ninth symbol is a check digit. The 10th symbol indicates model year: 3=2003. The 11th symbol indicates model line and assembly plant. The 12th symbol indicates the model and the last five symbols are sequential production numbers.

ENGINES

BASE V-6 X-TYPE 2.5 LITRE: Dual-overhead-cam "vee" type six-cylinder (32-valve). Aluminum block and heads. Displacement: 151 cid/2.5 litre (2495 cc). Bore & Stroke: 81.6 x 79.5 mm. Compression Ratio: 10.3:1. Brake Horsepower: 192 at 6800 rpm. Torque: 241 Nm. at 30000 rpm. Electronic sequential port fuel injection.

BASE V-6 X-TYPE 3.0 LITRE: Dual-overhead-cam "vee" type six-cylinder (32-valve). Aluminum block and heads. Displacement: 181 cid/3.0 litre (2967 cc). Bore & Stroke: 89 x 79.5 mm. Compression Ratio: 10.5:1. Brake Horsepower: 227 at 6800 rpm. Torque: 279 Nm. at 3000 rpm. Electronic sequential port fuel injection.

BASE V-6 S-TYPE 3.0 LITRE: Dual-overhead-cam "vee" type six-cylinder (32-valve). Aluminum block and heads. Displacement: 181 cid/3.0-litre (2967 cc). Bore & Stroke: 89 x 79.5 mm. Compression Ratio: 10.5:1. Brake Horsepower: 235 at 6800 rpm. Torque: 293 Nm. at 4100 rpm. Electronic sequential port fuel injection.

BASE 4.0 V-8 XJ8: Dual-overhead-cam "vee" type eight-cylinder (32-valve). Aluminum block and heads. Displacement: 243 cid (3980 cc). Bore & Stroke: 3.39 x 3.39 in. (86 x 86 mm). Compression Ratio: 9.0:1. Brake Horsepower: 280 at 6100 rpm. Torque: 376 lbs.-ft. at 4250 rpm. Electronic sequential port fuel injection.

BASE V-8 S-TYPE/XK8 4.2 LITRE: Dual-overhead-cam "vee" type eight-cylinder (32-valve). Aluminum block and heads. Displacement: 257 cid/4.2 litre (4196 cc). Bore & Stroke: 86 x 90.3 mm. Compression Ratio: 11.0:1. Brake Horsepower: 294 at 6000 rpm. Torque: 411 Nm. at 4100 rpm. Electronic sequential port fuel injection.

2003 Jaguars—from top to bottom, the X-type sedan, the XK8 convertible, the S-type sedan and the XJ8 sedan

2003 Jaguar XKR coupe *Jaguar Fox Valley*

MODEL	BODY TYPE & SEATING	ENGINE TYPE/ CID	P.O.E. PRICE	WEIGHT (LBS.)	PRODUCTION TOTAL
X-Type Series					
2.5L	4d Sedan-5P	V6/151	$29,305	3,428	**Note 1**
2.5L Sport	4d Sedan-5P	V6/151	$31,305	3,428	**Note 1**
3.0L	4d Sedan-5P	V6/181	$36,305	3,516	**Note 1**
3.0L Sport	4d Sedan-5P	V6/181	$38,305	3,516	**Note 1**
S-Type Series					
S-Type 3.0L SE	4d Sedan-5P	V8/181	$41,850	3,695	**Note 2**
S-Type 3.0L Sport	4d Sedan-5P	V8/181	$43,850	3,695	**Note 2**
S-Type 4.2L	4d Sedan-5P	V8/257	$49,330	3,874	**Note 2**
S-Type 4.2L Sport	4d Sedan-5P	V8/257	$51,330	3,874	**Note 2**
S-Type R	4d Sedan-5p	V8/257	$61,755	4,046	**Note 2**
XJ8 Series					
XJ8	4d Sedan-5P	V8/243	$56,330	3,995	**Note 3**
XJ8	4d Sedan Sport-5P	V8/243	$59,330	3,395	**Note 3**
XJ8	4d Vanden Plas-5P	V8/243	$68,330	4,006	**Note 3**
XJR	4d Sedan-5P	V8/243	$71,830	4,063	**Note 3**
XJ8 Super	4d Sedan-5p	V8/243	$79,330	4,129	**Note 3**
XK8	2d Coupe-2+2P	V8/257	$69,330	3,779	**Note 4**
XK8	2d Convertible-2+2P	V8/257	$74,330	3,980	**Note 4**
XKR	2d Coupe-2+2P	V8/257	$81,330	3,865	**Note 4**
XKR	2d Convertible-2+2P	V8/257	$86,330	4,042	**Note 4**

Note 1: Jaguar produced 61,609 X-Types in calendar-year 2003. **Note 2:** Jaguar produced 31,907 S-Types in calendar-year 2003. **Note 3:** Jaguar produced 26,949 XJs in calendar-year 2003. **Note 4:** Jaguar produced 5,656 XKs in calendar-year 2003.

BASE 4.0 V-8 XJR/XJ SUPER SUPERCHARGED: Dual-overhead-cam "vee" type eight-cylinder (32-valve). Supercharged. Aluminum block and heads. Displacement: 243 cid (3980 cc). Bore & Stroke: 3.39 x 3.39 in. (86 x 86 mm). Compression Ratio: 9.0:1. Brake Horsepower: 358 at 6150 rpm. Torque: 504 lbs.-ft. at 3600 rpm. Electronic sequential port fuel injection.

BASE V-8 XKR 4.2 LITRE SUPERCHARGED: Dual-overhead-cam "vee" type eight-cylinder (32-valve) with an Eaton supercharger and twin air-to-liquid intercoolers. Aluminum block and heads. Displacement: 257 cid/4196 cc. Bore & Stroke: 86 x 90.3 mm). Compression Ratio: 9.1:1. Brake Horsepower: 370 at 6150 rpm. Torque: 541 Nm. at 3600 rpm. Electronic sequential port fuel injection.

BASE V-8 S-TYPE R 4.2 LITRE SUPERCHARGED: Dual-overhead-cam "vee" type eight-cylinder (32-valve) with an Eaton supercharger and twin air-to-liquid intercoolers. Aluminum block and heads. Displacement: 257 cid/4196 cc. Bore & Stroke: 86 x 90.3 mm). Compression Ratio: 9.1:1. Brake Horsepower: 390 at 6100 rpm. Torque: 525 Nm. at 3600 rpm. Electronic sequential port fuel injection.

CHASSIS

X-TYPE: Wheelbase: 106.7 in. Overall length: 183.9 in. Width: 70.4 in. Height: 54.8 in.

S-TYPE: Wheelbase: 114.5 in. Overall length: 191.4 in. Width: 80.3 in. Height: 55.7 in.

XJ8, XJR: Wheelbase: 113.0 in. Overall length: 197.8. Width: 70.8 in. Height: 52.7 in.

XJ8 VANDEN PLAS, XJ8 SUPER: Wheelbase: 117.9 in. Overall length: 202.7 in. Width: 70.8 in. Height: 53.2 in.

XK8: Wheelbase: 101.9 in. Overall length: 187.4 in. Width: 70.8 in. Height: (coupe) 50.5 in., (convertible) 51 in.

XKR: Wheelbase: 101.9 in. Overall length: 187.4 in. Width: 70.8 in. Height: (coupe) 50.3 in., (convertible) 50.7 in.

TECHNICAL

X-TYPE: Layout: front-engine, rear-drive. Standard transmission: five-speed manual. Optional transmission: five speed automatic. Steering: rack-and-pinion. Brakes: 4-wheel ABS. Body Construction: steel unibody. Stability control: optional on X-Type 3.0. Traction control: Not available.

S-TYPE: Layout: front-engine, rear-drive. Standard transmission: six-speed automatic. Steering: rack-and-pinion. Brakes: 4-wheel ABS. Body Construction: steel unibody. Stability control: standard. Traction control: Not available.

XJ8, XJ8 VANDEN PLAS, XJR: Layout: front-engine, rear-

The interior of the 2003 Jaguar S-type sedan. *Phil Hall Collection*

drive. Standard transmission: six-speed automatic. Steering: rack-and-pinion. Brakes: 4-wheel ABS. Body Construction: steel unibody. Stability control: standard. Traction control: Not available.

XK8: Layout: front-engine, rear-drive. Standard transmission: six-speed automatic. Steering: rack-and-pinion. Brakes: 4-wheel ABS. Body Construction: steel unibody. Stability control: standard. Traction control: Not available.

XKR: Layout: front-engine, rear-drive. Standard transmission: six-speed automatic. Steering: rack-and-pinion. Brakes: 4-wheel ABS. Body Construction: steel unibody. Stability control: standard. Traction control: Not available.

PERFORMANCE: Acceleration (0-60 mph): (S-Type 3.0) 8.0 seconds; (S-Type 4.0) 6.5 seconds; (XJR) 6.7 seconds; (XK8 coupe) 6.5 seconds; (XK8 convertible) 6.7 seconds; (XKR) 6.9 seconds Acceleration (quarter mile): (S-Type 3.0) 15.9 seconds; (S-Type 4.0) 15.0 seconds; (XK8 coupe) 15.2 seconds; (XK8 convertible) 15.5 seconds; (XJR) 13.7 seconds; (XKR) 13.9 seconds EPA Fuel Economy City/Highway miles per gallon: (S-Type 3.0) 18/26; (S-Type 4.0) 17/23 (XK8 coupe) 17/25; (XK8 convertible) 17/24; (XKR coupe) 16/23; (XK8 convertible) 16/22; (XJ8, XJ8L) 17/24; (XJR VP SC) 16/21. Performance Figures by *Motor Trend*.

SALES/PRODUCTION: Jaguar cars produced 126,121 vehicles in England in calendar-year 2003. U.S. model-year sales of Jaguars totaled 55,290 cars. This included 15,716 S-Types, 27,534 X-Types, 7,493 XJ8s, 1,432 XJRs and 3,115 XK8s. U.S. calendar-year sales of Jaguars totaled 54,655 cars. This included 4,876 S-Types, 2,225 XJ8 Vanden Plas, 26,772 X-Types, 6,249 XJ8 and XJ6 models combined, 1,628 XJR models and 2,905 XK8 models.

MANUFACTURER: Jaguar Cars, Coventry, England.

DISTRIBUTOR: Aston Martin, Jaguar, Land Rover North America, Irvine, Calif.

Jaguar created this memorable "cat's paw" image in 2003 advertising.

A British 2003 Jaguar S-type 2.0-litre *diesel* sedan. Andrew Morland

A 2004 Jaguar S-Type on the road. *Jaguar Fox Valley*

2004

X-TYPE — V-6 — Jaguar's mid-size sedan had a sloping roof and a split "electric shaver" grille. It came in 2.5- and 3.0-litre models. Standard on the 2.5 were 16-in. alloys, leather upholstery, real wood interior and 1-touch power windows. The 3.0 added 17-in. wheels and a CD player. An optional Sport package added a stability-control system, alternate suspension configurations, and larger wheels. The Premium option included a moon roof and rear parking sensors.

S-TYPE – V-6/V-8 – The S-Type series was comprised of V-6 and V-8 versions of the mid-sized Jaguar sedan and an "R" version with a supercharged 4.2-litre V-8. Standard features included leather seats, bird's-eye maple wood interior trim, dual-zone climate control, a 140-watt stereo system with CD, auto up/down power windows, heated OSRV mirrors, alloy rims and a 3.0-litre V-6. The S-Type 4.2 included the V-8, power-adjustable memory seats, 17-inch wheels, and a power moon roof. A Sport package for both models included sport seats, sport steering wheel, special wood trim, big brakes and a computer-aided suspension system. The "R" version included the supercharged V-8, 18-in. alloy wheels, rear-park sensors, and a 10-speaker audio system.

XJ — V-8 — Jaguar XJ models had a split grille with horizontal bars, a bright surround and center divider and two vertical bars in each grille half. The XJ models came only as large four-door sedans. The standard XJ8 included traction control, 4-zone climate control, and a self-leveling suspension. Standard equipment included 12-way power seating, ABS, brake assist, side and head curtain airbags, added insulation, a new electronic parking brake and a standard 4.2-litre all-aluminum V-8 engine. The elegant Vanden Plas models included heated seats, and 16-position power seat adjusters. The XJR offered a supercharged version of the regular XJ8's 4.2-litre V-8 and a new ZF 6-speed automatic transmission.

XK — V-8 — The XK models had a touch of the classic E-Type Jaguar in their smooth, cigar-shaped body styling. A coupe and a convertible were offered, both with long lists of standard equipment including a 4.2-litre V-8, a 6-speed automatic transmission, 18-inch wheels, and leather upholstery. Heated seats with 12-way power adjusters, automatic climate control, reverse parking sensors, an Alpine stereo with 6-disc CD changer, and 4-wheel ABS with ventilated discs. The open-cockpit version had a power convertible top. The XKR was the supercharged version of the XK coupe and convertible. It included an Eaton supercharger, twin air-to-liquid intercoolers, and a standard 6-speed automatic transmission.

I.D. DATA: The VIN is located on a VIN plate attached to the top left of the dash and visible through the windshield. The black painted aluminum plate is etched with the full VIN. A white painted air bag symbol is to the left of the VIN and "Jaguar Cars Ltd." Is painted in white below the VIN. The VIN structure has 17 symbols. The first three symbols are the world manufacturer identifier SAJ=Jaguar. The fourth symbol indicates the market and air bag system. The fifth symbol indicates transmission and steering. The sixth and seventh symbols indicate body type. The eighth symbol indicates emissions control system. The ninth symbol is a check digit. The 10th symbol indicates model year: 4=2004. The 11th symbol indicates model line and assembly plant. The 12th symbol indicates the model. The last five symbols are the sequential production numbers.

ENGINES

BASE V-6 X-TYPE 2.5: Dual-overhead-cam "vee" type six-cylinder (32-valve). Aluminum block and heads. Displacement: 151 cid/2.5 litre (2495 cc). Bore & Stroke: 81.6 x 79.5 mm. Compression Ratio: 10.3:1. Brake Horsepower: 192 at 6800 rpm. Torque: 241 Nm. at 3000 rpm. Electronic sequential port fuel injection.

BASE V-6 X-TYPE 3.0: Dual-overhead-cam "vee" type six-cylinder (32-valve). Aluminum block and heads. Displacement: 181 cid/3.0 litre (2967 cc). Bore & Stroke: 89 x 79.5 mm. Compression Ratio: 10.5:1. Brake Horsepower: 227 at 6800 rpm. Torque: 279 Nm. at 3000 rpm. Electronic sequential port fuel injection.

BASE V-6 S-TYPE 3.0: Dual-overhead-cam "vee" type six-cylinder (32-valve). Aluminum block and heads. Displacement: 181 cid/3.0-litre (2967 cc). Bore & Stroke: 89 x 79.5 mm. Compression Ratio: 10.5:1. Brake Horsepower: 235 at 6800 rpm. Torque: 293 Nm. at 4100 rpm. Electronic sequential port fuel injection.

BASE V-8 S-TYPE 4.2, XJ8/XJ8 VANDEN PLAS/ XK8: Dual-overhead-cam "vee" type eight-cylinder (32-valve). Aluminum block and heads. Displacement: 257 cid/4.2 litre (4196 cc). Bore & Stroke: 86 x 90.3 mm. Compression Ratio: 11.0:1. Brake Horsepower: 294 at 6000 rpm. Torque: 411 Nm. at 4100 rpm. Electronic sequential port fuel injection.

BASE V-8 S-TYPE R, XJR/XKR: Dual-overhead-cam "vee" type eight-cylinder (32-valve) with an Eaton supercharger and twin air-to-liquid intercoolers. Aluminum block and heads. Displacement: 257 cid/4196 cc. Bore & Stroke: 86 x 90.3 mm). Compression Ratio: 9.1:1. Brake Horsepower: 390 at 6100 rpm. Torque: 541 Nm. at 4100 rpm. Electronic sequential port fuel injection.

CHASSIS

X-TYPE: Wheelbase: 106.7 in. Overall length: 183.9 in. Width: 70.4 in. Height: 54.8 in.

S-TYPE: Wheelbase: 114.5 in. Overall length: 192.0 in. Width: 81.1 in. Height: 56.0 in.

2004 Jaguar XJ8 coupe *Andrew Morland*

Model	Body Type & Seating	Engine Type/ CID	P.O.E. Price	Weight (lbs.)	Production Total
X-Type Series					
2.5L	4d Sedan-5P	V6/151	$29,995	3,428	N/A
3.0L	4d Sedan-5P	V6/181	$33,995	3,428	N/A
S-Type Series					
S-Type 3.0	4d Sedan-5P	V8/181	$43,895	3,777	N/A
S-Type 4.2L	4d Sedan-5P	V8/257	$49,995	3,874	N/A
S-Type R	4d Sedan-5P	V8/257	$63,120	4,046	N/A
XJ Series					
XJ8	4d Sedan-5P	V8/257	$59,995	3,806	N/A
XJ8 Vanden Plas	4d Sedan-5P	V8/257	$68,995	3,815	N/A
XJR	4d Sedan-5P	V8/257	$74,995	3,948	N/A
XK Series					
XK8	2d Coupe-2+2P	V8/257	$69,995	3,779	N/A
XK8	2d Convertible-2+2P	V8/257	$74,995	3,980	N/A
XKR	2d Coupe-2+2P	V8/257	$86,995	3,865	N/A
XKR	2d Convertible-2+2P	V8/257	$93,995	4,042	N/A

A view of the 2004 Jaguar S-type 4.2 sedan in motion. *Jaguar Fox Valley*

XJ8, XJ8 VANDEN PLAS, XJR: Wheelbase: 119.4 in. Overall length: 200.4 in. Width: 73.2 in. Height: 57.0 in.

XK8: Wheelbase: 101.9 in. Overall length: 187.4 in. Width: 70.8 in. Height: (coupe) 50.5 in., (convertible) 51 in.

XKR: Wheelbase: 101.9 in. Overall length: 187.4 in. Width: 70.8 in. Height: (coupe) 50.3 in., (convertible) 50.7 in.

TECHNICAL

X-TYPE: Layout: front-engine, rear-drive. Standard transmission: five-speed manual. Optional transmission: five speed automatic. Steering: rack-and-pinion. Brakes: 4-wheel ABS. Body Construction: steel unibody. Stability control: optional on X-Type 3.0. Traction control: Not available.

S-TYPE: Layout: front-engine, rear-drive. Standard transmission: six-speed automatic. Steering: rack-and-pinion. Brakes: 4-wheel ABS. Body Construction: steel unibody. Stability control: standard. Traction control: Not available.

XJ8, XJ8 VANDEN PLAS, XJR: Layout: front-engine, rear-drive. Standard transmission: six-speed automatic. Steering: rack-and-pinion. Brakes: 4-wheel ABS. Body Construction: steel unibody. Stability control: standard. Traction control: Not available.

XK8: Layout: front-engine, rear-drive. Standard transmission: six-speed automatic. Steering: rack-and-pinion. Brakes: 4-wheel ABS. Body Construction: steel unibody. Stability control: standard. Traction control: Not available.

XKR: Layout: front-engine, rear-drive. Standard transmission: six-speed automatic. Steering: rack-and-pinion. Brakes: 4-wheel ABS. Body Construction: steel unibody. Stability control: standard. Traction control: Not available.

PERFORMANCE

S-TYPE R: Acceleration (0-to-60 mph): 5.3 seconds. Top speed: (155 mph electronically limited).

XJR: Acceleration (0-to-60 mph): 5.0 seconds.

XKR: Acceleration (0-to-60 mph): Less than 5.5 seconds. (Quarter mile): Under 14 seconds.

SALES/PRODUCTION: Jaguar Cars in Europe further strengthened sales during 2004, helping to achieve the best ever results for the English and European markets overall. It was driven by expansion of the product lineup to include new Jaguar diesels and the X-Type Estate. Overall sales in the United Kingdom for 2004 reached record levels totaling 32,598 cars, an 11.2 percent improvement and 9.4 per cent up on the previous record in 2002. European sales of 24,337 cars helped achieve the best ever results with a 24.6 percent improvement over 2003.

MANUFACTURER: Jaguar Cars Ltd., Coventry, England.

DISTRIBUTOR: Aston Martin, Jaguar, Land Rover North America. Irvine, Calif.

HISTORICAL: Jaguar's overall 2004 performance was slowed by tough U.S. trading conditions, where a 16.4 percent downturn was seen. A significant shift by customers in the United States to premium SUVs, high incentive activity in the American premium car sector and the strength of sterling versus the dollar all contributed to this trend. Jaguar enjoyed success in the U.S., with the launch of its eagerly anticipated XJ long wheelbase model and late-in-the year X-Type Estate Wagon (called the Sportwagon in the United States). The XJ long-wheelbase version contributed to a 4.5 percent rise in its share of this key market.

2004 Jaguar XJ8 convertible *Andrew Morland*

S-TYPE R in Quartz.

2005 Jaguar S-type R sedan *Phil Hall Collection*

2005

X-TYPE — V-6 — The first ever Jaguar estate wagon, the 2005 X-Type Sportwagon, combined the driving confidence of the all-wheel-drive X-Type 3.0 with the versatility of a station wagon body. Standard exterior equipment for the wagon included 17-in. Cayman wheels with all-season tires, fixed silver roof rails and a tailgate window that opened independently from the rear door. Inside, the rear seat could be configured to provide seating for one, two or three passengers. The car came with 28 individual storage compartments. The X-Type 2.5 sedan featured impressive performance at a surprising price with a 192-hp, 2.5-liter V-6, ABS and a lightweight aluminum suspension. New for the 2005 X-Type Sport was an optional interior trim featuring Carbon Fiber veneer on the dash.

S-Type — SIX/V-8 — With a 235-hp, 3.0-liter V-6, six-speed automatic transmission, Dynamic Stability Control, ABS and lightweight aluminum suspension, the 2005 S-Type 3.0 delivered sporting luxury. The 3.0's striking 17-in. Kronos wheels were complemented by chrome-finish on the grille. A new instrument panel had two message centers to display information concurrently. The ultimate in S-Type luxury was the new Vanden Plas (VDP) Edition. It featured hand-polished Walnut veneer fascia and door trims, a walnut-and-

leather steering wheel, soft-grain leather-trimmed interior with contrasting seat piping, and 12-way electrically adjustable front passenger heated seats.

XJ8 — V-8 — With its powerful AJ-V-8 engine, smooth six-speed ZF automatic transmission, and Dynamic Stability Control. The 2005 XJ8 model was a true driver's car. Exterior features included 18-in. Dynamic wheels with all-season tires, and automatic headlights. A 320-watt Alpine Premium Sound System was standard. The ultimate XJ was the Super V-8, a new long-wheelbase model that combined the supercharged performance of a 390-hp V-8 engine with an uncompromised level of luxury. From the XJR, the Super V-8 took the 390-hp supercharged V-8, Brembo disc brakes with four piston calipers and radar-based adaptive cruise control. Inside, standard features included a DVD navigation system, rear multimedia entertainment system and 4-zone climate control.

XK8 — V-8 — With a 294-hp, 4.2-liter V-8, six-speed automatic transmission, Dynamic Stability Control (DSC) and Jaguar's Adaptive Restraint Technology System (A.R.T.S.), the 2005 XK8 coupe was Jaguar's closed sports car. New for 2005 were a restyled lower front bumper, side sills and rear bumper, as well as larger dual exhaust tailpipe finishers. The optional, radar-based Adaptive Cruise Control system added an unexpected measure of convenience.

I.D. DATA: (North America) The VIN is located on a VIN plate attached to the top left of the dash and visible through the windshield. The black painted aluminum plate is etched with the full VIN. A white painted air bag symbol is to the left of the VIN and "Jaguar Cars Ltd." is painted in white below the VIN. The VIN structure has 17 symbols. The first three symbols are the world manufacturer identifier SAJ=Jaguar. The fourth symbol indicates the market and air bag system. The fifth symbol indicates transmission and steering. The sixth and seventh symbols indicate body type. The eighth symbol indicates emissions control system. The ninth symbol is a check digit. The 10th symbol indicates model year: 5=2005. The 11th symbol indicates model line and assembly plant. The 12th symbol indicates the model. The last five symbols are the sequential production numbers.

ENGINES

BASE V-6 X-TYPE 2.5: Dual-overhead-cam "vee" type six-cylinder (32-valve). Aluminum block and heads. Displacement: 151 cid/2.5-litre (2495 cc). Bore & Stroke: 81.6 x 79.5 mm. Compression Ratio: 10.3:1. Brake Horsepower: 192 at 6800 rpm. Torque: 178 ft.-lbs. at 3000 rpm. Electronic sequential port fuel injection.

BASE V-6 X-TYPE 3.0: Dual-overhead-cam "vee" type six-cylinder (32-valve). Aluminum block and heads. Displacement: 181 cid/3.0-litre (2967 cc). Bore & Stroke: 89 x 79.5 mm. Compression Ratio: 10.5:1. Brake Horsepower: 227 at 6800 rpm. Torque: 206 ft.-lbs. at 3000 rpm. Electronic sequential port fuel injection.

BASE V-6 S-TYPE 3.0: Dual-overhead-cam "vee" type six-cylinder (32-valve). Aluminum block and heads. Displacement: 181 cid/3.0-litre (2967 cc). Bore & Stroke: 89 x 79.5 mm.

The front end of the 2005 Jaguar X-type 3.0 sedan.
Jaguar Fox Valley

Compression Ratio: 10.5:1. Brake Horsepower: 235 at 6800 rpm. Torque: 216 ft.-lbs. at 4100 rpm. Electronic sequential port fuel injection.

BASE V-8 S-TYPE 4.2, XJ8/XJ8 VANDEN PLAS/ XK8: Dual-overhead-cam "vee" type eight-cylinder (32-valve). Aluminum block and heads. Displacement: 257 cid/4.2 litre (4196 cc). Bore & Stroke: 86 x 90.3 mm. Compression Ratio: 11.0:1. Brake Horsepower: 294 ft.-lbs. at 6000 rpm. Torque: 303 at 4100 rpm. Electronic sequential port fuel injection.

BASE V-8 S-TYPE R, XJR/XKR: Dual-overhead-cam "vee" type eight-cylinder (32-valve) with an Eaton supercharger and twin air-to-liquid intercoolers. Aluminum block and heads. Displacement: 257 cid/4196 cc. Bore & Stroke: 86 x 90.3 mm). Compression Ratio: 9.1:1. Brake Horsepower: 390 at 3500 rpm. Torque: 399 ft.-lbs. at 3500 rpm. Electronic sequential port fuel injection.

CHASSIS

X-TYPE SEDAN: Wheelbase: 106.7 in. Overall length: 183.8 in. Width including mirrors: 78.8 in. Height: 56.7 in. Tires: (2.5) 205/55HR16 all-season, (3.0) 225/45HR17 all-season, (Sport) 225/40 ZR18 performance, (VDP) 225/45HR17 all-season.

X-TYPE SPORT WAGON: Wheelbase: 106.7 in. Overall length: 185.5 in. Width including mirrors: 78.8 in. Height: 58.4 in. Tires: 225/45HR17 all-season.

S-TYPE: Wheelbase: 114.5 in. Overall length: 193.1 in. Width including mirrors: 81.1 in. Height: 56.0 in. Tires: (3.0) 235/50R17, (4.2) 235/50R17, (VDP) 235/50R17, ("R") Front: 245/40Ra8, Rear: 275/35R18.

XJ8, XJR: Wheelbase: 119.4 in. Overall length: 200.4 in. Width including mirrors: 83.0 in. Height: 57.0 in. Tires: (XJ8) 235/50R18, (XJR) 255/40ZR19.

XJ8L, XJ8 VANDEN PLAS, SUPER V-8: Wheelbase: 124.4 in. Overall length: 205.3 in. Width including mirrors: 83.0 in. Height: 57.3 in. Tires: (XJ8L) 235/50R18, (VDP) 235/50R18, (Super V-8) 255/40ZR19

XK8: Wheelbase: 101.9 in. Overall length: 187.4 in. Width: 70.8 in. Height: (coupe) 50.5 in., (convertible) 51 in.

XKR: Wheelbase: 101.9 in. Overall length: 187.4 in. Width: 70.8 in. Height: (coupe) 50.3 in., (convertible) 50.7 in.

TECHNICAL

X-TYPE: Layout: front-engine, rear-drive. Standard transmission: five-speed manual. Optional transmission: five speed automatic. Steering: rack-and-pinion. Brakes: 4-wheel ABS. Body Construction: steel unibody. Stability control: optional on X-Type 3.0. Traction control: Not available.

Model	Body Type &Seating	Engine Type/ CID	P.O.E. Price	Weight (lbs.)	Production Total
X-Type Series					
2.5L	4d Sedan-5P	V6/151	$30,995	3,588	N/A
3.0L	4d Sedan-5P	V6/181	$34,995	3,630	N/A
3.0L	4d Sedan Sport-5P	V6/181	$37,945	3,677	N/A
3.0L	4d VDP Sedan-5P	V6/181	$38,745	3,663	N/A
3.0L	4d Sport Wagon-5P	V6/181	$36,995	3,761	N/A
S-Type					
S-Type 3.0	4d Sedan-5P	V8/181	$44,895	3,771	N/A
S-Type 4.2L	4d Sedan-5P	V8/257	$51,995	3,826	N/A
S-Type 4.2L	4d VDP Sedan-5P	V8/257	$55,295	N/A	N/A
S-Type R	4d Sedan-5P	V8/257	$58,995	3,969	
XJ Series					
XJ8	4d Sedan-5P	V8/257	$61,495	3,726	N/A
XJ8L	4d LWB Sedan-5P	V8/257	$63,495	3,777	N/A
XJ8	4d VDP Sedan-5P	V8/257	$70,995	3,841	N/A
XJR	4d Sedan-5P	V8/257	$75,995	3,947	N/A
Super V-8	4d Sedan-5P	V8/257	$89,995	4,059	N/A
XK8					
XK8	2d Coupe-2+2P	V8/243	$70,495	3,779	**Note 1**
XK8	2d Convertible-2+2P	V8/243	$75,495	3,980	**Note 1**
XKR	2d Coupe-2+2P	V8/243	$81,995	3,865	**Note 1**
XKR	2d Convertible-2+2P	V8/243	$86,995	4,042	**Note 1**

2005 Jaguar X-type 3.0 Sportwagon *Phil Hall Collection*

S-TYPE: Layout: front-engine, rear-drive. Standard transmission: six-speed automatic. Steering: rack-and-pinion. Brakes: 4-wheel ABS. Body Construction: steel unibody. Stability control: standard. Traction control: Not available.

XJ8, XJ8 VANDEN PLAS, XJR: Layout: front-engine, rear-drive. Standard transmission: six-speed automatic. Steering: rack-and-pinion. Brakes: 4-wheel ABS. Body Construction: steel unibody. Stability control: standard. Traction control: Not available.

XK8: Layout: front-engine, rear-drive. Standard transmission: six-speed automatic. Steering: rack-and-pinion. Brakes: 4-wheel ABS. Body Construction: steel unibody. Stability control: standard. Traction control: Not available.

XKR: Layout: front-engine, rear-drive. Standard transmission: six-speed automatic. Steering: rack-and-pinion. Brakes: 4-wheel ABS. Body Construction: steel unibody. Stability control: standard. Traction control: Not available.

PERFORMANCE

X-TYPE 2.5: Acceleration(0-to-60 mph, automatic): 8.5 seconds. Top speed: (121 mph electronically limited).

X-TYPE ALL SEDANS WITH 3.0: Acceleration (0-to-60 mph, automatic) 7.1 seconds. Top speed: (121 mph electronically limited).

X-TYPE SPORT WAGON WITH 3.0: Acceleration (0-to-60 mph, automatic) 7.3 seconds. Top speed: (121 mph electronically limited).

S-TYPE 3.0: Acceleration (0-to-60 mph, automatic): 7.5 seconds. Top speed: (121 mph electronically limited).

S-TYPE 4.2, VDP: Acceleration (0-to-60 mph, automatic): 6.2 seconds. Top speed: (121 mph electronically limited).

S-TYPE R: Acceleration (0-to-60 mph, automatic): 5.3 seconds. Top speed: (155 mph electronically limited).

XJ8, XJ8L, VDP: Acceleration (0-to-60 mph, automatic): 6.3 seconds. Top speed: (121 mph electronically limited).

XJR, SUPER V-8: Acceleration (0-to-60 mph, automatic): 5.0 seconds. Top speed: (155 mph electronically limited).

XK8: Acceleration (0-to-60 mph, automatic): Coupe: 6.1 seconds, Convertible: 6.3 seconds. Top speed: (155 mph electronically limited).

XKR: Acceleration (0-to-60 mph, automatic): Coupe: 5.2 seconds, Convertible: 5.3 seconds. Top speed: (155 mph electronically limited).

SALES/PRODUCTION: Not available at time of publication.

MANUFACTURER: Jaguar Cars, Coventry, England.

DISTRIBUTOR: Jaguar North America, Mahwah, New Jersey.

HISTORICAL: Introduced at the North American International Automobile Show in Detroit, early in January 2005, the Jaguar Advanced Lightweight Coupe heralded a new generation of stunning sports coupes and saloons which Jaguar described as, "Cars that will remain true to Jaguar's illustrious past, but more importantly will see the company leaping confidently forward into the future." The Lightweight Coupe was created by Jaguar's advanced design team under the watchful eye of renowned Design Director Ian Callum. Its lightweight aluminum body architecture was used on the new XJ saloon. Jaguar also announced that all diesel-powered X-Type saloons and estate models would be Euro IV emissions compliant starting in January 2005—a year ahead of the date demanded by legislation. The new Euro IV compliant X-Type 2.0 Diesel replaced the original model. It provided more responsive engine performance on top of improved mileage efficiency.

2005 Jaguar X-type VDP edition sedan *Phil Hall Collection*

VDP Edition in Quartz.

Jaguar

Vehicle Condition Scale

6	5	4	3	2	1
Parts car: May or may not be running, but is weathered, wrecked and/or stripped to the point of being useful primarily for parts.	**Restorable:** Needs complete restoration of body, chassis and interior. May or may not be running, but isn't weathered, wrecked or stripped to the point of being useful only for parts.	**Good:** A driveable vehicle needing no or only minor work to be functional. Also, a deteriorated restoration or a very poor amateur restoration. All components may need restoration to be "excellent," but the car is mostly useable "as is."	**Very Good:** Complete operable original or older restoration. Also, a very good amateur restoration, all presentable and serviceable inside and out. Plus, a combination of well-done restoration and good operable components or a partially restored car with all parts necessary to compete and/or valuable NOS parts.	**Fine:** Well-restored or a combination of superior restoration and excellent original parts. Also, extremely well-maintained original vehicle showing minimal wear.	**Excellent:** Restored to current maximum professional standards of quality in every area, or perfect original with components operating and apearing as new. A 95-plus point show car that is not driven.

	6	5	4	3	2	1
1946-48 3.5 Litre, 6-cyl., 125 hp, 120" wb						
Conv Cpe	3,160	9,480	15,800	35,550	55,300	79,000
Saloon	1,800	5,400	9,000	20,250	31,500	45,000
1949 Mk V, 6-cyl., 125 hp, 120" wb						
Conv Cpe	2,560	7,680	12,800	28,800	44,800	64,000
Saloon	1,800	5,400	9,000	20,250	31,500	45,000
1950 Mk V, 6-cyl., 160 hp, 120" wb						
Saloon	1,800	5,400	9,000	20,250	31,500	45,000
Conv Cpe	2,560	7,680	12,800	28,800	44,800	64,000
1950 XK-120, 6-cyl., 160 hp, 102" wb						
Rds	5,880	17,640	29,400	66,150	102,900	147,000

NOTE: Some XK-120 models delivered as early as 1949 models, use 1950 prices.

	6	5	4	3	2	1
1951 Mk VII, 6-cyl., 160 hp, 120" wb						
Saloon	920	2,760	4,600	10,350	16,100	23,000
1951 XK-120, 6-cyl., 160 hp, 102" wb						
Rds	3,960	11,880	19,800	44,550	69,300	99,000
Cpe	2,400	7,200	12,000	27,000	42,000	60,000
1952 Mk VII, 6-cyl., 160 hp, 120" wb, (twin-cam)						
Std Sed	1,120	3,360	5,600	12,600	19,600	28,000
DeL Sed	1,160	3,480	5,800	13,050	20,300	29,000
1952 XK-120S (modified), 160 hp, 102" wb						
Rds	4,240	12,720	21,200	47,700	74,200	106,000
Cpe	2,440	7,320	12,200	27,450	42,700	61,000
1952 XK-120, 6-cyl., 160 hp, 102" wb						
Rds	3,960	11,880	19,800	44,550	69,300	99,000
Cpe	2,400	7,200	12,000	27,000	42,000	60,000
1953 Mk VII, 6-cyl., 160 hp, 120" wb						
Std Sed	1,120	3,360	5,600	12,600	19,600	28,000

	6	5	4	3	2	1
1953 XK-120S (modified), 6-cyl., 160 hp, 102" wb						
Rds	4,240	12,720	21,200	47,700	74,200	106,000
Cpe	2,440	7,320	12,200	27,450	42,700	61,000
Conv	3,000	9,000	15,000	33,750	52,500	75,000
1953 XK-120, 6-cyl., 160 hp, 102" wb						
Rds	3,960	11,880	19,800	44,550	69,300	99,000
Cpe	2,400	7,200	12,000	27,000	42,000	60,000
Conv	2,960	8,880	14,800	33,300	51,800	74,000
1954 Mk VII, 6-cyl., 160 hp, 120" wb						
Sed	1,120	3,360	5,600	12,600	19,600	28,000
1954 XK-120S (modified), 6-cyl., 102" wb						
Rds	4,240	12,720	21,200	47,700	74,200	106,000
Cpe	2,440	7,320	12,200	27,450	42,700	61,000
Conv	3,000	9,000	15,000	33,750	52,500	75,000
1954 XK-120, 6-cyl., 160 hp, 102" wb						
Rds	3,960	11,880	19,800	44,550	69,300	99,000
Cpe	2,400	7,200	12,000	27,000	42,000	60,000
Conv	2,960	8,880	14,800	33,300	51,800	74,000
1955 Mk VII M, 6-cyl., 190 hp, 120" wb						
Saloon	1,160	3,480	5,800	13,050	20,300	29,000
1955 XK-140, 6-cyl., 190 hp, 102" wb						
Cpe	2,040	6,120	10,200	22,950	35,700	51,000
Rds	4,120	12,360	20,600	46,350	72,100	103,000
Conv	2,920	8,760	14,600	32,850	51,100	73,000
1955 XK-140M, 6-cyl., 190 hp, 102" wb						
Cpe	2,320	6,960	11,600	26,100	40,600	58,000
Rds	4,400	13,200	22,000	49,500	77,000	110,000
Conv	3,200	9,600	16,000	36,000	56,000	80,000

1955 XK-140MC, 6-cyl., 210 hp, 102" wb

	6	5	4	3	2	1
Cpe	2,600	7,800	13,000	29,250	45,500	65,000
Rds	4,680	14,040	23,400	52,650	81,900	117,000
Conv	3,480	10,440	17,400	39,150	60,900	87,000

1956 Mk VII M, 6-cyl., 190 hp, 120" wb

	6	5	4	3	2	1
Saloon	1,120	3,360	5,600	12,600	19,600	28,000

1956 XK-140, 6-cyl., 190 hp, 102" wb

	6	5	4	3	2	1
Cpe	2,040	6,120	10,200	22,950	35,700	51,000
Rds	4,120	12,360	20,600	46,350	72,100	103,000
Conv	2,920	8,760	14,600	32,850	51,100	73,000

1956 XK-140M, 6-cyl., 190 hp, 102" wb

	6	5	4	3	2	1
Cpe	2,320	6,960	11,600	26,100	40,600	58,000
Rds	4,400	13,200	22,000	49,500	77,000	110,000
Conv	3,200	9,600	16,000	36,000	56,000	80,000

1956 XK-140MC, 6-cyl., 210 hp, 102" wb

	6	5	4	3	2	1
Cpe	2,600	7,800	13,000	29,250	45,500	65,000
Rds	4,680	14,040	23,400	52,650	81,900	117,000
Conv	3,480	10,440	17,400	39,150	60,900	87,000

1956 2.4 Litre, 6-cyl., 112 hp, 108" wb

	6	5	4	3	2	1
Sed	1,080	3,240	5,400	12,150	18,900	27,000

1956 3.4 Litre, 6-cyl., 210 hp, 108" wb

	6	5	4	3	2	1
Sed	1,120	3,360	5,600	12,600	19,600	28,000

1956 Mk VIII, 6-cyl., 210 hp, 120" wb

	6	5	4	3	2	1
Lux Sed	1,240	3,720	6,200	13,950	21,700	31,000

NOTE: 3.4 Litre available 1957 only. Mk VIII luxury sedan available 1957.

1957 Mk VIII, 6-cyl., 210 hp, 102" wb

	6	5	4	3	2	1
Saloon	1,320	3,960	6,600	14,850	23,100	33,000

1957 XK-140, 6-cyl., 190 hp, 102" wb

	6	5	4	3	2	1
Cpe	2,040	6,120	10,200	22,950	35,700	51,000
Rds	4,120	12,360	20,600	46,350	72,100	103,000

1957 XK-140

	6	5	4	3	2	1
Conv	2,920	8,760	14,600	32,850	51,100	73,000

1957 XK-150, 6-cyl., 190 hp, 102" wb

	6	5	4	3	2	1
Cpe	2,400	7,200	12,000	27,000	42,000	60,000
Rds	3,520	10,560	17,600	39,600	61,600	88,000

1957 2.4 Litre, 6-cyl., 112 hp, 108" wb

	6	5	4	3	2	1
Sed	1,060	3,180	5,300	11,930	18,550	26,500

1957 3.4 Litre, 6-cyl., 210 hp, 108" wb

	6	5	4	3	2	1
Sed	1,100	3,300	5,500	12,380	19,250	27,500

1958 3.4 Litre, 6-cyl., 210 hp, 108" wb

	6	5	4	3	2	1
Sed	1,120	3,360	5,600	12,600	19,600	28,000

1958 XK-150, 6-cyl., 190 hp, 120" wb

	6	5	4	3	2	1
Cpe	2,400	7,200	12,000	27,000	42,000	60,000

1958 XK-150, 6-cyl., 190 hp, 120" wb (cont.)

	6	5	4	3	2	1
Rds	3,520	10,560	17,600	39,600	61,600	88,000
Conv	3,000	9,000	15,000	33,750	52,500	75,000

1958 XK-150S, 6-cyl., 250 hp, 102" wb

	6	5	4	3	2	1
Rds	5,000	15,000	25,000	56,250	87,500	125,000

1958 Mk VIII, 6-cyl., 210 hp, 120" wb

	6	5	4	3	2	1
Saloon	1,360	4,080	6,800	15,300	23,800	34,000

1959-60 XK-150, 6-cyl., 210 hp, 102" wb

	6	5	4	3	2	1
Cpe	2,400	7,200	12,000	27,000	42,000	60,000
Rds	3,520	10,560	17,600	39,600	61,600	88,000
Conv	3,000	9,000	15,000	33,750	52,500	75,000

1959-60 XK-150SE, 6-cyl., 210 hp, 102" wb

	6	5	4	3	2	1
Cpe	2,600	7,800	13,000	29,250	45,500	65,000
Rds	3,720	11,160	18,600	41,850	65,100	93,000
Conv	3,200	9,600	16,000	36,000	56,000	80,000

1959-60 XK-150S, 6-cyl., 250 hp, 102" wb

	6	5	4	3	2	1
Rds	5,000	15,000	25,000	56,250	87,500	125,000

1959-60 3.4 Litre, 6-cyl., 210 hp, 108" wb

	6	5	4	3	2	1
Sed	1,020	3,060	5,100	11,480	17,850	25,500

1959-60 Mk IX, 6-cyl., 220 hp, 120" wb

	6	5	4	3	2	1
Sed	1,480	4,440	7,400	16,650	25,900	37,000

NOTE: Some factory prices increase for 1960.

1961 XK-150, 6-cyl., 210 hp, 102" wb

	6	5	4	3	2	1
Cpe	2,400	7,200	12,000	27,000	42,000	60,000
Conv	3,000	9,000	15,000	33,750	52,500	75,000

1961 XKE, 6-cyl., 265 hp, 96" wb

	6	5	4	3	2	1
Rds	3,200	9,600	16,000	36,000	56,000	80,000
Cpe	2,200	6,600	11,000	24,750	38,500	55,000

1961 3.8 Litre Mk II, 6-cyl., 265 hp, 108" wb

	6	5	4	3	2	1
Sed	1,920	5,760	9,600	21,600	33,600	48,000

1961 Mk IX, 6-cyl., 265 hp, 120" wb

	6	5	4	3	2	1
Sed	1,480	4,440	7,400	16,650	25,900	37,000

1962 XKE, 6-cyl., 265 hp, 96" wb

	6	5	4	3	2	1
Rds	3,200	9,600	16,000	36,000	56,000	80,000
Cpe	2,200	6,600	11,000	24,750	38,500	55,000

1962 3.8 Litre Mk II, 6-cyl., 265 hp, 108" wb

	6	5	4	3	2	1
Sed	1,920	5,760	9,600	21,600	33,600	48,000

1962 Mk X, 6-cyl., 265 hp, 120" wb

	6	5	4	3	2	1
Sed	920	2,760	4,600	10,350	16,100	23,000

1963 XKE, 6-cyl., 265 hp, 96" wb

	6	5	4	3	2	1
Rds	3,200	9,600	16,000	36,000	56,000	80,000
Cpe	2,200	6,600	11,000	24,750	38,500	55,000

	6	5	4	3	2	1

1963 3.8 Litre Mk II, 6-cyl., 265 hp, 108" wb

	6	5	4	3	2	1
Sed	1,920	5,760	9,600	21,600	33,600	48,000

1963 Mk X, 6-cyl., 265 hp, 120" wb

	6	5	4	3	2	1
Sed	920	2,760	4,600	10,350	16,100	23,000

1964 XKE, 6-cyl., 265 hp, 96" wb

	6	5	4	3	2	1
Rds	3,200	9,600	16,000	36,000	56,000	80,000
Cpe	2,200	6,600	11,000	24,750	38,500	55,000

1964 Model 3.8 Liter Mk II, 6-cyl., 108" wb

	6	5	4	3	2	1
4d Sed	1,920	5,760	9,600	21,600	33,600	48,000

1964 Model Mk X, 6-cyl., 265 hp, 120" wb

	6	5	4	3	2	1
4d Sed	920	2,760	4,600	10,350	16,100	23,000

1965 XKE 4.2, 6-cyl., 265 hp, 96" wb

	6	5	4	3	2	1
Rds	3,240	9,720	16,200	36,450	56,700	81,000
Cpe	2,240	6,720	11,200	25,200	39,200	56,000

1965 Model Mk X 4.2

	6	5	4	3	2	1
4d Sed	1,000	3,000	5,000	11,250	17,500	25,000

1965 Model 3.8 Mk II

	6	5	4	3	2	1
4d Sed	1,920	5,760	9,600	21,600	33,600	48,000
S Sed	1,200	3,600	6,000	13,500	21,000	30,000

1966 XKE 4.2, 6-cyl., 265 hp, 96" wb

	6	5	4	3	2	1
Rds	3,240	9,720	16,200	36,450	56,700	81,000
Cpe	2,240	6,720	11,200	25,200	39,200	56,000

1966 Model Mk X 4.2

	6	5	4	3	2	1
4d Sed	1,000	3,000	5,000	11,250	17,500	25,000

1966 Model 3.8 Mk II

	6	5	4	3	2	1
4d Sed	1,920	5,760	9,600	21,600	33,600	48,000
S 4d Sed	1,200	3,600	6,000	13,500	21,000	30,000

1967 XKE 4.2, 6-cyl., 265 hp, 96" wb

	6	5	4	3	2	1
Rds	3,200	9,600	16,000	36,000	56,000	80,000
Cpe	2,200	6,600	11,000	24,750	38,500	55,000
2 plus 2 Cpe	1,440	4,320	7,200	16,200	25,200	36,000

1967 420, 6-cyl., 255 hp, 108" wb

	6	5	4	3	2	1
4d Sed	960	2,880	4,800	10,800	16,800	24,000

1967 340, 6-cyl., 225 hp, 108" wb

	6	5	4	3	2	1
4d Sed	920	2,760	4,600	10,350	16,100	23,000

1967 420 G, 6-cyl., 245 hp, 107" wb

	6	5	4	3	2	1
4d Sed	1,000	3,000	5,000	11,250	17,500	25,000

1968 Model XKE 4.2, 245 hp, 96" wb

	6	5	4	3	2	1
Rds	2,320	6,960	11,600	26,100	40,600	58,000
Cpe	1,480	4,440	7,400	16,650	25,900	37,000
2 plus 2 Cpe	1,120	3,360	5,600	12,600	19,600	28,000

1969 Model XKE, 246 hp, 96" wb

	6	5	4	3	2	1
Rds	2,160	6,480	10,800	24,300	37,800	54,000

1969 Model XKE, 246 hp, 96" wb (cont.)

	6	5	4	3	2	1
Cpe	1,440	4,320	7,200	16,200	25,200	36,000
2 plus 2 Cpe	1,080	3,240	5,400	12,150	18,900	27,000

1969 Model XJ, 246 hp, 96" wb

	6	5	4	3	2	1
4d Sed	800	2,400	4,000	9,000	14,000	20,000

1970 Model XKE, 246 hp, 96" wb

	6	5	4	3	2	1
Rds	2,160	6,480	10,800	24,300	37,800	54,000
Cpe	1,440	4,320	7,200	16,200	25,200	36,000
2 plus 2 Cpe	1,080	3,240	5,400	12,150	18,900	27,000

1970 Model XJ, 246 hp, 96" wb

	6	5	4	3	2	1
4d Sed	800	2,400	4,000	9,000	14,000	20,000

1971 Model XKE, 246 hp, 96" wb

	6	5	4	3	2	1
Rds	2,160	6,480	10,800	24,300	37,800	54,000
Cpe	1,440	4,320	7,200	16,200	25,200	36,000
V-12 2 plus 2 Cpe	1,480	4,440	7,400	16,650	25,900	37,000
V-12 Conv	2,520	7,560	12,600	28,350	44,100	63,000

1971 Model XJ, 246 hp, 96" wb

	6	5	4	3	2	1
4d Sed	800	2,400	4,000	9,000	14,000	20,000

1972 Model XKE V-12, 272 hp, 105" wb

	6	5	4	3	2	1
Rds	2,520	7,560	12,600	28,350	44,100	63,000
2 plus 2 Cpe	1,480	4,440	7,400	16,650	25,900	37,000

1972 Model XJ6, 186 hp, 108.9" wb

	6	5	4	3	2	1
4d Sed	720	2,160	3,600	8,100	12,600	18,000

1973 Model XKE V-12, 272 hp, 105" wb

	6	5	4	3	2	1
Rds	2,520	7,560	12,600	28,350	44,100	63,000
2 plus 2 Cpe	1,480	4,440	7,400	16,650	25,900	37,000

1973 Model XJ, 186 hp, 108.9" wb

	6	5	4	3	2	1
4d XJ6	680	2,040	3,400	7,650	11,900	17,000
4d XJ12	840	2,520	4,200	9,450	14,700	21,000

1974 Model XKE V-12, 272 hp, 105" wb

	6	5	4	3	2	1
Rds	2,400	7,200	12,000	27,000	42,000	60,000

1974 Model XJ

	6	5	4	3	2	1
4d XJ6	640	1,920	3,200	7,200	11,200	16,000
4d XJ6 LWB	680	2,040	3,400	7,650	11,900	17,000
4d XJ12L	800	2,400	4,000	9,000	14,000	20,000

1975 Model XJ6

	6	5	4	3	2	1
C Cpe	800	2,400	4,000	9,000	14,000	20,000
4d L Sed	640	1,920	3,200	7,200	11,200	16,000

1975 Model XJ12

	6	5	4	3	2	1
C Cpe	880	2,640	4,400	9,900	15,400	22,000
4d L Sed	720	2,160	3,600	8,100	12,600	18,000

1976 Model XJ6

	6	5	4	3	2	1
C Cpe	800	2,400	4,000	9,000	14,000	20,000

	6	5	4	3	2	1

1976 Model XJ6 (cont.)

	6	5	4	3	2	1
4d L Sed	640	1,920	3,200	7,200	11,200	16,000

1976 Model XJ12

	6	5	4	3	2	1
C Cpe	880	2,640	4,400	9,900	15,400	22,000
4d L Sed	720	2,160	3,600	8,100	12,600	18,000

1976 Model XJS

	6	5	4	3	2	1
2 plus 2 Cpe	800	2,400	4,000	9,000	14,000	20,000

1977 Model XJ6

	6	5	4	3	2	1
C Cpe	800	2,400	4,000	9,000	14,000	20,000
4d L Sed	640	1,920	3,200	7,200	11,200	16,000

1977 Model XJ12L

	6	5	4	3	2	1
4d Sed	720	2,160	3,600	8,100	12,600	18,000

1977 Model XJS

	6	5	4	3	2	1
GT 2 plus 2 Cpe	800	2,400	4,000	9,000	14,000	20,000

1978 Model XJ6L

	6	5	4	3	2	1
4d Sed	640	1,920	3,200	7,200	11,200	16,000

1978 Model XJ12L

	6	5	4	3	2	1
4d Sed	720	2,160	3,600	8,100	12,600	18,000

1978 Model XJS

	6	5	4	3	2	1
Cpe	800	2,400	4,000	9,000	14,000	20,000

1979 Model XJ6

	6	5	4	3	2	1
4d Sed	600	1,800	3,000	6,750	10,500	15,000
4d Sed Series III	640	1,920	3,200	7,200	11,200	16,000

1979 Model XJ12

	6	5	4	3	2	1
4d Sed	720	2,160	3,600	8,100	12,600	18,000

1979 Model XJS

	6	5	4	3	2	1
Cpe	800	2,400	4,000	9,000	14,000	20,000

1980 Model XJS

	6	5	4	3	2	1
4d Sed XJ6	600	1,800	3,000	6,750	10,500	15,000
2d XJS 2 plus 2 Cpe	840	2,520	4,200	9,450	14,700	21,000

1981 Model XJS

	6	5	4	3	2	1
4d XJ6 Sed	600	1,800	3,000	6,750	10,500	15,000
2d XJS Cpe	840	2,520	4,200	9,450	14,700	21,000

1982 Model XJS

	6	5	4	3	2	1
4d XJ6 Sed	600	1,800	3,000	6,750	10,500	15,000
Vanden Plas 4d XJ6 Sed	760	2,280	3,800	8,550	13,300	19,000
2d XJS Cpe	840	2,520	4,200	9,450	14,700	21,000

1983 Model XJS

	6	5	4	3	2	1
4d XJ6 Sed	600	1,800	3,000	6,750	10,500	15,000
Vanden Plas 4d XJ6 Sed	760	2,280	3,800	8,550	13,300	19,000

1983 Model XJS (cont.)

	6	5	4	3	2	1
2d XJS Cpe	840	2,520	4,200	9,450	14,700	21,000

1984 Model XJS

	6	5	4	3	2	1
4d XJ6 Sed	600	1,800	3,000	6,750	10,500	15,000
Vanden Plas 4d XJ6 Sed	760	2,280	3,800	8,550	13,300	19,000
2d XJS Cpe	840	2,520	4,200	9,450	14,700	21,000

1985 Model XJ6

	6	5	4	3	2	1
4d Sed	600	1,800	3,000	6,750	10,500	15,000
Vanden Plas 4d Sed	760	2,280	3,800	8,550	13,300	19,000

1985 Model XJS

	6	5	4	3	2	1
2d Cpe	840	2,520	4,200	9,450	14,700	21,000

1986 Model XJ6

	6	5	4	3	2	1
4d Sed	600	1,800	3,000	6,750	10,500	15,000
Vanden Plas 4d Sed	760	2,280	3,800	8,550	13,300	19,000

1986 Model XJS

	6	5	4	3	2	1
2d Cpe	840	2,520	4,200	9,450	14,700	21,000

1987 Model XJ6

	6	5	4	3	2	1
4d Sed	600	1,800	3,000	6,750	10,500	15,000
Vanden Plas 4d Sed	760	2,280	3,800	8,550	13,300	19,000

1987 Model XJS

	6	5	4	3	2	1
2d Cpe	880	2,640	4,400	9,900	15,400	22,000
2d Cpe Cabr	1,000	3,000	5,000	11,250	17,500	25,000

1988 Model XJ6

	6	5	4	3	2	1
4d Sed	680	2,040	3,400	7,650	11,900	17,000

1988 Model XJS

	6	5	4	3	2	1
2d Cpe	880	2,640	4,400	9,900	15,400	22,000
2d Cpe Cabr	1,000	3,000	5,000	11,250	17,500	25,000
2d Conv	1,080	3,240	5,400	12,150	18,900	27,000

1989 Model XJ6

	6	5	4	3	2	1
4d Sed	720	2,160	3,600	8,100	12,600	18,000

1989 Model XJS

	6	5	4	3	2	1
2d Cpe	920	2,760	4,600	10,350	16,100	23,000
2d Conv	1,120	3,360	5,600	12,600	19,600	28,000

1990 Model XJ6

	6	5	4	3	2	1
4d Sed	760	2,280	3,800	8,550	13,300	19,000
4d Sovereign Sed	800	2,400	4,000	9,000	14,000	20,000
Vanden Plas 4d Sed	840	2,520	4,200	9,450	14,700	21,000
4d Majestic Sed	880	2,640	4,400	9,900	15,400	22,000

1990 Model XJS

	6	5	4	3	2	1
2d Cpe	920	2,760	4,600	10,350	16,100	23,000
2d Conv	1,120	3,360	5,600	12,600	19,600	28,000

NOTE: Add 10 percent for Collection Rouge Ed.

1991 Model XJ6

	6	5	4	3	2	1
4d Sed	760	2,280	3,800	8,550	13,300	19,000
4d Sovereign Sed	800	2,400	4,000	9,000	14,000	20,000
Vanden Plas 4d Sed	840	2,520	4,200	9,450	14,700	21,000

1991 Model XJS

	6	5	4	3	2	1
2d Cpe	900	2,750	4,600	10,350	16,100	23,000
2d Conv	1,120	3,360	5,600	12,600	19,600	28,000

1992 Model XJ6

	6	5	4	3	2	1
4d Sed	800	2,400	4,000	9,000	14,000	20,000
4d Sovereign Sed	850	2,500	4,200	9,450	14,700	21,000
Vanden Plas 4d Sed	880	2,640	4,400	9,900	15,400	22,000
4d Majestic Sed	900	2,750	4,600	10,350	16,100	23,000

1992 Model XJS

	6	5	4	3	2	1
2d Cpe	960	2,880	4,800	10,800	16,800	24,000
2d Conv	1,160	3,480	5,800	13,050	20,300	29,000

1993 Model XJ6

	6	5	4	3	2	1
4d Sed	840	2,520	4,200	9,450	14,700	21,000
Vanden Plas 4d Sed	880	2,640	4,400	9,900	15,400	22,000

1993 Model XJS, V-12

	6	5	4	3	2	1
2d Cpe	960	2,880	4,800	10,800	16,800	24,000
2d Conv	1,160	3,480	5,800	13,050	20,300	29,000

NOTE: Deduct 10 percent for 6-cyl.

1994 XJ6, 6-cyl.

	6	5	4	3	2	1
4d Sed	840	2,520	4,200	9,450	14,700	21,000
Vanden Plas 4d Sed	880	2,640	4,400	9,900	15,400	22,000
4d Sed XJ12	1,000	3,000	5,000	11,250	17,500	25,000

1994 XJS

	6	5	4	3	2	1
2d Cpe, 6-cyl.	860	2,580	4,300	9,680	15,050	21,500
2d Cpe, V-12	960	2,880	4,800	10,800	16,800	24,000
2d Conv, 6-cyl.	1,040	3,120	5,200	11,700	18,200	26,000
2d Conv, V-12	1,160	3,480	5,800	13,050	20,300	29,000

1995 XJ6, 6-cyl. & V-12

	6	5	4	3	2	1
4d Sed	840	2,520	4,200	9,450	14,700	21,000
Vanden Plas 4d Sed	880	2,640	4,400	9,900	15,400	22,000

1995 XJ6, 6-cyl. & V-12 (cont.)

	6	5	4	3	2	1
4d XJR Sed (sc)	940	2,820	4,700	10,580	16,450	23,500
4d XJ12 Sed	1,000	3,000	5,000	11,250	17,500	25,000

1995 XJS, 6-cyl. & V-12

	6	5	4	3	2	1
2d Cpe, 6-cyl.	900	2,700	4,500	10,130	15,750	22,500
2d Cpe, V-12	1,000	3,000	5,000	11,250	17,500	25,000
2d Conv, 6-cyl.	1,080	3,240	5,400	12,150	18,900	27,000
2d Conv, V-12	1,200	3,600	6,000	13,500	21,000	30,000

1996 XJ6, 6-cyl.

	6	5	4	3	2	1
4d Sed	840	2,520	4,200	9,450	14,700	21,000
Vanden Plas 4d Sed	880	2,640	4,400	9,900	15,400	22,000
XJR 4d Sed (sc)	940	2,820	4,700	10,580	16,450	23,500

1996 XJ12, V-12

	6	5	4	3	2	1
XJ12 4d Sed	1,000	3,000	5,000	11,250	17,500	25,000

1996 XJS, 6-cyl.

	6	5	4	3	2	1
2d Conv	1,080	3,240	5,400	12,150	18,900	27,000

1997 XJ6, 6-cyl.

	6	5	4	3	2	1
4d Sed	840	2,520	4,200	9,450	14,700	21,000
L 4d Sed	860	2,580	4,300	9,680	15,050	21,500
Vanden Plas 4d Sed	880	2,640	4,400	9,900	15,400	22,000
XJR 4d Sed (sc)	940	2,820	4,700	10,580	16,450	23,500

1997 XK8, V-8

	6	5	4	3	2	1
2d Cpe	980	2,940	4,900	11,030	17,150	24,500
2d Conv	1,160	3,480	5,800	13,050	20,300	29,000

1998 XJ8, V-8

	6	5	4	3	2	1
4d Sed	880	2,640	4,400	9,900	15,400	22,000
L 4d Sed	900	2,700	4,500	10,130	15,750	22,500
Vanden Plas 4d Sed	920	2,760	4,600	10,350	16,100	23,000
XJR 4d Sed (sc)	960	2,880	4,800	10,800	16,800	24,000

1998 XK8, V-8

	6	5	4	3	2	1
2d Cpe	1,020	3,060	5,100	11,480	17,850	25,500
2d Conv	1,200	3,600	6,000	13,500	21,000	30,000

1999 XJ8, V-8

	6	5	4	3	2	1
4d Sed	760	2,280	3,800	8,550	13,300	19,000
L 4d Sed	800	2,400	4,000	9,000	14,000	20,000
Vanden Plas 4d Sed	840	2,520	4,200	9,450	14,700	21,000
XJR 4d Sed (sc)	1,040	3,120	5,200	11,700	18,200	26,000

1999 XK8, V-8

	6	5	4	3	2	1
2d Cpe	1,020	3,060	5,100	11,480	17,850	25,500
2d Conv	1,200	3,600	6,000	13,500	21,000	30,000

(sc) = supercharged

A racing version of the 1954 Jaguar XK 120 roadster.

Appendix A: Model Specifications

(Source XKS Unlimited, San Luis Obispo, California)

Jaguar XK-120, XK-140 and XK-150

The Roadster (or OTS, for Other Than Sedan) was the basic sports model designed for the enthusiast who wanted top-down performance and was willing to sacrifice some creature comforts. The XK-120 and XK-140 roadsters had a minimal top, cut down doors and side curtains instead of roll-up door windows. In many ways this was the purest form of the XK design. The XK-150 roadster did feature roll-up door windows, but was still Spartan compared to the Drop Head Coupe or the Fixed Head Coupe models.

The Drop Head Coupe (DHC) was the British equivalent to a convertible. The top was retractable and much more substantial than the roadster. It featured a fully padded headliner and better weather protection. The Drop Head Coupe also featured roll-up door windows and a plusher interior with wood veneer used extensively on both the XK-120 and XK-140. The Drop Head Coupe was considered the convertible for the gentleman who required a Grand Touring car with open-air capabilities.

The Fixed Head Coupe (FHC) is the fully enclosed hardtop model. On the XK-120 and XK-140 models, the interior featured wood veneer. On the XK-140 and XK-150, you'll find small occasional seats in the rear. All Fixed Head Coupes came with roll-up door windows.

Jaguar XK-120

Dan Lyons

Distinctive front end of a 1954 Jaguar XK 120
Engine: DOHC in-line 6 cylinder.
Bore & Stroke: 83 x 106.
Displacement: 3442cc (3.4 Liter).
Compression Ratio: 7:1, 8:1 with optional Special Equipment package and 9:1 with C-head.
Carburetion: Twin SU.
BHP: 160 Standard or 180 with Special Equipment and M packages.
Transmission: 4-speed synchro (except first).
Rear suspension: Semi-elliptical leaf springs.
Gear ratios: 3.64, 4.98, 7.22 and 12.29:1.
Front suspension: Independent with torsion bars.

Frame: Reinforced cross-braced steel.
Wheelbase: 102" Track: 51" front and 51" rear.
Brakes: Lockheed 2LS Hydraulic.
Tires: 6.00 x 16 front and rear.
Wheels: Steel disc. Wires available in Special Equipment and M.

Jaguar XK-140

Richard Dance Collection

1955 Jaguar XK 140 roadster
Engine: DOHC in-line 6 cylinder.
Bore x Stroke: 83 x 106.
Displacement: 3422cc (3.4 Liter).
Compression Ratio: 8:1, 9:1 with C-head.
Carburetion: Twin SU.
BHP: 190 Standard and 210 with C-head.
Transmission: 4-speed synchro (except first).
(Late DHC and FHC had an automatic Borg-Warner option.)
Rear suspension: Semi-elliptical springs.
Gear ratio: 3.54, 4.83, 7.01 and 11.95.1.
Front suspension: Semi-elliptical springs.
Wheelbase: 102." Track: 51 1/2" front and rear.
Brakes: Lockheed 2LS, hydraulic.
Tires: 16" front and rear.
Wheels: Steel disc. Wire available in Special Equipment or M.

Jaguar XK-150

Dan Lyons

1958 XK 150 drophead coupe
Engine: DOHC in-line 6 cylinder.
Bore x Stroke: 83 x 106 (3.4 L) and 87 x 106 (3.8 L).
Displacement: 3442cc (3.4) and 3781cc (3.8).
Compression ratio: 7:1, 8:1, 9:1 on S model.
Carburetion: Twin SU. Triple SU on S model.
BHP: 190 Standard, 210 with Special Equipment and 250 with S package.
Transmission: 4-speed synchro (except first). Overdrive

on S models. Optional automatic transmission.
Rear suspension: Semi-elliptical spring.
Gear ratio: 3.54, 4.54, 6.58 and 11.91:1. 3.18, 4.09, 5.247, 7.60 and 13.8:1 Overdrive, S model.
Front suspension: Independent.
Frame: Cross-braced steel.
Wheelbase: 102." Track: 51 ½" front and rear.
Brakes: Dunlop disc with servo assist.
Tires: 16 inch Dunlop RS-4.

Wheels: Wire. Pressed steel are optional and very rare.

Jaguar E-Types

The E-type was offered in three body styles and five different models. The three body styles are: Roadster, Coupe and 2 + 2.

Roadster: Any model of E-type where the top folds down is considered a roadster. All three series of E-types were offered in the roadster body style.

Coupe: Any E-type with a fixed top and strictly two seats. Only Series I and II were offered in the pure coupe body.

2 + 2: This body style was offered on all three series of E-types from 1965 and on. On the Series III, all hardtops were 2 + 2 bodies. All Series III cars were built on the long wheelbase chassis and never came in the pure coupe form. They also have a more steeply raked windshield than the coupe.

The E-type was offered in five different models:

1. Series I 3.8-liter. This was the first model and still considered the purest form of the design, being uncompromised by comfort or safety regulations. This model was offered from 1961 to 1964 in the coupe and roadster body styles.

2. Series I 4.2-liter. This model was virtually identical in appearance to the earlier 3.8-liter cars, but had some important mechanical changes, including a larger displacement engine, all-synchro gearbox, an alternator rather than a generator, a brake servo and improved cooling. This model also featured much more comfortable seating. Shortly after the introduction of the Series I 4.2 came the debut of the 2 + 2 body style. When ordering parts for your "hardtop" car, please always be specific as to whether you have a coupe or a 2 + 2. Many parts do not interchange.

3. Series I½ 4.2-liter. This model was offered from late 1967 through late 1968 and gives its owners more problems than any other model. It was a transition car and for about a year and a half Jaguar would slowly change different items from Series I to II (and sometimes back again, just for fun) such as carburetion, cooling systems, electrics, and various trim bits. Be very specific when ordering parts for these cars. They look like Series I cars (with the tail lamps and front turn signal lamps above the bumpers) but do not have glass-covered headlamps. Also, the headlamp trim is unique to this model—even though they look like Series II they will not interchange. The Series I½ came in all three body styles: roadster, coupe and 2 + 2.

4. Series II 4.2-liter. This model was offered from 1969 to early 1971. Many changes were made to the car to meet safety and emissions requirements. While performance and looks suffered, in reality these cars were more reliable and comfortable than the earlier models and more practical to drive. They were offered in coupe, roadster or 2 + 2 body styles. Ordering parts for these models is somewhat more difficult than the earlier models because Jaguar never produced an illustrated parts manual. In addition, there are many subtle differences between early and late Series II cars as Jaguar attempted to comply with American safety and emissions standards.

5. Series III V-12s. This model was offered from 1971 to 1974 and came only as a roadster or 2 + 2. The roadsters were built on the long wheelbase chassis of the 2 + 2. This model featured the new V-12 engine and many other new features. While the Series III cars were more grand tourers than sports cars (losing some of the nimble feel of the six-cylinder cars in the process), they are by far the most comfortable and civilized E-Types with available automatic transmission and air conditioning. Power steering was also made standard equipment on the V-12 cars.

Jaguar Sedans

1950-1968

This group of Jaguar models can be divided into three groups, the Mk VII, VIII and IX; Mk I and II; 3.8S and 420; Mk X and 420G.

The **Mk VII, VIII and IX** sedans are the stately models built during the 1950s to 1961. Much of the trim—such as inner door handles, window winders and switches—is interchangeable. The Mk VII started out with the 3.4-liter engine and XK suspension. The Mk VIII is very similar but has a one-piece windshield and slightly different interior and exterior trim. The Mk IX offered many mechanical changes, including a 3.8-liter engine, four-wheel disc brakes, and power steering. These cars make great restoration projects. They are modestly priced, are great looking when restored, and are very drivable even by modern standards. They are also very rugged and reliable by Jaguar standards of the era.

The **"Small Sedans"** started in the mid 1950s with the Mk I and continued with variations until 1967. These models represent Jaguar's first foray into unibody construction and included the Mk I, Mk II, 340, 3.8S and 420. They were all variations on the same theme. From the late Mk Is on, they feature four-wheel disc brakes and engines from 2.4—not officially imported to the U.S.—to 4.2-liters in the 420 sedan. All sedans are increasing in value, but unrestored examples are still quite reasonable. These cars make great drivers. They are comfortable and fast.

One other model of the 1960s was the Mk X and 420G series, what we call the "Big Sedans."

Many of the mechanical and trim parts are interchangeable with other models. Remember, though, a 420 and 420G are two completely different animals.

Like all Jaguars, the sedans are rust-prone. Be sure to thoroughly inspect any potential purchase, preferably while the car is up on a garage lift. While these cars are rewarding to restore, starting out with the right car makes all the difference. Also, check for general completeness. These are complex cars compared to an XK or an E-Type, and lots of missing bits can add substantially to restoration costs and time. Luckily there is a fairly ample supply of healthy sedans, so look at several before lightening your wallet.

XJ Sedans and XJ-S

Richard Dance Collection

1965 Jaguar Mark X saloon

The XJ sedans started in 1968 and continue up to today. There are four basic series of the XJ-6 and three versions of the XJ-S.

The XJ-6 and XJ-12:

Phil Hall Collection

1990 Jaguar XJ-S convertible

Series I: 1968 to early 1974. All these models were built on the short-wheelbase chassis, at least all those imported to the U.S. They featured chrome bumpers and a large front grille. This model was available in 1973 with the V-12 engine, called the XJ-12. While later XJ cars were improved in many ways over the Series I, this version is many enthusiast's favorite because of its tidier dimensions and simpler trim.

Series II: 1974 through 1978. All four-door models were built on the long-wheelbase chassis and featured higher rubber bumpers and the smaller radiator grille—both changes necessitated by the new U.S. crashworthiness laws. While many of the trim items are becoming scarce for the Series II, much of the Series III trim bolts right on. A 12-cylinder version was also available. Later Series II cars, both six- and 12-cylinder versions, were supplied with fuel injection. Jaguar also built a limited number of Series II two-door coupes on the short wheelbase chassis.

Series III: 1979 through 1987. Jaguar made big improvements in quality and reliability for these cars. All Series IIIs are fuel injected and feature much improved trim and components. If you're considering a Jaguar for daily transport, the Series III is perhaps the best all-around choice. Properly cared for, the Series III can provide many trouble-free miles.

XJ-40: 1988 through 1994. This is a completely new model and does not share any components with earlier XJs. It also features the all-new twin-cam AJ-6 engine that displaced 3.6 liters until 1990, when it was enlarged to 4 liters. Early cars tend to be troublesome and many parts are already not available. We recommend the 4-liter cars.

1975 Jaguar XKC coupe

Kevin Manley photo/Jerry Liudahl, owner

The XJ-S:

1990 Jaguar XJ-S convertible

XJ-S: 1976 through 1981: Many people do not realize how fast these cars really were. They are a good value and good examples are available for under $10,000. Also, many of the improved components from the HE series will bolt on.

XJ-S HE: 1981 – on: This version perhaps saved the XJ-S. Great improvements were made in quality and reliability. The engine features the HE cylinder heads that improve mileage and performance while meeting stricter emissions standards. Again, older versions of these cars are a great value offering lots of performance and style for relatively little money. The V-12 used in these cars is rugged and if taken care of will last 150,000 miles.

XJS: 1992 – on: Jaguar restyled the XJ-S with new rear quarter panels and windows, tail lamps and Euro-style single-lens headlamps. This is a substantial re-do that improved quality while reducing assembly costs (but not the sticker price!) The 4.0 six-cylinder engine was offered as well as a 6.0-liter V-12 in later cars.

1967 Jaguar Mk II sedan

Kevin Manley photo/Jerry Liudahl, owner

The exotic Jaguar Advanced Lightweight. *Phil Hall Collection*

Appendix B:
Jaguar Terms and Abbrevations

Abbreviations

ABS .... Antilock Braking System
ASC .... Automatic Stability Control
Cam .... Camshaft
Cc .... cubic centimeters
CID .... cubic inch displacement
Co. .... Company
DIN .... standard, DIN 70020, for hp
                (very close to SAE net hp)
DOHC .... double overhead camshaft
Dr. .... door (2d, 4d)
EFI .... Electronic Fuel Injection
Hp .... horsepower
I6 .... inline six-cylinder
In. .... inches
Inc. .... Incorporated
Jag .... Jaguar
Lbs.-ft. .... foot-pounds
LED .... Liquid emulsion display
LHD .... left-hand drive
Ltd. .... Limited
LWB .... Long-wheelbase
MK .... Mark
MM .... millimeters
N/A .... not available
P.O.E. .... Port of Entry
RHD .... right-hand drive
Rpm .... revolutions per minute
SAE .... Society of Automotive Engineers
SOHC .... single overhead camshaft
SS .... Swallow Sidecars

SUV .... sport utility vehicle
UK .... United Kingdom
U.S. .... United States
VDP .... Vanden Plas
WWII .... World War II
2+2 .... Four seater

Understanding the Jaguar book

Liter vs. litre – "Litre" is the British spelling. Although we generally use American terminology throughout the text, "litre" is used due to the fact that the word, spelled the English way, was part of the official "model name" for some Jaguars. In some cases, Litre is part of the car series model name.

Likewise, "drophead" is used in some places (instead of "convertible") and "saloon" is used in other places instead of "sedan." When "convertible" and "sedan" are the official model designators, they are used in this book.

XK-E is used until 1965, when the "E-TYPE" designation appeared on the cars. It appears that in England, E-Type was generally used from the start of production.

Jaguar sales and production totals often require qualifications. Production is usually production in England for worldwide distribution. Originally Jaguar kept records on cars shipped to the U.S, during the company's financial year, which ran from July to July. For some years, no figures were reported. In later years, production totals become available again. Sales are generally for the calendar year. Sales can be cars sold by U.S. dealers or cars sold by U.S. dealers, plus tourist deliveries overseas. Jaguar

The rear view of the Jaguar Advanced Lightweight. *Phil Hall Collection*

sometimes made slight changes (usually increases) to sales totals reported to industry trade journals. In this book we have tried to qualify the numbers we have published. In some cases, the totals do not include prototypes or race cars. The totals for the rare XK-SS are those for "street" cars.

NOTE 1: The "Standard Equipment" listed in this catalog is not complete. We have attempted to list some standard features to help the reader differentiate models without listing every equipment detail. To a large degree, Jaguars have similar features, but one or two differences can help to identify a particular model.

NOTE 2: In all instances, the text and tables in this catalog should be considered an effort to give a good "sketch" of Jaguar's product history. We have attempted to make the

information as accurate as possible, but we do not claim this to be "complete in every detail."

Helpful British terms

Accumulator	Battery
Bonnet	Hood
Boot	Trunk
Bulkhead	Firewall
Dipping mirror	Prismatic mirror
Dipping switch	Dimmer
Drop-head coupe	Convertible
Dynamo	Generator
Estate/ estate wagon	Station wagon (In Jaguar's case, a Sportwagon)
Fascia	Dashboard
Fixed-head coupe	Two-door sport coupe
Hood	Convertible top
Marque	Car maker
Monocoque	Unibody assembly
Nacelle	Housing for a switch or light
O.E. or O.E.M.	Original equipment or original equipment manufacturer
Overriders	Bumper guards
Quarterlight	Vent window
Rear or back light	Rear window
Rev counter	Tachometer
Saloon	Four-door sedan
Scuttle	Cowl
Side curtains	Removable, usually plastic, side windows
Spanner	Wrench
Tail locker	Trunk
Trafficators	Semaphore-style signals
Windscreen	Windshield

The cockpit view of the Jaguar Advanced Lightweight.

Phil Hall Collection